THE MICHIGAN ESTATE PLANNING BOOK

BY MICHAEL MARAN · MICHIGAN LAWYER

**A COMPLETE
DO-IT-YOURSELF
GUIDE TO
PLANNING AN
ESTATE IN MICHIGAN**

The Michigan Estate Planning Book: A Complete Do-It-Yourself Guide to Planning an Estate in Michigan
by Michael Maran

Published by:
Grand River Press
P.O. Box 1342
E. Lansing, MI 48826

Printing history:
First edition: July 2000
ISBN 0-936343-09-5
Printed in the United States of America

Order Form

■ **The Michigan Estate Planning Book: A Complete Do-It-Yourself**
Guide to Planning an Estate in Michigan $29.95

ALSO AVAILABLE:

■ **After the Divorce: A Do-It-Yourself Guide to Enforcing or**
Modifying a Divorce Judgment in Michigan $24.95

■ **The Michigan Divorce Book: A Guide to Doing an Uncontested**
Divorce without an Attorney (without minor children) $24.95

■ **The Michigan Divorce Book: A Guide to Doing an Uncontested**
Divorce without an Attorney (with minor children) $29.95

TITLE	PRICE	QUANTITY	TOTAL

Method of Payment:

		Subtotal	
		Add 6% Sales Tax	
		Postage	
		TOTAL	

☐ Check or money order (payable to **Grand River Press)**

☐ Charge: ☐ Visa ☐ MasterCard

Account # ☐☐☐☐☐☐☐☐☐☐☐☐☐☐☐☐☐

_____
Expiration Date   Signature

_____
NAME

_____
ADDRESS

_____
CITY   STATE   ZIP

Please send form to: **Grand River Press, P.O. Box 1342, East Lansing, Michigan 48826**

Design and layout:
Altese Graphic Design

Editing:
Mark Woodbury

Thanks to Tammie Havermahl, of Gift of Life, in Ann Arbor,
for helpful information and suggestions about the anatomical
gifts section

And thanks to the New Jersey Bioethics Commission for its
kind permission allowing adaptation of their advance directive
forms for use in this book

Table of Contents

Forms:

Statutory Will

Separate List

Self-Proving Declaration (for will execution)

Self-Proving Declaration (for previously-signed will)

Custodial Power of Attorney

(separate) Guardian Appointment

Living Trust Agreement (pet trust)

Quit Claim Deed

Transfer under the Michigan Uniform Transfers to Minors Act

Letter of Instruction

Anatomical Donor Document

Durable Power of Attorney

Attachment (to durable power of attorney)

Revocation of Power of Attorney

Living Will

Revocation of Advance Directive

Do-Not-Resuscitate Order (general)

Do-Not-Resuscitate Order (religious)

Patient Advocate Designation

Affidavit in Support of Patient Advocate Designation

Preface

This book is destined for a lukewarm public reception, and respectable but modest sales. It's not because the book itself is deficient; on the contrary, I'm confident it's the best and most comprehensive estate planning book available today.

I'm also convinced that most people could benefit enormously from this book. They may not use everything inside, but almost everyone needs a basic estate plan of: 1) will (or separate guardian appointment) 2) durable power of attorney 3) advance directive (living will or patient advocate designation) 4) anatomical gift (optional).

Yet a 1997 survey revealed that 62% of adults in Michigan don't have wills. A recent national poll found that although 90% of Americans like the idea of advance directives, only 10-20% had gotten around to making one.

Why don't more people make wills and plan their estates? Perhaps it's a legacy of the old superstition that to make a will is to invite death. My hunch is that the entire subject is unpleasant, so most people avoid estate planning entirely, or put it off until a personal crisis makes it unavoidable.

This attitude exists even among people should know better. There are countless cobbler-going-shoeless examples of lawyers and legal experts dying without an estate plan or even so much as a will.

My favorite is the sad case of Mary Severns, a Delaware living will advocate and active member of the Euthanasia Council in that state. Severns lobbied tirelessly for living will legislation during the 1970s, and all her effort paid off: Delaware was one of the first states to authorize living wills. Then in 1979, Severns was in a terrible automobile accident, leaving her in a coma. Her doctors looked for her living will but found none. Friends remembered that Severns had often talked about making a living will, but apparently had never gotten around to actually doing this.

Don't you fall into this trap of good intentions, but no follow-through. Take the time to make an estate plan, if not with this book, then with another similar publication, or by going to a lawyer.

Chapter 1
Planning Your Estate

Families

1A: Inventory of Property

    Inventory Form

1B: Basics of Estate Planning

Families' Estate Plans

Estate planning isn't an easy subject to grasp. You encounter complicated legal and financial questions. You must face wrenching decisions about your property, family and self. Adding to the difficulty, estate planning is, by its very nature, speculative. You're looking 10, 20 or 30 years into the future and providing guidance about your affairs then.

As hard as it is, estate planning is even knottier when you deal with it in the abstract. That's why this book uses two fictional families to show the practical side of estate planning.

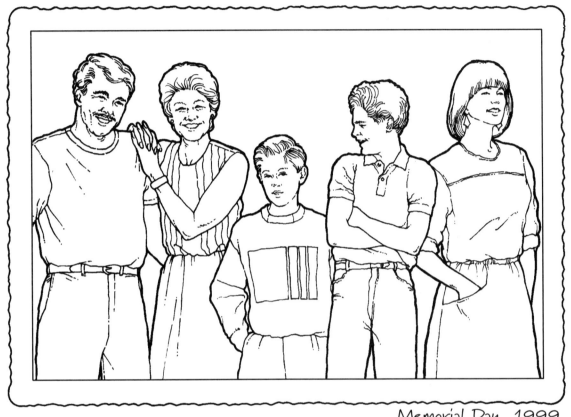

Memorial Day, 1999

Frisbie Family

George and Margo Frisbie are married with three children: Thelma, 21, Dewey, 15, and Woodrow, 12. Thelma has recently wed Dudley Mangrove; they have no children. The family lives in Lake City, Michigan, where George, 48, is a police officer and Margo, 45, manages a convenience store. All are in excellent health. George and Margo own the following property:

	Ownership	Value
House	JT (h&w)	80,000
Cottage in northern Michigan	S (h)	20,000
Vacant lot in Florida	S (w)	5,000
Certificate of deposit	JT (h&w)	20,000

Group term life insurance	S (h)	50,000
Retirement plan	S (h)	25,000
Automobile	S (h)	20,000
Automobile	S (w)	15,000
Household goods	JT (h&w)	10,000
Personal goods	S (h)	2,000
Personal goods	S (w)	3,000
		$250,000

After death, the Frisbies want to distribute their property first to each other and then to their children equally. But they want to give $20,000 now to Thelma for a down-payment on a house she and Dudley are buying. The Frisbies wish to avoid probate as much as possible, and so hold a lot of property jointly. Both Frisbies want to die a "natural death" if their medical condition becomes hopeless. George dislikes funerals and burials, and wants to be cremated followed by a simple memorial ceremony.

Eugene's Visit, 1998

Millsaps Family

Edith Millsaps, 54, is a widow whose husband died five years ago. Since his death, Edith has gone back to work as a beautician. She has four children: Grover, 34, Eugene, 30, Shirley, 28, and Wanda, 24. Grover has four children: three with his second wife Doreen and a son Garth from his first marriage, which ended in divorce. Eugene is married with two children. Shirley has a daughter, Rhonda, but was recently divorced from her husband Gus. Wanda is single and lives with her boyfriend, Luther. All the Millsaps live in Michigan except Eugene who lives in California.

Edith also has a beloved dog, a Welsh corgi named Digger, which she regards as part of the family.

Edith has diabetes, high blood pressure and was hospitalized recently after a minor stroke. She has recovered fully from the stroke. While she was in the hospital, Grover and Shirley looked after her property, which includes:

	Ownership	*Value*
House	S	50,000
Bank account	JT (w/ Shirley)	10,000
Stock	S	1,000
Automobile	S	5,000
Household goods	S	2,000
Antiques	S	2,000
		$70,000

After death, Edith wants to give property to just three of her children: Grover, Shirley and Wanda. She wants to exclude Eugene because he seldom calls or visits her. Edith wants to give several heirlooms to people and leave money to her church. She is also worried about what might happen to Digger after her death, and would like to provide some security for him.

Right now, Edith wants to give $1,000 to grandson Garth, whom she feels has been neglected by Grover after his divorce, to pay for school and incidental expenses. Edith also realizes that she may need help if she becomes sick again, but fears losing control of her property now.

Chapter 1A Inventory of Property

Estate planning begins with a complete inventory of all property and liabilities. In the inventory, list all your property and indicate the form of ownership and value of the property. Your liabilities must also be added up.

An inventory of property has several purposes. Making an inventory reacquaints you with your property and liabilities, so you don't omit anything from your estate plan. You need to know the kind of property you own for probate planning. And above all, an inventory establishes your net worth, which tells whether you face an estate tax bill.

Making an Inventory

You can make an inventory any way you want, as long as it includes all the necessary information. Many financial institutions and insurance companies distribute inventory forms, and these may be fine. For your convenience, an inventory form is included after this section, and can be used with the following instructions.

Listing Property and Liabilities

In sec. 1 of the inventory, list all the property you own or have an interest in. Include both real property (land and anything permanently attached, such as houses, buildings, demobilized mobile homes, etc.) and personal property (everything else, including financial assets like bank accounts, stocks, bonds, etc.). The list must include things you might not normally think of as property, such as legal judgments for you, patents, trademarks, copyrights, etc.

Ordinarily, married couples should combine their property in one inventory because spouses usually give their property to each other, and are therefore treated as a unit by the estate tax. But if married couples have earmarked large amounts of property for nonspouses, they should make separate inventories and plan their estates separately.

With a few exceptions, liabilities belong in sec. 2 of the inventory. Debts against property (mortgages, land contracts, secured debts, etc.) and business debts are listed in sec. 1 (as explained below, you deduct these liabilities from the indebted property to figure the equity value of the property). Leave these debts out of sec. 2. The rest of your debts, such as bank loans, personal loans, credit card debts, etc., should go into sec. 2, the liabilities section.

Ownership of Property

The ownership of your property appears in these property records:

Real property. Ownership is designated in the grantee section of deeds. If you don't have the original deed, you can get a copy from the office of the register of deeds where the property is located.

Personal property. The following title documents reveal ownership:

Bank accounts—signature cards on file at a bank, savings and loan association, or credit union.

Stocks and bonds—stock and bond certificates.

Insurance—insurance policies.

Motor vehicles—certificates of title.

Miscellaneous personal property—Personal goods (clothing, furs, jewelry, stamps, coins, antiques, etc.) don't have title documents, so the person who bought the item is the owner. In Michigan, household goods (furniture, appliances, dishes, etc.) are presumed to be the sole property of husbands because of their financial duty to support the household. But this presumption can be disproved with evidence of joint ownership by the husband and wife, or sole ownership by the wife.

Real and personal property can be held in several forms of ownership:

Solely-owned property. Owned by you alone, when no one else is listed or named on the document of title.

Joint tenancy. A type of joint property giving each owner (joint tenant) an equal but undivided interest in the property. Joint tenancy also provides rights of survivorship, so the surviving joint tenant gets full ownership when the other joint tenant dies.

In deeds to real property, the designation of two or more people as "joint tenants" or "joint tenants with rights of survivorship," or any variation creates some type of joint tenancy. A deed to a husband and wife without saying more automatically creates a tenancy by the entirety-type of joint tenancy.

For personal property, such as bank accounts, stocks, bonds, and motor vehicles, the joint tenancy designations resemble deeds. Frequently, the designation is abbreviated as either JT TEN or JT WROS (joint tenancy with rights of survivorship), or as TEN ENT (for the tenancy by the entirety-type of joint tenancy between spouses).

Tenancy in common. A type of joint property giving each owner (tenant in common) a fractional share of the property, which is transferable by sale, gift, will or inheritance. Sometimes, title documents abbreviate tenancy in common as TEN COM.

Value of Property

Use fair market value to value all property. Fair market value is the price property brings in a sale between a willing seller and a willing buyer. If the property is subject to a debt, an adjustment is necessary. For indebted property, the equity value of the property—fair market value minus the debt against the property—should be used instead of simple fair market value.

For the fair market value of real property, you can either: 1) compare your property to the sale prices of similar property sold recently in your neighborhood, or 2) double the amount of your property's tax assessment, since assessments are usually around 50% of fair market value.*

You should be able to establish the fair market value of most kinds of personal property without much effort. Cash or near-cash assets (bank accounts, certificates of deposit, money market funds, etc.) are worth their present account balances. The value of stocks, corporate bonds and other securities are listed daily in *The Wall Street Journal*. Use the current redemption value for series E/EE U.S. savings bonds, and the face or par value for series H/HH bonds.

The value of life insurance is the so-called face amount of the insurance policy (the amount of insurance proceeds payable at death). The value of retirement plan death benefits is harder to establish. If you need help with valuation, contact the retirement plan administrator.

Valuing a business is also difficult. If the business cannot be sold as a going concern, the book value of the business (tangible business assets minus business liabilities) may be used. But if the business is marketable, consider valuing the business by multiplying the average annual net earnings (before taxes) by a multiplier (1, 1½, 2, etc.) customary for that type of business. If you own a business jointly with others, you may have a buy-sell agreement with the co-owners fixing the value of your share, and you can use this value.

The fair market value of motor vehicles can be obtained from National Automobile Dealer Association (NADA) bluebooks. There are also price

---

* In some cases, you can value farm real property at the agricultural value instead of fair market value.

guides for jewelry, stamps, coins and antiques. You can estimate the fair market value of personal and household goods by comparing these to the value of similar used items.

Value of Joint Property

For joint tenancy property, the value of your share corresponds to the percentage of your contribution toward purchase of the item, as follows:

Example: Edith contributed $900 (⁹⁄₁₀) and Shirley $100 (¹⁄₁₀) toward the purchase, as joint tenants, of stock for $1,000. The stock now has a fair market value of $2,000, making Edith's share worth $1,800.

For tenancy in common property, include the value of your fractional share. Tenants in common are presumed to have equal shares, unless the deed or document of title assigns unequal shares.

Example: Edith is a co-owner, as a 50-50 tenant in common, of a lot worth $10,000. The value of her share is $5,000.

Inventory Form

There is an inventory form following this section which you can use to list your property and liabilities. As you record ownership of property, use the following symbols: S for solely-owned, JT for joint tenancy, and TC for tenancy in common. Married couples with solely-owned property should indicate which spouse owns the item ("h" for husband and "w" for wife). If you own property jointly with a nonspouse, name the co-owner in parentheses.

INVENTORY

Ownership   *Value*

1. Property

A. Real property

Residence

Address

————— $ —————

Other real property (list business real property under business interests in sec. B)

Type of land

Address

————— $ —————

Type of land

Address

————— $ —————

B. Personal property

Cash and financial accounts (include cash, savings, checking, money market accounts, certificates of deposit, etc.)

Name of institution holding account

Account or certificate no.

————— $ —————

Name of institution holding account

Account or certificate no.

————— $ —————

Name of institution holding account

Account or certificate no.

————— $ —————

Other accounts (include seller's interest in land contracts, mortgages, notes, debts owed to you, etc.)

Describe:

————— $ —————

Stocks (include only publicly traded stocks; list stock in small corporations under business interests later in this section)

Company

Type of stock

Certificate no.

Number of shares

_____ $ _____

Company

Type of stock

Certificate no.

Number of shares

_____ $ _____

Company

Type of stock

Certificate no.

Number of shares

_____ $ _____

Bonds

Issuer

Type or series of bond

Maturity date

_____ $ _____

Issuer

Type or series of bond

Maturity date

_____ $ _____

Issuer

Type or series of bond

Maturity date

_____ $ _____

Life insurance (include insurance you own on your life and insurance you own on the lives of others)

Term life insurance

Name of company

Policy no.

Insured

Primary beneficiary

Secondary beneficiary

Face amount   _____ $ _____

Whole life insurance

Name of company

Policy no.

Insured

Primary beneficiary

Secondary beneficiary

Face amount   _____ $ _____

Retirement plan death benefits from employer-provided and individual (IRA, SEP, Keogh (HR-10), etc.) retirement plans

Employer/Payor

Type of plan

Type of death benefit

Primary beneficiary

Secondary beneficiary

Current value of death benefit   _____ $ _____

Employer/Payor

Type of plan

Type of death benefit

Primary beneficiary

Secondary beneficiary

Current value of death benefit   _____ $ _____

Business interests

Sole proprietorship

Name of business

Type of business

Value of business   _____ $ _____

Partnership

Name of business

Type of business

Value of your interest in business   _____ $ _____

Small corporation

Name of business

Type of business

Value of your interest in business   _____ $ _____

Motor vehicles (include automobiles, watercraft, aircraft, recreational vehicles, etc.)

Type of vehicle

Year/make/model

     _____ $ _____

Type of vehicle

Year/make/model

     _____ $ _____

Type of vehicle

Year/make/model

     _____ $ _____

Machinery, tools and equipment

Describe:

     _____ $ _____

Household goods (furniture, appliances, dishes, etc.)   _____ $ _____

Personal effects (clothing, furs, jewelry, etc.)   _____ $ _____

Antiques, collectibles (stamps, coins, etc.) and art objects   _____ $ _____

Legal judgments   _____ $ _____

Refunds (income tax, insurance, etc.)   _____ $ _____

Interests in trusts and estates   _____ $ _____

Patents, copyrights, trademarks and royalties   _____ $ _____

Other personal property   _____ $ _____

2. Liabilities

Personal debts (bank loans, personal loans, credit card debts, charge accounts, etc.)

Creditor

Type of debt

Persons obligated

Current balance   _____ $ _____

Creditor

Type of debt

Persons obligated

Current balance   _____ $ _____

Creditor

Type of debt

Persons obligated

Current balance   _____ $ _____

Tax and legal obligations (tax debts, legal judgments owed, unpaid child support, etc.)

Creditor

Type of debt

Persons obligated

Current balance   _____ $ _____

Total liabilities   _____ $ _____

Net worth (total of sec. 1 minus total of sec. 2)   _____ $ _____

Chapter 1B Basics of Estate Planning

When people think about death—a topic most of us prefer to avoid—everyone expects to exit quickly and painlessly. Maybe that's why estate planning often looks no further than death. Estate planning has customarily focused on the distribution of property *after* death, and related issues like avoiding estate taxes and probate. All this is fine because these things are as important as ever.

The reality is that fewer and fewer deaths are sudden. With advances in medicine and new life-sustaining technology, most people today decline slowly from chronic or terminal illnesses, which often cause mental or physical incapacitation of the patient.

Incapacity isn't only a worry at the end of life either. Mental or physical incapacity can strike anyone, even the young, after a severe illness or accident. In fact, incapacity is far more likely than death for everyone, including the elderly.

As a result, the scope of estate planning must be expanded to consider incapacity as well as death. And today, no estate plan is complete without planning for both death and incapacity by dealing with the following issues.

Distributing Property

At death, your property is divided into two categories: probate and non-probate estates. The probate estate contains probate property, such as:

- property you own by yourself (solely-owned property)
- your percentage share of tenancy in common property (a type of joint property)

Married person with children/descendants when at least one is also child/descendant of surviving spouse	[Spouse square] + [Spouse / Children/descendants by representation circle]
Married person with children/descendants when none is child/descendant of surviving spouse	[Spouse triangle] + [Spouse / Children/descendants by representation circle]
Married person without children/descendants, but with parents	[Spouse square] + [Parents / Spouse circle]
Married person without children/descendants or parents	[Spouse circle]
Single person with children/descendants	[Children/descendants by representation circle]
Single person without children/descendants, but with parents	[Parents circle]
Single person without children/descendants or parents, but with brothers or sisters/their descendants	[Brothers and sisters/their descendants by representation circle]
All distributions beyond this point are to other heirs	

□ = first $150,000 of residuary estate

△ = first $100,000 of residuary estate

○ = 1) any remainder of residuary estate after spouse's share has been deducted 2) otherwise, entire residuary estate

Note: the fixed-dollar shares allotted to spouse will be adjusted for inflation annually

- proceeds from insurance on your life if your estate receives the proceeds
- retirement plan death benefits if your estate receives the benefits

Your nonprobate estate is all your nonprobate property, including:

- joint tenancy and tenancy by the entirety property
- proceeds from insurance on your life received by someone other than your estate
- retirement plan death benefits received by someone other than your estate
- property held in a living (*inter vivos*) trust

Die without a will and your probate estate is distributed by Michigan's inheritance law. This law allocates property in rigid patterns, which might be very different from what you want. The chart on the opposite page depicts the inheritance law pattern.

A will is your chance to devise your own pattern of property distribution. With few exceptions, a will gives you complete freedom to distribute your probate estate. Chapter 2, "Wills," has information and directions for making two types of simple wills available in Michigan: a fill-in-the-blanks Michigan statutory will (Chapter 2A) and a handwritten will (Chapter 2B).

Your nonprobate estate is distributed according to its own rules, and isn't affected by the inheritance law or a will. For example, most joint property goes to the surviving joint owner(s). Life insurance proceeds and retirement plan death benefits go to designated beneficiaries.

Just as you plan for distribution of your probate estate, you should plan for distribution of your nonprobate estate. Chapter 5, "Joint Property," explains who gets your joint property when you die. Chapter 6, "Insurance," and Chapter 7, "Retirement Benefits," have planning tips on designating beneficiaries of these assets.

Avoiding Estate Taxes

Michigan residents face two estate taxes: 1) federal estate tax (FET) 2) Michigan estate tax (MET). These taxes are assessed against a deceased person's probate and nonprobate property. That's why you must figure your total net worth before estimating possible estate taxes.

Federal Estate Tax

The FET is a graduated tax, with rates that increase as the value of the estate does. These rates are quite stiff. They start at 37% and climb to a staggering 55% on estates over $2.5 million. Luckily, the FET has several generous exemptions, including:

Marital exemption. Unlimited exemption covering all distributions to spouses who are U.S. citizens (if a spouse is a noncitizen, no marital exemption is allowed).

General exemption. Exemption for transfers of estate property or lifetime gifts to anyone. The general exemption is $675,000 until 2001, but will then rise sharply, as follows:

20002 and 2003	$700,000
2004	850,000
2005	950,000
2006 and after	1 million

Thanks to these exemptions, single persons or married couples with a combined net worth of $675,000 (or whatever the general exemption is in future years) or less normally don't owe any FET. On the other hand, single persons or married couples who plan to leave their property to each other face a possible FET bill if they own more than $675,000.

Example: George has property worth $300,000 and Margo has $100,000. George dies and passes his property to Margo. No FET is due because the marital exemption covers the transfer. Margo dies and gives $400,000 to their three children. Again, no FET is due because the $675,000 general exemption exempts the transfer.

Example: George owns property worth $800,000 and Margo has $200,000. George dies and passes his property onto Margo. No FET is due then because of the marital exemption. Margo dies and gives $1 million to their three children. The FET's general exemption exempts $675,000 of the transfer, but the remaining $325,000 is taxable.

Had George split his estate between Margo and others (children, siblings or anybody else), no tax would be owed. The $400,000 given to Margo is covered by the marital exemption and the $400,000 for the others is exempted by the $675,000 general exemption. When Margo dies and gives property worth $600,000 to the children, her general exemption easily covers the transfer.

To see how you stand with the FET, take your net worth from the last line of your inventory, and compare this figure with the general exemption. Single persons or married couples with a net worth of $675,000 or less usually won't owe any FET. Those with more than $675,000 may owe some tax.

In reality, you may consume some of your wealth before you die, leaving a smaller estate than your inventory shows. Or you may add to your wealth before death increasing the estate. Both things are speculative, as is your life span. Thus, you must plan as if you will die tomorrow, with your estate as it is now. As your wealth grows or shrinks in the future, you may have to revise your estate plan.

Even those with a potential FET bill shouldn't despair, because they can avoid or minimize the tax with proper estate planning. In fact, the FET can be avoided completely on estates up to $1.35 million (or double the amount of the general exemption, as the exemption increases after 2001), and taxes can be reduced on larger estates.

Gifts are one tax-reduction technique. As explained in Chapter 4, "Gifts," you can give away property during your lifetime reducing your estate and estate tax bill, while avoiding gift tax. There are other more sophisticated tax strategies, such as trusts (especially so-called bypass trusts), which professional estate planners can design for you.

All these tax avoidance schemes are effective. According to recent U.S. Department of Treasury figures, only around 25,000 estates owe FET annually, which is slightly more than 1% of all Americans who die each year.

Michigan Estate Tax

In 1993, Michigan replaced the inheritance tax, which had been around since 1899, with the MET. The MET is directly linked to the FET. In FET returns, estates can take credits for estate taxes paid to states. The MET makes clever use of this state tax credit. The MET expands to equal the maximum amount of the state tax credit available for estates.

> *Example*: Edith dies leaving $800,000 to her children. The FET allows a $960 state tax credit for the $125,000 taxable portion of her estate. Edith's MET tax equals the credit: $960. Her estate pays this amount to the state of Michigan and then receives a credit for the payment on her FET return.

You don't owe any MET unless you owe FET. Thus, estates of $675,000 or less don't have to worry about the MET. And curiously, neither do $675,000-plus estates. When the MET is paid, the full amount of the tax comes off the FET bill. As a result, the estate suffers no out-of-pocket cost for the MET. In effect, the federal government pays the MET indirectly by reducing the FET bill in the amount of the MET.

Probate Planning

No matter how much you try, it's difficult to avoid probate entirely, and almost everyone leaves a few things requiring probate transfer after death. Thus, you should do some planning for probate, if nothing more than appointing a personal representative to handle the probate.

Avoiding Probate

Probate is the settlement of a deceased person's probate estate. During the procedure, the deceased's probate property is collected, any charges against the estate (final disposition and death ceremony expenses, estate taxes, debts, etc.) are paid, and the remainder is distributed by the inheritance law or will.

Probate has a bad reputation, which isn't totally deserved. When

Norman Dacey wrote *How to Avoid Probate!* in the 1960s, probate was truly a chamber of horrors. Probate was complicated and lawyers were eager to stretch it out to earn maximum fees.

These days, there is less reason to fear probate. For one thing, fewer assets than ever are subject to probate. During the last 50 years, people have put more of their wealth in nonprobate assets, such as joint property, life insurance and retirement plans, leaving much less property for probate.

And as complaints about probate grew louder, states revised their probate laws. Among other reforms, states introduced "small estate" procedures making probate cheaper and quicker. In Michigan, eligibility for small estate probate depends on several factors: the value of and kind of property in the probate estate and the identity of the survivors. The chart below depicts the small estate eligibility rules:

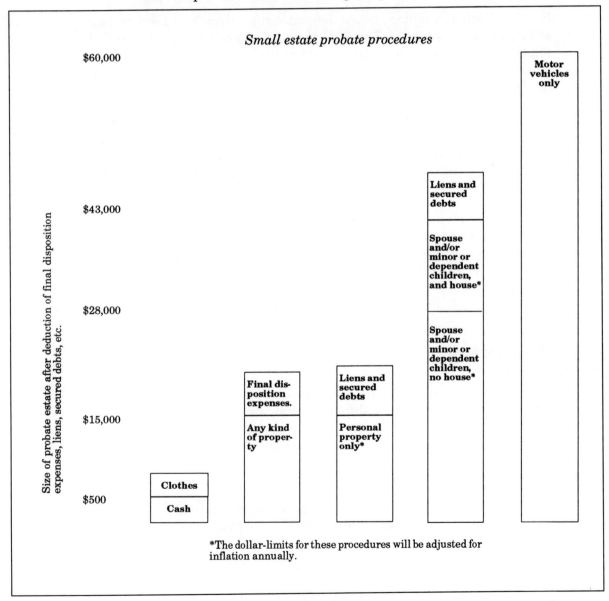

Small estate probate procedures

Size of probate estate after deduction of final disposition expenses, liens, secured debts, etc.

$60,000

$43,000

$28,000

$15,000

$500

Motor vehicles only

Liens and secured debts

Spouse and/or minor or dependent children, and house*

Spouse and/or minor or dependent children, no house*

Final disposition expenses.

Any kind of property

Liens and secured debts

Personal property only*

Clothes

Cash

*The dollar-limits for these procedures will be adjusted for inflation annually.

Use your inventory to see which small estate probate, if any, you qualify for. Estimate the size of your probate estate by totaling all your probate property in Michigan. Working from your inventory, add up all your solely-owned property, your share of tenancy in common property, and proceeds from life insurance and retirement plan death benefits your estate will receive. Compare this figure to the levels in the chart above.

If you want to avoid or minimize probate, convert probate property into nonprobate form. Chapter 5, "Joint Property," explains how to create various types of joint property, which are usually nonprobate property.

It isn't always possible to eliminate your probate estate completely. Single people in particular may not want to put property in joint ownership or other nonprobate form. And no matter how determined you are to avoid probate, almost everyone ends up leaving some probate property.

If you have a probate estate, which you estimate is too large for a small estate probate, consider asking for unsupervised probate. This is an efficient probate procedure with little or no court supervision.

Your will can include a request for unsupervised probate, which must be followed except in extraordinary situations. Part II of Chapter 2B explains how to add such a request to a handwritten will.

Choosing Someone to Probate Your Estate

In Michigan, the person responsible for probating your estate is known as a personal representative. The personal representative also has some authority to carry out instructions about "final matters" (final disposition of your body and a death ceremony).

If you die without a will, the probate court appoints a personal representative for you. The appointee is usually chosen from among your close relatives. But there's no guarantee of this choice, and you have no control over the selection.

By making a will, you can handpick a first-choice personal representative and a successor if the first choice can't serve. Both wills in Chapter 2 have provisions for choosing personal representative.

Leaving "Liquid Assets"

After death, there's often an urgent need for spendable liquid assets, such as cash or near-cash (bank accounts, money market accounts, certificates of deposit, etc.). Survivors may need these liquid assets to pay the deceased's final expenses or their own living expenses.

You may have liquid assets in your probate or nonprobate estates to meet all the liquidity needs of your estate and survivors. For example, you can leave a solely-owned or joint bank account with funds to satisfy these needs (see Chapter 5, "Joint Property" about using several kinds of joint property for this purpose).

Or the beneficiaries of life insurance or retirement plan death benefits can make these available to your estate, providing liquidity. Chapter 6,

"Insurance," and Chapter 7, "Retirement Benefits," explain this technique. Chapter 8, "Final Matters,"tells how to prepay final expenses, minimizing the need for liquidity.

Caring for Dependent People and Animals

Anyone with dependents—whether human or animal—is naturally anxious about who will care for them when they can't. Caretakers may need temporary substitutes during a spell of incapacity or absence. And certainly, someone must take over when they die.

For temporary transfers of custody, Michigan offers a special custodial power of attorney, which can last up to six months (it can be renewed for longer periods). Chapter 3, "Taking Care of Dependents," has all the details about this handy device.

Guardianship is the way to protect dependents whose current caretakers have died. Courts will step in and appoint guardians to take custody of these dependents (and conservators to manage their property, if necessary). But you can appoint guardians and conservators before death. Your guardian appointment is binding (subject only to veto by a teenage dependent); a conservator appointment is nonbinding, but carries great weight and is usually followed by the court.

You can appoint guardians and conservators for many of your human dependents in a will, as explained in Chapter 2. It's also possible to provide care for your pet animals after you die by setting up a special living trust for pets. These pet trusts are explained in Chapter 3.

Or if you don't want to make a will just yet, you can appoint guardians for many of your dependents in a separate guardian appointment, outside a will. Chapter 3 explains how to make these nonwill guardian appointments.

Arranging Final Matters

After death, your body must be disposed of in an acceptable way. Most people also want a ceremony marking the death. By planning ahead for these final matters, you take pressure off your survivors to decide. And you get the kind of final disposition and death ceremony you want.

It's permissible to leave directions for final matters in a will. But wills aren't always available at death, so the directions might not be heeded. A better place for these directions is a letter of instruction, addressed to your personal representative. In the letter, you can give directions about most aspects of a final disposition and death ceremony. Special forms are necessary for anatomical gifts (gifts of whole bodies and organ/tissue donations).

Chapter 8, "Final Matters," has information about all these issues. Chapter 8A, "Final Disposition," covers final disposition options like burial, cremation and anatomical gifts. "Death Ceremony," Chapter 8B, deals with the most popular death ceremonies: funeral, memorial, and committal.

Planning for Incapacity

Planning for incapacity is doubly important. A mental or physical incapacity can suddenly leave you unable to manage your financial affairs. Incapacity can also rob you of the ability to make health care decisions for yourself.

As always, the court system takes over when you fail to plan. A court can appoint a conservator to manage your financial affairs and/or a guardian to make health care decisions for you. But you can avoid these court interventions by planning ahead.

Financial management help is available in the form of a durable power of attorney (DPA). With this instrument, you appoint an agent to manage your financial affairs. The DPA lasts throughout your incapacity because of its durability. Chapter 9, "Durable Power of Attorney," has complete information about making two kinds of DPAs: one effective immediately and a so-called springing power of attorney which is dormant until your become incapacitated.

Advance directives are designed to assist incapacitated persons with their health care. Frequently, advance directives have end-of-life instructions, about if and when life-sustaining treatment should be terminated. There are two main types of advance directives: living will and patient advocate designation (PAD), which is a kind of power of attorney.

These advance directives do similar things, but they work differently. A living will gives instructions about health care in advance of incapacity. Then after incapacity, your health caregivers use the document as a guide for your health care. With a PAD, you appoint an agent (called a patient advocate) to make health care decisions for you during incapacity. You can also add health care directions to a PAD to guide the patient advocate.

Living wills and PADs are detailed documents, and may take your medical caregivers a while to read and interpret. These advance directives aren't really designed for on-the-spot medical decisions, such as when your heart or breathing stops and emergency caregivers have to decide whether to administer cardiovascular resuscitation (CPR). Michigan law allows you to give a special advance directive, called a do-not-resuscitate (DNR) order, forbidding CPR when your vital signs have stopped. A DNR order can be a written document or a wearable medical-alert bracelet.

Chapter 10, "Advance Directives" has more on advance directives. Chapter 10A, "Living Will," tells you how to make a living will and DNR order, while Chapter 10B, "Patient Advocate Designation," has similar information about making a PAD and DNR order.

Conclusion

Before you begin your estate plan, decide what you want to accomplish. Do you want to distribute property after death, avoid estate taxes, plan for incapacity, etc., or do all these things? After you decide, combine the various estate planning devices—wills, gifts, advance directives, etc.—into an estate plan to achieve your estate planning goals.

Wills, gifts, joint property, powers of attorney, it can all seem confusing until you see how the pieces fit together into a complete estate plan. To show you how estate planning works, consider the estate plans of the Frisbie and Millsaps families.

Frisbie Estate Plan

The Frisbies review their estate planning goals: distribute property after death to the surviving spouse, then children; make a gift now to Thelma; avoid probate as much as possible; die natural deaths, etc. With this in mind, the Frisbies put together the following estate plan.

Winter 1999

Wills. The Frisbies' inventory reveals that they don't own enough to worry about estate taxes, allowing them to use simple wills. They are pleased to find that the pattern of property distribution provided by a Michigan statutory will (all to the spouse, then to children equally) is the pattern they want. The statutory will also allows them to name guardians and conservators for Dewey and Woodrow. The Frisbies make statutory wills.

Gift. The Frisbies cash in their certificate of deposit and make a $20,000 gift to Thelma for a down-payment on her house. By making the gift together, they can avoid gift tax on the gift.

Joint property. The Frisbies already hold much of their property jointly, to avoid probate and for peace of mind. They decide to stick with this arrangement and even expand their joint property. George puts his northern Michigan cottage in joint tenancy with Margo. This leaves his automobile as his sole probate asset, making it eligible for special small estate transfer. Similarly, Margo puts her Florida lot in joint tenancy with George. With this transfer, she won't have any property requiring probate in another state.

Life insurance and retirement benefits. After reviewing George's employee benefits, the Frisbies decide that his term life insurance and retirement plan death benefits, when added to their financial assets, will provide enough liquidity after George's death.

The Frisbies find that George's life insurance goes to Margo as primary beneficiary and then the children as secondary beneficiaries. This is the pattern of distribution they want.

But the Frisbies are shocked that George's parents are the beneficiaries of his retirement plan death benefits. Apparently, he made this designation years ago, before he was married, and neglected to change it later. George contacts his benefits office and designates Margo as primary and the children as secondary beneficiaries of his retirement plan death benefits.

Final matters. With his dislike of funerals and burials, George makes a letter of instruction requesting cremation followed by a simple memorial. Both Frisbies are in favor of organ/tissue donations. They discuss these donations, enroll in Michigan's Organ and Tissue Donor Registry, and make anatomical donor documents.

Durable power of attorney and advance directives. The Frisbies enjoy good health, but realize that a mental or physical incapacity could strike anytime, leaving them unable to manage their financial affairs and/or health care. The couple decides to make durable powers of attorney (DPAs) with each other as agents. Since the Frisbies are healthy now, they make so-called springing DPAs, which don't go into effect until the actual onset of incapacity.
 The Frisbies also make patient advocate designations (PADs), with each other as patient advocates. Besides basic health care powers, the Frisbies include powers to terminate life-sustaining treatment in several situations in their PADs.

Millsaps Estate Plan

Edith has firm estate planning goals. She wants to: distribute her property to all her children except Eugene, while making specific gifts of certain items and money; make a gift now to grandson Garth; provide care for Digger, her dog; obtain help during incapacity; etc. She accomplishes these goals with the following estate plan.

Will. Like the Frisbies, Edith can use a simple will since she doesn't have enough property to owe estate taxes. Edith rejects a Michigan statutory will because it distributes property to all her children, including Eugene. To leave him out, Edith makes a handwritten will with a special provision "disinheriting" Eugene. A handwritten will can also easily accommodate Edith's gifts of heirlooms and cash to her church. Both gifts are permissible in a Michigan statutory will, but an extra form would be necessary to transfer the heirlooms.

Pet trust. Worried about who will take care of her dog Digger after her death, Edith makes a modest pet trust (a living trust), with Digger as sole beneficiary, Shirley as trustee and Grover as trust enforcer. Money to fund the trust comes from a pour-over provision in Edith's handwritten will.

Gift. Edith wants to give $1,000 to Garth, but knows the risk of giving the money to him directly. Instead, she creates a bank account under the

Uniform Transfers to Minors Act (UTMA) for Garth. Edith names Garth's mother (Grover's ex-wife), whom Edith likes and trusts, as custodian. The custodian can draw money from this account to help Garth, and Edith can add to it in the future.

Joint property. Since Edith has a small estate and isn't worried about probate, she has most of her property in sole ownership. She did put her bank account in joint tenancy with Shirley, so one of her children would have access to the account if she became incapacitated.

Edith realizes now that creation of the joint bank account with Shirley was a mistake. Edith wants to give her property to her children (minus Eugene) equally. But the $10,000 bank account is one-seventh of Edith's total wealth, and when she dies, Shirley will get the account plus one-third of the probate estate. Shirley would end up with more than Grover and Wanda, which might create hard feelings among them.

Edith considers adding Grover and Wanda to the bank account as additional joint tenants. She rejects this idea because Wanda, who is kind of a spendthrift, would have complete access to the account.

A better option is conversion of the joint tenancy bank account into a convenience account with Shirley. With this type of account, Edith and Shirley both control the account during Edith's lifetime, but at her death it remains part of her probate estate (and goes by will to Grover, Shirley and Wanda equally).

Ultimately, Edith decides that a durable power of attorney (DPA) is the best way to manage her bank account and other property. The power of attorney provides maximum control with more protection if she becomes incapacitated. With Shirley's cooperation, Edith puts the bank account back into her sole name, so it will pass through her will and probate estate to Grover, Shirley and Wanda equally.

Durable power of attorney and advance directive. After her recent illness, Edith realizes that she may soon need help with her financial affairs. She makes an immediate DPA, which is effective right away. Edith names Grover as agent with Shirley as the standby.

Edith also makes a patient advocate designation (PAD), with Grover and Shirley as patient advocates, for health care decision-making. Because her church frowns on termination of life-sustaining treatment, Edith omits this power from the PAD.

As you can see, it doesn't take a lot of fancy planning to put together an estate plan. Most people of modest means can achieve all their goals with just a few simple devices. The Frisbies are typical. Their estate plan of wills, incidental gifts, DPAs, PADs, letters of instruction, and anatomical gift documents, is all most people need.

Chapter 2
Wills

Chapter 2
Introduction to Wills

Besides gifts, wills have the oldest pedigree of any estate planning device. Scholars speculate that wills and related inheritance laws were devised by primitive people to prevent squabbling over property of the dead. The oldest surviving will was made in 2601 B.C. by Nek'ure, the son of the Egyptian Pharaoh Khafre, who built the Great Pyramid. Nek'ure's will, inscribed on the wall of his tomb, disposes of 14 towns and 2 estates near his father's pyramid.

In the modern era, by far the most important will law was the English Wills Act of 1837, which spelled out rules for making wills. For the first time, all wills, except those made by soldiers and sailors, had to be written. The Wills Act also erased the previous distinction between a will (transferring real property) and a testament (passing personal property). Henceforth, wills governed both types of property, although even today some people still refer to a will as a last will and testament.

Types of Wills

Unlike most countries, the United States doesn't have a single, national law of wills. Instead, wills are left to state control. As states adopted will laws in the 19th century, they often borrowed from the English Wills Act of 1837. Thus, there are similarities between state will laws. Yet many differences also exist. Nowhere are these more noticeable than in the types of wills states recognize.

Written wills. Most states require that wills must be written, although states authorize a variety of will documents.

¶ *Regular will.* Regular wills are tailor-made wills that people get from lawyers and sign before witnesses. You don't need a lawyer for a regular will; you can make one yourself. But most people go to lawyers for regular wills because they're familiar with the rules of will-writing and execution (the procedure for signing a will and having it witnessed).

¶ *Statutory will.* A statutory will is a form will which you can make without a lawyer. You complete a statutory will by filling in blanks on the will form. Statutory wills don't need lawyers, but they do require witnesses for execution.

California adopted the first statutory will in 1983, followed by Maine and Wisconsin a year later, and New Mexico in 1991. Michigan adopted its statutory will in 1986.

¶ *Handwritten will.* In a handwritten will (technically known as a holographic will) the willmaker handwrites the entire will. Unlike other wills, a handwritten will doesn't have to be witnessed. The reasoning is that a handwritten will can be authenticated by verification of the handwriting, so witnesses are unnecessary.

Handwritten wills are a creation of French and Spanish law, and existed in several southern and western states influenced by those legal traditions. Now, other states have adopted handwritten wills. Michigan has permitted them since 1979.

¶ *International will.* A new kind of will in Michigan, which can be in any language and is valid all over the world. There are special execution rules for international wills, and they must be witnessed by two ordinary witnesses and a special international wills witness (any lawyer or a U.S. foreign service official), who must certify the proper execution of the will.

¶ *Self-proved will.* A self-proved will isn't really a separate kind of will; any *witnessed* will (regular, statutory, but not handwritten) can become self-proved. After self-proving, the signatures in the will are assumed to be valid, doing away with the need of witness testimony to support the will during the main types of probate. A will is self-proved by execution of a self-proving document, in which the willmaker and witnesses swear to (under oath, before a notary public) or verify (by signing a verification statement, without a notary public) the correctness of the will signing.

¶ *Joint will.* A joint will is made by several people together. Years ago, joint wills were popular, particularly among married couples, because they were a bargain (you got two wills for the price of one). But joint wills have a big flaw. The making of a joint will can legally bind the joint willmakers to the will. This prevents the joint willmakers from changing the will later, even after the death of one of them. Because of this problem, few people make joint wills today.

¶ *Living will.* A living will isn't really a will at all, since it doesn't distribute any property. A living will is actually a type of advance directive, where you give instructions about health care.

Unwritten wills. Centuries ago, when most people were illiterate, wills were usually unwritten. Unwritten wills were often whispered to friends or relatives just before death. Since these wills were ripe for misinterpretation, states have steadily curbed unwritten wills.

¶ *Oral will.* Some states have permitted oral wills in emergency circumstances. For example, several states allowed dying patients or military servicemen during war to make oral wills. Before 1979, Michigan permitted oral wills by active-duty military personnel, or anybody when the value of the property transferred was $300 or less. But since 1979, Michigan, like most states today, has forbidden all oral wills.

¶ *Video will.* Someday, written wills may be replaced by wills recorded on videotape or other electronic means. But currently, no state authorizes video wills. A few states, such as Indiana, have laws regulating the videotaping of will executions, although the wills themselves must be written.

Making Your Own Will

Not everyone should make their own will. Some people have special estate planning needs or problems demanding lawyer-made regular wills (often with special trusts built into the wills). Here are several situations where you should go to a lawyer for a will:

- you (and your spouse) have a net worth of more than $675,000, creating a potential estate tax problem
- your spouse is a noncitizen without a marital exemption from the estate tax
- you wish to place unusual conditions or restrictions on distribution of your property
- you suspect that a relative may contest your will
- you have dependents, such as a handicapped child or elderly aged parent, whose dependency, unlike a minor child, continues indefinitely and requires special support

But if you don't need a lawyer-made will, you're in luck because Michigan has two do-it-yourself wills: a statutory will and a handwritten will. Both are simple wills designed for people with basic estate plans. These wills are also simple to make, so you can prepare one yourself, without a lawyer.

Despite these similarities, statutory and handwritten wills differ in several important ways. Keep these differences in mind as you choose the will that's right for you.

Distribution of Property

Statutory Will

Like the inheritance law, a statutory will distributes property in a fixed pattern. The pattern isn't as rigid as the inheritance law. For example, a statutory will offers two distribution choices if you die without any close relatives. Nevertheless, a statutory will's pattern of distribution, depicted below, is basically fixed and cannot be modified.

Married person with or without children/descendants	◯ Spouse
Single person with children/descendants	◯ Children/descendants by representation
Single person without children/descendants	◯ Heirs

◯ = residuary estate

The statutory will's pattern of property distribution is based on a survey of deceased people filed in probate courts. These wills show that a majority of married people with children want to give property first to their spouses, then to children/descendants. The surveyed wills also reveal that single people with children or descendants favor these relatives over others. And heirs are the preferred beneficiaries of childless single persons.

Despite its popularity, a statutory will's property distribution pattern isn't right for everyone. It's the wrong choice if you want to disinherit your spouse (which in most cases is impossible to do completely). You should also avoid a statutory will when you want to divide your property unequally, since the will usually distributes property in equal shares.

Example: Edith wants to give her estate to just three of her children, excluding Eugene. She also wants to reduce Grover's share because she once helped him buy a house. A statutory will doesn't allow Edith to disinherit Eugene or give Grover a smaller share of property.

A statutory will adopts Michigan's estates code definition of children (see "Children" in the glossary for a full explanation of this definition). The code definition excludes some children, such as stepchildren and certain illegitimate children of men. As a result, you cannot benefit these excluded children in a statutory will (except by cash gift). The code definition includes other children such as legally adopted children. These children are automatically included in any distributions of property to children in a statutory will, making it impossible to leave them out.

Example: Grover's wife Doreen wants to include her stepson Garth in any distribution of property to her children in her will. And if the distribution reaches her sister Margaret and her children, she wants to exclude Margaret's adopted children. Doreen cannot include Garth or exclude Margaret's adopted children in a statutory will.

A statutory will distributes property to blood relatives or spouses; nonrelatives are totally excluded (unless you give them cash gifts). Thus, you cannot distribute your estate to friends or organizations, such as charities, religious or service organizations, etc., in a statutory will.

Example: Edith wants to divide her property equally among her children and church. She cannot include the church as co-taker with her children in a statutory will because it doesn't distribute property to nonrelatives.

Handwritten Will

A handwritten will offers much greater flexibility in property distribution. With a few exceptions, you can devise your own pattern of distribution and give your property to whomever you want.

You can stick with a conventional distribution pattern, echoing the pattern in the statutory will. Or you can do things you couldn't do in a statutory will. You can limit your spouse's share to the legal minimum or completely disinherit your children/descendants. You can benefit children excluded from the estates code definition of children, or cut out children included in the code definition. You can distribute your property in unequal shares, or include nonrelatives like friends or organizations in the distribution.

37

Specific Gifts

Statutory Will

One benefit of a will is the ability to make specific gifts, earmarking specific items of property for particular recipients. Typically, willmakers give personal property, such as cash, jewelry or heirlooms, in these gifts.

A Michigan statutory will permits a maximum of two specific gifts, of cash only. You can give the money directly to the recipients, or to their custodians under the Uniform Transfers to Minors Act (UTMA), delaying payment until age 18-21 (you can pick the age for payment).

Michigan's statutory will is a little stingy with specific gifts of cash (Wisconsin's statutory will allows five). You can compensate a bit by making specific gifts of personal and household items outside a statutory will in a separate list. But this method doesn't allow distribution of noncash financial assets, which fall outside the category of personal and household items, or transfer of any real property.

A statutory will also limits the distribution of frustrated specific gifts. A frustrated specific gift is a will gift to a person who dies before you, or an organization that goes defunct before your death, and isn't available to take the gift as planned.

Example: George prepares a statutory will and makes two specific gifts: $5,000 to his brother Chester and $1,000 to a policemen's charity. His brother dies before George does and the charity goes out of business before his death. What happens to these frustrated gifts?

In other types of wills, you can address the problem of frustrated gifts by naming second takers, who take the gift when the first taker fails to survive you. The specific gift provisions of a statutory will don't allow for that. Instead, a statutory will relies on a Michigan law that passes frustrated gifts according to a prescribed pattern. This pattern may not always be what you want.

Example: George makes a statutory will, dies and leaves two frustrated specific gifts: $5,000 to his deceased brother Chester and $1,000 to a defunct policemen's charity. According to Michigan law, the $5,000 goes to Chester's children/descendants and the $1,000 passes with the rest of the estate. The distribution of the $1,000 was what George wanted, but he would have preferred to give the $5,000 to his other brother Wesley, instead of Chester's children/descendants.

Handwritten Will

You can make an unlimited number of specific gifts in a handwritten will, directly to recipients or in a trust-like way under the Uniform Transfers to Minors Act (UTMA). What's more, these gifts may include any kind of personal property or real property. With this flexibility, there's seldom a need for a separate list with a handwritten will.

A handwritten will allows you to name second or even third takers of specific gifts. By planning ahead that way, you can prevent the gifts from becoming frustrated and going to someone you don't want.

Example: In his handwritten will, George makes a $5,000 specific gift to his brother Chester. If Chester fails to survive him, he wants to give the money to Wesley. So George adds a provision to the gift naming Wesley as second taker of the $5,000.

Appointment of Fiduciaries

In a will, you can appoint several kinds of fiduciaries, who represent you after death. You may appoint personal representatives (to settle your estate), guardians (to take care of your dependent children), and conservators (to manage minor children's property). You can also appoint substitutes to serve in these roles when your first choices are unable or unwilling to serve.

These appointments are either binding on the probate court, or have clout and are followed by the court in most cases. Appointment of a personal representative is nonbinding, but the appointee has top priority and can qualify easily. A guardian appointment is the most forceful; it's binding unless a teenage dependent vetoes the appointment. A conservator appointment has perhaps the least influence. The appointee has high priority, but a mature teenage dependent can nominate his/own candidate, which the court must consider.

Statutory Will

If you make a statutory will, you can appoint all three kinds of fiduciaries in the will. Still, a statutory will's fiduciary provisions have some limitations. One thing you can't do is name several fiduciaries to act collectively. Collective fiduciaries take several forms, including joint and split appointments.

Joint appointment. In a joint appointment, fiduciaries act together sharing the powers given to them. For example, naming co-personal representatives to settle your estate is a joint appointment. If a will permits joint appointments, you can appoint joint personal representatives, guardians or conservators.

Split appointment. Split fiduciaries are assigned separate powers and duties which they perform independently of each other. For example, you could split a guardian appointment by naming different guardians for different children. If a will permits split appointments, you may split guardian or conservator appointments; Michigan's estates code forbids true splitting of personal representative's duties.

Sometimes, collective fiduciaries makes sense; other times they're more trouble than they're worth. Good or bad, appointment of collective fiduciaries isn't allowed in a Michigan statutory will. A statutory will has space for only one appointee per fiduciary position, ruling out all kinds of joint and split appointments.

Ordinarily, willmakers appoint guardians for their minor children. But in some circumstances you can appoint guardians for dependent adults by will. Parents of developmentally disabled (DD) adult children often have this right. And parents of legally incapacitated (LI) unmarried adults, or spouses of LI mates, who are already serving as guardians, can appoint successor guardians to take over when they're gone.

In a statutory will, you can appoint guardians for children (minor or adult) only. Thus, parents of DD adult children can appoint guardians, or parents serving as guardians of LI unmarried adult children can appoint successor guardians. But spouses of LI adults cannot appoint successors in statutory wills.

A statutory will adopts broad fiduciary powers drawn from Michigan's estates code. The powers assigned to a personal representative are particularly wide in scope (these are summarized in "Powers of Personal Representative" in the glossary). Granting broad fiduciary powers is usually good, since your fiduciaries must have full authority to act for you.

There are a few small deficiencies in the personal representative's powers to manage and operate a small business during probate. Some willmakers with businesses may wish to expand these powers. Others might want to go in the opposite direction and limit the powers given to fiduciaries. Neither modification is permissible in a statutory will. If you make a statutory will, you must accept the standard fiduciary powers the will adopts from the estates code.

Handwritten Will

In a handwritten will, you can make personal representative, guardian and conservator appointments, just as in a statutory will. But these appointments are more flexible in a handwritten will.

You can make joint or split fiduciary appointments in a handwritten will. Spouses may also appoint successor guardians for their LI spouses. And you may assign standard code powers to your personal representative, as in a statutory will, or craft your own statement of powers.

Survival

Statutory Will

When you give property in a will—either a specific gift or distribution of your entire estate—you assume that the takers will survive you. If they don't, they cannot take the property and the gifts are frustrated. There are ways to deal with the frustration of will gifts. You can anticipate the problem and name second takers of the gifts. Or if there's time, you can revise your will and name new takers to replace the deceased ones.

A similar problem happens when a will gift-taker barely survives you for a brief time. Ordinarily, the survivors (or their estates) might be entitled to the gifts. But does it make sense to give the property to them, and probate it through their estates, when they never get a chance to use it?

> *Example:* George and Margo have wills giving all their property to each other, then to their children. George dies first, followed by Margo two days later. Without any survival rules or provisions, George's property goes to Margo since she survived him. All of Margo's property, which now includes George's property, is then transferred from her estate to the children.

As you can see, this isn't the most efficient way to transfer property. Passing George's property through Margo's estate to the children delays distribution of the property to them . It also adds to the size and expense of Margo's probate.

Luckily, Michigan law has rules about survival. One rule says that, unless a will states otherwise, all takers from a will must survive the will-maker by 120 hours (five days). Although it doesn't say so, a statutory will adopts this five-day survival rule. Thus, had George and Margo made statutory wills in the example above, George's property would skip Margo (because she did not survive him by five days), and go directly to the children.

The five-day survival rule, but doesn't completely solve the survival problem. Had, in the above example, Margo survived George by seven days instead of two, the survival problem would still exist. The solution is to extend the survival period beyond the automatic 120 hours. A statutory will doesn't allow such an extension.

Handwritten Will

When lawyers write regular wills, they usually extend the 120-hour survival period to around 30 days. You can extend the survival period this way in a handwritten will.

Final Directions

Statutory Will

A statutory will doesn't give you much chance to make final directions. You can say whether your fiduciaries must post bonds. Otherwise, there's no place to give directions about final matters (final disposition of your body and death ceremonies), or other things. You can compensate by taking care of final matters outside the will, in separate documents, which is usually a better method anyway.

Handwritten Will

You may include any type of final direction in a handwritten will: instructions about final matters, fiduciary bond requirements, the kind of probate you want, cancellation of debts owed to you, satisfaction of will gifts (deduction of lifetime gifts from will gifts), etc. Despite this opportunity, most final directions, such as instructions about final matters, are best made outside the will, in separate documents.

Will Preparation

Statutory Will

The biggest advantage of a statutory will is ease of preparation; all you have to do is fill in some blanks. The execution of the will is more bother because you must gather several witnesses for the signing of the will. Even so, the execution procedure takes just a few minutes, even if you make the will self-proving.

Handwritten Will

Compared to a statutory will, a handwritten will is much more difficult to prepare. You have to choose the correct will provisions and assemble these into a coherent will. You must then write out the entire will in your own handwriting. On the other hand, a handwritten will is easy to execute because it doesn't need witnesses; all you have to do is date and sign the will.

Choosing a Will

As a no-frills will, a statutory will plainly has several limitations. It possesses a fairly fixed pattern of property distribution, with few opportunities for specific gifts. It also has minor deficiencies with fiduciary appointments and survival requirements.

You cannot modify a statutory will to correct these shortcomings. Any modification of a statutory will, by adding or subtracting from the will form, can jeopardize the modified section or even the entire will. A statutory will is either take-it-or-leave-it.

Despite these limitations, a statutory will has distinct advantages. It has a popular pattern of property distribution. You can add to the specific gifts available in a statutory will by making other gifts in a separate list, outside the will. And above all, a statutory will is almost foolproof; it's easy to prepare and execute, making it a very reliable instrument (the reliability can be increased by making the will self-proving).

A handwritten will is a far more flexible instrument. You can adopt almost any pattern of property distribution and make unlimited specific gifts. You have great freedom in fiduciary appointments and may extend the survival period. On the minus side, a handwritten will takes more effort to prepare, since you must compose the will and write it out.

All in all, a statutory will should be suitable for most people. A handwritten will is the best choice for those with special needs or problems, such as when you want to disinherit relatives, make out-of-the-ordinary specific gifts or appoint joint or split fiduciaries.

Chapter 2A Before You Make a Statutory Will

Part 1

A Michigan statutory will has an abundance of notices, warnings, instructions, and even its own glossary of terms. Despite all this information, the will doesn't tell you everything you need to know about making the document. This part fills that gap and provides extra information about making a statutory will.

Who Can Make a Statutory Will?

Age and Mental Capacity

In Michigan, any adult (a person 18 years of age or older) with a sound mind can make a will. Sound mind has a two-fold meaning. In one sense, it means that a willmaker must have the proper mental capacity to make a will. To have this mental capacity, a willmaker must possess the ability to know:

- the "natural objects of one's bounty" (those a willmaker would be expected to benefit, such as close relatives)
- the nature and extent of the willmaker's property
- that s/he is providing for distribution of property in the will
- the manner in which the will distributes property

Sound mind also means that the willmaker's judgment isn't clouded by an insane delusion. An insane delusion is a belief in things that don't exist. If a willmaker distributes property under such a delusion, the willmaker's mind might be unsound, jeopardizing the will.

Undue Influence, Duress and Fraud

Besides having a sound mind, a willmaker must make the will without undue influence, duress or fraud. Undue influence is when someone influences you to the extent the will is not really your free choice. Undue influence usually comes from those you trust, such as relatives, friends or advisors. Duress is like undue influence, but worse. With duress, someone actually forces you to make a will. Normally, the force must be physical force or the threat of it. But in some cases, extreme psychological pressure can qualify as duress. A fraudulent will is based on a misrepresentation (falsification) of a fact that you relied on in making the will.

When a willmaker is underage or has an unsound mind, the will is completely invalid. A will made under undue influence, duress or fraud may be declared invalid, or just the tainted provisions are removed, allowing the rest of the will to remain.

As strict as the mental capacity rules are, they apply only at the exact moment you make a will. In other words, you must have a sound mind and be free of undue influence, duress and fraud when you make your will. Spells of mental incapacity before or after are excusable.

Example: George suffers a serious stroke. For several days he is confined to an intensive care ward where he is under heavy sedation and semiconscious. He recovers his senses and makes a statutory will. Before long, George has another stroke and becomes mentally incapacitated again. Despite his spells of incapacity, the will is valid because it was made during a period of mental capacity.

Residence

As explained in the introduction, wills are regulated by state law. One consequence of state control is that you must reside in the state where you make your will. Thus, you must be a resident of Michigan before you can make a Michigan statutory will.

If you move out of state, will other states accept your Michigan will? Luckily, all states have will reciprocity laws recognizing out-of-state wills. According to these laws, a will is enforceable anywhere if it was valid when and where it was made.

Despite will reciprocity laws, you still should consider making a new will after moving out of state. Not every state has statutory wills, so courts in your new state might not be familiar with these. Also, a move out of state may require appointment of new fiduciaries who live near you. You can avoid these problems by making a new will under the law of the state where you reside.

Michigan residency is necessary for your statutory will; presence in the state is not. For example, you can make the will outside Michigan during a temporary absence, such as a vacation or business trip. Military servicepersons from Michigan can make Michigan statutory wills wherever they are stationed, because they normally keep the state residence they had before enlistment.

Residence is important for willmaking; citizenship is not. Thus, Michigan residents who aren't U.S. citizens can make Michigan statutory wills. These wills will be recognized throughout the United States because of the will reciprocity laws mentioned before. At the same time, noncitizens with property in their native countries may want to make an international will (see "Types of Wills" on page 33 for more about this option).

Specific Gifts

You can make a maximum of two specific gifts—of cash only—in a statutory will. Extra specific gifts of personal and household items are permissible in a separate list, outside the will. With either type of specific gift, you must know some will gift basics.

Who Can Take a Specific Gift?

You can make specific gifts to any person.* But some recipients, such as incapacitated adults and minors, may need special arrangements before they can take the gift. At one time, it was often necessary to put complicated trusts in wills, to hold will property for incapacitated adults or minors. These days, there are simpler management options, described below.

For will gifts to incapacitated adults, the gift can be transferred to:

- a conservator, if one is known to exist
- a specially-appointed trustee named during probate
- any agent from a power of attorney, such as a durable power of attorney
- 1) if the amount or value of the gift is $5,000 or less annually, and 2) a conservator has not been appointed, the gift goes to:
    - a spouse, parent or close relative taking care of the incapacitated adult
    - a guardian
    - a special savings account at a financial institution

For will gifts to minors, the gift can be transferred to:

- a conservator, if one is known to exist
- a specially-appointed trustee named during probate
- a custodian under the Uniform Transfers to Minors Act (UTMA) who already exists, is appointed in the will, or whom the personal representative names during probate

---

* Most of the following information about specific gifts also applies to the transfer of the remainder of the estate (the residuary estate).

- 1) if the amount or value of the gift is $5,000 or less annually, and 2) a conservator has not been appointed, the gift goes to:
  - the minor personally, if married
  - a current caretaker, such as a parent
  - a special savings account at a financial institution

There aren't any geographical limits on specific gifts. You can make gifts to people outside the state of Michigan, or even beyond the United States. Years ago, there were restrictions on making gifts to some noncitizens, particularly in communist countries, but these have now been abolished.

Besides giving to people, you can make specific gifts to a variety of organizations: charities, religious and service organizations, schools, foundations, governments, business and nonprofit organizations, fraternal associations and political parties. All that's necessary is that the organization has a formal legal identity. You cannot make specific gifts to informal organizations, like your softball or bowling team, because these groups aren't legally capable of taking a will gift.

People and organizations can take will gifts; animals cannot receive property directly from wills. You can make a specific gift to a charity or service organization providing animal care, like a humane society.

Michigan used to ban animals from benefiting from trusts. But Michigan's new estates code now allows special trusts for "domestic or pet animals." If you create a pet trust, you can name the primary animal beneficiaries, the secondary human beneficiaries (who take over when the pets have died), the trustee, and even a special trust enforcer. Pet trusts are explained in detail in Chapter 3, in "Permanent Care for Pets" on page 141. There is also a pet trust form you can use in the forms section.

Designating Specific Gift-Takers

As you make specific gifts, designate the gift-takers with care. People sometimes have look-alike or sound-alike names. The correct legal name of an organization is often far different from its popular name. Be absolutely sure you use the right name to avoid confusion.

Selecting Fiduciaries

Everyone should appoint personal representatives in their wills. Parents with minor children will want to appoint guardians and conservators for their children. DD adult children may also need guardians. And if you're already serving as guardian for a LI unmarried adult child, you can appoint a guardian to succeed you.*

---

* Keep in mind that you cannot make split appointments in a statutory will. Thus, if you have a mixture of minor children and LI or DD adult children, you must appoint one guardian for all your children.

For each fiduciary slot, you need two picks: a first choice and a substitute. If all goes well, your first choice will serve as fiduciary. But if the first choice cannot or will not serve, your substitute choice can step in.

Don't worry about making final fiduciary selections now. Use the information below to narrow the field of fiduciary candidates down to a few. Then make your final picks after the reviewing the sections of Part II dealing with qualifications for the various types of fiduciaries.

Fiduciaries: Legal Eligibility

You can appoint any adult person, except someone who is mentally incompetent, to serve as a fiduciary. Ordinarily, avoid appointing minors because they cannot serve if they are still underage when the time comes for them to assume their duties.

Michigan used to bar residents of other states or countries from serving as fiduciaries in many circumstances. But these days families are often far-flung, and willmakers often want to name out-of-state fiduciaries. In 1984, the fiduciary law was changed and now nonresidents and noncitizens can serve as fiduciaries in most cases.

Some financial institutions can act as personal representatives or conservators. To be eligible for appointment, a financial institution must possess trust powers. In Michigan, only banks and savings and loan associations can get these powers (although not all such institutions have them); credit unions and other financial service companies cannot receive trust powers.

Much as nonresidents were once excluded, Michigan law used to bar out-of-state financial institutions from fiduciary service here. But a recent amendment to the banking law allows out-of-state banks (with trust powers) to serve if they are doing business in the state.

In some cases, you can appoint qualified nonprofit corporations, such as religious, charitable, or social welfare organizations, as guardians and conservators. The appointment will take effect only if: 1) it's in the best interests of the dependent 2) no other suitable person is willing to serve. As a result, nonprofit corporations are better as second-choice fiduciaries, or first choices for someone without any surviving relatives or friends.

Fiduciaries: Practical Qualities

Most people and several kinds of organizations are legally eligible to serve as fiduciaries. But for practical reasons, some make better choices than others. These are a few of the practical qualities that you should look for in a fiduciary:

Honesty. Honesty is by far the most important quality because a fiduciary often handles money or manages other property. Probate courts supervise fiduciaries, but the supervision isn't very close. Thus, a dishonest fiduciary can do considerable harm before detection and removal. Select an honest fiduciary and you can also excuse bond for the fiduciary, saving the cost of a bond premium.

Suitability. Fiduciaries should be matched to the tasks they perform. They don't necessarily need special skills or expertise, but they should have an aptitude for the job. So, personal representatives and conservators should have good financial judgment, and guardians must get along well with children.

Willingness to serve. A fiduciary's job is strictly voluntary; a fiduciary can decline to serve before appointment or resign afterward. To avoid disappointment, always ask fiduciary candidates whether they are willing to serve before you appoint them. Financial institutions should also be asked because they might decline to serve if the estate is too small or difficult to manage.

Availability. Select fiduciaries who are going to be around when you need them. Ordinarily, your picks should be your age or younger, and in good health. Organizations don't face physical infirmities, but they can fail financially. Before you choose an organization, make sure it enjoys financial "good health."

Nonresidents of Michigan are legally eligible to serve as fiduciaries. But nonresidents may find it difficult to carry out fiduciary duties long-distance. Thus, you may want to give preference to those who live near you in Michigan.

Affordability. Your fiduciaries must also be affordable. As explained below, fiduciaries may receive fees for their work. Financial institutions and professionals (lawyers, accountants, financial advisers, etc.) in particular may want fiduciary fees. If these are too expensive, select someone else.

Fiduciary Fees

Years ago, it was customary to give small will gifts to personal representatives. These gifts encouraged the fiduciary to carry out the will, and rewarded the fiduciary for his service.

These days, fiduciaries are entitled to fees for service. You can set fiduciary fees in a will, but few do (there's no place for fiduciary fees in a statutory will). Instead, fiduciaries are entitled to "reasonable compensation" for their services. The probate court may review these fees, judging the reasonableness of the fees by the: 1) difficulty of the fiduciary tasks 2) amount of time spent 3) any fee schedule the fiduciary uses.*

Not all fiduciaries ask for fees. Relatives serving as guardians or conservators often give up fees because they know that the fees come out of the estates. A personal representative who is also a taker of the estate, such as a spouse or child, may surrender fees to save taxes. Fiduciary fees are taxable as income to a fiduciary, while estate distributions are not. By waiving fees, personal representatives-estate takers have a larger estate to

---

* Institutional and professional fiduciaries often use fee schedules,
  which typically compute fees as a percentage of the value of an estate.

take from (because it hasn't been reduced by fiduciary fees), without income taxation (since estate distributions are income tax-free). This makes up for the loss of fiduciary fees. Needless to say, financial institutions and professional fiduciaries don't have these incentives for giving up fees, and seldom waive fees.

Selecting Witnesses

Besides fiduciaries, you must choose witnesses for your will. The witnesses observe you as you sign/acknowledge your will, a procedure known as execution of the will. After your death, during probate, the witnesses must be ready to testify about the execution of your will.

In reality, the witnesses probably won't have to testify. Michigan has liberal rules about probating wills, and the actual live testimony of witnesses is seldom necessary, particularly if the will is self-proved. Nevertheless, the witnesses should be available if needed.

Michigan used to have strict will witness rules, which, in effect, required disinterested witnesses during will execution. A disinterested witness is someone who doesn't have a direct stake or interest in your will, such as taking a will gift.* When disinterested witnesses were used, the will, or parts of it, was invalid.

Michigan's new will law relaxed the will witness rules. The only requirement is that the witnesses be mentally competent adults. The disinterested-witness rules were thrown out because in emergencies, such as a will execution during a medical crisis in the hospital, disinterested witnesses are often difficult to find (many hospitals now forbid medical staff from witnessing legal documents, for liability reasons). Thus, many times interested persons, family usually, are often the only available witnesses.

Despite these new rules, it's still best to use disinterested witnesses whenever possible. Interested witnesses may create a suspicion of undue influence, duress or fraud (see "Undue Influence, Duress and Fraud" on page 44 for more about these dangers), which could provide grounds for a challenge to the will. Interested witnesses are permissible in emergencies, such as a deathbed will execution, when no one else is available.

In Michigan, all wills except handwritten wills must have a minimum of two witnesses. Wills without the required pair of witnesses are invalid. Two witnesses are required, but three are better when a third person is available to witness. The extra witness comes in handy if testimony about the will is necessary, and the other two witnesses are unavailable.

---

* A fiduciary appointment doesn't count as an interest in a will, because fiduciaries earn any fees they receive by performing services.

49

How to Make a Statutory Will

Part II walks you through a statutory will section-by-section. But before you sit down to make a statutory will, here are some general rules about willmaking:

- Use a typewriter or pen with dark, permanent ink. Never use a pencil or a pen with erasable ink.

- In blanks asking for "Your signature," sign your name longhand as you would sign a check. The witnesses must also sign that way in the blanks designated "Signature of witness."

- Your name in the title of the will and the names of the witnesses in the statement of witnesses section must be printed (by hand or typewriter), not written. Printing is required for clarity.

- The rest of the blanks can be completed by either printing (by hand or typewriter) or writing. All sections must be legible, so consider printing if your handwriting is hard to read.

- As you describe people or organizations, use their full legal names (and addresses, if called for) to avoid confusion.

- Names should be consistent in the will. If a name is mentioned more than once, the form of the name should be the same wherever it appears.

- If you don't use a section of your statutory will, leave it blank. Don't cross out the unused section.

- Don't attempt to customize your statutory will by crossing out words or adding new ones to the form. At best, these changes are ineffective. At worst, they may invalidate the modified provision or even the entire will. If the statutory will doesn't fit your needs, don't use it!

Chapter 2A Making a Statutory Will

Part II

You make a statutory will on a Michigan statutory will form. Two of these are included in the forms section, and a sample statutory will appears at the end of this part. If you want to make your statutory will self-proving, add a self-proving declaration to the will. There are two copies of each kind of self-proving declaration (as explained in Part III, there are two kinds of self-proving declarations, for different types of will execution) in the forms section, and a sample declaration follows the sample statutory will.

Notices and Instructions

A Michigan statutory will begins with several notices and instructions providing basic information about the will. Most of this information has been covered in Part I, but you may wish to review it again. The information about will execution and storage is dealt with later, in Parts III and IV.

Title

Insert your name in the title section, stating your full legal name. Use this form of your name throughout the will, in the signatures in arts. 2 and 3, and in the final signature at the end of the will.

Article 1: Declarations

In art. 1, you endorse the will as your own. You also revoke any prior wills you may have made. A revocation statement like this is fine. But as explained in "Destroying Prior Wills" on page 73, you should also revoke by destroying prior wills and all copies.

You must state the Michigan county where you live. As mentioned in Part I, you should be a Michigan resident when you make a Michigan statutory will. This residency declaration helps establish your residence here.

Identify your spouse and children, if any, in art. 1. Your spouse is whom you are *legally* married to when you make your will (see "Spouse" in the glossary to determine which marriages are recognized in Michigan).

A statutory will adopts Michigan's estates code definition of children. Besides children born during a marriage, this definition includes adopted children and most illegitimate (out-of-wedlock) children, but excludes stepchildren. See "Children" in the glossary for more about the code definition of children.

When you identify your children, list living children only. Deceased children should be omitted because they cannot take property from your will (although their children/descendants can). If you are single and childless, skip the family information section of art. 1.

Article 2.1: Cash Gifts

With the introductory material out of the way, you're ready to get down to business and distribute property in art. 2.

In art. 2.1, you can make a maximum of two specific gifts of cash. One taker per cash gift is allowed; you cannot make a joint cash gift, with multiple takers of the same gift. You can give the money directly to the taker. Or if the taker is a minor, you can give the cash to the minor in trust-like form under the Uniform Transfers to Minors Act (UTMA).

Before you make any cash gifts, keep in mind how they are satisfied from your estate. Payment of cash gifts has high priority during distribution of an estate (see "Article 2.3: Residuary Estate" on page 55 for the exact order of distribution). A big cash gift can deplete the estate if there aren't enough liquid assets to go around.

Example: Edith makes a cash gift of $10,000 to her church. After her death, Edith's estate has only $1,000 in cash and no other liquid assets. To raise money to pay the cash gift, other property in the estate, which Edith wanted her children to share, might have to be sold.

It's easy to see that cash gifts can affect or even upset the pattern of property distribution you have chosen in your will. Before you make cash gifts, especially large ones, consider the impact of these gifts on the rest of your estate.

Frustrated cash gifts also affect the distribution of your estate. A frustrated gift is a will gift to a person who dies before you (or an organization that goes defunct before your death), and isn't around to take the gift as planned. Michigan law specifies how frustrated will gifts pass. If the deceased taker is a close relative,* the cash gift goes to the taker's children/descendants by representation (see "Representation" in the glossary for more about this pattern of distribution). But if the taker is a distant relative, a nonrelative or an organization, the frustrated cash gift fails and the cash passes through the residuary estate (art. 2.3 of a statutory will). Thus, a frustrated cash gift gets distributed, but not always in the way you anticipated.

Example: In her statutory will, Edith makes two cash gifts of $1,000 to her daughter Shirley and a charity. Before Edith's death, Shirley dies and the charity goes out of business. Since Shirley is Edith's close relative, the cash gift to Shirley goes to her daughter Rhonda. The cash gift to the charity fails, and the money passes through art. 2.3 of Edith's statutory will.

As art 2.1 says, cash gifts are optional; if you don't want to make any, leave the lines in art. 2.1 blank and move on. If you want to make a cash gift, you must choose which kind: a direct gift or one in UTMA form.

To make a direct cash gift, print the name and address of the taker on the top lines of the first cash gift portion of art. 2.1. On the next two lines, write the amount of the gift in numbers and words. Sign your name on the line below that. If you want to make another direct cash gift, repeat this procedure in the second cash gift section of art. 2.1.

For an UTMA cash gift, you must put the gift in UTMA form. You give the cash to the UTMA custodian for the minor under the act. If you like, you can extend the final distribution of the cash gift from the normal age of 18, to any age between 18 and 21.

See "Making UTMA Gifts" on page 168 for complete information about giving under the act. The second cash gift in the sample statutory will is an UTMA cash gift with an age extension, which you can use as a guide for your UTMA cash gifts.

Article 2.2: Giving Personal and Household Items

Art. 2.2 distributes personal and household items, which the statutory will describes as "books, jewelry, clothing, automobiles, furniture, and other personal and household items." The will doesn't define "other personal and household items." But presumably these are things you have around the house: dishes, utensils, appliances, tools, art objects, electronic equip-

---

* Close relatives include those who can qualify as your heirs, except your spouse, plus your stepchildren. See "Heirs" in the glossary for a list.

ment (televisions, stereos, personal computers, etc.), and recreational vehicles (bicycles, motorcycles, boats, etc.).

All these items go first to the spouse; if none, to the children; if none, onto the takers of the residuary estate (see below for the pattern of distribution for this estate).

Making a Separate List

If you don't like this pattern of distribution, you can modify it by making a separate list outside your statutory will. Art. 2.2 of the statutory will allows you to give any personal and household items in a separate list. In the list, you may give personal and household items to your spouse and children in a different pattern than the one prescribed in art. 2.2, or you can give these items to other persons or organizations.

> *Example:* George has two favorite guns. He wants to give one gun to his son Dewey and the other to his friend Ivan. George makes a separate list giving the guns to Dewey and Ivan. If George hadn't made these gifts in a separate list, art. 2.2 of his statutory will would distribute the guns to Margo, or all his surviving children if Margo failed to survive him.

When you give personal and household items in a separate list, you're really making a specific gift of the items. See "Specific Gifts" on page 45 for information about who may take specific gifts and how to identify the takers. In addition, follow these rules when you make a separate list:

- You can make a separate list anytime: before, during, or after you make your will.
- Use a typewriter or pen with dark, permanent ink. Never use a pencil or a pen with erasable ink.
- Your separate list can be printed (by hand or typewriter) or written. All the provisions must be legible, so consider printing if your writing is hard to read.
- The items you give must be described in enough detail so your personal representative can find them after your death. Any distinctive characteristics, marks or identification numbers should be mentioned in the gift of the item.
- Avoid joint gifts in which one item is given to multiple takers.
- The gifts should be clear and direct, without any conditions or stipulations.
- If you can't fit all the gifts on a one-page separate list form, add extra pages (using blank paper) to the form. But make sure that you: 1) number all the pages 2) date and sign the last page of your list below the final provision 3) staple all the pages of the list together.
- You must date and sign the list at the end. It doesn't have to be witnessed or notarized.

- After you make a separate list, you can amend the list anytime. For minor changes, just cross out old material and/or write in additions on the list, then initial the amendment. If the changes are extensive, prepare a new separate list.

For convenience, a separate list form is included in the forms section of this book. Or you can make a list on a blank sheet of paper (which you should label as the separate list for your will). Either way, simply list the gifts and gift-takers, as in the sample separate list at the end of this part.

Article 2.3: Residuary Estate

Art. 2.3 is really the heart of a statutory will because it distributes the residuary estate (the statutory will calls this estate "all other assets"). The residuary estate is the remainder of a probate estate after deduction, in order, of the following items:

- final expenses (costs of probate, final disposition, death ceremony, estate taxes, and costs of last illness)
- family rights (see "Family Rights" in the glossary for an explanation of these rights)
- claims against the estate
- specific gifts from art. 2.1 or a separate list
- personal and household items from art. 2.2 (if a spouse or children survive)

These deductions can take a bite out of the residuary estate, particular for small probate estates. But for most people, there is a residuary estate remaining which transfers the bulk of the probate estate.

Art. 2.3 provides a basic pattern for distribution of the residuary estate: all to the spouse, and then to the children/descendants. Distribution to the children/descendants is by representation. In representation, a deceased child's share goes to his/her surviving children or descendants, who split it, usually equally, among themselves (see "Representation" in the glossary for more about this pattern of distribution). For single people without children, art. 2.3 follows the inheritance law and distributes residuary estates to their heirs, as if they didn't have a will.

Art. 2.3 offers two distribution options (clauses (a) and (b)) if your spouse and children/descendants all fail to survive you. Dying without surviving close relatives is a particular concern for small families, because the deaths of a few close relatives can leave them without any residuary estate-takers. But larger families should also be concerned, because a common disaster could quickly wipe out their entire family.

Example: The Frisbie family is traveling in a car to a wedding when they get into a terrible automobile accident. The entire family dies together in the accident, leaving George and Margo without any surviving spouse or children/descendants to take their residuary estates.

For married people, the statutory will offers two distribution choices if your spouse and children/descendants fail to survive you. These choices are clauses (a) and (b) of art. 2.3, which are as follows:

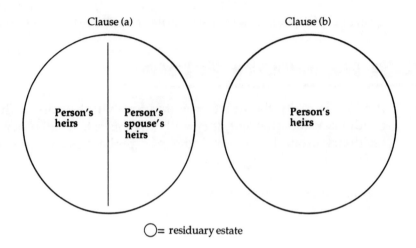

Clause (a)   Clause (b)

Person's heirs | Person's spouse's heirs

Person's heirs

◯ = residuary estate

For married willmakers considering these options, clause (a) might seem like a strange choice. Why would you want to give your in-laws half your residuary estate? In fact, there are very good reasons for that distribution.

Example: The Frisbies, who have not made wills, have been in the automobile accident described above. But in this scenario, Margo doesn't die right away. She lingers and dies one week after the accident. Because she survived everybody, Margo inherits George's and most of the rest of the family's estates. After her death, all this property goes to her brother Stu, her only relative, whom George and she always disliked. So the bulk of the Frisbies' wealth ends up on only one side of the family, with someone they never liked, excluding the Frisbie side of the family.

Had the Frisbies made statutory wills and selected clause (a), they could have kept Stu from getting everything. Their choice of clause (a) would have divided Margo's residuary estate into two equal shares, and distributed one share to her heirs (still Stu) and the other share to George's heirs. As in many tragic cases like this, that distribution may be the fairer one.

On the other hand, some people might not want to benefit their spouse's heirs under any circumstances. They might be estranged from their in-laws. Or the in-laws may be well-off and don't need more property. Whatever the reason, if you want to keep the distribution among your heirs exclusively, select clause (b).

Married willmakers should choose either clause (a) or (b) by signing their names on the line immediately below the correct clause. If you sign below both clauses by mistake, or fail to sign below either clause, clause (b) is assigned to you.

Single persons (with or without children/descendants) can't choose clause (a) because, without a spouse or in-laws, the clause doesn't apply. Single willmakers should choose clause (b) by signing their names below that paragraph. Single willmakers selecting clause (a) by mistake are assigned clause (b) anyway.

Article 3: Appointment of Fiduciaries

So far, the statutory will has dealt with distribution of property. Next is another important topic: appointment of fiduciaries. In a statutory will, you can appoint three types of fiduciaries: personal representative, guardian, and conservator.*

Everyone, regardless of their family situation, should appoint a personal representative. If you have minor children, you should appoint a guardian and a conservator for them. Parents with DD children, or parents serving as guardians for LI unmarried adult children, may also want to appoint original or successor guardians for these special-needs children.

For the rules about legal eligibility to serve as a fiduciary, review "Selecting Fiduciaries" on page 46. Or see the chart on the next page summarizing many of these eligibility rules. The practical qualities for fiduciaries are covered below.

Article 3.1: Personal Representative

The chief task of a personal representative is to settle your estate during probate. A personal representative doesn't have to do that personally (s/he/it may hire a lawyer or other professional to handle the probate), but the personal representative must supervise the procedure. The personal representative also has some authority to carry out instructions from the deceased about final matters (final disposition and death ceremony). These are important things requiring the following practical qualities:

Financial decision-making. Since your personal representative will be managing property during probate, the appointee must be able to make sound financial decisions for you.

¶ *Honesty.* Above all else, your personal representative must be honest. In a small estate or unsupervised probate, which should be the norm in

---

* If you make a cash gift in UTMA form, you will also be naming a fourth kind of fiduciary: a custodian of the gift.

Fiduciaries

	Function	Legal eligibility	Practical factors
(1) Guardian of minor children	Care for dependent and manage small amounts of property; same for (2), (3), and (4) below	Financial institutions cannot serve; some nonprofits can in certain cases; same for (2), (3), and (4) below	Single parent must consider rights of other parent; teenager may veto appointment
(2) Guardian of legally incapacitated (LI) children		Parent can appoint successor guardian for unmarried adult LI child if serving as guardian now	
(3) Guardian of legally incapacitated (LI) spouse		Other spouse can appoint successor guardian if currently serving as guardian	
(4) Guardian of developmentally disabled (DD) child		Parent can appoint guardian for adult DD child if: 1) serving as guardian now, or 2) child has no guardian and parent is surviving parent	
Conservator	Manage property for dependent when it is of amount or kind needing management	Many financial institutions and some nonprofits can serve	Teenager can nominate own conservator
Personal representative	Settle deceased's estate and carry out final instructions	Many financial institutions can serve	

Michigan, a personal representative operates with scant court supervision. A dishonest personal representative can considerable harm before removal, making honesty an absolute necessity.

¶ *Good financial judgment.* In most cases, good financial judgment simply means common sense. But if your estate property is difficult to manage, special skills might be necessary. For example, if you own a small business, your personal representative must know how to supervise it during probate.

Capacity to help. Your personal representative must have the time and inclination to give close attention to settlement of your affairs.

¶ *Commitment.* A personal representative's job is strictly voluntary; the appointee can refuse to serve, or quit anytime after beginning to serve. To prevent this, always ask candidates whether they are willing to serve before you appoint them. By getting prior consent, you reduce the chance they will fail to serve later.

¶ *Health and stability.* Some candidates, such as elderly people, may seem like good choices now, but will they be around when you need them? Ditto for casual friends you might drift away from.

Location. Michigan law doesn't disqualify nonresident personal representatives. But nonresidents may have difficulty supervising probate long-distance. Because of this problem, you might want to give preference to Michigan residents.

As you select your personal representative, don't forget about your spouse. Spouses are often excellent choices as personal representative. A spouse usually has all the practical qualities you look for in a fiduciary. What's more, spouses have an incentive to do a good job because they usually take the estates. On the other hand, you aren't required to select your spouse, and there are certainly situations in which your spouse is a poor choice.

After you've made the final picks, appoint the personal representatives in art. 3.1 You'll need a two picks for each fiduciary slot: a first choice and a substitute if the first choice is unavailable. Remember, in a statutory will joint appointments aren't allowed, so two people can't share a slot. To make the appointments, insert the names and addresses of the appointees in the lines in art. 3.1.

Article 3.2: Guardian and Conservator

Choose guardians and conservators with special care, because their responsibilities are enormous. Guardians will be stepping into your shoes as caretakers of your children or dependents. Guardians can also manage small amounts of property. A conservator manages property only, and uses the property to provide support for your dependents. With so much at stake, you will certainly want to look for these practical qualities in guardians and conservators:

Capacity for care or help. Above all, your guardians and conservators must be willing and able to provide good care or financial management help for your dependents.

¶ *Commitment.* Is the guardian or conservator willing to care for or help your minor dependents until they reach adulthood, which may be many years away? An even greater degree of commitment is necessary for special-needs dependents such as DD or LI adults. Find out the level of commitment by asking guardian or conservator candidates whether they are up to the task. Even if they say "Yes," judge how realistic this is.

¶ *Experience as caregiver.* You don't want to thrust caretaking on someone not ready to handle it. For example, a childless person may not be able to cope with newfound custodial responsibilities. All this goes double for special-needs dependents.

¶ *Child-rearing methods.* You may want someone who shares your values and beliefs about raising children. Or you may want to pick someone who belongs to the same religion, or has similar interests and hobbies as you and your children.

¶ *Health and stability.* Some candidates, such as elderly grandparents, may seem like good guardian or conservator choices now, but will they have sufficient health and longevity to provide care or help 5, 10 or 15 years from now?

Financial decision-making. Since the conservator will be managing your dependents' finances, the appointee must be able to make sound financial decisions for them.

¶ *Honesty.* Above all else, the conservator must be honest. A conservator handles financial matters with minimal court supervison. A dishonest appointee can do considerable harm before removal, making honesty an absolute necessity.

¶ *Good financial judgment.* In most cases, good financial judgment simply means common sense. But if the dependents' financial affairs are complex or difficult to manage, special skills might be necessary.

Location. Dependents usually move to live with their guardians, not the other way around. If you appoint an out-of-state guardian, or even one faraway in Michigan, could your dependents adjust to a move like that? Nonresident conservators may also have trouble managing property long-distance. Thus, you may want to choose guardians and conservators who live near you.

Financial resources. A dependent's living expenses are supposed to be paid by the guardian from the dependent's own property (managed by the guardian, if small, or a conservator, if large). But guardians inevitably spend some of their own money on dependents, without reimbursement. Consider whether your guardians can afford these extra expenses.

On the other hand, conservators can impose costs on the dependent (or the dependent's property), if they seek fees for financial management services. Institutional conservators, such as banks, will most often charge fees, which can be stiff. Relatives, friends or nonprofit conservators will often seek minimal fees, or none at all.

Children's preferences. You should clear guardian and conservator appointments with teenage children. In Michigan, children 14 years of age and older can veto guardian appointments or nominate their own conservators. After a child objects to parental appointments, the probate court must hold a hearing and make suitable appointments. You can avoid all this trouble by discussing guardian and conservator appointments with your teenage children and appointing someone acceptable to them.

Younger children don't have a guardian veto, but their feelings should also be respected. Find out by asking them whether they will be happy living with the guardian you want to appoint.

Combining guardian and conservator. You should seriously consider appointing the same person guardian and conservator, as in the appointment in the sample will. Combining these positions makes sense, because the appointee will have the funds for support at hand, without having to ask another person for these. If you want combined guardians and conservators, remember to do this for both your first choice and substitute appointments.

On the other hand, some might not like the coziness of combining guardian and conservator in one person. They might prefer to have different persons or institutions fill these positions so they can check on each other.

Coordinating Appointments between Parents

Parents should coordinate guardian and conservator appointments, or risk making different appointments. If the appointments aren't in synch, Michigan law says that the will of the parent who dies last controls guardianship.

Example: George and Margo make statutory wills. They thought they appointed the same person as guardian of their children. However, they actually made different appointments. George dies before Margo. Because Margo died last, the guardian appointment in her will is the one that's effective.

Example: Same as above except that George and Margo die simultaneously in an airplane crash. Since neither of them died last, neither one's guardian appointments have priority. Making matter worse, both appointees want to be guardian of the children, and they contest the issue in a guardianship proceeding in court.

Parents can avoid these and similar problems by coordinating guardian and conservator appointments. On the other hand, parents aren't legally required to appoint the same guardians and conservators, and may choose different appointees if they wish.

Appointments by Parents with Broken Families

More than most, parents with broken families want different guardians and conservators. Parents with broken families include parents who are single after a separation, divorce or annulment, parents who have remarried after a divorce or annulment, and unwed parents who never married and now live apart.

If the break-up was bitter, these parents may wish to have someone besides the other parent serve as guardian. With this in mind, the parent may hope to use a guardian appointment in a will as a means of taking custody of a child away from the other parent and giving custody to a nonparent third party, such as a new spouse, family member or friend.

What parents with broken families often forget is that guardians are only necessary for orphaned children. If one parent survives, s/he automatically gets or keeps custody as the natural guardian of the children* (unless s/he is legally incapacitated). Moreover, the surviving parent can control the future custody of the children by making guardian appointments in a will (since the guardian appointment of the last parent to die prevails).

Parents with broken families can still appoint the third parties they want as guardians. They must realize that their appointments will take effect only if the other parent: 1) is legally incapacitated 2) dies first 3) dies last but didn't make guardian appointments in a will.

> *Example:* Shirley and her ex-husband Gus went through a bitter divorce. Shirley got custody of their daughter Rhonda. Shirley would like to deprive Gus of custody of Rhonda after her death by naming her brothers as guardians of the child in her will.
>
> Shirley discovers that Gus, if he survives her, will get custody of Rhonda regardless of her will. Thus, Shirley makes a statutory will naming Grover and Eugene as Rhonda's guardians and conservators. She realizes that the guardian appointment will take effect only in the three exceptional situations described above.

Appointing a third party as conservator has a better chance of success. A surviving parent doesn't automatically become conservator, although parents have high priority for appointment. Thus, an appointed third party could possibly vie with the surviving parent for appointment as conservator and win.

Appointments for Special-Needs Children

Ordinarily, you appoint guardians for your minor children in a will. But you can usually appoint successor guardians for your LI or DD adult children, who will take over as guardian when you die. Or if you aren't serving as guardian for a DD adult child, and no else is either, you can make a guardian appointment in your will. This appointment takes effect at your death if you are the sole surviving parent of the DD child.

If you have an adult LI or DD child, and no minor children, simply

---

* As consolation, Michigan law gives the parents of the deceased parent (the grandparents) the right to seek visitation with the grandchildren in these situations.

appoint the guardian in art. 3.2 If you have a mixture of LI or DD adult children and minor children, you must appoint the same person as guardian of all your children, because you cannot split guardian appointments in a statutory will. If you want different guardians for your adult and minor children, you'll have to make another kind of will.

Appointing Guardians and Conservators

Make your guardian and conservator appointments in art. 3.2. You need a first choice and a substitute for each fiduciary slot. Keep in mind that in a statutory will joint or split appointments aren't allowed. For the appointments, insert the names and addresses of the appointees in the correct lines of art. 3.2.

Article 3.3: Fiduciary Bonds

When fiduciaries handle property, they may have to give bonds. Personal representatives and conservators face bond requirements because they control money and other property. Guardians don't post bonds since they don't handle much property.

A bond is a promise by a fiduciary that s/he will pay any financial losses up to the amount of the bond. In some cases, this promise must be backed by a bonding company, which charges a premium for the guarantee. If a bond is required, the court sets the amount of the bond. It may mirror the value of the property the fiduciary controls, or it may be a nominal ($1,000) amount.

The court has the final say whether your personal representative or conservator must post bond. At the same time, you can make a recommendation about bond in your will which the judge must take into account.

Should you require bond or excuse it? Ordinarily, bond shouldn't be necessary. You select your personal representative and conservator for their honesty and trustworthiness, so a bond shouldn't be needed to ensure good behavior. If you think a bond is necessary to keep them honest, pick different fiduciaries. Keep in mind that bond premiums are expensive and can be a financial drain on the estates of the deceased or child, which must pay them.

Don't worry about bond if you've appointed financial institutions or nonprofit organizations as fiduciaries. By law, organizations eligible to serve as fiduciaries have large bonds on deposit with the state treasurer to cover fiduciary losses. They don't have to post bond in individual cases.

If you want bonds for your personal representative and conservator, sign your name on the line under clause (a). Sign under clause (b) to excuse bonds for these fiduciaries.

Article 3.4: Definitions and Extra Clauses

Art 3.4 tacks several definitions and additional clauses onto the will. The additional clauses section gives various powers to the fiduciaries. Basically, these provisions give your fiduciaries broad powers granted to them by the estates code, with a few more added for good measure.

Signature

In the signature section, you date and sign/acknowledge the will during execution. Leave this section blank for now.

Witness Provisions

During execution, several witnesses must watch as you sign the will. The notice regarding witnesses provides information about the witnesses and the execution procedure. See "Selecting Witnesses" on page 49 for more about the number and qualifications of witnesses. Execution is covered in more detail in Part III.

The statement of witnesses is what lawyers call an attestation clause. This clause is a statement by the witnesses describing the signing or acknowledgment of the will. The clause is important because it makes the will easier to probate.

In the attestation clause, the witnesses state that the willmaker: 1) appeared to have a sound mind and was free of duress, fraud or undue influence 2) acknowledged that s/he has read the will (or has it read to him/her) 3) and that s/he understood it. The witnesses read and sign the attestation clause during execution, after the willmaker signs the will.

Making a Statutory Will Self-Proving

You can make a statutory will self-proving by making a self-proving declaration. A self-proved will is easier to establish during probate, reducing the chance of a will contest.

There are two kinds of self-proving declarations: 1) declaration for a will signed during execution by the willmaker personally or by proxy 2) declaration for an acknowledged will, when the willmaker acknowledges a previously-signed will to witnesses. Both declarations say that the will was correctly signed under Michigan will execution rules.

If you decide to self-prove your statutory will, make sure you use the correct declaration or declarations (as explained in Part III, you often must use both kinds of declarations for execution by acknowledgment of a previously-signed will). Make several copies of the declaration(s), and bring everything with you to the will execution.

MICHIGAN STATUTORY WILL

1. An individual age 18 or c
2. There are several kinds
   this will does not meet y
   will.
3. Warning! It is strongly
   in the blanks because
4. This will has no effect
   have named a benefic
5. This will is not design
6. This will treats adop
   without a will the sa
7. You should keep thi
   in your county's pr
8. You may make and
   and sign a new will

1. To have a Michig
   direct someone t
   your presence.
2. Read the entire
   not understand

This is my wil

My spouse is

My children

Pe

ARTICLE 2. DISPOSITION OF MY ASSETS

2.1 CASH GIFTS TO PERSONS OR CHARITIES. (Optional)

I can leave no more than two (2) cash gifts. I make the following cash gifts to the persons or charities in the amount stated here. Any transfer tax due upon my death shall be paid from the balance of my estate and not from these gifts.

Full name and address of person or charity to receive cash gift (name only 1 person or charity here):

POLICEMEN'S BENEVOLENCE FUND
(Insert name of person or charity)
121 S. MAIN, LAKE CITY, MI 48800
(Insert address)

Amount of gift (In figures): $ 1,000

Amount of gift (In words): ONE THOUSAND AND NO/100 _____ Dollars

George Edward Frisbie
(Your signature)

Full name and address of person or charity to receive cash gift (name only 1 person or charity here):

CHESTER DEAN FRISBIE, AS CUSTODIAN FOR JOHN GEORGE FRISBIE, UNTIL AGE 21, UNDER
(Insert name of person or charity)   MICHIGAN UNIFORM TRANSFER
                                        TO MINORS ACT
701 W. ELM, LAKE CITY, MI 48800
(Insert address)

Amount of gift (In figures): $ 1,000

Amount of gift (In words): ONE THOUSAND AND   *Edward Frisbie*

2.2 PERSONAL AND HOUSEHOLD ITEMS.

I may leave a separate list or statement, either in my
books, jewelry, cl____ automobiles, furniture, and o

I give my spo_____ clothing
included on such _____
my personal repr_____
children surviv

2.3 ALL OTH

I give eve
me, I give thes
children surviv
sign on both t
(b).
Distribu
(a) One
as i

(b) A

3.1 PERSONAL REPRESENTATIVE. (Name at least 1)

I nominate MARGO ANN FRISBIE
of 900 S. WASHINGTON, LAKE CITY, MI 48800
(Insert name of person or eligible financial institution)
to serve as personal representative.
(Insert address)

If my first choice does not serve, I nominate
CHESTER DEAN FRISBIE
of 701 W. ELM, LAKE CITY, MI 48800
(Insert name of person or eligible financial institution)
to serve as personal representative.
(Insert address)

3.2 GUARDIAN AND CONSERVATOR.

Your spouse may die before you. Therefore, if you have a child under age 18, name an individual as guardian of the child, and an individual or eligible financial institution as conservator of the child's assets. The guardian and the conservator may, but need not be, the same person.

If a guardian or conservator is needed for any child of mine, I nominate
RUTH JEAN SMITH
of 1601 S. MAPLE, LAKE CITY, MI 48800
(Insert name of individual)
(Insert address)
and RUTH JEAN SMITH
of 1601 S. MAPLE, LAKE CITY, MI 48800 _____ as guardian
(Insert name of individual or eligible financial institution)
to serve as conservator.
(Insert address)

If my first choice cannot serve, I nominate
CHESTER DEAN FRISBIE
of 701 W. ELM, LAKE CITY, MI 48800
(Insert name of individual)
(Insert address)
and CHESTER DEAN FRISBIE
of 701 W. ELM, LAKE CITY, MI 48800 _____ as guardian
(Insert name of individual or eligible financial institution)
to serve as conservator.
(Insert address)

3.3 BOND.

A bond is a form of insurance in case your personal representative or a conservator performs improperly and jeopardizes your assets. A bond is not required. You may choose whether you wish to require your personal representative and any conservator to serve with or without bond. Bond premiums would be paid out of your assets.
(Select only 1)
(a) My personal representative and any conservator I have named shall serve with bond.

(b) My personal representative and any conservator I have named shall serve without bond.
(Your signature)

George Edward Frisbie
(Your signature)

3.4 DEFINITIONS AND ADDITIONAL CLAUSES.

Definitions and additional clauses found at the end of this form are part of this will.

I sign my name to this Michigan statutory will on

You m_____

JAN

Frisbie

to have 3 adult
or have you tell

und mind and
king this will
il.

age

SEPARATE LIST

for the Michigan statutory will of

GEORGE EDWARD FRISBIE
(Full name)

JAN. 1, 2000
(Date of will)

According to sec. 2.2 of my Michigan statutory will and sec. 2513 of the Estates and Protected Individuals Code of of Michigan, I give the following personal and household items to the persons designated below:

WESTMINSTER MODEL 700 .17-CALIBER RIFLE TO
DEWEY JOHN FRISBIE, 900 S. WASHINGTON, LAKE CITY, MI 48800

SMITH & JAMES 1955 MODEL 25 .22-CALIBER REVOLVER TO
IVAN EDGAR GOOCH, 279 W. CHERRY, LAKE CITY MI 48800

SELF-PROVING DECLARATION
(for will execution)

I, GEORGE EDWARD FRISBIE _____, the testator sign my name to this document on JAN. 1, 2000. I declare under penalty for perjury under the law of the state of Michigan that this document is my will; that I sign it willingly or willingly direct another to sign it for me; that I execute it as my voluntary act for the purposes expressed in the will, and that I am 18 years of age or older, of sound mind, and under no constraint or undue influence.

George Edward Frisbie
(Signature) Testator

We, ARCHIE LOUIS SAVAGE _____

GUY FRANCIS FISH _____

and LUTHER ERNEST DOOLITTLE _____

the witnesses, sign our names to this document under penalty for perjury under the law of the state of Michigan, and declare that all of the following statements are true: the individual signing this document as testator executes the document as his or her will, signs it willingly or willingly directs another to sign for him or her, and executes it as his or her voluntary act for the purposes expressed in this will; each of us, in the testator's presence, signs this will as witness to the testator's signing; and, to the best of our knowledge, the testator is 18 years of age or older, of sound mind, and under no constraint or undue influence.

JAN. 1, 2000
Date

JAN. 1, 2000
Date

JAN. 1, 2000
Date

Archie Louis Savage
(Signature) Witness

Guy Francis Fish
(Signature) Witness

Luther Ernest Doolittle
(Signature) Witness

Chapter 2A Executing a Statutory Will
Part III

Execution is the procedure for making a will or other document legally effective. For a statutory will, execution means three things: dating, signing and witnessing the will.

Copying the Will

Before execution, make a few photocopies of the unsigned will. Later, you will probably want a copy to keep around the house, for review, while the original is stored in a safe place. You may also want copies for your fiduciaries, particularly the personal representative. In fact, financial institutions often request copies before they accept appointment as personal representative.

On the other hand, don't copy your will indiscriminately. When a will is revoked and/or replaced by a new will, the prior will and all copies should be destroyed (see "Destroying Prior Wills" on page 73 for more about this procedure). If multiple copies of the will are in circulation, it's difficult to collect and destroy them all. A copy of the repudiated will might survive and be used as a rival for the new will. It's easier to do this if the will is signed; that's why you should make copies of the unsigned will.

No matter how many copies you make, you won't need the copies for execution. But don't distribute the copies just yet. As explained in Part IV, you should add some will execution information to the copies before distribution. After you add this information, you're ready to distribute the copies.

Methods of Execution

Michigan once had complicated will execution requirements, which had to be followed precisely. During the last 20 years, these have been relaxed a bit. Today, Michigan law provides for three simple methods of execution.

- signature before witnesses
- signature by proxy before witnesses
- previous signature of the will followed by acknowledgment of the signature (or the will) to witnesses

With each method of execution, the original will must be signed (or acknowledged) before two, but preferably three, disinterested witnesses

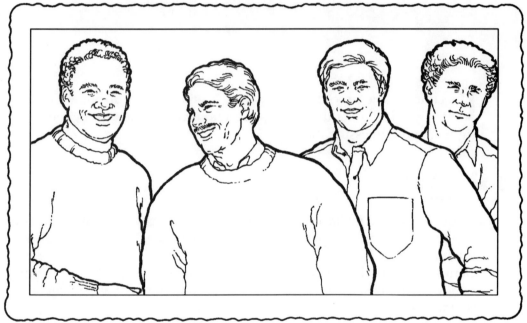

George's Bowling Team, 1997

(see "Selecting Witnesses" on page 49 for more about the number and qualifications of witnesses). In emergencies, it's permissible to have just two witnesses, and even ones with an interest in the will (the right to take property from the will). If you use two witnesses, or interested ones, consider making a self-proved will, to make the will more secure.

You and your witnesses are all you need to execute your will. In fact, it's best to have *only* the witnesses on hand during the execution. The presence of others during execution isn't prohibited, but it can raise questions of undue influence or duress.

Despite the flexibility of Michigan's will execution requirements, you must follow one important rule: The witnesses must be present with and observe you during the execution by one of the three execution methods.

Signature before Witnesses

To sign before witnesses, gather witnesses in the same room and use the procedure described below. The sample statutory will on page 65 shows a will executed by this method.

- Tell the witnesses that you've read the will (or had it read to you) and you understand it.
- Date and sign the will in the final signature section.
- Ask the witnesses to read the statement of witnesses in the will, and have them sign their names below this paragraph.
- Ask the witnesses to print their names and addresses on the lines to the left of their signatures.
- If you are self-proving the will, you and the witnesses must date and sign the self-proving declaration (for will execution).

Signature by Proxy

If you're physically disabled, it may be difficult to make and/or sign a statutory will. Luckily, Michigan law allows you to sign by proxy. A proxy is someone authorized by you to make and/or sign the will on your behalf. The procedure for making and executing a statutory will by proxy (with a sample proxy signature) is described below:

- Before execution, direct the proxy during the completion of the title and articles of the will. Any signatures in articles 2 and 3 should be signed by the proxy on your behalf as shown in the sample proxy signature below.
- After the will is made, you and the proxy should meet with the witnesses in the same room. (Incidentally, the proxy can be one of the witnesses.)
- Tell the witnesses that you've read the will (or had it read to you) and that you understand it.
- Tell the witnesses that the proxy is signing the will on your behalf and at your direction.
- Have the proxy date and sign the will in the final signature section as in the sample below:

George Edward Frisbie by Archie Louis Savage
AT THE FORMER'S DIRECTION AND IN HIS PRESENCE
_____
(Your signature)

- Ask the witnesses to read the statement of witnesses in the will, and have them sign their names below this paragraph.
- Ask the witnesses to print their names and addresses on the lines to the left of their signatures.
- If you are self-proving the will, you (or your proxy) and the witnesses must date and sign the self-proving declaration (for will execution).

- If the willmaker can't sign the will, s/he probably won't be able to sign the self-proving declaration either. The proxy can sign for the will-maker. Use the proxy procedure and proxy-style signature described above.

  When a willmaker cannot speak, the proxy procedure must be modified. Instead of receiving instructions from the willmaker, the proxy should ask the willmaker if s/he should do the things described above. In answer to each question, the willmaker can give consent by nodding or showing approval another way.

Acknowledgment of Previous Signature

You can sign a will personally or by proxy, outside the presence of one or more of the witnesses, and then acknowledge the signature to the absent witness(es) later. For an acknowledgment, the execution should be as follows:

- The will shall have been previously dated and signed (by you personally or on your behalf by a proxy) in the final signature section. If the previous signature was before one or two witnesses, one of the other execution methods should be used for them. If you are also self-proving the will, the willmaker and witness(es) present should date and sign the self-proving declaration (for will execution).

  Example: George wants to execute his will quickly before admission into the hospital for major surgery. He cannot get all three witnesses together because one works at night. He signs the will before the first two witnesses and then acknowledges the signature later to the absent witness.

- Gather the absent witness(es) in the same room and tell them that you've read the will (or had it read to you) and you understand it.
- Point to the previous signature in the final signature section and tell the witness(es) that it's your signature (if signed personally), or was made on your behalf (if signed by proxy).
- Ask these witness(es) to read the statement of witnesses and have them sign their names below that paragraph.
- Ask these witness(es) to print their names and addresses on the lines to the left of their signatures.
- If you are self-proving the will, the willmaker and the witness(es) who were absent during the execution session should date and sign the self-proving declaration (for previously-signed will). In this way, both self-proving declarations will be completed and ultimately attached to the statutory will.

Selecting a Will Execution Method

Although three execution methods are available, the first method (signature before witnesses) is by far the safest, and should be used whenever possible. Don't use either of the other two methods merely for the sake of convenience; postpone the execution of your will until the first method is available.

Nevertheless, in emergencies the proxy or acknowledgment methods might have to be used. If you must use these execution methods, consider self-proving the will, to bolster its reliability.

Chapter 2A After You Make a Statutory Will

Part IV

After you execute your statutory will, staple the pages together. Do the same for any photocopies you made. Fastening the pages this way keeps them from getting scattered later.

While you still have the original will and photocopies together, use information from the original will to do two things to the copies: 1) print the date your will was signed in the dateline in the final signature sections of the copies (but don't sign the copies) 2) print the names and addresses of the witnesses who signed your will in the lines below the statement of witnesses sections of the copies. By adding this information, your unexecuted copies will show the date of your will and who witnessed it. This information could come in handy later if your original will is lost or destroyed and a copy has to serve as a substitute.

Repeat this procedure for the self-proving declaration, if you self-proved the will during execution. Take information (about dates, names of witnesses), from the original declaration and print this on the copies of the declaration.

Afterward, collate everything: put the original will with the original self-proving declaration, and match copies with copies.

Destroying Prior Wills

As you recall, art. 1 revoked any prior wills you made. Nevertheless, it's still a good idea to revoke prior wills by destroying them and all copies. Some people hesitate to do this. But if you leave prior wills around, there's always a chance that one could be put forward as a rival to your new will. By destroying prior wills, that's practically impossible. Thus, soon after you make your will, collect your prior wills and all copies. Destroy the documents by tearing them up and putting them in the trash.

Storing the Will

In *The Pickwick Papers,* Charles Dickens tells of Susan Weller who left her will in a teapot for her husband Tony to find after her death. You shouldn't be so casual about storing your will. Store your will where it's secure during your lifetime. At the same time, the storage place must be accessible to your survivors so they don't have to scavenge for the will. These are the most popular places to store the original will and original self-proving declaration, if used:

Home safe. A safe located in your home is a good place to store your will if the safe is fireproof and waterproof. By storing your will at home, it's accessible to your survivors after your death.

Safe deposit box. Most financial institutions and some private storage companies have safe deposit boxes available for lease. A safe deposit box is a secure storage place, but access can be restricted.

When a safe deposit box has been leased by a box-holder alone, the box-holder's survivors or personal representative must obtain an order from the probate court to get access after the boxholder's death. This procedure might delay probate of the will.

Access is much easier if a safe deposit box has been leased jointly. The surviving box-holder has the right to remove the deceased box-holder's will or other papers from the box without obtaining official permission. Thus, if you store your will in a safe deposit box, consider leasing the box jointly with others, such as your spouse or children.

Vault at a financial institution. As a courtesy, some financial institutions allow you to store wills in their vaults, without charge, when you have appointed them as fiduciaries.

Probate court. You can also store your will in the probate court of the county where you live. After storage, the probate court keeps the will until you decide to withdraw it or until your death. Until then, the will is kept confidential and cannot be revealed to anyone.

Michigan probate courts charge a one-time fee of $25 for storage of a will. They also ask that the will be submitted for storage in a sealed envelope or wrapper. The envelope or wrapper must be labeled with the will-maker's: 1) name 2) place of residence 3) social security number or driver's license number 4) date the will was submitted for storage 5) name of the person who submitted it for storage.

Whichever storage method you use, it's important to tell your family and/or personal representative appointees where your will is located. When you have stored your will in a home safe or safe deposit box, give these people the key or combination to the storage place.

Revising the Will

The will that you have made should reflect your current wishes about the distribution and settlement of your estate. But as your personal situation changes, the will may become outdated and need revision.

Small changes in your personal situation shouldn't affect the will. For example, if you move to another county or your daughter has a new name after marriage, the personal information in art. 1 will be outdated. However, it isn't necessary to revise the will to add this new information. On the other hand, important events, like those listed below, may require revision.

- your marriage, separation, divorce, or annulment of your marriage
- birth or adoption of children
- death of relatives or takers of your property
- wish to change the pattern of property distribution your statutory will provides
- wish to change fiduciary appointments
- growth in the value of your net worth to a level that might result in estate taxation
- change of residence to another state

If revision is necessary, don't revise by crossing out words or writing in new ones. After a will is made, it's complete and mustn't be changed. At best, the modifications are ineffective. At worst, they are treated as an obliteration of the will, which is regarded as a revocation. This could result in revocation of the obliterated sections or even the entire will!

The correct way to revise a will is by codicil. A codicil is a will amendment changing or supplementing the will. Codicils must describe the modification and be executed with some of the formalities used for wills. In the end, making a codicil is a lot like making the will itself. What's more, there's always a risk that a codicil may be lost or separated from the will it modifies. If that happens, the codicil is ineffective.

Because of these problems, it's best to avoid codicils and make a whole new will when you want to revise your statutory will. If a statutory will still fits your needs, simply repeat the procedure described above and make a new statutory will.

Chapter 2B Before You Make a Handwritten Will

Part I

Before you make a will, you need some basic information about will-making. This is especially true for a handwritten will, which you must compose and assemble yourself.

Who Can Make a Handwritten Will?

Age and Mental Capacity

In Michigan, any adult (a person 18 years of age or older) with a sound mind can make a will. Sound mind has a two-fold meaning. In one sense, it means that a willmaker must have the proper mental capacity to make a will. To have this state of mind, a willmaker must possess the ability to know:

- the "natural objects of one's bounty" (those a willmaker would be expected to benefit, such as close relatives)
- the nature and extent of the willmaker's property
- that s/he is providing for distribution of property in the will
- the manner in which the will distributes property

Sound mind also means that the willmaker's judgment isn't clouded by an insane delusion. An insane delusion is a belief in things that don't exist. If a willmaker distributes property under such a delusion, the will-maker's mind might be unsound, jeopardizing the will.

Undue Influence, Duress and Fraud

Besides having a sound mind, a willmaker must make the will without undue influence, duress or fraud. Undue influence is when someone influences you to the extent the will is not really your free choice. Undue influence usually comes from those you trust, such as relatives, friends or advisors. Duress is like undue influence, but worse. With duress, someone actually forces you to make a will. Normally, the force must be physical force or the threat of it. But in some cases, extreme psychological pressure can qualify as duress. A fraudulent will is based on a misrepresentation (falsification) of a fact that you relied on in making the will.

When a willmaker is underage or has an unsound mind, the will is completely invalid. A will made under undue influence, duress or fraud may be declared invalid, or just the tainted provisions are removed, allowing the rest of the will to remain.

As strict as these rules about mental capacity are, they apply only at the exact moment you make a will. In other words, you must have a sound mind and be free of undue influence, duress and fraud when you make your will. Spells of mental incapacity before or after are excusable.

Example: George suffers a serious stroke. For several days he is confined to an intensive care ward where he is under heavy sedation and semiconscious. He recovers his senses and makes a handwritten will. Before long, George has another stroke and becomes mentally incapacitated again. Despite his spells of incapacity, the will is valid because it was made during a period of mental capacity.

Physical Capacity

With most wills, you don't have to worry about physical capacity to make the will. A willmaker, no matter how feeble, usually has enough strength to sign the will. But some physical capacity is necessary for a handwritten will since the willmaker must handwrite the entire will.

Residence

As explained in the introduction to this chapter, wills are regulated by state law. One consequence of state control is that you must reside in the state where you make your will. Thus, you must be a resident of Michigan before you can made a Michigan handwritten will.

If you move out of Michigan, will other states accept your Michigan will? Luckily, all states have will reciprocity laws recognizing out-of-state wills. According to these laws, a will is enforceable anywhere if it was valid when and where it was made.

Despite will reciprocity laws, you still should consider making a new will after moving out of state. Not every state has handwritten wills, so courts in your new state might not be familiar with these. Also, a move out of state may require appointment of new fiduciaries who live near you.

You can avoid these problems by making a new will under the law of the state where you reside.

Michigan residency is necessary for your handwritten will; presence in the state is not. For example, you can make the will outside Michigan during a temporary absence, such as a vacation or business trip. Military servicepersons from Michigan can make Michigan handwritten wills wherever they are stationed, because they normally keep the state residence they had before enlistment.

Residence is important for willmaking; citizenship is not. Thus, Michigan residents who aren't U.S. citizens can make Michigan handwritten wills. These wills will be recognized throughout the United States because of the will reciprocity laws mentioned before. At the same time, noncitizens with property in their native countries may want to make an international will (see "Types of Wills" on page 33 for more about this option).

Specific Gifts

You can make an unlimited number of specific gifts—of any kind of property—in a handwritten will. Making a specific gift may seem simple and straightforward: You select an item and give it to someone. But in fact, will gifts are loaded with complications, as explained below.*

What Can Be Given in a Specific Gift?

In a specific gift, you can give virtually any type of real or personal property. Keep in mind that the property must be solely-owned (property you own by yourself). If you try to give joint property, the gift is ineffective since a will doesn't normally affect this kind of property. Even worse, if you give a jointly-owned item to someone besides the other joint owner, you can create a legal dispute between the specific gift-taker and the other joint owner. This dispute could wind up in court after your death.

Describing Specific Gifts

Whether you give real or personal property, the item given must be described in enough detail so it can be identified after your death and transferred to the gift-taker. Personal property should be described by citing distinctive characteristics, marks or identification numbers:

> *Example:* George has two gold watches. He wants to give one to his brother Wesley, or to his brother Chester if Wesley fails to survive him. George makes a specific gift of the watch, describing it in detail to avoid confusion with his other watches.

---

* Most of the following information about specific gifts also applies to the transfer of the remainder of the estate (the residuary estate).

One: I give my gold-filled, seven-jewel, Hamilton pocket watch, serial no. 444881, to my brother Wesley Francis Frisbie. If Wesley Francis Frisbie fails to survive me, this watch shall be given to my brother Chester Dean Frisbie.

Describe real property by street address whenever possible. For rural land without an address, use a general description of the land. A full legal description, which appears in deeds and other legal documents, usually isn't necessary.

Example: George wants to give a house he owns to Woodrow, or to Dewey if Woodrow fails to survive him. George makes a specific gift of the house as follows:

One: I give my house at 217 S. Washington, Lake City, Michigan, and all its contents, to my son Woodrow James Frisbie. If Woodrow James Frisbie fails to survive me, this house and contents shall be given to my son Dewey John Frisbie.

Example: George has 40 acres of rural hunting land that he wants to give to his brothers. He makes a specific gift of the land to them:

One: I give my 40 acres of land in Sumpter Township, Lake County, Michigan, to my brother Wesley Francis Frisbie. If Wesley Francis Frisbie fails to survive me, this land shall be given to my brother Chester Dean Frisbie.

A specific gift of real property only includes the land and permanent attachments, such as houses, buildings and demobilized mobile homes. The gift doesn't include the contents of the houses, buildings or mobile homes, which are separate personal property, unless you say so. In the first example above, the contents are given with the house.

Who Can Take a Specific Gift?

You can make specific gifts to any person. But some recipients, such as incapacitated adults and minors, may need special arrangements before they can take the gift. At one time, it was often necessary to put complicated trusts in wills, to hold will property for incapacitated adults or minors. These days, there are simpler management options, described below.

For will gifts to incapacitated adults, the gift can be transferred to:

- a conservator, if one is known to exist
- a specially-appointed trustee named during probate
- any agent from a power of attorney, such as a durable power of attorney
- 1) if the amount or value of the gift is $5,000 or less annually, and 2) a conservator has not been appointed, the gift goes to:
  - a spouse, parent or close relative taking care of the incapacitated adult

- a guardian
- a special savings account at a financial institution

For will gifts to minors, the gift can be transferred to:

- a conservator, if one is known to exist
- a specially-appointed trustee named during probate
- a custodian under the Uniform Transfers to Minors Act (UTMA) who already exists, is appointed in the will, or whom the personal representative names during probate
- 1) if the amount or value of the gift is $5,000 or less annually, and 2) a conservator has not been appointed, the gift goes to:
  - the minor personally, if married
  - a current caretaker, such as a parent
  - a special savings account at a financial institution

There aren't any geographical limits on specific gifts. You can make gifts to people outside the state of Michigan, or even beyond the United States. Years ago, there were restrictions on making gifts to some noncitizens, particularly in communist countries, but these have now been abolished.

Besides giving to people, you can make specific gifts to a variety of organizations: charities, religious and service organizations, schools, foundations, governments, business and nonprofit organizations, fraternal associations and political parties. All that's necessary is that the organization has a formal legal identity. You cannot make specific gifts to informal organizations, like your softball or bowling team, because these groups aren't legally capable of taking a will gift.

People and organizations can take will gifts; animals cannot receive property directly from wills. You can make a specific gift to a charity or service organization providing animal care, like a humane society.

Michigan used to bar animals from benefiting from trusts. But Michigan's new estates code now allows special trusts for "domestic or pet animals." If you create a pet trust, you can name the primary animal beneficiaries, the secondary human beneficiaries (who take over when the pets have died), the trustee, and even a special trust enforcer. Pet trusts are explained in detail in Chapter 3, in "Permanent Care for Pets" on page 141. There is also a pet trust form you can use in the forms section.

Designating Specific Gift-Takers

As you make specific gifts, designate gift-takers with care. People sometimes have look-alike or sound-alike names. The correct legal name of an organization is often far different from its popular name. Be absolutely sure you use the right name to avoid confusion. It also helps if you precede the gift-taker's name with a description of his/her relationship, if any, to you. This designation method is used in the sample handwritten wills in this book, so specific gifts are made to, "my wife X," "my brother Y," and "my son Z," etc.

You must be even more careful with specific gifts to groups of people in categories or classes, such as children, brothers, sisters, etc. Lawyers call these class gifts. Identify the class accurately, and make sure the class includes everyone you want to benefit, but nobody else.

Example: Eugene wants to make a specific gift to his brother's and sisters' children. He decides the best way to phrase the gift is to "my brother's and sisters' children." Had he made the gift to the "children of my brother and sisters," there might be confusion about whether the gift goes to Eugene's brother's and sisters' children, or to his brother's children and his sisters personally.

Joint Gifts

Sometimes, you may want to make a joint gift to multiple takers. It's easy to make joint specific gifts of real property, because Michigan law permits several forms of joint ownership in real property. In fact, Michigan law says that a will gift of real property to two or more persons automatically creates a tenancy in common between them.

Tenancy in common ownership is described in more detail in Chapter 5. Simply put, it gives the joint owners, called tenants in common, fractional shares of the property. The share is the tenant's solely-owned property, which s/he can transfer by sale, gift, will or inheritance. These characteristics make tenancy in common ideal for joint gifts. The following specific gift provides for a tenancy in common, in equal shares, between two takers:

> One: I give my 40 acres of land in Sumpter Township, Lake County, Michigan, to my brothers Wesley Francis Frisbie and Chester Dean Frisbie, in equal shares. If either Wesley Francis Frisbie or Chester Dean Frisbiee fails to survive me, this land shall be given to the one of them who survives me.

Ordinarily, tenants in common get equal shares. But that doesn't always have to be so. You can provide for joint gifts with unequal shares, as in the following provision:

> One: I give my 40 acres of land in Sumpter Township, Lake County, Michigan, to my brothers Wesley Francis Frisbie and Chester Dean Frisbie, as follows: 75% share to Wesley Francis Frisbie and 25% share to Chester Dean Frisbie. If either Wesley Francis Frisbie or Chester Dean Frisbie fails to survive me, this land shall be given to the one of them who survives me.

Unlike real property, Michigan law doesn't permit joint ownership of every kind of personal property. What's more, there are practical problems with joint ownership of personal property that don't exist for real property.

Example: George considers making a joint gift of a watch to his brothers. Even if such a gift were legally possible, how could the brothers share the watch? Who would get possession of the watch and be responsible for it?

Whatever form they take, joint gifts must be intentional; they don't happen by accident. For example, if you give a specific gift to a married person, the gift goes to this person alone.* It won't benefit the person's spouse unless you make a joint gift to both spouses.

Conditional Gifts

It's tempting to use wills to influence the behavior of others by making conditional specific gifts. A conditional gift comes with strings attached, making the gift effective if the taker does or doesn't do something (the condition).

Most conditional gifts are a recipe for trouble. The gifts are often hard to interpret, and even harder to enforce. Say you give $1,000 to your son provided he never gets a tattoo. Who is going to watch his appearance? Is it the personal representative? If so, must the estate be kept open indefinitely while the personal representative looks for a tattoo on the son?

Worse yet, conditional gifts often encourage unacceptable behavior. Suppose you make a specific gift to your daughter provided she isn't married to your "lazy son-in-law Ted." Won't this gift encourage your daughter to divorce Ted to get the gift? Many courts think so and have set aside similar conditional gifts as contrary to public policy.

Thus, as a general rule, avoid conditional gifts. If you want to influence the behavior of others post-mortem, set up a trust. A trust is more flexible than a conditional will gift, and can influence the behavior of the beneficiaries for years. The only condition that should be placed on will gifts is survival, which Michigan law automatically attaches to every will for a 120-hour period (as suggested in "Survival" on page 40, you may want to extend this survival period).

Selecting Fiduciaries

Everyone should appoint personal representatives in their wills. Parents with minor children will also want to appoint guardians and conservators for their children. Parents of DD children can also appoint guardians. Parents of LI unmarried adult children, or spouses of LI mates, who are

---

* But if the gift-taker and spouse divorce later, the gift could possibly be divided during their divorce. Michigan divorce law throws all property, including lifetime gifts, will gifts and inheritances received before or during the marriage, into the pot for possible division. However, except in hardship cases, Michigan courts usually allow divorce parties to keep their gifts and inheritances.

currently serving as guardians, can appoint guardians to succeed them.

For each fiduciary slot, you need two picks: a first choice and a substitute. If all goes well, your first choice will serve as fiduciary. But if the first choice cannot or will not serve, your substitute choice can step in.

Don't worry about making final fiduciary selections now. Use the information below to narrow the field of fiduciary candidates down to a few. Then make your final picks after reviewing the sections of Part II dealing with qualifications for the various types of fiduciaries.

Fiduciaries: Legal Eligibility

You can appoint any adult person, except someone who is mentally incompetent, to serve as a fiduciary. Ordinarily, avoid appointing minors because they cannot serve if they are still underage when the time comes for them to assume their duties.

Michigan used to bar residents of other states or countries from serving as fiduciaries in many circumstances. But these days families are often far-flung, and willmakers often want to name out-of-state fiduciaries. In 1984, the fiduciary law was changed and now nonresidents and noncitizens can serve as fiduciaries in most cases.

Some financial institutions can act as personal representatives or conservators. To be eligible for appointment, a financial institution must possess trust powers. In Michigan, only banks and savings and loan associations can get these powers (although not all such institutions have them); credit unions and other financial service companies cannot receive trust powers.

Much as nonresidents were once excluded, Michigan law used to bar out-of-state financial institutions from fiduciary service here. But a recent amendment to the banking law allows out-of-state banks (with trust powers) to serve if they are doing business in the state.

In some cases, you can appoint qualified nonprofit corporations, such as religious, charitable, or social service organizations, as guardians and conservators. The appointment will take effect only if: 1) it's in the best interests of the dependent 2) no other suitable person is willing to serve. As a result, nonprofit corporations are better as second-choice fiduciaries, or first choices for someone without any surviving relatives or friends.

Fiduciaries: Practical Qualities

Most people and several kinds of organizations are legally eligible to serve as fiduciaries. But for practical reasons, some make better choices than others. These are a few of the practical qualities that you should look for in a fiduciary:

Honesty. Honesty is by far the most important quality because a fiduciary often handles money or manages other property. Probate courts supervise fiduciaries, but the supervision isn't very close. Thus, a dishonest fiduciary can do considerable harm before detection and removal. Select an honest fiduciary and you can also excuse bond for the fiduciary, saving the cost of a bond premium.

Suitability. Fiduciaries should be matched to the tasks they perform. They don't necessarily need special skills or expertise, but they should have an aptitude for the job. So, personal representatives and conservators should have good financial judgment, and guardians must get along well with children.

Willingness to serve. A fiduciary's job is strictly voluntary; a fiduciary can decline to serve before appointment or resign afterward. To avoid disappointment, always ask fiduciary candidates whether they are willing to serve before you appoint them. Financial institutions should also be asked because they might decline to serve if the estate is too small or difficult to manage.

Availability. Select fiduciaries who are going to be around when you need them. Ordinarily, your picks should be your age or younger, and in good health. Organizations don't face physical infirmities, but they can fail financially. Before you choose an organization, make sure it enjoys financial "good health."

Nonresidents of Michigan are legally eligible to serve as fiduciaries. But nonresidents may find it difficult to carry out fiduciary duties long-distance. Thus, you may want to give preference to those who live near you in Michigan.

Affordability. Your fiduciaries must also be affordable. As explained below, fiduciaries may receive fees for their work. Financial institutions and professionals (lawyers, accountants, financial advisers, etc.) in particular may want fiduciary fees. If these are too expensive, select someone else.

Fiduciary Fees

Years ago, it was customary to give will gifts to personal representatives. These gifts encouraged the fiduciary to carry out the will, and rewarded the fiduciary for his service.

These days, fiduciaries are entitled to fees for service. You can set fiduciary fees in a will, but few do. Instead, fiduciaries are entitled to "reasonable compensation" for their services. The probate court may review these fees, judge the reasonableness of the fees by the: 1) difficulty of the fiduciary tasks 2) amount of time spent 3) any fee schedule the fiduciary uses.*

Not all fiduciaries ask for fees. Relatives serving as guardians or conservators often give up fees because they know the fees come out of the estates. A personal representative who is also a taker of the estate, such as

---

* Institutional and professional fiduciaries often use fee schedules, which typically compute fees as a percentage of the value of an estate.

a spouse or child, may surrender fees to save taxes. Fiduciary fees are taxable as income to a fiduciary, while estate distributions are not. By waiving fees, personal representatives-estate takers have a larger estate to take from (because it hasn't been reduced by fiduciary fees), without income taxation (since estate distributions are income tax-free). This makes up for the loss of fiduciary fees. Needless to say, financial institutions and professional fiduciaries don't have these incentives for giving up fees, and seldom waive fees.

Executing a Handwritten Will

A handwritten will is easy to execute. You just date and sign the will and it's executed. You don't need others to witness or self-prove the will, because a handwritten will can be tied to the willmaker by analysis of the handwriting.

How to Make a Handwritten Will

The next part shows you how to put together a handwritten will, paragraph by paragraph. But before you begin, here are some general rules about making a handwritten will:

- The entire will—from the caption at the top to the date and signature at the bottom—must be handwritten. If you typewrite or print by hand any part of the will, you risk invalidation of the whole will.

- Your handwriting must be legible. If you have bad penmanship, you must write carefully so the will is readable.

- Avoid penmanship errors. And don't try to fix any errors by blocking or lining out errors because this may make it look like someone has altered the will. If you make a serious error, rewrite the entire page.

- Except for ruled lines, the paper you write the will on should be completely blank. Using paper with writing on it, even a business or personal letterhead, is risky. The printed material might be considered part of the will, violating the rule that the entire will must be handwritten. To avoid this risk, use blank paper only.

- Use a pen with dark, permanent ink. Never use a pencil or a pen with erasable ink.

- When you identify a person, organization or financial institution, use their full legal names to avoid confusion.

- Your will should be consistent. If a name is mentioned more than once, the form of the name should be same whenever it appears.

Every will is different because it's such a personal document. Nevertheless, people with similar family and property tend to have similar wills. This resemblance makes it possible to explain willmaking in terms of four typical situations:

George Frisbie: married people with children

Thelma Mangrove: married people without children

Edith Millsaps: single people with children

Wanda Millsaps: single people without children

These character's wills appear in their entirely below. Excerpts from the wills also appear in Part II, as examples to guide you in your will-making. In addition, the wills of other characters are excerpted to describe special situations.

Will of George Edward Frisbie

I, George Edward Frisbie, of Lake City, Michigan, revoke previous wills and make this my will.

My wife is Margo Ann Frisbie, and we have three children: Thelma Alice Mangrove, Dewey John Frisbie and Woodrow James Frisbie.

One: I give my gold-filled, seven-jewel, Hamilton pocket watch, serial no. 444881, to my brother Wesley Francis Frisbie. If Wesley Francis Frisbie fails to survive me, this watch shall be given to my brother Chester Dean Frisbie.

Two: I give my residuary estate to my wife Margo Ann Frisbie. If Margo Ann Frisbie fails to survive me, the residuary estate shall go to my children and descendants by representation.

Three: Anyone taking a distribution from this will must survive me by 30 days.

Four: I appoint my sister Ruth Jean Smith as guardian of my minor children. If she does not serve, I appoint my brother Chester Dean Frisbie as guardian.

If my children need a conservator, I appoint Ruth Jean Smith as conservator. If she does not serve, I appoint Chester Dean Frisbie as conservator.

Five: I appoint my wife Margo Ann Frisbie as personal representative. If she does not serve, I appoint my brother Chester Dean Frisbie as personal representative.

The personal representative shall have all powers of administration given by Michigan law to personal representatives, and may do any act the representative determines to be in the best interests of my estate.

No bond shall be required for the personal representatives or conservators.

Signed this first day of January 1, 2000, at Lake City, Michigan.

George Edward Frisbie

Will of Thelma Alice Mangrove

I, Thelma Alice Mangrove, of Lake City, Michigan, revoke previous wills and make this my will.

My husband is Dudley X. Mangrove.

One: I give $5,000 cash to Willard P. Archey, as custodian for Woodrow James Frisbie, until age 21, under the Michigan Uniform Transfers to Minors Act.

Two: I give my residuary estate to my husband Dudley X. Mangrove.

If Dudley X. Mangrove fails to survive me, the residuary estate shall be divided equally between my brothers Dewey John Frisibe and Woodrow James Frisbie. If either Dewey John Frisbie or Woodrow James Frisbie fails to survive me, the deceased one's share shall go to the other one who survives me. If both Dewey John Frisbie and Woodrow James Frisbie fail to survive me, the residuary estate shall be divided equally between my parents George Edward Frisbie and Margo Ann Frisbie.

Three: Anyone taking a distribution from this will must survive me by 30 days.

Four: I appoint my husband Dudley X. Mangrove as personal representative. If he does not serve, I appoint my father George Edward Frisbie to serve as personal representative.

The personal representative shall have all powers of administration given by Michigan law to personal representatives, and may do any act the representative determines to be in the best interests of my estate.

No bond shall be required for the personal representatives.

Signed this first day of January 1, 2000, at Lake City, Michigan.

Thelma Alice Mangrove

Will of Edith Mae Millsaps

I, Edith Mae Millsaps, of Lake City, Michigan, revoke previous wills and make this my will.

My children are Grover Edward Millsaps, Eugene Arthur Millsaps, Shirley Noreen Millsaps and Wanda Sue Millsaps. It is my intention to exclude my son Eugene Arthur Millsaps and his descendants from the provisions of this will, for personal reasons. Therefore, any reference in this will to my children or descendants shall not include Eugene Arthur Millsaps or his descendants.

One: I give my five-piece silver tea service to my daughter Shirley Noreen Millsaps. If Shirley Noreen Millsaps fails to survive me, I give this tea service to my daughter Wanda Sue Millsaps.

I give $1,000 to United Charities of Lake City, Michigan.

Two: I give my residuary estate to my children and descendants by representation.

Three: Anyone taking a distribution from this will must survive me by 30 days.

Four: I appoint my son Grover Edward Millsaps and daughter Shirley Noreen Millsaps as co-personal representatives. If one of them does not serve, I appoint the other as sole personal representative.

The personal representative shall have all powers of administration given by Michigan law to personal representatives, and may do any act the representative determines to be in the best interests of my estate.

No bond shall be required for the personal representatives.

Signed this first day of January 1, 2000, at Lake City, Michigan.

Edith Mae Millsaps

Will of Wanda Sue Millsaps

I, Wanda Sue Millsaps, of Lake City, Michigan, revoke previous wills and make this my will.

One: I give my residuary estate to Luther Ray Hooper. If Luther Ray Hooper fails to survive me, I give the residuary estate to my mother Edith Mae Millsaps.

Two: Anyone taking a distribution from this will must survive me by 30 days.

Three: I appoint Luther Ray Hooper as personal representative. If he does not serve, I appoint my brother Grover Edward Millsaps as personal representative.

The personal representative shall have all powers of administration given by Michigan law to personal representatives, and may do any act the representative determines to be in the best interests of my estate.

No bond shall be required for the personal representatives.

Signed this first day of January 1, 2000, at Lake City, Michigan.

Wanda Sue Millsaps

Chapter 2B Making a Handwritten Will

Part II

By now, you should know what you want to do in your will. But you may have trouble putting this into words, especially legal language. That's where this section comes in; it shows how to phrase and write a handwritten will.

Title

Will of George Edward Frisbie

For the purpose of identification, the will should be entitled your will, using your full legal name. This form of your name should be repeated in the introduction and signature at the end of the will.

Introduction

I, George Edward Frisbie, of Lake City, Michigan, revoke previous wills and make this my will.

My wife is Margo Ann Frisbie, and we have three children: Thelma Alice Mangrove, Dewey John Frisbie and Woodrow James Frisbie.

The introduction to a will doesn't transfer any property, yet it has several important functions. It introduces you and says that this is your will. The introduction also revokes any prior wills you may have made. As explained in "Destroying Prior Wills" on page 119, you should also revoke by destroying prior wills and all copies.

In the introduction, say where in Michigan you live. As mentioned in Part I, you should be a Michigan resident when you make a Michigan handwritten will. This residency declaration helps establish your residence here.

Identify your spouse and children, if any, in the introduction. Your spouse is whom you are *legally* married to when you make your will (see "Spouse" in the glossary to determine which marriages are recognized in Michigan).

Unless you say otherwise, your children are defined by the Michigan estates code and include children born during your marriage, adopted children and most illegitimate (out-of-wedlock) children. See "Children" in the glossary for more about the code definition of children.

One advantage of a handwritten will is that you can redefine your children to handle special situations. For example, you can expand the definition of children to include stepchildren, who are normally excluded. Or you may narrow the definition to exclude illegitimate children. There is more about redefining children later in this part, with sample redefinition provisions.

When you identify your children, list living children only. Deceased children should be omitted because they cannot take property from your will (although their children/descendants can). If you are single and childless, leave out the family information from the introduction.

Specific Gifts

With the introductory material out of the way, you're ready to get down to business and distribute property in the main part of the will. Start with specific gifts. In a handwritten will, you can make unlimited specific gifts, of any kind of property, either directly or in trust-like form under the Uniform Transfers to Minors Act (UTMA).

Despite this flexibility, make specific gifts to transfer important items, such as cash or heirlooms, which you want to earmark for particular recipients. Don't try to transfer your estate piecemeal by making a lot of specific gifts. This clutters up your will and isn't an effective way to transfer property.

Before you make any specific gifts, keep in mind how they are satisfied from your estate. The satisfaction of specific gifts has high priority during the distribution of an estate (see "Distributing the Residuary Estate" on page 94 for the exact order of distribution). A large or valuable specific gift can deplete the estate if there isn't a lot of property to go around.

Example: Edith makes a specific gift of $10,000 to her church. After her death, Edith's estate has only $1,000 in cash and no other liquid assets. To raise money to pay the cash gift, other property in the estate, which Edith wanted her children to share, might have to be sold.

As you can see, specific gifts can affect or even upset the pattern of property distribution you have chosen in your will. Before you make specific gifts, especially large ones, consider the impact of these gifts on the rest of your estate.

Making Specific Gifts

Make specific gifts in the first numbered paragraph of the will. If you want to make several gifts, put them all in paragraph one, before you transfer the rest of your estate (the so-called residuary estate) in paragraph two. If you don't want to make any specific gifts, skip these and make the transfer of the residuary estate paragraph one.

> One: I give my gold-filled, seven-jewel, Hamilton pocket watch, serial no. 444881, to my brother Wesley Francis Frisbie. If Wesley Francis Frisbie fails to survive me, this watch shall be given to my brother Chester Dean Frisbie.

As you make specific gifts, remember the rules for making gifts explained in "Specific Gifts" on page 79. Make sure you have sole ownership of the gift item. A specific gift must accurately identify the item and the recipient. Avoid joint gifts of personal property and gifts with unusual conditions or stipulations.

Besides these rules, you must also make gifts which are definite and forceful, leaving no doubt about your intention to make the gift. Consider this pair of specific gifts by Edith:

> One: I would like my daughter Shirley Noreen Millsaps to get my five-piece silver tea service after I am gone.

> One: I give my five-piece silver tea service to my daughter Shirley Noreen Millsaps.

In the first gift, you aren't really sure Edith wants to give the tea service to Shirley. Avoid such fuzzy, wishful language because it might not be definite enough to transfer the item. The second gift is much better because it clearly gives the tea service to Shirley. All specific will gifts should be phrased in this way.

If the recipient of your specific gift is a minor, you may want to change the form of the gift. You can make the gift directly to the minor, but the minor may need help managing it (see "Who Can Take a Specific Gift?" on page 80 for more about this management problem.)

You can also make a trust-like specific gift to a minor under the Uniform Transfers to Minors Act (UTMA). You may give any kind of property this way, and name a custodian to manage the property. In addition, you can extend final distribution of the custodial property from the normal 18 years of age, to anytime between 18 and 21. For complete information about UTMA giving, see "Making UTMA Gifts" on page 168.

All the sample gifts in this chapter are direct, except for one in

Thelma's will. She has made an UTMA gift of cash to her favorite brother, and extended the final payout to age 21. See Thelma's will on page 88 for guidance on making an UTMA will gift designation.

To make a will gift complete, you should think about possible frustration of the gift. A frustrated gift is one whose recipient is dead (if a person) or defunct (if an organization) at your death.

Example: In her will, Edith makes two specific gifts: a silver tea service to her daughter Shirley and $1,000 to a charity. Before Edith's death, Shirley dies and the charity goes out of business. What happens to these specific gifts, which are now frustrated?

Michigan law specifies how frustrated specific gifts pass. If the deceased taker is a close relative,* the gift goes to the taker's children/descendants by representation (see "Representation" in the glossary for more about this pattern of distribution). But if the taker is a distant relative, a nonrelative or an organization, the frustrated gift fails and passes through the residuary estate. Thus, a frustrated gift gets distributed, but not always in the way you anticipated.

Michigan law allows you to override the frustrated gift law and provide your own distribution pattern. In a handwritten will, you have the opportunity to control frustrated gifts by designating alternate takers of the item.

Example: Edith wants to make two specific gifts in her will: a silver tea service to her daughter Shirley and $1,000 to a charity. If Shirley isn't around to take the tea service, Edith wants to give it to Wanda. Frustration of the cash gift to the charity doesn't bother Edith, since she won't mind if the money goes into her residuary estate for division among her children. Edith makes the following specific gifts:

One: I give my five-piece silver tea service to my daughter Shirley Noreen Millsaps. If Shirley Noreen Millsaps fails to survive me, I give this tea service to my daughter Wanda Sue Millsaps.

I give $1,000 to United Charities of Lake City, Michigan.

Distributing the Residuary Estate

The next paragraph is really the heart of the will because it distributes the residuary estate. The residuary estate is the remainder or residue of a probate estate after deduction, in order, of the following items:

---

* Close relatives include those who can qualify as your heirs, except your spouse, plus your stepchildren. See "Heirs" in the glossary for a list.

- final expenses (costs of probate, final disposition, death ceremony, estate taxes, and costs of last illness)
- family rights (see "Family Rights" in the glossary for an explanation of these rights)
- claims against the estate
- specific gifts

These deductions can take a bite out of the residuary estate. For example, high final expenses or big specific gifts may drain a residuary estate. But for most people, there is a residuary estate remaining which transfers the bulk of the probate estate.

The paragraph giving the residuary estate is paragraph two if you made specific gifts. If not, it's the first numbered paragraph of the will.

Estate Distributions for Married People with Children

Married persons with children usually want to give residuary estates to their spouses first, then to their children. This is the pattern of distribution the Frisbies want. The provision below, from George's will, accomplishes that:

Two: I give my residuary estate to my wife Margo Ann Frisbie. If Margo Ann Frisbie fails to survive me, the residuary estate shall go to my children and descendants by representation.

This provision names first (spouse) and second (children) takers of the residuary estate. But it does more. When your spouse is deceased and a child(ren) has also failed to survive you, the residuary estate goes to your surviving children/descendants by representation. The representation pattern passes a deceased child's share onto his/her surviving children or other descendants (grandchildren, great-grandchildren, etc.), who split it among themselves. For a full explanation of the representation pattern, see "Representation" in the glossary.

Representation is popular because it offers a comprehensive pattern of distribution to several generations of descendants. Both the inheritance law and statutory will use it. However, there are other distribution patterns, such as *per capita* and *per stirpes* schemes. "Representation" in the glossary has more about these alternatives. You may also want to give your residuary estate to someone besides your spouse and children/descendants. If so, see "Special Estate Distributions" on page 98.

Estate Distributions for Married People without Children

Married persons without children will probably want their spouses to be the first takers of their residuary estates. As for second takers, the choice is unlimited: parents, grandparents, brothers and sisters, nephews and nieces, aunts and uncles, cousins, friends, organizations, etc. In the example below, Thelma Mangrove has chosen her husband as first taker, followed by her brothers:

> Two: I give my residuary estate to my husband Dudley X. Mangrove.
>
> If Dudley X. Mangrove fails to survive me, the residuary estate shall be divided equally between my brothers Dewey John Frisbie and Woodrow James Frisbie. If either Dewey John Frisbie or Woodrow James Frisbie fails to survive me, the deceased one's share shall go to the other one who survives me. If both Dewey John Frisbie and Woodrow James Frisbie fail to survive me, the residuary estate shall be divided equally between my parents George Edward Frisbie and Margo Ann Frisbie.

Notice how this provision names first (spouse), second (brothers), and even third (parents) takers. By carrying the distribution this far, you guard against the loss of all takers in a common disaster, leaving no one to take the estate.

Naturally, other patterns of distribution are possible. See "Special Estate Distributions" on page 18 for distribution patterns without a spouse as first taker.

Estate Distributions for Single People with Children

Single persons with children usually want to make children/descendants the first takers of their residuary estates. The paragraph below from the will of Edith Millsaps, as brief as it is, does that using the representation pattern of distribution:

> Two: I give my residuary estate to my children and descendants by representation.

This provision gives the residuary estate to the children in equal shares. When a child fails to survive Edith, the representation pattern passes the deceased child's share onto to his/her children or other descendants (grandchildren, great-grandchildren, etc.), who split it among themselves. For a full explanation of the representation pattern, see "Representation" in the glossary.

Representation is popular because it offers a comprehensive pattern of distribution to several generations of descendants. Both the inheritance law and statutory will use it. However, there are other distribution patterns, such as *per capita* and *per stirpes* schemes. "Representation" in the glossary has more about these alternatives.

For some single-parent families, distribution of the residuary estate to children/descendants is enough. If the family is large and far-flung, there is likely to be someone around to take the estate even if a disaster happens. For example, Edith's family spans three generations living in several states. It's unlikely that a common disaster would wipe out everyone.

Edith can safely give her residuary estate to her children/descendants and leave it there.

On the other hand, small single-parent families may want to name more takers than just children/descendants. Taking the distribution further guards against the risk of a common disaster wiping out the entire family.

Example: Shirley is a divorcee with a young child, Rhonda. Shirley wants her residuary estate to go to Rhonda or her descendants. But she is worried that she and her daughter could die together in an accident, leaving no estate takers. In that case, Shirley wants her brother Grover and sister Wanda to take the estate. She makes the following residuary gift:

Two: I give my residuary estate to my children and descendants by representation.

If all my children and descendants fail to survive me, the residuary estate shall be divided equally between my brother Grover Edward Millsaps and my sister Wanda Sue Millsaps.

Shirley, Rhonda, Grover and Wanda could die together in an accident, frustrating Shirley's residuary gift. But the odds of that are small enough, so Shirley can safely leave the distribution at this point.

Not every single person with children wants to give their residuary estates to children/descendants. Other distributions are permissible. See "Special Estate Distributions" on page 98 for other possibilities.

Estate Distributions for Single People without Children

Single persons without children can distribute their residuary estates to whomever they wish: close relatives, distant relatives, nonrelatives, organizations, or any combination of them. Whatever the distribution, the residuary gift must describe the takers and the shares they are entitled to, as in the following example from the will of Wanda Millsaps:

One: I give my residuary estate to Luther Ray Hooper. If Luther Ray Hooper fails to survive me, I give the residuary estate to my mother Edith Mae Millsaps.

Both first and alternate takers of the residuary estate should be designated. This controls the disposition of the estate if the first taker fails to survive you. How many alternate takers should you name? That depends on who they are and where they live. If the takers are apt to be together, particularly travel together, name several alternate takers to prevent a common disaster from wiping out all your choices.

In the example above, Wanda has named only a second taker of her estate (Edith, her mother). That's because her friend Luther and her mother are seldom together (Edith doesn't approve of Wanda's relationship with Luther), so there's only a small risk of Wanda, Luther and Edith perishing together. If Luther and Edith were together more, Wanda should name second and third takers after Luther.

Special Estate Distributions

Ordinarily, you can distribute your residuary estate to whomever you like. But some individuals (your spouse and children/descendants) have legally protected rights or interests in your estate. You must make special provisions in your will to leave these people out, or limit their shares, so you can give to others. Special provisions are also necessary to expand or narrow the definition of children to handle special family situations.

Limiting a Spouse's Share

Most married people want to give residuary estates to their spouses. But this isn't always true. Some people, for a variety of reasons, want to "disinherit" or exclude their spouses from their wills. Michigan law makes it very difficult to exclude a spouse totally, because the law gives spouses guaranteed rights in the estates of their mates.*

	Surviving spouse is a widow	Surviving spouse is a widower
	Marital Rights	
Surviving spouse included in will distribution	(1) any one of: a) will gift b) dower c) ½ of intestate share (elective share) reduced by ½ of nonprobate transfers received (2) plus probate allowances	(1) either: a) will gift b) ½ of intestate share (elective share) reduced by ½ of nonprobate transfers received (2) plus probate allowances
Surviving spouse omitted from will because it was made before marriage	(1) either: a) dower b) full intestate share (2) plus probate allowances	(1) full intestate share (2) plus probate allowances
Surviving spouse omitted from will made after marriage	(1) either: a) dower b) ½ of intestate share (elective share) reduced by ½ of nonprobate transfers received (2) plus probate allowances	(1) ½ of intestate share (elective share) reduced by ½ of nonprobate transfers received (2) plus probate allowances

Probate allowances include homestead, family and exempt property allowances. See "Family Rights" in glossary for more information about these.

These marital rights can be given up in a marital contract, such as a prenuptial agreement.

---

* Michigan law allows spouses to surrender or limit their estate rights, in marital contracts like prenuptial agreements, giving the other spouse freedom to choose other estate takers.

As the chart shows, Michigan law protects spouses with several types of marital rights. Some of these are modest, such as the probate allowances, or unpopular, such as dower. This leaves the guaranteed share as the primary protection for spouses. Lawyers sometimes call this the elective share, since the surviving spouse must file a document choosing or electing the share with the probate court to receive it.

If you want to exclude your spouse, you must realize that complete disinheritance is usually unrealistic, and that the spouse is entitled to something from your probate estate. The disinheritance strategy changes from one of exclusion to limitation: How do you reduce your spouse's share to the legal minimum?

The one thing a disinheriting spouse wants to avoid is omission of the spouse from a will s/he made before marriage (a premarital will). Such an omission gives the omitted spouse the full inheritance share, twice the elective share. Naturally, you should always make a new will after an important life event like marriage (see "Revising the Will" on page 121 for a list of life events that trigger a need for will revision). But the danger of omission is another incentive for revision, when you want to limit a spouse's share.

Example: Margo made a will before she married George, and never got around to changing it, so George is left out of the will. Margo dies with an estate of $200,000. George qualifies as an omitted spouse and takes his inheritance law share: $175,000 (first $150,000 and one-half of the remainder), plus probate allowances.

If you make a will after you are married, and want to limit your spouse's share, your will should specifically exclude the spouse, leaving the spouse to the elective share (or dower, if a widow), plus the probate allowances.

Example: Margo made a will after marriage, mentioning George and giving him nothing. Margo dies with an estate of $200,000. George doesn't qualify as an omitted spouse, so he takes his elective share of one-half of what the inheritance law gives him: $87,500 (one-half of the first $150,000 and one-half of one-half (one-fourth) of the remainder), plus the probate allowances.

For the limitation provision itself, just mention the spouse by name and say s/he gets nothing. It's risky to go into the reasons for disfavoring the spouse. If you state a reason that's factually untrue, the spouse could use the error as grounds for attacking the limitation provision. Or if you say something unkind or malicious, the spouse could possibly sue your estate for testamentary libel or libel-by-will. It's better to say the spouse gets nothing for personal reasons without saying more.

Example: Margo wants to limit George's share to the legal minimum. She makes a handwritten will with the introduction below. Then she gives the residuary estate to her children in paragraph two of the will.

99

I, Margo Ann Frisbie, of Lake City, Michigan, revoke previous wills and make this my will.

My husband is George Edward Frisbie, and we have three children: Thelma Alice Mangrove, Dewey John Frisbie and Woodrow James Frisbie. I have intentionally excluded my husband George Edward Frisbie from the provisions of this will, for personal reasons.

Disinheriting Children and Descendants

Parents usually name their children as first or second takers in their wills. But some parents choose to leave the children out of the distribution, which is often called disinheritance.

Parents disinherit children for many reasons. They may decide the children are well-off and don't need any more property. Conversely, parents sometimes disinherit poor children receiving public benefits, such as developmentally disabled (DD) children, if a will gift would jeopardize these benefits. And naturally, children sometimes get disinherited out of anger or spite.

Whatever the reason—good or bad—it's entirely permissible to disinherit children. Unlike spouses, children don't have a legally guaranteed right to a share of their parents' estates except for one kind of child: afterborn children.

An afterborn child is one born (or adopted) after a willmaker made his/her will. Frequently, willmakers provide for afterborns by making so-called class gifts to "children." Even childless people do this, looking ahead to the day when they have offspring. For example, the late John F. Kennedy Jr.'s will reportedly provided for distribution to his children, although he died without any. Not-so-farsighted willmakers simply revise their wills to add children, individually or as a class, after they become parents for the first time.

But if you fail to plan and omit after-born children from your will, the omitted child is entitled to a possible share of your estate. The amount of the omitted child's share is complicated, influenced by several factors. In fact, if you benefited some children but not afterborns, the afterborns share equally with the living children.

On the other hand, if you want to disinherit afterborn children, you must say so in your will. Willmakers do this most often after entering second or later marriages, while still wanting to benefit living children from earlier marriages. Whatever the reason, use the following provision to disinherit after-born children:

It is my intention to exclude from the provisions of this will any children born to me after I make this will. Therefore, any reference in this will to my children shall not include my children born after I make this will.

The more far common disinheritance scenario is exclusion of children alive when you make your will. Unlike after-born children, living children don't have any claim on your estate, and you can disinherit them by leaving them out of the distribution. Nevertheless, the better practice is to disinherit the child(ren) personally in a disinheritance provision in the will.

In the provision, mention the disinherited child by name and state clearly that s/he gets nothing from the will. It isn't a good idea to disinherit by leaving a dollar or other small gift to the child, because this can sometimes complicate the probate (the disinherited child might refuse to give a receipt for the gift, delaying closing of the estate). The most convenient place to disinherit children is in the introduction of the will, where you introduce your family:

Example: Edith wants to disinherit Eugene and his children because they seldom call or visit her. In the introduction of her handwritten will, Edith states her intention to disinherit.

> I, Edith Mae Millsaps, of Lake City, Michigan, revoke previous wills and make this my will.
>
> My children are Grover Edward Millsaps, Eugene Arthur Millsaps, Shirley Noreen Millsaps and Wanda Sue Millsaps. It is my intention to exclude my son Eugene Arthur Millsaps and his descendants from the provisions of this will, for personal reasons. Therefore, any reference in this will to my children or descendants shall not include Eugene Arthur Millsaps or his descendants.

Notice the reason for Eugene's disinheritance (unspecified "personal reasons") is left vague. This is deliberate. If you give a specific reason for a disinheritance, which is untrue, the disinherited child might use this error to challenge the disinheritance. It's even riskier to disinherit with unkind or malicious language. As mentioned before, Michigan recognizes testamentary libel. The disinherited child could cite the clause, claim libel and sue your estate for damages.

When you disinherit a child, the disinheritance might not always cut off the disinherited child's descendants. If you want to disinherit a child and his/her descendants, mention the descendants as a group, as in the example above. Or you can disinherit descendants selectively by name, as in the provision below, leaving open the possibility that other descendants from the family might benefit:

Example: Edith has a grudge against Eugene and his sons, Ronald and Donald Millsaps, because they have neglected her. Edith decides to disinherit these three, but leave Eugene's other children in the distribution pattern.

> I, Edith Mae Millsaps, of Lake City, Michigan, revoke previous wills and make this my will.
>
> My children are Grover Edward Millsaps, Shirley Noreen Millsaps and Wanda

Sue Millsaps. It is my intention to exclude my son Eugene Arthur Millsaps and my grandsons Ronald Earl Millsaps and Donald Jay Millsaps from the provisions of this will, for personal reasons. Therefore, any reference in this will to my children or descendants shall not include Eugene Arthur Millsaps, Ronald Earl Millsaps or Donald Jay Millsaps.

Limiting a Child's Share

Sometimes, you may want to reduce a child's share, instead of totally disinheriting the child. Like disinheritance, limitation of a child's share may be motivated by anger or spite. But often there are good reasons for an unequal distribution. For example, parents may have given extra financial help to one of their children, and now want to even things out by reducing the child's share. No matter why, it's perfectly permissible to provide for an unequal distribution, like this one:

Two: I give my residuary estate to my wife Margo Ann Frisbie.

If Margo Ann Frisbie fails to survive me, the residuary estate shall be divided in percentage shares among my children as follows: 40% to my daughter Thelma Alice Mangrove, 30% to my son Dewey John Frisbie and 30% to my son Woodrow James Frisbie. The share of a child who fails to survive me shall go to the child's descendants by representation.

If you split the residuary estate unequally, use fractional (one-half, one-third, etc.) or percentage (50%, 40%, 30%, etc.) shares, not fixed dollar amounts. Your residuary estate may increase or decrease in value during your lifetime. Distribution in fractional or percentage shares automatically adjusts for these changes. Also, make sure that the shares allocated add up to 100%!

Redefining Children

Michigan's estates code, which governs wills and inheritance, has a standard definition of children. The code definition applies to statutory wills and other types of wills, unless you say otherwise. See "Children" in the glossary for a full explanation of the code definition.

One advantage of a handwritten will is that you can depart from the estates code definition of children. You can expand the definition to include stepchildren, foster children, unacknowledged illegitimate children of men, or children given up for adoption; or narrow the definition to exclude children. Just state your intention in the introduction of the will.

Example: Grover's wife Doreen wants to make her stepson Garth a second taker of her residuary estate, along with her own children. She does that in the introduction to her will:

My husband is Grover Edward Millsaps, and we have three children: Michael Allen Millsaps, Mark Paul Millsaps and Susan Anne Millsaps. I also have a stepson, Garth Joseph Millsaps. It is my intention to include Garth Joseph Millsaps and his descendants in the provisions of this will. Therefore, any reference in this will to my children or descendants shall include Garth Joseph Millsaps and his descendants.

On the other hand, you may want to benefit stepchildren, illegitimate or foster children, but not on equal terms with your other children. If so, it may make more sense to give a fixed specific gift to the child, and leave the child out of the distribution of the residuary estate.

Example: If Grover dies, Doreen wants to benefit Garth in her will. But she doesn't want him to share her residuary estate along with her own children. She decides to make a specific gift of some stock to Garth, conditioned on Grover's failure to survive her. In the introduction of her will, Doreen lists Michael, Mark and Susan as her children, leaving out Garth. Then in paragraph one, she makes the following specific gift:

One: If my husband Grover Edward Millsaps fails to survive me, I give 1,000 shares of ABC Corporation to my stepson Garth Joseph Millsaps.

In a handwritten will, it's also possible to exclude children who are normally included within the code definition of children. It's usually more efficient to do this by disinheritance. In the introduction to the will, mention the disinherited child by name and say that s/he is excluded. See "Disinheriting Children and Descendants" above for complete information on the technique.

Survival

As mentioned in "Survival" on page 40, Michigan's survival law requires all takers to survive the willmaker by 120 hours (5 days). For reasons explained in that section, it's smart to extend this survival period to 30 days. By making this extension, you can provide for an orderly transfer of your estate, but without delaying probate unreasonably. The paragraph below can accomplish this:

Three: Anyone taking a distribution from this will must survive me by 30 days.

Appointment of Fiduciaries

So far, your will has dealt with distribution of property. Next is another important topic: appointment of fiduciaries. In a simple handwritten will, you can appoint three types of fiduciaries: guardian, conservator and personal representative.*

---

* If you make specific gifts in UTMA form, you will also be naming a fourth kind of fiduciary: a custodian of the gifts.

If you have minor children, you should appoint a guardian and a conservator for them. Parents with DD adult children, or parents serving as guardians for LI unmarried adult children, or spouses serving as guardians for LI mates, may also want to appoint original or successor guardians for these special-needs dependents. And everyone, regardless of their family situation, should appoint a personal representative.

For the rules about legal eligibility to serve as a fiduciary, review "Selecting Fiduciaries" on page 83. Or see the chart below summarizing many of these eligibility rules. The practical qualities for fiduciaries are covered below.

Fiduciaries

	Function	Legal eligibility	Practical factors
(1) Guardian of minor children	Care for dependent and manage small amounts of property; same for (2), (3), and (4) below	Financial institutions cannot serve; some nonprofits can in certain cases; same for (2), (3), and (4) below	Single parent must consider rights of other parent; teenager may veto appointment
(2) Guardian of legally incapacitated (LI) children		Parent can appoint successor guardian for unmarried adult LI child if serving as guardian now	
(3) Guardian of legally incapacitated (LI) spouse		Other spouse can appoint successor guardian if currently serving as guardian	
(4) Guardian of developmentally disabled (DD) child		Parent can appoint guardian for adult DD child if: 1) serving as guardian now, or 2) child has no guardian and parent is surviving parent	
Conservator	Manage property for dependent when it is of amount or kind needing management	Many financial institutions and some nonprofits can serve	Teenager can nominate own conservator
Personal representative	Settle deceased's estate and carry out final instructions	Many financial institutions can serve	

Guardian and Conservator

Choose guardians and conservators with special care, because their responsibilities are enormous. Guardians will be stepping into your shoes as caretakers of your children or dependents. Guardians can also manage small amounts of property. A conservator manages property only, and uses the property to provide support for your dependents. With so much at stake, you will certainly want to look for these practical qualities in guardians and conservators:

Capacity for care or help. Above all, your guardians and conservators must be willing and able to provide good care or financial management help for your dependents.

¶ *Commitment.* Is the guardian or conservator willing to care for or help your minor dependents until they reach adulthood, which may be many years away? An even greater degree of commitment is necessary for special-needs dependents such as DD or LI adults. Find out the level of commitment by asking guardian or conservator candidates whether they are up to the task. Even if they say "Yes," judge how realistic this is.

¶ *Experience as caregiver.* You don't want to thrust caretaking on someone not ready to handle it. For example, a childless person may not be able to cope with newfound custodial responsibilities. All this goes double for special-needs dependents.

¶ *Child-rearing methods.* You may want someone who shares your values and beliefs about raising children. Or you may want to pick someone who belongs to the same religion, or has similar interests and hobbies as you and your children.

¶ *Health and stability.* Some candidates, such as elderly grandparents, may seem like good guardian or conservator choices now, but will they have sufficient health and longevity to provide care or help 5, 10 or 15 years from now?

Financial decision-making. Since the conservator will be managing your dependents' finances, the appointee must be able to make sound financial decisions for them.

¶ *Honesty.* Above all else, the conservator must be honest. A conservator handles financial matters with minimal court supervision. A dishonest appointee can do considerable harm before removal, making honesty an absolute necessity.

¶ *Good financial judgment.* In most cases, good financial judgment simply means common sense. But if the dependents' financial affairs are complex or difficult to manage, special skills might be necessary.

Location. Dependents usually move to live with their guardians, not the other way around. If you appoint an out-of-state guardian, or even one faraway in Michigan, could your dependents adjust to a move like that? Nonresident conservators may also have trouble managing property long-distance. Thus, you may want to choose guardians and conservators who live near you.

Financial resources. A dependent's living expenses are supposed to be paid by the guardian from the dependent's own property (managed by the guardian, if small, or a conservator, if large). But guardians inevitably spend some of their own money on dependents, without reimbursement. Consider whether your guardians can afford these extra expenses.

On the other hand, conservators can impose costs on the dependent (or the dependent's property), if they seek fees for financial management services. Institutional conservators, such as banks, will most often charge fees, which can be stiff. Relatives, friends or nonprofit conservators will often seek minimal fees, or none at all.

Children's preferences. You should clear guardian and conservator appointments with teenage children. In Michigan, children 14 years of age and older can veto guardian appointments or nominate their own conservators. After a child objects to parental appointments, the probate court must hold a hearing and make suitable appointments. You can avoid all this trouble by discussing guardian and conservator appointments with your teenage children and appointing someone acceptable to them.

Younger children don't have a guardian veto, but their feelings should also be respected. Find out by asking them whether they will be happy living with the guardian you want to appoint.

Combining guardian and conservator. You should seriously consider appointing the same person guardian and conservator, as in the sample appointment clause below. Combining these positions makes sense, because the appointee will have the funds for support at hand, without having to ask another person for these. If you want combined guardians and conservators, remember to do this for both your first choice and substitute appointments.

On the other hand, some might not like the coziness of combining guardian and conservator in one person. They might prefer to have different persons or institutions fill these positions so they can check on each other.

After you've made your final guardian and conservator selections, appoint them in paragraphs like these from the will of George Frisbie.

Four: I appoint my sister Ruth Jean Smith as guardian of my minor children. If she does not serve, I appoint my brother Chester Dean Frisbie as guardian.

If my children need a conservator, I appoint Ruth Jean Smith as conservator.

If she does not serve, I appoint Chester Dean Frisbie as conservator.

Coordinating Appointments between Parents

Parents should coordinate guardian and conservator appointments, or risk making different appointments. If the appointments aren't in synch, Michigan law says that the will of the parent who dies last controls guardianship.

Example: George and Margo make handwritten wills. They thought they appointed the same person as guardian of their children. However, they actually made different appointments. George dies before Margo. Because Margo died last, the guardian appointment in her will is the one that's effective.

Example: Same as above except that George and Margo die simultaneously in an airplane crash. Since neither of them died last, neither one's guardian appointments have priority. Making matter worse, both appointees want to be guardian of the children, and they contest the issue in a guardianship proceeding in court.

Parents can avoid these and similar problems by coordinating guardian and conservator appointments. On the other hand, parents aren't legally required to appoint the same guardians and conservators, and may choose different appointees if they wish.

Appointments by Parents with Broken Families

More than most, parents with broken families may want different guardians and conservators. Parents from broken families include parents who are single after a separation, divorce or annulment, parents who have remarried after a divorce or annulment, and unwed parents who never married and now live apart.

If the break-up was bitter, these parents may wish to have someone besides the other parent serve as guardian. With this in mind, the parent may hope to use a guardian appointment in a will as a means of taking custody of a child away from the other parent and giving custody to a nonparent third party, such as a new spouse, family member or friend.

What parents with broken families often forget is that guardians are only necessary for orphaned children. If one parent survives, s/he automatically gets or keeps custody as the natural guardian of the children* (unless s/he is legally incapacitated). Moreover, the surviving parent can control the future custody of the children by making guardian appointments in a will (since the guardian appointment of the last parent to die prevails).

Parents with broken families can still appoint the third parties they

---

* As consolation, Michigan law gives the parents of the deceased parent (the grandparents) the right to seek visitation with the grandchildren in these situations.

want as guardians. They must realize that their appointments will take effect only if the other parent: 1) is legally incapacitated 2) dies first 3) dies last but didn't make guardian appointments in a will.

Example: Shirley and her ex-husband Gus went through a bitter divorce. Shirley got custody of their daughter Rhonda. Shirley would like to deprive Gus of custody of Rhonda after her death by naming her brothers as guardians of the child in her will.

Shirley discovers that Gus, if he survives her, will get custody of Rhonda regardless of her will. Thus, Shirley makes a handwritten will naming Grover and Eugene as Rhonda's guardians and conservators. She realizes that the guardian appointment will take effect only in the three exceptional situations described above.

Appointing a third party as conservator has a better chance of success. The surviving parent doesn't automatically become conservator, although parents have high priority for appointment. Thus, an appointed third party could possibly vie with the surviving parent for appointment as conservator and win.

Joint Appointments

In a handwritten will, you can make joint appointments of guardians and conservators, where several persons combine to carry out a fiduciary role. Despite this opportunity, in most cases you should avoid joint appointments. They're no guarantee that things will go smoother than with a single fiduciary. And joint appointments can create all sorts of practical problems.

Example: George and Margo prepare wills naming George's brother Chester and his sister-in-law Selma as co-guardians of their children. George and Margo die and the pair become guardians of Dewey and Woodrow. Chester wants to transfer the boys to a private school, while Selma wants to leave them in public school. Their dispute ends up in court, where the judge decides that the boys should stay in public school.

Example: Later, Chester and Selma divorce. Both want to remain guardians of Dewey and Woodrow. Again, a court hearing is necessary to decide who becomes sole guardian of the children.

On the other hand, there are some situations in which joint appointments make sense. For instance, you might appoint a close relative, who has no financial expertise, and a financial expert, such as a friend or financial institution, as joint conservators for children. With this arrangement, the personal attention of the close relative complements the financial expertise of the other appointee. To make a joint appointment, use a provision like this from George's will providing for a joint conservatorship:

Four: I appoint my sister Ruth Jean Smith as guardian of my minor children. If she does not serve, I appoint my brother Chester Dean Frisbie as guardian.

If my children need a conservator, I appoint Ruth Jean Smith and John David Mason as co-conservators. If one of them does not serve, I appoint the other as sole conservator.

Split Appointments

You can also split guardian and conservator appointments by dividing the fiduciary's role among several appointees, who perform their tasks separately. For example, you can split guardian or conservator appointments by assigning children to different guardians or conservators.

Split guardian appointments are often frowned upon because they may separate brothers and sisters. Nevertheless, split guardian appointments make sense in some situations, especially among the blended families that are more common these days.

Example: After several years, Shirley remarries and has another daughter with her new husband. Rhonda, who is now a teenager, has difficulty adjusting to her stepfather and new half-sister.

In her will, Shirley decides to split her guardian appointments. She names Grover and Eugene as Rhonda's guardians, and relatives of her new husband as guardians for the baby.

Split conservator appointments are less controversial than split guardian appointments because the children aren't physically separated. If you decide to split guardian or conservator appointments, use a provision like this from George's will, with a split conservator appointment:

Four: I appoint my sister Ruth Jean Smith as guardian of my minor children. If she does not serve, I appoint my brother Chester Dean Frisbie as guardian.

If my children need a conservator, I appoint Ruth Jean Smith as conservator for my son Woodrow James Frisbie, and Chester Dean Frisbie as conservator for my son Dewey John Frisbie. If one of them does not serve, I appoint the other as conservator for both children.

Appointments for Special-Needs Dependents

Ordinarily, you appoint guardians for your minor children in a will. But you can often appoint guardians for your DD adult children. If you are currently serving as guardian, the appointee normally succeeds you as guardian; if you're not the guardian now, and no one else is either, the appointment takes effect at your death if you are the sole surviving parent. You may also appoint successor guardians for your LI unmarried adult children. To appoint a guardian for LI or DD adult children, use a paragraph like this from Grover's will appointing a successor guardian for his DD adult son Michael:

Four: I appoint my brother Eugene Arthur Millsaps to succeed me as guardian of my son Michael Allen Millsaps after my death. If he does not serve, I appoint my sister Shirley Noreen Millsaps to succeed me as guardian of Michael Allen Millsaps.

The same rules apply to a guardianship of a LI spouse. A spouse currently serving as guardian has the right to appoint a successor guardian for the spouse, who takes over when the guardian-spouse dies. George, who serves as guardian for recently incapacitated Margo, has appointed a successor in the following paragraph:

Four: I appoint my sister-in-law Joan Susan Clark to succeed me as guardian of my wife Margo Ann Frisbie. If she does not serve, I appoint my brother-in-law Donald Richard Clark to succeed me as guardian of Margo Ann Frisbie.

Personal Representative

The chief task of a personal representative is to settle your estate during probate. A personal representative doesn't have to do that personally (s/he/it may hire a lawyer or other professional to handle the probate), but the personal representative must supervise the procedure. The personal representative also has some authority to carry out instructions from the deceased about final matters (final disposition and death ceremony). These are important things requiring the following practical qualities:

Financial decision-making. Since your personal representative will be managing property during probate, the appointee must be able to make sound financial decisions for you.

¶ *Honesty.* Above all else, your personal representative must be honest. In a small estate or unsupervised probate, which should be the norm in Michigan, a personal representative operates with scant court supervision. A dishonest personal representative can considerable harm before removal, making honesty an absolute necessity.

¶ *Good financial judgment.* In most cases, good financial judgment simply means common sense. But if your estate property is difficult to manage, special skills might be necessary. For example, if you own a small business, your personal representative must know how to supervise it during probate.

Capacity to help. Your personal representative must have the time and inclination to give close attention to settlement of your affairs.

¶ *Commitment.* A personal representative's job is strictly voluntary; the appointee can refuse to serve, or quit anytime after beginning to serve. To prevent this, always ask candidates whether they are willing to serve before you appoint them. By getting prior consent, you reduce the chance they will fail to serve later.

¶ *Health and stability.* Some candidates, such as elderly people, may seem like good choices now, but will they be around when you need them? Ditto for casual friends you might drift away from.

Location. Michigan law doesn't disqualify nonresident personal representatives. But nonresidents may have difficulty supervising probate long-distance. Because of this problem, you might want to give preference to Michigan residents.

As you select your personal representative, don't forget about your spouse. Spouses are often excellent choices as personal representative. A spouse usually has all the practical qualities you look for in a fiduciary. What's more, spouses have an incentive to do a good job because they usually take the estates. On the other hand, you aren't required to select your spouse, and there are certainly situations in which your spouse is a poor choice.

After you've made the final picks, appoint your first choice and substitute personal representatives in a paragraph like this one from George's will:

> *Five: I appoint my wife Margo Ann Frisbie as personal representative. If she does not serve, I appoint my brother Chester Dean Frisbie as personal representative.*
>
> *The personal representative shall have all powers of administration given by Michigan law to personal representatives, and may do any act the representative determines to be in the best interests of my estate.*

Joint Appointments

You have considerable flexibility in appointing fiduciaries in a handwritten will. You may not make a true split appointment because the powers of a personal representative cannot be split up between several appointees. But you may appoint joint personal representatives who share the powers.

Despite this flexibility, in most cases avoid joint personal representatives. Multiple personal representatives are no guarantee that things will go smoother than with just one. When one appointee is unable or unwilling to serve, there may be temporary confusion about whether the other(s) can act without him/her.

A joint appointment might also result in disputes over settlement of the estate, which could wind up in court. Michigan law requires unanimous decisions by joint personal representatives, so a court is the only place to settle disputes. However, the law allows you waive the unanimous consent rule in your will. It's a good idea to do that if you name co-personal representatives, as in Edith's appointment below.

On the other hand, sometimes it's necessary to appoint joint personal representatives for the sake of family harmony. Several relatives may be expecting appointment, and a joint appointment can avoid disappointing them. Or there may be other good reasons for a joint appointment.

Example: Edith wants to appoint Shirley as personal representative because she's good with money. However, Shirley has recently moved out of state, and won't be able to handle the probate personally. Grover is Edith's other choice since he lives nearby, and is honest, ready, and willing to help. The trouble is, Grover is terrible at managing financial affairs. Edith decides to make a joint personal representative appointment, so she gets Shirley's financial skill with Grover's personal attention.

Five: I appoint my son Grover Edward Millsaps and daughter Shirley Noreen Millsaps as co-personal representatives. If one of them does not serve, I appoint the other one as sole personal representative. I do not require unanimous consent by these co-personal representatives during settlement of my estate.

The personal representatives shall have all powers of administration given by Michigan law to personal representatives, and may do any act the representatives determine to be in the best interests of my estate.

Powers of Personal Representative

In settling estates, personal representatives use the powers assigned to them by law (in Michigan's estates code), or by the wills that appoint them. Personal representatives receive 32 separate powers from the estates code (see "Powers of Personal Representative" in the glossary for a summary of these powers), allowing them to perform almost any task.

Some wills cite many or all the powers assigned to the personal representatives. But to save space, most wills simply adopt the estates code powers, and perhaps add a few more. This method makes sense for handwritten wills because you would get writer's cramp trying to write out all the personal representative's powers.

As mentioned before, it's best to give personal representatives broad powers so they don't have to get constant court approval of their activities. The easiest way to do that is to incorporate all the powers the estates code gives to personal representatives into your will. The sample wills in this book use this method, with a few modifications.

Despite their broad scope, the code powers of personal representatives have a few omissions. It's often worthwhile to add a catch-all power, allowing a personal representative to do anything that's in the best interests of the estate. The sample wills add this power.

The business powers the estates code assigns also have deficiencies and can be improved. The code says that a personal representative can operate an unincorporated business for a maximum of four months. After that, the personal representative must either seek court approval to run the business longer, or incorporate the business.

If you own an unincorporated business (a sole proprietorship or partnership), consider enlarging the personal representative's ability to operate it after your death. You can give the personal representative the power to operate the business indefinitely, until it's sold or distributed, without prior court approval or incorporation. As you expand the business powers of your personal representative, you're also exposing him/her to extra liability for business losses. Thus, you may also want to shield the personal representative from liability for any good faith business losses.

Example: George owns an unincorporated one-man business. He wants to give his personal representative the power to run this business during probate until it is sold. He also wants to exempt the personal representative from liability for any ordinary business losses incurred during the wind-up of the business. George includes the following provision in his will:

Five: I appoint my wife Margo Ann Frisbie as personal representative. If she does not serve, I appoint my brother Chester Dean Frisbie as personal representative.

The personal representatives shall have all powers of administration given by Michigan law to personal representatives, and may do any act the representatives determine to be in the best interests of my estate.

In addition, my personal representative shall have the power to operate a business until the assets are distributed or sold. This power shall be exercised without prior court approval and without the necessity of incorporation. During the operation of a business, my personal representative shall not be personally liable for any good faith business losses, nor shall the business be liable to my estate for the use of any business assets.

In most cases, it's best to give your personal representative broad powers. But there may be situations in which you want to limit powers. If so, all you have to do is take back selected powers from the personal representative:

Example: In the past, George has had bad luck with installment sales of real property. He wants to make sure that real property sold from his estate is for cash only. George notices that the estates code allows personal representatives to sell real property for "cash, credit, or part cash and part credit." He wants to remove the power to sell real property for credit from his will:

Five: I appoint my wife Margo Ann Frisbie as personal representative. If she does not serve, I appoint my brother Chester Dean Frisbie as personal representative.

The personal representatives shall have all powers of administration given by Michigan law to personal representatives, and may do any act the representatives

113

determine to be in the best interests of my estate, except: the personal representative must sell real property for cash only.

Fiduciary Bonds

When fiduciaries handle property, they may have to give bonds. Personal representatives and conservators face bond requirements because they control money and property. Guardians don't post bonds since they don't handle much property.

A bond is a promise by a fiduciary that s/he will pay any financial losses up to the amount of the bond. In some cases, this promise must be backed by a bonding company, which charges a premium for the guarantee. If a bond is required, the court sets the amount of the bond. It may mirror the value of the property the fiduciary controls, or it may be a nominal ($1,000) amount.

The court has the final say whether your personal representative or conservator must post bond. At the same time, you can make a recommendation about bond in your will which the judge must take into account.

Should you require bond or excuse it? Ordinarily, bond shouldn't be necessary. You selected your personal representative and conservator for their honesty and trustworthiness, so a bond shouldn't be needed to ensure good behavior. If you think a bond is necessary to keep them honest, pick different fiduciaries. Bond premiums are expensive and can be a financial drain on the estates of the deceased or child, which may pay them.

Don't worry about bond if you've appointed financial institutions or nonprofit organizations as fiduciaries. By law, organizations eligible to serve as fiduciaries have large bonds on deposit with the state treasurer to cover fiduciary losses. They don't have to post bond in individual cases.

If you decide to excuse bond, give this direction near the end of the will, as follows:

No bond shall be required for the personal representatives or conservators.

Other Will Provisions

The will paragraphs above should cover the estate planning needs of most people. But in special situations, you may need extra will provisions, such as the ones described below.

Cancellation of Debts

Debts owed to you are property of your estate which your personal representative is obliged to collect, by suing if necessary. However, it's permissible to cancel some debts in your will. You can cancel any debt owed to you personally.* Personal loans, balances on land contracts, and mortgages from the sale of land to relatives are the debts canceled most often in wills.

A cancellation of debt is actually a specific gift, in the amount of the debt, from you to the debtor. Therefore, insert any debt cancellations in paragraph one of your will along with other specific gifts. The cancellation of debt provision must identify the debt and the debtor, as in the example below:

Example: George sold a house to Thelma on a land contract. He wants to forgive the debt owed on the land contract at his death.

One: I cancel any money owed to me at my death by my daughter Thelma Alice Mangrove from a land contract dated March 1, 1999.

Instead of an outright cancellation, you might want to cancel the debt, but deduct it from other will distributions the debtor receives. This arrangement might be fairer to others in the family.

Example: George wants to cancel a land contract balance owed by Thelma. But he fears that the cancellation would show favoritism toward her, offending her brothers. George decides to set off the debt cancellation against other will distributions Thelma may receive:

One: I cancel any money owed to me at my death by my daughter Thelma Alice Mangrove from a land contract dated March 1, 1999. However, the value of this canceled debt shall be deducted from the value of other property Thelma Alice Mangrove receives from this will, and she shall receive this reduced share of property.

Satisfaction of Will Gifts

People often help others with both lifetime gifts and will gifts. You can keep these gifts separate. Or you can treat the lifetime gifts as satisfactions of the will gifts, and have the lifetime gifts deducted from the will gifts. To do that, you must include a satisfaction provision in your will. Add it as a miscellaneous provision at the end of the will.

Example: Edith has given Grover $10,000 to help him buy a house. She didn't do this for the other children and worries that they are resentful. Edith decides to treat the $10,000 lifetime gift to Grover as a satisfaction of his will gift.

Six: I have previously made a gift of $10,000 to my son Grover Edward Millsaps. The value of this gift shall be deducted from the value of property

---

* If a debt is owed to you and other(s) jointly, your cancellation alone won't cancel the debt.

Grover Edward Millsaps receives from my will, and he shall receive this reduced share of property.

Exoneration of Property

Your personal representative pays your personal debts out of your estate. Nonpersonal debts secured by property, such as mortgages and liens, are treated differently. According to Michigan law, these aren't paid from your estate and pass to the recipient of the property which secures them. It's the responsibility of the recipient to pay these off.

You can reverse this rule and provide for the payment of secured debts from your estate. All you have to do is add a so-called exoneration provision to the specific gift of property.

Example: George makes a specific gift of real property, subject to a $10,000 mortgage, to Woodrow. George wants to pay off the mortgage before the property goes to his son. He includes the following exoneration provision in the specific gift:

One: I give my house located at 217 S. Washington, Lake City, Michigan, and all its contents, to my son Woodrow James Frisbie. If Woodrow James Frisibe fails to survive me, this house and contents shall be given to my son Dewey John Frisbie.

I direct that any mortgage indebtedness against this property be paid as an expense of my estate.

Exoneration is a nice gesture, but be careful. It may be unnecessary if the debt is covered by insurance. Debtors often obtain private mortgage insurance (PMI) for real property, or similar credit insurance for other debts. The insurance pays off the debt when the debtor dies. This arrangement makes exoneration of the property unnecessary.

Keep in mind that exoneration can cause havoc with your estate. The payment of a large secured debt from the estate could deplete it, leaving nothing for others. Make sure that your estate is sufficient to pay the debt and accomplish your other goals.

Unsupervised Probate

Unsupervised probate is a good choice for larger estates that don't qualify for small estate probate. Unsupervised probate is quicker and less expensive than supervised probate, while offering the same protections to estate-takers and creditors.

Michigan law allows you to request unsupervised probate in your will. With the request, the probate judge must order unsupervised probate except in unusual cases. To make the request, include a provision in your will as follows:

Five: I request unsupervised administration of my estate.

Finishing the Will

According to Michigan law, a handwritten will must be dated and signed at the end. Also, add the place where it was signed. This isn't legally required, but helps establish residency in Michigan. Dating and signing are absolutely necessary for a handwritten will. Without these, the entire will is invalid.

When you sign the will, place your signature at the end of the will, so the entire body of the will appears above the signature. Don't add anything below the signature, as a postscript. Michigan law no longer requires handwritten wills to end with a signature. But a court interpreting the will might view below-the-signature material as surplus, and disregard it.

If you forget something, redo the will and work in the omitted material into the body of the will. If you want to amend the will later, see Part III on the correct way to amend a handwritten will.

Signed this first day of January 1, 2000, at Lake City, Michigan.

George Edward Frisbie

If your will has extended beyond a single page, it's smart to paginate the bottom of each page, by writing "Page One," "Page Two," etc. Pagination aids interpretation of the will later if the pages get scattered. To prevent scattering, staple the pages of the will together.

Lawyers sometimes have clients sign or initial each page of their ordinary wills. This isn't legally required, and is unnecessary with a handwritten will because your handwriting appears on every page already.

Chapter 2B After You Make a Handwritten Will

Part III

With your will complete, make a few photocopies of the document. Later, you will probably want a copy to keep around the house, for review, while the original is stored in a safe place. You may also want copies for your fiduciaries, particularly the personal representative. In fact, financial institutions often request copies before they accept appointment as personal representative.

On the other hand, don't make copies of your will indiscriminately. When a will is revoked and/or replaced by a new will, the prior will and all copies should be destroyed (see below for more about this procedure). If multiple copies of the will are in circulation, it's difficult to collect and destroy them all. A copy of the repudiated will might survive and be put forward as a rival for the new will. Because of this risk, make copies of your will sparingly, perhaps three or four at most.

Destroying Prior Wills

As you recall, the introduction to your will revoked any prior wills you made. Nevertheless, it's still a good idea to revoke prior wills by destroying these and all copies. Some people hesitate to do this. But if you leave prior wills around, there's always a chance that it could be used as a rival to your new will. By destroying prior wills, that's practically impossible. Thus, soon after you make your will, collect your prior wills and codicils and all copies. Destroy these documents by tearing them up and putting them in the trash.

Storing the Will

In *The Pickwick Papers*, Charles Dickens tells of Susan Weller who left her will in a teapot for her husband Tony to find after her death. You shouldn't be so casual about storing your will. Store your will where it's secure during your lifetime. At the same time, the storage place must be accessible to your survivors so they don't have to scavenge for the will. These are the most popular places to store an original will.

Home safe. A safe located in your home is a good place to store your will, if the safe is fireproof and waterproof. By storing your will at home, it's accessible to your survivors after your death.

Safe deposit box. Most financial institutions and some private storage companies have safe deposit boxes available for lease. A safe deposit box is a secure storage place, but access can be restricted.

When a safe deposit box has been leased by a box-holder alone, the box-holder's survivors or personal representative must obtain an order from the probate court to get access after the boxholder's death. This procedure might delay probate of the will.

Access is much easier if a safe deposit box has been leased jointly. The surviving box-holder has the right to remove the deceased box-holder's will or other papers from the box without obtaining official permission. Thus, if you store your will in a safe deposit box, consider leasing the box jointly with others, such as your spouse or children.

Vault at a financial institution. As a courtesy, some financial institutions allow you to store wills in their vaults, without charge, when you have appointed them as fiduciaries.

Probate court. You can also store your will in the probate court of the county where you live. After storage, the probate court keeps the will until you decide to withdraw it or until your death. Until then, the will is kept confidential and cannot be revealed to anyone.

Michigan probate courts charge a one-time fee of $25 for storage of a will. They also ask that the will be submitted for storage in a sealed envelope or wrapper. The envelope or wrapper must be labeled with the will-maker's: 1) name 2) place of residence 3) social security number or driver's license number 4) date the will was submitted for storage 5) name of the person who submitted it for storage.

Whichever storage method you use, it's important to tell your family and/or personal representative appointees where your will is located. When you have stored your will in a home safe or safe deposit box, give these people the key or combination to the storage place.

Revising the Will

The will you have made should reflect your current wishes about the distribution and settlement of your estate. But as your personal situation changes, the will may become outdated and need revision.

Small changes in your personal situation shouldn't affect the will. For example, if you move to another city in Michigan or your daughter has a new name after marriage, the personal information in the introduction to your will would be outdated. However, it isn't necessary to revise the will to add this new information. On the other hand, important life events, like those listed below, may require revision:

- your marriage, separation, divorce, or annulment of your marriage
- birth or adoption of children
- death of relatives or takers of your property
- wish to change the pattern of property distribution provided in your will
- wish to change fiduciary appointments
- growth in the value of your net worth to a level that might result in estate taxation
- change of residence to another state

If revision is necessary, don't revise by crossing out words or writing in new ones. After a will is made, it's complete and mustn't be changed. At best, the modifications are ineffective. At worst, they are treated as an obliteration of the will, which is regarded as a revocation. This could result in revocation of the obliterated sections or even the entire will!

Don't attempt to revise the will by adding material at the end of the will, below your signature. As mentioned in "Finishing the Will" on page 117, a postscript like that could be interpreted as surplus material, and disregarded.

The correct way to revise a will is by codicil. A codicil is a will amendment changing or supplementing the will. A codicil must describe the modification and be executed with some of the formalities used for wills. Thus, it's easy to make a handwritten codicil, which must be handwritten, dated and signed, for minor revisions to your handwritten will.

Example: After quarreling with his brother Chester and sister Ruth, George wants to appoint different guardians and conservators for his children in his handwritten will. He takes a blank sheet of paper and handwrites the following codicil:

Codicil to Will of George Edward Frisbie

I, George Edward Frisbie, of Lake City, Michigan, make this codicil to my will of January 1, 2000.

I revoke paragraph four of this will and replace it with the following paragraph:

Four: I appoint my sister-in-law Joan Susan Clark as guardian of my minor children. If she does not serve, I appoint my brother-in-law Donald Richard Clark as guardian.

If my children need a conservator, I appoint Joan Susan Clark as conservator. If she does not serve, I appoint Donald Richard Clark as conservator.

Except for this change, I affirm my will of January 1, 2000

Signed May 1, 2000, at Lake City, Michigan.

George Edward Frisbie

To be effective, a codicil must be read along with the will it modifies. This means that the codicil should be stored with the original will so the two documents are found and interpreted together. Wherever you have stored your original will—at home, in a financial institution, or at the probate court—make sure you store the original codicil in the same place.

The storage problem emphasizes one risk of using a codicil; it's ineffective unless read along with the will. But even if the two documents are together, it's sometimes difficult to make them mesh, particularly when the codicil makes many modifications. For these reasons, it's best to use a codicil for the simplest changes only, such as appointment of new fiduciaries or addition or removal of a specific gift.

For other changes, it's much better to revise by preparing a whole new will. Simply repeat the procedure described above and make a new will, with the modifications included.

After the Wedding, 1979

Chapter 3 Taking Care of Dependents

If someone is dependent on you, there's a natural anxiety about who will care for the dependent when you can't. Appointment of a guardian for the dependent, either by will or court order, is the customary remedy. But there are exciting new options—custodial powers of attorney, appointment of guardians without having to make a will, even trusts for pets!—to take care of dependents when you cannot provide care.

Nature of Caretaking

A caretaker is someone with custody of a dependent and/or control of their property and financial affairs. A guardian is one kind of caretaker, who has received custody from a court. But there are other kinds of caretakers: parents of minor children, conservators managing the financial affairs of protected persons, and even owners of pets.

Dependents are those who cannot take care of themselves and need caretakers to manage their personal or financial affairs. One kind of dependent is a ward, whose custody has been assigned to a guardian by a court. But probably the most familiar kind of dependents are minor (under-18) children, who usually remain dependent on their parents until adulthood. This natural custody of parents over children exists by law, without court intervention.

Not all dependents are human. These days, people are forming closer bonds with pet animals, often treating them as virtual members of the family. Pets, unlike wild animals, are unable to fend for themselves and are dependent on their owners for care.

You often have caretaking thrust upon you so quickly—as a parent to a newborn, a caregiver for a sick parent, a pet-owner—that you scarcely think about what you are doing. But really, there are two basic parts to caretaking, which can overlap a little:

Custody. The right and responsibility to look after a dependent's physical well-being, such as providing food, clothing, shelter, health care, etc. In addition, the caretaker may decide the dependent's education, religion and social life. Custody also includes limited power to manage small amounts of a dependent's property.* For example, a caretaker can receive income on behalf of a dependent, and apply it to the cost of his/her physical care or education.

Financial management. The responsibility for managing a dependent's real property (land and attachments to the land, such as houses and buildings) and personal property (all other kinds of property). The property or income from the property is applied toward care of the dependent.

This chapter focuses on the custody side of caretaking, not financial management. In particular, it looks at custody of human and animal dependents in two situations: 1) temporary transfer of custody from the current caretaker to another caretaker 2) permanent custody arrangements after the current caretaker's death.

There are a number of financial management options for dependent adults: conservatorship, protective arrangement, representative payeeship, living trust, joint ownership of property, and the best choice of all: durable power of attorney. All these remedies are covered in Chapter 9.

Conservatorship is the usual way to manage the finances of dependent children, and is beyond the scope of this book. A simple alternative to conservatorship is a gift under the Uniform Transfers to Minors Act (UTMA), covered in Chapter 4.

Temporary Caretaking

Here's the problem: You have custody of a human or animal dependent, but must give up custody temporarily because of absence during a vacation, business trip, military tour of duty, illness, or some other reason. Is it necessary to make legal arrangements for the separation, and if so, what kind?

Temporary Care of People

Facing a temporary separation from dependents, it's tempting to just transfer custody to friends or relatives informally. The risk? Informal care-

---

* Nevertheless, any property a caretaker receives for a dependent remains the dependent's own. If the property is valuable or difficult to manage, a conservator may have to be appointed to manage the property.

takers don't have legal authority over dependents. If a dependent needs legal consent for medical treatment or a school activity, informal caretakers have no right to speak for the children.

Guardianship is another option. But a guardian must be appointed by a court, after a formal hearing. What's more, a guardianship is sometimes difficult to undo, so former caretakers may have a hard time regaining custody of their dependents.

Guardians themselves sometimes have to give up their court-assigned custody briefly, during a temporary absence for one the reasons described above. They can go back to court for custody modification, but this is often inconvenient.

Luckily, Michigan law offers an easy solution to temporary transfer of custody of dependents: custodial power of attorney (CPA).

Custodial Power of Attorney

The concept of a power of attorney is simple, and familiar if you made a durable power of attorney (DPA) or a patient advocate designation (PAD), a special kind of power of attorney for health care, as part of your estate plan. A power of attorney creates a legal relationship known as agency, in which a principal gives powers to an agent to act for the principal.

With a CPA, the current caregiver (principal) transfers custody and related powers to another caregiver (agent). Like other powers of attorney, a CPA is an informal device made outside of court. You, not a judge, pick the temporary caregiver and assign the custodial powers you want. A CPA is also freely revocable, so you can cancel the arrangement anytime and get back custody immediately.

According to Michigan law, a CPA can last for a maximum of six months. However, you can renew the CPA and pick up additional six-month periods indefinitely. Powers of attorney lapse if the principal becomes mentally incapacitated, except when they're durable (see the introduction to Chapter 9 on page 251 for more about durability). The CPA in this book is durable to guard against the slight chance of incapacity after transfer of custody.

Who Can Make a Custodial Power of Attorney?

Custody for Transfer

Needless to say, you must have custody before you can transfer it. Parents ordinarily have natural custody of their minor (under-18) children.* Parental custody can be interrupted by a divorce, separate maintenance, annulment, independent custody, paternity, juvenile delinquency, protective (abuse/neglect or dependency), guardianship, mental commitment, or adoption case. If so, the parent may not have any custody left to transfer.

---

* A minor child who has been "emancipated" (by marriage, enlistment in the military, or court order) is regarded as an adult, and isn't subject to the natural custody of parents.

Guardians have custody of their wards through their guardianship powers. But not all guardians can use CPAs to transfer custody of wards. The CPA says that only guardians of: 1) minors 2) legally incapacitated (LI) adults* may use CPAs to transfer custody. Guardians of other wards, such as developmentally disabled (DD) adults, can't use CPAs, and must go back to court to modify custody.

It's possible that both you and your spouse want to transfer custody of your minor children. Or co-guardians of minors or LI adults may want to do the same thing. Either way, the CPA law permits parents or co-guardians to act as joint principals and transfer custody of their dependents in a single document.

Age and Mental Capacity

There aren't any age requirements for making a CPA. For example, a teenage mother, who is a minor herself, could make a CPA to transfer custody of her child.

But regardless of age, you must possess the proper mental capacity to make a CPA. The test for this is simple: You must be able to consent to having an agent act for you. This is a very low threshold of competency, lower than the mental capacity to sign a contract or the sound mind required for a will.

Undue Influence, Duress and Fraud

Besides having the proper mental capacity, you must also make your CPA free of undue influence, duress, and fraud. Undue influence is when someone influences you to the extent the power of attorney isn't really your free choice. Duress is like undue influence but worse. With duress, you are actually forced (usually by physical force or the threat of it) to make a power of attorney. A fraudulent power of attorney is one based on a misrepresentation (falsification) of a fact that you have relied on in making the power of attorney. Any CPA tainted by undue influence, duress or fraud would probably be invalid.

Residence

You should be a resident of Michigan when you make a CPA. There aren't any residency rules for these kinds of instruments. But to be on the safe side, it's best to be a Michigan resident.

Who Can Be an Agent?
Legal Eligibility

When you make a CPA, you transfer custody of your dependent to an agent, who has the responsibility to take care of him/her. Almost any

---

* See glossary for who qualifies as a legally incapacitated (LI) or developmentally disabled (DD) adult.

person—possibly even a minor or mentally incompetent person—could serve as your agent. Nevertheless, you won't want to choose minors as agents because they lack the maturity and judgment to be good caretakers. Mentally incompetent persons are also poor choices for the same reason.

Practical Qualities

As you can see, almost anyone is legally eligible to serve as an agent. But for practical reasons, some people make better agents than others. When you select your agent, look for the following practical qualities:

Capacity for care. Above all, the agent must be willing and able to provide good care for your dependents full-time.

¶ *Commitment.* Is the agent willing to care for your minor dependents for the time specified in your custodial power of attorney? If you have doubts about the agent's commitment, consider another agent. Even more commitment is necessary for the care of special-needs dependents such as LI adults. Find out the level of commitment by asking agent candidates whether they are up to the task. Even if they say "Yes," judge how realistic this is.

¶ *Experience as caregiver.* You don't want to thrust caretaking on someone unready to handle it. For example, a childless person may not be able to cope with newfound custodial responsibilities. All this goes double for special-needs dependents.

¶ *Child-rearing methods.* You may want someone who shares your values and beliefs about supervising and disciplining children. Or you may want to pick someone who belongs to the same religion as you and your children.

¶ *Health and stability.* Some candidates, such as elderly grandparents, may seem like good choices now, but will they have sufficient health and stamina to provide care for the time specified in your CPA?

Location. Whenever possible, avoid selecting agents who live outside the state of Michigan. Out-of-state agents are not legally barred from serving. But sometimes a child or ward is subject to a court order (from a divorce, guardianship, or other case) fixing his/her "domicile" (residence) in Michigan. Transferring the dependent outside the state could violate this order. What's more, your dependent may not like moving out of state, away from family and friends, even for a brief period of time.

Financial resources. A dependent's living expenses are supposed to be paid by the agent from the dependent's own property (managed by the guardian, if small, or a conservator, if large). But agents inevitably spend some of their own money on dependents, without reimbursement. Consider whether your agents can afford these extra expenses.

Dependent's preferences. You should always take into account the dependent's own feelings. Find out by asking the dependent whether they will be happy living with the agent.

As you pick an agent, relatives will probably be at the top of the list. That's natural because relatives are usually ready, willing, and able to serve as agents. Dependents may adjust better to relatives because they're familiar with them.

Relatives enjoy another advantage over nonrelatives when a dependent is going to be transferred outside his/her school district. In 1979, Michigan's Attorney General ruled that children crossing school districts during a custody transfer can become residents of the new school district only if placed with a relative.* Transfer to a nonrelative never creates residency after a cross-district move.

Today, with new school-of-choice laws in Michigan, transferring between school districts is much easier and cheaper (if the transfer is allowed, the state funding for the child follows the child, avoiding payment of nonresident school tuition).Thus, under the school-choice program, residency isn't the important issue it once was.

On the other hand, not every school district participates in the school-choice program. Transfer may still be possible into a nonparticipating school district, but under the old transfer rules, with tuition due for nonresident transferees. However, all school districts must educate resident children free of charge. And as described above, a child can become a resident through a CPA with a relative as agent. As a result, appointing a relative is still a consideration even with liberal school choice.

After you review your candidates, select at least one agent. Since a CPA won't last long (a maximum of six months), the risk of losing your agent is perhaps small. But it could happen. So it might be wise to select two agents: a first choice and a successor. That way, the successor agent can take over if the first choice fails to serve.

---

* Whether the child qualifies for residency in the new school district depends on the intent behind the transfer. If it's to find a new home for the child, s/he becomes a resident. But when the transfer is motivated by an intent to get educational benefits from the new school district, the child won't qualify for residency.

Collective Agencies

As with any power of attorney, it's possible to appoint several agents to act collectively. Collective agencies take several forms, including joint and split agencies. With a joint custodial agency, two or more co-agents share the responsibility of taking care of the dependents. In a split custodial agency, the dependents are assigned to the custody of different agents and care for them separately.

Joint agencies are legally permissible, but they can be difficult to manage. When one agent is unable or unwilling to serve, there may be confusion about whether the other(s) can act without him/her. Worst of all, co-agents may disagree about decisions, and the disagreement could wind up in court. As a result, the CPA in this book doesn't have space for joint agents.

Split agencies can also be a problem because they can separate children, such as brothers and sister, who are used to living together. But sometimes split custodial agencies make good sense.

Example: George and Margo will be out of the country for several months. They want to transfer custody of sons Dewey and Woodrow to George's brother Wesley. The problem is, Dewey dislikes Wesley. Dewey does get along with George's other brother, Chester. Although George and Margo hate to separate the boys, they decide to transfer custody of Woodrow to Wesley and Dewey to Chester in their CPA.

The CPA in this book allows you to transfer custody of several dependents together. However, it transfers these dependents to a single agent, ruling out split agencies in one CPA. But you can get around this limitation and create split agencies by making multiple CPAs. Simply make a separate CPA for each set of agent-dependent(s).

Making a Custodial Power of Attorney

The CPA in this book begins immediately, so custody is transferred to the agent as soon as you date and sign the document. Thus, make your CPA just before the temporary absence causing you to make the instrument.

When you make CPA, complete the form by printing or typing. If you print, use an ink pen, instead of a pencil, to make a permanent document. This prevents someone from altering the document.

Begin with the introductory paragraph of the CPA, and insert your name and address as the principal. As mentioned above, two persons, such as parents or co-guardians, can make a CPA jointly. If you and another person want to do that, include both names and address(es) in the introductory paragraph.

Below the next paragraph, list the names and dates of birth of the dependents whose custody you want to transfer. The CPA has space for four dependents. But you can add more by squeezing their names in this space, or by adding an attachment.

Put the name and address of your agent in paragraph #1. As suggested earlier, you should also name a successor agent, and put his/her name and address below your first choice.

In paragraph #2, you can specify the duration of your CPA. By law, the CPA can last as long as six months. When you want yours to last for the maximum six-month period, leave paragraph #2 as it is. But for a shorter duration, insert an earlier expiration date in the space for the date and cross out the phrase "for six months."

Paragraph #3 assigns broad powers of care, custody and property management to the agent. Custody (which is the same as care) is the most important power. As explained before, limited powers of property management normally go along with custody.

For emphasis, subparagraphs #3(a)-(c) spell out several specific care, custody and property management powers. These specific powers are actually included within the general powers given at the beginning of the paragraph. But they're added for the benefit of third parties like schools, medical caregivers and financial institutions, who often like to see specific powers mentioned.

However, you can modify those powers to fit your own situation. Subparagraph #3(d) gives you the opportunity to add extra powers. On the other hand, you can take away powers by striking out any powers in paragraph #3, or by inserting restrictions in paragraph #4.

Several powers are withheld from agents, by law. The CPA law bars a guardian of a minor ward from transferring powers to: 1) release the ward for adoption 2) consent to the adoption of the ward 3) consent to the marriage of the ward. Apparently, the law regards these powers as so special that guardians cannot give them up. Whatever the reason, paragraph #4 of the CPA withholds them from the agent as powers "prohibited by law" from transfer.

Finish the CPA by dating and signing it at the end. If you're making the instrument jointly with another person, both of you must sign (an extra signature space is included for this reason). You may also want to have your signature witnessed (by one or two witnesses) and/or notarized by a notary public. Witnessing and notarization aren't required, but they make your CPA more acceptable to third parties who deal with your agent.

Using a Custodial Power of Attorney

When a guardian (not a parent) makes a CPA, the guardian must give the court that appointed him/her notice of the transfer. The notice must be given within seven days after the CPA was signed by the guardian. Written notice is best. The guardian should write a letter to the court stating the name, address and telephone number of the agent, and include a copy of the CPA along with the letter.

Schools want to know who has the legal power to make educational decisions for students. And medical caregivers must ordinarily get consent from patients (or those legally responsible for them) before they can treat. Your agent can use the CPA to make these decisions for your dependent. But before the agent can act, third parties like schools and medical caregivers must accept the CPA.

To aid acceptance, paragraph #5 says that third parties can rely on the power of attorney, generally without liability to you. Signing the document before witnesses and/or a notary public also helps acceptance. But you can increase the acceptability of the CPA even more by distributing copies to third parties, such as your dependent's school and medical caregivers. That way, the third parties will be familiar with the CPA when your agent uses it.

Naturally, your agent should also get a copy of the CPA. In fact, you may want to give your agent the original power of attorney. Despite paragraph #6, which says that copies of the power of attorney can substitute for the original document, some third parties may want to see the original. When you have the original power of attorney and have gone away, the agent may have difficulty getting it. But if you leave the original with the agent, s/he will have it handy. If you give the agent the original document, make sure that you keep a copy.

Terminating a Custodial Power of Attorney

As long as you remain mentally capable, you can revoke your CPA anytime. To revoke, prepare a written revocation using the revocation of power of attorney contained in the forms section of this book. All you need to do is date and sign the revocation; it doesn't have to be witnessed or notarized. If you made the CPA jointly with your spouse of someone else, both of you must sign the revocation (just add the second signature below the single signature line in the revocation form).

According to the law of agency, a revocation of a power of attorney is only effective when the agent and/or third parties receive notice of it. Until this notice, your agent can still sometimes deal with third parties. Therefore, give notice of revocation immediately after revocation.

To give the agent notice, deliver a copy of the revocation of power of attorney to the agent personally. If that's inconvenient, send a copy of the revocation to the agent by certified mail, return receipt requested. The receipt proves that the agent got the revocation. Likewise, deliver or send copies of the revocation to third parties who have dealt with the agent.

After you revoke your CPA, destroy the original document and as many copies as you can get back from third parties (but keep a copy for your records). Destroying the power of attorney leaves absolutely no doubt that you intend to revoke the instrument. Destruction also makes it impossible for someone to get the document and attempt to exercise it against your wishes.

Another way to revoke a CPA is to make a new one. The introductory paragraph says that, by making the instrument, you intend to revoke any prior CPA for the dependent. Consequently, the CPA you make for the dependent is the one that's effective. Nevertheless, it's also a good idea to destroy any prior CPA (and all copies except yours) you have made for that dependent, for the reasons described above.

Besides revoking the instrument, there are several other ways a CPA can terminate:

Death. The CPA ends around the time of your death. The power of attorney can actually survive you because it remains in effect until your agent and/or third parties find out about your death. But when they do, the power of attorney ends immediately.

Loss of agents. The CPA terminates when your agent dies or quits, and the successor agent is also unable to serve.

Loss of dependent. The CPA terminates when your dependent dies, becomes an adult (at age 18), or is emancipated while still a minor (by marriage, enlistment in the military service, or court order).

Expiration. The CPA ends after six months, or sooner if you have specified an earlier expiration date.

Revising a Custodial Power of Attorney

After you have made a CPA, you can always revise it. For example, you may wish to appoint a different agent if you discover that s/he isn't taking good care of your dependent.

When you want to revise your custodial power of attorney, don't make revisions by scratching out parts of the power of attorney and/or writing in new ones. After a CPA is dated and signed, it's complete and shouldn't be altered. There are ways to amend the instrument, but amendment is difficult. Instead, the best way to revise your CPA is to start over and make a new one.

Temporary Care of Pets

Every pet-owner has made short-term arrangements for pet care when away on a vacation or trip. But have you thought about who will provide extended care if you're temporarily incapacitated after an accident or illness?

Careful pet-owners make plans for these emergencies. They will have someone, such as a friend, relative, veterinarian or kennel, ready to step in and provide care.

As an extra precaution, you may want to carry a card with you in your purse or wallet saying that you have a pet needing care. The card should name the substitute caregiver and include that person's address and telephone number. During an emergency, emergency workers or medical caregivers will find this card and notify the caregiver about taking care of your pet until you're ready to resume care.

Caretaking after Death

Temporary caretaking is a worry, but easily fixed by a CPA or other arrangements. Much more planning is necessary to provide for long-term custody of your human or animal dependents after your death.

Caretaking for People

Parents of minor children should always make caretaking arrangements for their children if they should die. Likewise, parents of developmentally disabled (DD) or legally incapacitated (LI) unmarried adult children, or spouses with LI mates, should do the same.

CPAs won't help in any of these situations. Like all powers of attorney, custodial powers expire at the principal-caretaker's death, and therefore are never a long-term custody solution.

At the other extreme, caretakers near death could make permanent custody arrangements. For example, a caretaker could make a deathbed release of parental or custodial rights, paving the way for foster care or even adoption of the dependent. These are rather unappealing solutions. What if the dying caretaker surrenders custody rights, recovers from the illness, and can't get the rights back?

The fact is, there is a much better remedy for long-term custody of dependents: guardianship. If necessary, a court will appoint a guardian for your helpless dependents after your death, but the appointment is out of your control. You can appoint a guardian in your will, or outside the will in a separate guardian appointment. Both appointments are legally binding, with one small exception explained later.

Guardian Appointment in a Will

The customary way to appoint a guardian is by will. This is still a good method. It has the benefit of being familiar and well-recognized by courts. A will appointment is also a little more flexible than a separate guardian appointment outside a will. You can appoint a guardian for DD adult child, or appoint conservators for minor children. These are things you cannot do in a separate guardian appointment.

Whichever type of will you make, take advantage of the opportunity to appoint guardians (and conservators). Chapter 2A has information and instructions for guardian and conservator appointments in a statutory will; Chapter 2B has the same for handwritten wills.

Separate Guardian Appointment

Wills are a good place to appoint guardians. The trouble is, people seem to dread making wills, losing their chance to appoint. A 1997 survey found that 62% of Michigan adults don't have wills; among parents with young children, who need to make guardian appointments the most, it's been estimated that this figure is higher and that perhaps as many as 90% of new parents are will-less.

Michigan's new will law tries to fix this problem by, for the first time, allowing guardian appointments outside wills in separate documents. The separate appointment of a guardian has the same force and effect as an appointment by will: The appointment goes into effect as soon as the appointee files an acceptance with the probate court, unless a teenage dependent vetoes the appointment (this veto right is explained in "Who Can Be a Guardian?" below).

The law permits separate appointments of guardians only, not conservators. Parents may appoint guardians for their minor children, or LI unmarried adult children if currently serving as guardians. Spouses acting as guardians for LI mates may also name successor guardians by separate appointment.

Who Can Appoint a Guardian?

Custody for Transfer

Needless to say, you must have custody, or some custodial rights, before you can assign custody in a separate guardian appointment. Parents ordinarily have custody of their minor (under-18) children.* Parental custody can be interrupted by a divorce, separate maintenance, annulment, independent custody, paternity, juvenile delinquency, protective (abuse/neglect or dependency), guardianship, mental commitment, or adoption case. But even after interruption, noncustodial parents retain some custody rights, such as the right to parenting time (formerly known as visitation), and this is enough custody to make a guardian appointment.

On the other hand, parents can have their parental rights, including custody, terminated in a protective (abuse/neglect and dependency) or adoption case. If so, these parents would not have any custody left to transfer.

Parents of LI unmarried adult children, who are serving as guardians, can appoint successor guardians in a separate appointment. Similarly, a spouse acting as guardian of a LI mate can do the same.

Age and Mental Capacity

To make a will, and appoint a guardian in the will, you must be at least 18 and have a sound mind. A separate guardian appointment isn't a will, so those age and state-of-mind requirements don't apply.

As a result, a minor, such as a teenage parent, can make a separate guardian appointment. There must be mental capacity for the appointment. This state of mind is knowledge of the legal significance of the appointment (what it is and what it does), which is similar to the mental capacity for other legal documents like contracts.

---

* A minor child who has been "emancipated" (by marriage, enlistment in the military, or court order) is regarded as an adult, and isn't subject to the natural custody of parents.

Undue Influence, Duress and Fraud

Besides having the proper mental capacity, you must also make your separate guardian appointment free of undue influence, duress, and fraud. Undue influence is when someone influences you to the extent the appointment isn't really your free choice. Duress is like undue influence but worse. With duress, you are actually forced (usually by physical force or the threat of it) to make the appointment. A fraudulent guardian appointment is one based on a misrepresentation (falsification) of a fact that you have relied on in making the document. Any separate guardian appointment tainted by undue influence, duress or fraud would probably be invalid.

Residence

You should be a resident of Michigan when you appoint guardians outside a will. There aren't any residency rules for making these appointments, as there are for wills. But to be on the safe side, it's best to be a Michigan resident.

All states have will reciprocity laws recognizing out-of-state wills. But a separate guardian appointment isn't a will, so those will reciprocity laws don't necessarily apply. Moreover, many states allow guardian appointments in wills only, and don't allow separate appointments. As a result, if you move outside of Michigan later, make new guardian appointments under the law of your new home state.

Who Can Be a Guardian?
Legal Eligibility

You can appoint any mentally competent adult as guardian. Avoid appointing minors because they cannot serve if they are still underage when the time comes for them to begin caretaking. And even if they were to reach adulthood, young adults are seldom suitable guardians.

Your spouse shouldn't be chosen because your children won't need a guardian until both you and your spouse are deceased or incapacitated. In fact, your surviving spouse automatically gets custody when you die, without court action, thanks to the natural custody parents enjoy.

The same thing happens in broken families (marriage terminated by divorce, separate maintenance or annulment; parents never married and have separated): The surviving parent gets or keeps custody, and there isn't much you can do to prevent this (see "Appointments by Parents with Broken Families" on page 107 for more about this situation).

Michigan used to bar residents of other states or countries from serving as guardians in many circumstances. But these days families are often far-flung, and parents must sometimes name out-of-state guardians. In 1984, the law was changed and now nonresidents or noncitizens can serve as guardians in most cases. But there are still practical reasons for choosing local guardians (see "Location" below).

A few organizations can serve as guardian. Obviously, financial institutions, which can act as personal representatives or conservators, cannot become guardians because they cannot provide care directly. Some non-profit corporations, such as religious, charitable or social welfare organizations, can serve as guardians. But they usually fill in as last-resort choices, when no one else is available to serve. It's hard to imagine why you would want to appoint a nonprofit corporation as guardian, unless absolutely no one else is willing to serve.

Practical Qualifications

Most people and even some organizations are legally eligible to serve as guardian. But for practical reasons, some make better choices than others. These are a few of the practical things to consider before you appoint:

Capacity for care. Above all, the guardian must be willing and able to provide good care for your dependents.

¶ *Commitment.* Is the guardian willing to care for your minor dependents until they reach adulthood, which may be many years away? An even greater degree of commitment is necessary for the care of special-needs dependents such as LI adults. Find out the level of commitment by asking guardian candidates whether they are up to the task. Even if they say "Yes," judge how realistic this is.

¶ *Experience as caregiver.* You don't want to thrust caretaking on someone not ready to handle it. For example, a childless person may not be able to cope with newfound custodial responsibilities. All this goes double for special-needs dependents.

¶ *Child-rearing methods.* You may want someone who shares your values and beliefs about supervising and disciplining children. Or you may want to pick someone who belongs to the same religion as you and your children.

¶ *Health and stability.* Some candidates, such as elderly grandparents, may seem like good choices now, but will they have sufficient health and longevity to provide care 5, 10 or 15 years from now?

Location. Dependents usually move to live with their guardians, not the other way around. If you appoint an out-of-state guardian, or even one faraway in Michigan, could your dependents adjust to a move like that?

Financial resources. A dependent's living expenses are supposed to be paid by the guardian from the dependent's own estate (managed by the guardian, if small, or a conservator, if large). But guardians inevitably spend some of their own money on dependents, without reimbursement. Consider whether your guardians can afford these extra expenses.

Children's preferences. You should clear guardian and conservator appointments with teenage children. In Michigan, children 14 years of age and older can veto guardian appointments. After a child objects to parental a appointment, the probate court must hold a hearing and make suitable appointments. You can avoid all this trouble by discussing guardian appointments with your teenage children, and appointing someone acceptable to them.

Younger children don't have a guardian veto, but their feelings should also be respected. Find out by asking them whether they will be happy living with the guardian you want to appoint.

Coordinating Guardian Appointments between Parents

Parents should coordinate guardian appointments, or risk making different appointments. If the appointments aren't in synch, Michigan law says that the appointment of the parent who dies last controls guardianship.

Example: George and Margo make separate guardian appointments. They thought they appointed the same person as guardian of their children. However, they actually made different appointments. George dies before Margo. Because Margo died last, her guardian appointment is the one that's effective.

Example: Same as above except that George and Margo die simultaneously in an airplane crash. Since neither of them died last, neither one's guardian appointments have priority. Making matter worse, both appointees want to be guardian of the children, and they contest the issue in a guardianship case in court.

Parents can avoid these and similar problems by coordinating guardian appointments. On the other hand, parents aren't legally required to appoint the same guardians, and may choose different appointees if they wish.

Guardian Appointments by Parents with Broken Families

More than most, parents with broken families may want different guardians. Parents from broken families include parents who are single after a separation, divorce or annulment, parents who have remarried after a divorce or annulment, and unwed parents who never married and now live apart.

If the break-up was bitter, these parents may wish to have someone besides the other parent serve as guardian. With this in mind, the parent may hope to use a guardian appointment—whether by will or in a separate appointment—as a means of taking custody of a child away from the other parent, and giving custody to a nonparent third party, such as a new spouse, family member or friend.

What parents with broken families often forget is that guardians are only necessary for orphaned children. If one parent survives, s/he automatically gets or keeps custody as the natural guardian of the children* (unless s/he is legally incapacitated). Moreover, the surviving parent can control the future custody of the children by making guardian appointments by will or in a separate appointment document (since the guardian appointment of the last parent to die prevails).

Parents with broken families can still appoint the third parties they want as guardians. They must realize that their appointments will take effect only if the other parent: 1) is legally incapacitated 2) dies first 3) dies last but didn't make guardian appointments in a will or separate appointment document.

Example: Shirley and her ex-husband Gus went through a bitter divorce. Shirley got custody of their daughter Rhonda. Shirley would like to deprive Gus of custody of Rhonda after her death by naming her brothers as guardians of the child in an appointment document.

Shirley discovers that Gus, if he survives her, will get custody of Rhonda regardless of her appointment. Thus, Shirley makes a separate guardian appointment naming Grover and Eugene as Rhonda's guardians. She realizes that the guardian appointment will take effect only in the three exceptional situations described above.

Joint Guardian Appointments

In a separate guardian appointment, you can name joint guardians, who combine to carry out guardian duties. Despite this opportunity, in most cases avoid joint appointments. They're no guarantee that things will go smoother than with a single guardian. And joint appointments can create all sorts of practical problems.

Example: George and Margo make separate guardian appointments naming George's brother Chester and his sister-in-law Selma as co-guardians of their children. George and Margo die and the pair become guardians of Dewey and Woodrow. Chester wants to transfer the boys to a private school, while Selma wants to leave them in public school. Their dispute ends up in court, where the judge decides that the boys should stay in public school.

Example: Later, Chester and Selma divorce. Both want to remain guardians of Dewey and Woodrow. Again, a court hearing is necessary to decide who becomes sole guardian of the children.

But right or wrong, sometimes joint appointments are unavoidable. For instance, you might have several relatives expecting appointment as

---

* As consolation, Michigan law gives the parents of the deceased parent (the grandparents) the right to seek visitation with the grandchildren in these situations.

guardian. To avoid offending them, you make a joint appointment, for the sake of family harmony.

Split Guardian Appointments

You can also split guardian appointments by dividing the caretaking role among several appointees, who perform their tasks separately. For example, you can split a guardian appointment by assigning children to different guardians.

Split guardian appointments are often frowned upon because they may separate brothers and sisters. Nevertheless, split guardian appointments make sense in some situations, especially among the blended families that are more common these days.

> *Example:* After several years, Shirley remarries and has another daughter with her new husband. Rhonda, who is now a teenager, has difficulty adjusting to her stepfather and new half-sister.
>
> In her separate guardian appointments, Shirley decides to split her guardian appointments. She names Grover and Eugene as Rhonda's guardians in one appointment document, and relatives of her new husband as guardians for the baby in another appointment document.

The separate guardian appointment document in this book transfers all minor children to one guardian. This rules out split appointments in one document. But you can get around this limitation and create split appointments by making multiple appointment documents. Simply make a separate guardian appointment for each set of guardian-dependent child(ren), as in the example above.

Guardian Appointments for Special-Needs Dependents

Ordinarily, you appoint guardians for your minor children. But you may also appoint guardians for your LI unmarried adult children or LI mates, *if you are already serving as guardian.* With the appointment, the appointee takes over guardian duties from you at your death. You make these appointments like you do for children.

Making a Separate Guardian Appointment

When you make your final guardian picks, you should have two selections: a first choice and a substitute if the first choice cannot serve. You make the appointments in the guardian appointment form. There is a sample form at the end of this chapter, and blank ones in the forms section of this book.

In the first paragraph, insert your name and place of residence. There are two sections in the form: one for guardians of minor or LI unmarried adult children (if you're already serving as guardian for the LI adult child), and another for guardian of a LI spouse (if you're already serving as guardian for the LI spouse). Insert the names of your first- and second-choice guardians in the correct spaces of one (or both) section.

After you complete the form, you must date and sign the form before two witnesses. Any mentally competent adult can witness your signature. After you sign, the witnesses must sign in the spaces provided.

After You Make a Separate Guardian Appointment

After you complete the separate guardian appointment, make several copies of the document. You should give copies to your first- and second-choice appointees, so they are aware of the appointment.

Store the original in a safe place, but where it will be accessible after your death. See "Storing the Will" on page 120 for tips on storing vital documents likes wills and separate guardian appointments.

Revising a Separate Guardian Appointment

You may want to revise your appointments and name different guardians at some point. Don't try to amend the old appointment document. Simply make a new one. Then, destroy the prior document and all copies.

Terminating a Separate Guardian Appointment

You can terminate a prior guardian appointment by destroying the document. Or you can make a new appointment, which revokes the previous one.

Another way to revoke a separate guardian appointment is to make a will with new guardian appointments in the will. The will, as the most recent document, cancels the prior separate guardian appointment. If you do this, it's wise to destroy the prior guardian appointment document and all copies.

Conflicting Will and Separate Guardian Appointments

When guardian appointments in and outside a will conflict, the will appointments should always control. Will appointments are superior even if they were made first, and the separate guardian appointments second. This happens because wills are a more authoritative document than separate guardian appointments.

Try to avoid these conflicts by making all your guardian appointments in either a will or separate appointment document, not both. If you make both kinds of appointments, see that the appointments are consistent, or revoke the prior instrument before you make a new one with different guardian appointments.

Permanent Care for Pets

Until recently, there wasn't much pet-owners could do to provide security for pets after their death. Pet-owners could make informal arrangements with family and friends for care. They could also leave money, in a lifetime or will gift, to a caretaker with an understanding the money is going to be spent on care of the pet. None of these things was legally enforceable, and all depended on the good faith of survivors, who may not be as fond of the pet as the original owner is.

More formal options include entering into a long-term pet-care contract with a veterinarian or boarding kennel. With this arrangement, the veterinarian or kennel agrees to provide life-long pet care for a fixed price. If you can afford it, this is a good option. It's even better when combined with one of Michigan's new pet trusts described below. By adding a trust to the picture, the veterinarian or kennel takes care of the pet, while the trustee of the pet trust pays periodically for the care.

Another option is arranging for adoption of your pet after your death. Some animal welfare organizations and societies provide informal pet-adoption services or referrals. The problem is, they receive far too many requests for placement, and can only handle a fraction. If your pet is a pure-bred dog, there may be a breed rescue program providing foster care or adoption of the animal.

When all else fails, some pet-owners must face the hardest choice of all: destruction of the pet. Sometimes destruction is unavoidable. If the pet is old, sick, or unable to get along with anyone except its owner, the pet may have to be destroyed after the pet-owner's death.

But for healthy pets, destruction is controversial. It's particularly a problem if the pet-owner orders destruction of the pet in his/her will. Courts have had great difficulty with pet-destruction provisions. On the one hand, courts are supposed to enforce wills, carrying out the wishes of the willmaker. On the other hand, wills are designed to distribute property, not destroy it. Michigan law is unclear about the legality of pet-destruction provisions, with no reported cases on the issue.

But Michigan law was always clear about one thing: Pets were things and things cannot be the direct beneficiaries of wills or trusts. Michigan's new will law changes this entirely. The new law not only allows the creation of special trusts for pets, the law has detailed rules about the operation of pet trusts.

Other states have allowed honorary trusts for pets. Honorary trusts are unenforceable trusts in which the trustee volunteers to carry out the trust purpose. Voluntary and nonbinding, honorary pet trusts end up resembling informal pet-care arrangements relying on the good faith of survivors. Michigan's pet trust is akin to an honorary trust, but with a big difference; it provides for enforcement of the trust through a trust enforcer who acts as a watchdog for the trust.

Pet Trusts

Concept of a Trust

Trusts are triangular arrangements in which the trust creator, called the settlor, transfers property to a trustee, to be managed for the benefit of third parties, the beneficiaries of the trust.

Trusts take many different forms, but they generally fit into two main categories: a testamentary trust or a living (*inter vivos*) trust. A testamentary trust is part of a will, and like other will provisions, doesn't become effective until the willmaker-settlor dies. A living trust is made in a separate trust document, and goes into effect during the settlor's lifetime. Living trusts can either be revocable, and subject to amendment or cancellation by the settlor anytime before death, or irrevocable and not open to future alteration.

A living trust may be funded or unfunded. With a funded living trust, you transfer property to the trust during your lifetime, and the trust becomes operational then. If the trust is unfunded, it goes into effect while you're alive, but it's just an empty shell, without any property to do anything.

An unfunded living trust can draw property from your probate estate, through a "pour-over" provision in your will. The pour-over provision takes probate property, earmarked for transfer by the will, and "pours it over" into the empty trust, filling it with property. An unfunded living trust may also receive nonprobate property, such as life insurance proceeds, at the settlor's death.

With a living trust, the trust document creating the trust, called a trust agreement, spells out how the trust property shall be held, managed and distributed to the beneficiaries. Typically, there are periodic distributions for ongoing support, then a final distribution, during termination of the trust.

Design of a Pet Trust

The pet trust in this book is an unfunded revocable living trust, which needs a pour-over provision in the settlor's will to get probate property to fund the trust. All this may seem complicated, but there's a good reason for the arrangement.

A pet trust can be testamentary, or placed inside a will. But this is impossible with a Michigan statutory will, which cannot be added to or modified in any way, and difficult with a handwritten will (the entire trust would have to be handwritten, verbatim). Thus, a living trust is a more practical choice.

The pet trust is unfunded because you can provide support for your pets while you're alive. Thus, there's no really no need for the trust during your lifetime. What's more, keeping the trust empty gives you full control over your property during your lifetime.

This is also the reason why the trust property comes from your probate estate, through the pour-over provision in your will. To be sure, the poured-over property must pass through probate, which has a cost. But the amount of property at stake should be small; sometimes, everything may even qualify for one of Michigan's small estate probates (see "Probate Planning" on page 21 about qualifying for these procedures). By taking property this way, you have maximum lifetime control of your property.

The pet trust is revocable, so you can amend or revoke it if circumstances change later. You may want to amend the trust, adding or subtracting pet-beneficiaries. Or you may decide to cancel the arrangement entirely. You couldn't do any of these things if the pet trust were irrevocable.

Who Can Make a Pet Trust?

Any mentally competent person can make a trust. But the kind of pet trust in this book needs a companion will, with a pour-over provision, for funding the trust. As a result, you must satisfy all will rules about age, soundness of mind, residence, etc. See "Who Can Make a Statutory Will?" on page 43, or "Who Can Make a Handwritten Will?" on page 77 for an explanation of these willmaking rules.

Presumably, the pet-owner is the settlor of the pet trust. It's possible that someone else could make a pet trust for a pet they are fond of, but don't own. But the pet trust in this book is really designed for pet-owners only; for others its not going to work correctly. For example, if a nonowner makes a pet trust and dies after the pet-owner, there's a hiatus between the two deaths when the pet might not receive any support.

In this regard, the will that goes with a pet trust should also transfer ownership of the pet to the trustee. Make sure you have clear ownership of the pet, allowing you to give the pet in your will. You can obtain ownership of pets by sale, gift (lifetime or will), inheritance, breeding (ownership of female animals provides ownership of offspring), or capture of wild or stray animals.

Who Can Be Beneficiaries of a Pet Trust?

There are two classes of beneficiaries of a pet trust: animals and humans. The animals are the primary beneficiaries, and the humans are the secondary or default beneficiaries who take the final distribution of trust property when the trust fails or terminates.

The new Michigan law permitting pet trusts says that only "domestic or pet" animals may become beneficiaries of a pet trust. The difference between domestic animals (which includes pets as a sub-category) and wild animals is not very clear in the law. Basically, domestic animals are those entire species of animals (horses, cats, or dogs), or individual members of wild species (a trained monkey, for example), which are tame and peaceful enough to live among humans. See "Domestic Animal" and "Pet" in the glossary for more information about the legal classification of animals.

The secondary human beneficiaries of a pet trust can be anybody qualified to take a will gift (see "Who Can Take a Specific Gift?" on page 45 for a full explanation). As explained in that section, some organizations, such as charities, can also take will gifts. These organizations should also be able to qualify as secondary beneficiaries of a pet trust. For example, a real animal-lover might make a trust for a pet, and name the humane society as secondary beneficiary of the trust. Either way, you specify who the secondary beneficiaries are in the trust agreement.*

Who Can Be a Trustee of a Pet Trust?

A trustee is a fiduciary, like a personal representative, guardian or conservator. Many of the rules about legal eligibility and practical qualities for those fiduciaries also apply to trustees. See "Selecting Fiduciaries" on page 46 for complete information.

But there are some special considerations for trustees of a pet trust. A financial institution may be legally eligible to serve as trustee, but probably would decline to serve. The trust department of a financial institution couldn't supervise the care of an animal. And even if someone else provided actual care, financial institutions shy away from managing small trusts like pet trusts.

As mentioned before, it's most efficient to have the caretaker of the pet, who receives ownership of the pet from the will, also act as trustee. Thus, the trustee must combine certain guardian qualities (capacity for care, commitment, etc.) with the good financial judgment of a conservator.

Needless to say, it's important to check with the trustee about these things before you make your pet trust and will. You may be very fond of your pet, but the trustee might not share your warm feelings for the animal. This goes double for difficult-to-handle or exotic pets like large dogs or reptiles.

Who Can Be a Pet Trust Enforcer?

A unique feature of Michigan's pet trust is the right given to the settlor to designate an enforcer, who can enforce the trust by going to court if necessary. The enforcer can be any mentally competent adult, who has the capacity to file lawsuits (minors and mentally incompetent people cannot sue in court themselves).

Avoid naming the trustee as enforcer. The enforcer is supposed to keep an eye on the trustee, watching for mismanagement. Combining the roles defeats this check the law offers.

How Much Should I Give to My Pet Trust, and from Which Sources?

Your experience as a pet-owner should tell you how much to earmark for your pet trust. Estimate the annual cost of food, shelter, grooming, and veterinarian care, and then multiply this by the remaining life expectancy of the pet. Or you can fix these pet care costs by entering into a long-term

---

* If you don't name any secondary beneficiaries or your named ones don't survive to the end of the pet trust, the final distribution goes to your heirs.

pet care contract with a veterinarian or kennel, paid for by money from the pet trust.

There is a risk of not leaving enough to the pet trust, but also a danger of leaving too much. There are countless examples of people leaving vast amounts to pets. In one of the best known, Eleanor Ritchey, heir to the Quaker State Motor Oil fortune, left $4.5 million in her will to 150 stray dogs she had befriended (the will gift was thrown out because animals cannot take directly from wills). The Michigan pet trust law allows the probate court to reduce the property given to a pet trust, if the amount is excessive.

The real danger of excessive generosity is depletion of your estate, leaving insufficient property for your main estate distribution. The pour-over of money to fund the pet trust is really a specific gift to the trust, which is satisfied before distribution of your main estate. If you give too much to the pet trust, you may not leave enough for your main estate distribution to your spouse and/or children. See "Specific Gifts" on page 45 for more about the danger of draining an estate by excessive specific gifts.

If estate depletion is a problem, you can pour nonprobate property into the pet trust. All you have to do is name the trustee of your pet trust as the beneficiary of nonprobate assets like life insurance. Your insurance agent or employee benefits office can help with the correct wording of the designation. Retirement plan death benefits are another possible source of funds, but these plans often have restrictions on distribution, and may not allow payment to a pet trust.

Making a Pet Trust

The pet trust, which after all is a *living* trust, must be created during your lifetime. You do this by completing the living trust agreement, signing the document, and having the trustee sign it. Ideally, you should make the pet trust around the time you make your will, because the trust depends on the will for funding; one won't work without the other.

In sec. 1 of the trust, put your name as settlor, designate the trustee, successor trustee, trust enforcer, and name the trust as yours.

In sec. 1F(1), designate the pets which are the primary beneficiaries receiving ongoing support. Use the name by which the pet is known, and any other means of identification, such as species, breed, or pedigree information. In subsection (2), list the secondary beneficiaries (people or organizations) who take the final distribution from the trust.

Most of the rest of the trust is what lawyers call boilerplate. These are standard provisions about trust purpose, powers and property suitable for an unfunded revocable living trust. After you fill out the trust agreement, but before you and the trustee sign it, make several photocopies of the document.

At the end of the living trust agreement, sign and date the document as settlor. Witnessing and notarization are optional. At the same time, or soon after, the trustee must also sign and date the trust agreement. Sign the original trust agreement only. Give the trustee one of the unsigned photocopies, for his/her records.

The Michigan pet law excuses pet trusts from the normal filing, registration, reporting, accounting, and fees required of other trusts. Thus, there isn't anything that has to be filed or registered before or after your death.

Amendment or Revocation of a Pet Trust

As a revocable trust, you can amend or even revoke the pet trust anytime during your lifetime.

For a minor amendment, just add an attachment to the trust document spelling out the change. As an example, you may acquire new pets which you want to benefit, and can add them as beneficiaries in an amendment.

If you want to make a large revision, or cancel the pet trust, destroy the trust agreement and all copies. To revise, just make a new pet trust, with the new provisions.

Will Provisions Required for a Pet Trust

As explained before, the pet trust in this book needs a companion will with a: 1) pour-over provision funding the pet trust 2) specific gift of the pet(s) to the pet trustee.

Pet Provisions for a Statutory Will

It takes a little finesse to add the necessary pet provisions to a Michigan statutory will. The trouble is, a statutory will is a fixed form, and you cannot add anything to the will. It does allow two specific gifts of cash, one of which you can use as the pour-over provision.

In art. 2.1, make the cash gift payable to your pet trustee, in his/her capacity as trustee of the pet trust. Cite the official name of the pet trust, as it appears in the living trust agreement. (For guidance about phrasing the cash gift to the trust, see the similar sample pour-over provision from a handwritten will at the end of this chapter.) Add the amount of money pouring into the trust in figures and words. Then sign the cash gift on the signature line.

A Michigan statutory will doesn't permit specific gifts of any property except cash. But you may add a separate list to the will and give specific items of personal and household property. Pets undoubtedly fall into that category, and can be given to the trustee like other property in the separate list. See "Making a Separate List" on page 54 for complete instructions.

Pet Provisions for a Handwritten Will

A handwritten will is more flexible than a statutory will, allowing you to make specific gifts of any kind of property. Thus, it's easy to add pour-over and gift-of-pet provisions, which are both specific gifts, to a hand-written will.

See "Specific Gifts" on page 79 for information about phrasing and placing specific gifts within a handwritten will. That section advises against attaching conditions to specific gifts. But you might want to break that rule here and attach a pet survival condition to the pour-over provision. This way, if the pet doesn't survive you, the pet trust will terminate quickly for lack of funds.

Otherwise, without the survival condition, the money would pour out of your estate and into the trust. But with no surviving pet-beneficiary, the trust would go into final distribution and the secondary beneficiaries would get the money. All in all, this is much less efficient than immediate failure of the trust for lack of funds.

You can combine the pour-over provision and gift-of-pet into a single pet provision. Put this provision in the first numbered paragraph of your handwritten will, where you make other specific gifts, and before you give your residuary estate. Here is a sample combined pour-over/gift-of-pet provision, from Edith's will:

> One: I give my Welsh corgi dog named Digger to my daughter Shirley Noreen Millsaps. If my dog Digger survives me, I also give $2,500 to Shirley Noreen Millsaps, as trustee of the Edith Mae Millsaps Living Trust, dated January 1, 2000.

CUSTODIAL POWER OF ATTORNEY

I _GEORGE AND MARGO FRISBIE_ the principal

of _LAKE CITY, MI_

make this power of attorney according to sec. 5103 of the Estates and Protected Individuals Code of Michigan. I also revoke any prior power of attorney I may have made dealing with the dependent's custody as described below.

I am either the parent of the minor child(ren) or guardian of the ward(s) (who shall be referred to as the "dependent") named below:

DEWEY JOHN FRISBIE   2-11-85
Name   Date of Birth

WOODROW JAMES F   11-15-88

1. Appointment of Agent.

I appoint _CHESTER D_

of _LAKE CITY, MI_

as my agent.

If that person fails, for any

sor agent _RUTH JEA_

of _LAKE CIT_

2. Duration. This po
shall remain in effect for
This power of attorney s

3. Powers of Age
all my powers regard
named above, includi

   (a) provide for the
     ing any diagnos
   (b) provide for t
   (c) manage the
   (d) other:

---

4. Restrictions on Agent's Powers. The agent shall not have the power to do anything prohibited by law, or as stated below:

5. Reliance by Third Parties. Third parties can rely on this power of attorney without liability to me or my estate, unless they have actual notice that the power of attorney has been amended or terminated.

6. Miscellaneous. This power of attorney shall be governed by Michigan law, although it may be used out of state. The singular nouns and pronouns in the power of attorney shall refer to plural principals or dependents as the case may be. Photocopies of this document shall have the same legal authority as the original.

JAN. 1, 2000
Date

JAN. 1, 200
Date

George Edward Frisbie
Principal

Margo Ann Frisbie
Principal

Witnesses:

Chester Frisbie

Archie Savage

State of Michigan

County of _____

This instrument was acknowledged before me on _____

by _____

_____

_____
Notary Public

_____ County, Michigan

My commission expires _____

GUARDIAN APPOINTMENT

I __GEORGE EDWARD FRISBIE__

of __LAKE CITY, MI__

make the following guardian appointments as authorized by the Estates and Protected Individuals Code of Michigan. I also revoke any prior guardian appointments I have made outside a will.

I. Guardian for Children

A. Guardian for Minor Children

If any of my minor children needs a guardian after my death, I appoint __RUTH JEAN SMITH__ as guardian.

If that person fails, for any reason, to serve as guardian, I appoint as guardian __CHESTER DEAN FRISBIE__

B. Guardian for Legally Incapacitated Adult Children

I am currently serving as guardian for my legally incapacitated unmarried adult child(ren), and I appoint the following person to succeed me as guardian after my death _____

If that person fails, for any reason, to serve as guardian, I appoint as successor guardian _____

II. Guardian for Spouse

I am currently serving as guardian for my legally incapacitated spouse, and I appoint the following person to succeed me as guardian after my death _____

If that person fails, for any reason, to serve as guardian, I appoint as successor guardian _____

__JAN. 1, 2000__
Date

Witnesses:

Margo Ann Frisbie

Ruth Jean Smith

George Edward Frisbie
Parent or Spouse

(2) *Individual beneficiaries.* The following people or organizations shall be the individual beneficiaries of this trust. (List additional individual beneficiaries in an attachment)

SHIRLEY NOREEN MILLSAPS
_____
Name

GROVER EDWARD MILLSAPS
_____

2. Distr
trustee shal

A. *Regu*
reasonabl
beneficiar

In mak
the care
providin

B. *Fin*
propert
individ
individ

(1)
anima
menc

(2)
trust
sour
distr

3.
dur
giv

th
na

g

LIVING TRUST AGREEMENT

1. Creation of Trust. This is a trust agreement creating a living trust for the primary benefit of designated pet and domestic animals, as authorized by sec. 2722 of the Estates and Protected Individuals Code of Michigan (EPIC),

between ___EDITH MAE MILLSAPS_____

of_____LAKE CITY, MI_____ settlor, and

___SHIRLEY NOREEN MILLSAPS_____

of_____LAKE CITY, MI_____ trustee

A. *Name of trust.* This living trust shall be named and be known as the

___EDITH MAE MILLSAPS_____Living Trust.

B. *Trustee succession.* If the trustee named above cannot serve, that person

shall be replaced by ___GROVER EDWARD MILLSAPS_____

of_____LAKE CITY, MI_____

C. *Trust enforcement.* If necessary, this trust shall be enforced by

___GROVER EDWARD MILLSAPS_____

of_____LAKE CITY, MI_____

as provided by sec. 2722(3)(d) of EPIC.

D. *Trust property.* The principal source of trust property shall be transfers from the settlor's will, receivable after the settlor's death. The trust may also receive nontestamentary transfers from the settlor after his/her death. This property, and any income from these assets, shall constitute the trust property.

E. *Trust purpose.* The primary purpose of this trust is to provide funds for the care of the animal beneficiaries after the death of the settlor. Before then, the trust shall exist without trust property, and do nothing.

F. *Beneficiaries of trust.* There shall be two classes of beneficiaries of this trust: 1) animals 2) individuals (people and organizations), who shall receive distributions from the trust as specified in section 2.

(1) *Animal beneficiaries.* The following pet or domestic animals shall be the animal beneficiaries of this trust. (List additional animal beneficiaries in an attachment)

DIGGER   WELSH CORGI DOG
_____   _____
Name   Species and/or breed

_____   _____

_____   _____

_____   _____

---

erned by Michigan
ns and pronouns in
Photocopies of this
l.

Millsaps

Millsaps

Michigan

Chapter 4 Gifts

Not everyone makes a will, trust, or power of attorney, but all of us have made gifts sometime. According to Giving USA, the authority on generosity, Americans made more than $134 billion in charitable gifts in 1998. And this figure omits private gifts among relatives and friends.

Gifts are so ordinary it's easy to take them for granted. But the fact is, gifts are one of the most powerful estate planning devices around, particularly when made in a well-conceived gift plan.

The concept of a gift is seemingly simple: You transfer property to someone else without getting anything back. Yet gifts have a way of getting mixed up with other transfers like sales, leases, loans and storage arrangements. For example, if you sold a house worth $100,000 for $50,000, is it a sale, a gift or maybe a combination of the two? To avoid confusion, the law has a strict definition of gifts, which says that a gift transfer must be:

- motivated by an intent to give
- delivered from the giver (donor) to the recipient (donee)
- accepted by the donee

The intent-to-give element means that the donor must give the gift gratuitously, or without expecting anything in return. If return value is expected, the donor didn't really have an intent to give and the transfer fails as a gift.

Naturally, it's difficult to know a donor's state of mind. That's why the law often looks at the circumstances surrounding a gift to determine whether an intent to give existed. The relationship of the donor and the donee is especially important. If they're related, an intent to give is often presumed from gratuitous transfers between them. On the other hand, similar transfers between unrelated persons, made at arm's length, don't have this presumption and might not qualify as gifts.

The second and third elements, delivery and acceptance, are really opposite sides of the same coin. They require removal of the gift from the donor's control and placement under control of the donee. If either delivery or acceptance is missing, the gift is incomplete and fails as a gift.

Estate Planning with Gifts

There are basically two ways to pass property gratuitously: will gift and (lifetime) gift.* Both permit the transfer of any type of probate property, in unlimited amounts, to selected takers. But there are important differences in the two techniques.

The main distinction between will gifts and gifts is the time of their effectiveness. A will gift doesn't take effect until the willmaker dies; a gift is effective immediately. This difference has enormous practical and tax consequences.

Since a gift is effective immediately, the donee usually gets control of the gift right away. Donees like this because they may use the gift for immediate needs, such as support, education, purchase of a house, etc. With a will gift, the recipient must wait until the willmaker dies to receive the gift, which may be many years.

Donors may also like the immediate impact of gifts. In fact, helping donees with support or other daily needs is often why donors give gifts in the first place. Donors may also appreciate the security of gifts. Unlike a will gift, there's no chance of frustration with a gift; it's completed when made. Donors also get to see the effects of their generosity on donees—whether good or bad—and can adjust any future giving accordingly. A will gift, by contrast, is all-or-nothing; you make it and hope for the best.

The immediate impact of gifts has a negative side. With a gift, the donor must surrender complete control of the item. The donor might develop a bad case of "donor's remorse" if s/he wants to take the gift back. Even worse, donors can risk impoverishment with their generosity. The lesson? Only give what you can afford to give. If you can't afford to part with the gift, save it for a will gift or joint ownership.

Gifts can also have bad effects on donees. Immature or irresponsible donees may squander gifts. For them, postponing the gift, as a will gift does, makes good sense.

The elderly or incapacitated sometimes use gifts for financial management. If their property becomes a burden, they give it to donees, who can manage the property better. This may work, but the donors lose all control over the property. There are better financial management devices, joint

---

* See "Gift" in the glossary for more about the double meaning of gift as both a will and lifetime transfer.

ownership of property, protective arrangements, and, above all, durable powers of attorney, guaranteeing more control for the propertyowner.

Other donors protect property by making gifts to put property out of the reach of creditors. This is permissible unless the donor is already insolvent or about to file for bankruptcy. Gifts by already insolvent donors or transfers making the donor insolvent may be canceled as fraudulent conveyances. Similarly, transfers made just before bankruptcy can be set aside as voidable preferences.

Another advantage of gifts is that they usually stay private. Except for transfers of property covered by a public recording system, such as real property or motor vehicles, there is no public disclosure of gifts. The private nature of gifts is important, particularly when a gift could create family disharmony or jealousy. A will gift, by contrast, inevitably comes to light when the will is probated following the death of the willmaker.

Needless to say, a gift reduces your probate estate by the amount of the gift. This reduces the size of the probate, saving probate fees and expenses. What's more, the reduced probate estate may be eligible for a small estate probate, with even larger savings.

Above all, gifts possess important tax advantages. They can reduce federal estate taxes and, in some cases, even save income taxes. At the same time, gifts can produce their own taxes—gift taxes—unless you know the ways to avoid them.

Taxation of Gifts

Gift and Estate Taxation

The federal estate tax (FET) was adopted in 1916. At that time there wasn't any gift tax. Thus, it was possible to give away all your property before death tax-free, and also completely avoid estate taxation. This loophole was partially closed in 1932 with passage of the federal gift tax. However, gift tax rates were lower than those for estate taxes, so it still paid to give away property before death. Finally, in 1977 gift and estate taxes were unified, ending the tax advantage gifts enjoyed.

Nevertheless, you still can use gifts to avoid estate taxes. The gift tax has a generous system of exemptions* protecting many gifts from taxation. By fitting your gifts within these exemptions you can both reduce your estate and avoid gift taxation. In fact, this is the aim of estate planning with gifts.

Annual Exclusion

From the beginning, the federal gift tax sought to exclude small gifts, such as birthday, graduation and wedding gifts, from gift taxation. For years,

---

* Technically, these exemptions are exclusions, deductions and credits. But they have the effect of exemptions because they exempt qualifying gifts from gift taxation.

the tax code allowed a $3,000 annual exclusion to exempt small gifts. In 1982, the annual exclusion was raised to $10,000 (this amount will be increased periodically in the future, to adjust for inflation). With this increase, the annual exclusion became even more important in estate planning. When properly used, the exclusion can exempt substantial amounts of wealth from gift taxation. The annual exclusion allows donors to give gifts of property worth up to $10,000 to any number of donees during a calendar year. Because this exclusion is available annually, it can be used repeatedly in future years.

> *Example*: Thanks to the annual exclusion, Edith could give $10,000 to each of her four children in 1992 and then repeat these gifts in 1993, 1994, 1995, etc., without any gift taxation.

An enormous amount of property can be given this way without gift taxation. Edith, if she were to make the gifts above from 1992 to 1995, could transfer $160,000 tax-free by using the annual exclusion. Even more can be given tax-free when spouses combine their annual exclusions by making joint gifts. This method is explained in "Gift-Splitting" below.

Annual exclusions are available for gifts to anyone, not just children or other relatives. They also can be used for gifts to organizations that aren't charities and don't qualify for the charitable deduction (see below). Annual exclusions can also be applied against larger gifts to reduce the amount of the gifts subject to gift taxation, as in the example below.

> *Example*: Edith gave $15,000 to a grandchild in 1995. She could use the annual exclusion to reduce the taxable portion of this gift to $5,000 (the taxable portion might also be exempted under one of the other exemptions described below).

The annual exclusion is actually the lesser of the amount of annual gifts to a donee or $10,000 per donee. Thus, you cannot save a portion of the annual exclusion and carry it over into the next year for the same donee, or apply it against gifts to other donees in the year.

> *Example*: Edith gave $3,000 to Grover and $15,000 to Shirley in 1997. Edith also gave $17,000 to Grover in 1996. Edith can't save the unused portion of the 1996 exclusion for Grover ($7,000) and carry it over into 1997 to exclude $7,000 of the $17,000 gift to Grover this year. Nor can she apply the unused portion of the exclusion toward the larger gift to Shirley because Edith's 1996 exclusion for Grover is actually only $3,000 (the amount of the gift or $10,000, whichever is smaller).

All this shows the wisdom of making smaller gifts over several years, instead of making big gifts in one or two years. By spreading gifts out, you take maximum advantage of the annual exclusion in each year to exempt all or parts of the gifts.

Marital Deduction

Federal tax law often treats married couples as a taxable unit, allowing them to transfer property freely among themselves. The marital gift tax deduction is an example of this philosophy. The deduction exempts all qualifying gifts between spouses regardless of amount. To qualify for the exemption, the spouses must be legally married when the gift is made. The donor-spouse must be a U.S. citizen or resident and the donee-spouse must be a U.S. citizen.* Finally, the gift must be complete, giving the donee-spouse complete control of the gift.

> *Example*: George wins $1 million in a lottery, and gives $500,000 of the prize to Margo. George doesn't owe any gift tax on this gift because he can give an unlimited amount of money to his spouse without gift taxation, courtesy of the marital deduction.

Charitable Deduction

Like the income tax law, the gift tax law has a charitable deduction to encourage charitable giving. Qualified gifts in any amounts above the annual exclusion are exempt from gift taxation under the charitable gift tax deduction. What's more, almost any type of gift—money, other personal property or real property—is eligible for the gift tax charitable deduction.

> *Example*: Edith gives a gift worth $20,000 (of any type of property) to her church in 1995. The first $10,000 of this gift is exempt under Edith's annual exclusion and the rest is exempt under the charitable deduction.

To claim the charitable gift tax deduction, the donor must be a U.S. citizen or resident. The donee must be one of the following types of organizations:

- federal, state or local government body for use for exclusively public purposes
- any corporation, trust, community chest, fund or foundation organized and operated for religious, charitable, scientific, literary or educational purposes
- fraternal society, order or association operating under the lodge system if the gift is used for the purposes mentioned immediately above
- any U.S. war veterans organization or auxiliary if no one benefits privately from the organization

---

* If the donee-spouse isn't a U.S. citizen, a substitute for the marital deduction is available which is currently $101,000 (and which will be adjusted for inflation in the future).

Political Contributions

Contributions to qualified political organizations (political parties, lobbies, etc.) aren't subject to gift tax. In fact, these contributions aren't even regarded as gifts under the tax law.

Medical and Tuition Payments

The law also rewards other forms of generosity by providing gift tax exclusions for several qualified transfers made to others for the benefit of donees. To qualify for the exclusion, a gift must be made for either of the following purposes:

- payment of the donee's medical care
- payment of the donee's educational or vocational tuition, if the:
  - gift pays for tuition only, not dormitory fees, books, supplies, etc.
  - the school providing the education or training is an organization with a regular faculty, student body and curriculum
  - donee is a part- or full-time student

In each case, the gift must be paid directly to the medical or educational provider for the donee's benefit; the donee cannot receive the gift personally. The donor and donee don't have to be related in order to use this exclusion.

Example: George's nephew owes $15,000 to a hospital for medical bills. George pays these bills for him at the hospital. No gift tax is due on this gift because it was made directly to a medical provider for the benefit of the donee.

General Exemption

A general exemption is available to everyone as a means of reducing or eliminating gift taxes. As mentioned in Chapter 1B, the general exemption, which also exempts estates from estate taxes, is currently worth $675,000 (and is scheduled to rise to $1 million by 2006). The general exemption is applied to taxable gifts only. Thus, the various exclusions and deductions cited before are subtracted from a gift first, the gift tax is figured on the taxable remainder, and then the general exemption is applied to cover the gift tax.

Example: Edith gives $20,000 to Grover. She hasn't made any taxable gifts in prior years. The annual exclusion for Grover covers $10,000 of the gift, leaving $10,000 as a taxable gift. The gift tax on the gift is $1,800. This amount is applied from Edith's general exemption to eliminate the gift tax.

Gift-Splitting

Most married people know that income tax can be reduced by filing a joint income tax return. Filing jointly saves income tax because the couple's income is divided equally between the spouses, regardless of which spouse earned it, and taxed at lower rates. Tax experts call this technique income-splitting.

The tax law allows similar splitting for gifts by married people. If a married donor makes a gift, and the proper steps are taken, the gift can be split with the donor's spouse. The splitting allows each spouse to apply his/her $10,000 annual exclusion and general exemption against the gift. Moreover, any remaining taxable portion of the gift is divided equally between the spouses, which usually results in taxation of the gift in lower brackets.

> *Example*: George and Margo take $40,000 of George's money and make a split gift to Thelma. They haven't made any previous taxable gifts. If they claim the gift as a split one, each is regarded as having made a gift of $20,000. They can deduct $10,000 annual exclusions from the gift leaving only $10,000 taxable to each spouse. The gift tax on these gifts is $1,800 per spouse, which their general exemptions cover completely.

Gift-splitting is available only for persons who are legally married at the time the gift is made. Split gifts can be claimed for gifts of property owned by the spouses jointly, or of property owned by just one spouse, as in the example above.

Either way, the spouse of the donor must consent to the gift-splitting because it affects his/her future tax situation. The consent must be voluntary, you cannot force a spouse to split gifts, and shown in the donor-spouse's gift tax return. The gift tax return has a place for this consent. Furthermore, after a spouse consents to gift-splitting, all other gifts made during the year must also be split.

Payment of Gift Tax

All gifts to non-spouse donees above the annual exclusion of $10,000 must be reported in a gift tax return. Gifts above $10,000 covered by the gift-splitting of spouses must be reported to show that the other spouse consented to the split gift. Gifts to a spouse, which are exempt under the marital deduction, don't have to be reported regardless of value.

Gift tax returns are due just as income tax returns are: April 15 of the year following the year when the gift is made. However, the gift tax isn't normally paid with the return. If the gift is covered by the general exemption, payment of the gift tax is delayed until the donor's death. Then, there's a sort of final gift and estate tax reckoning. All your lifetime gifts are added to your estate transfers, the estate tax is figured on the total and the general exemption is applied to the tax.

When gift tax is owed, the donor is primarily liable for it. But if the donor fails to pay the tax, the donee must step in and pay the tax.

Taxation of Gifts in Michigan

Like most states, Michigan doesn't have a gift tax. Thus, you can give property in Michigan without worrying about a separate state gift tax. A handful of states have gift taxes, and Michigan donors who live or own property in these states may owe gift taxes there.

As described above, giving is one way to reduce FET. The same strategy works for the Michigan estate tax (MET). MET is due only when FET is also owed. So by using gifts to avoid FET you also eliminate or reduce your MET bill.

Income Taxation

Besides gift taxation, a donor must consider the impact of income taxes on the gift, because these are often misunderstood. For instance, many people incorrectly believe that gifts are income tax deductible. It's true, an income tax deduction can be claimed for some gifts to charities,* but this is exceptional. In the beginning, a gift usually has a neutral effect on income taxes; it provides no income tax deduction to the donor and creates no income for the donee. Instead, the income tax consequences of gift-giving often show up later, when the gift is in the hands of the donee.

Income Shifting with Gifts

A gift of income-producing property to a donee transfers both the property and the income it produces to the donee. When the donee is in a lower income tax bracket than the donor, income tax is saved. For example, a high-bracket father might give rental property to his low-income children, who pay income tax on the rent at a lower rate than their parent. Wealthy people have used this income-splitting dodge for years. In a refinement of the technique, they also made gifts in special trusts, called "Clifford trusts," which allowed the donor to get the property back after a while.

The Tax Reform Act (TRA) of 1986 curbed many of these income-shifting strategies. Clifford trusts have essentially been abolished by the act. Furthermore, the TRA has a provision, dubbed the kiddie tax, taxing the unearned income of $1,400 (this threshold amount will be adjusted for inflation in the future) or more of under-14 children at their parents' top rates. Except for gifts of income property producing little income (around $1,300 or less), the kiddie tax reduces the value of giving to young children for income tax splitting purposes.

For gifts to others, the TRA's consolidation of income tax rates from 15 to 5 (15%, 28%, 31%, 36% and 39.6%) means that there is less of a gap between the income tax rates of donors and donees. This flattening of the rates diminishes the savings available from income-splitting.

---

* The income tax rules for charitable deductions are much more complicated than those in the gift tax area. See IRS Tax Pub. 526, "Charitable Contributions," for the income tax rules.

Nevertheless, the 24.6-point spread in tax rates guarantees that some income-splitting can still be achieved by gifts.

Gifts and Capital Gains

There are two kinds of income which are taxed: ordinary income and capital gain. Property given in a gift can produce both kinds of income. In fact, capital gain often results in the biggest tax bill for a donee. In the example of the gift of rental property above, the rent from the property is ordinary income for the owner. If the property were sold, the profit would probably be capital gain to the owner-seller. This profit or capital gain is calculated as the amount by which sales proceeds exceed the owner's basis in the item. Subject to several adjustments, your basis in market property (property you bought) is the cost, or what you paid for it. This is called the cost basis.

Example: Edith buys vacant land for $10,000. The cost of the property, $10,000, is also her basis in the property. She sells the property for $20,000. Assuming no adjustments to the basis, her capital gain is $10,000, the sales proceeds minus the basis.

This example involved market property which cost the owner something. What is the basis of property received at no cost, such as from a gift, will, inheritance or nonprobate transfer? Special basis rules apply in these situations. For gifts, the tax law says that a donee's basis is the same as the donor's, with a few minor adjustments. This is called the carry-over basis. It's usually what the donor paid for the gift when s/he bought it.

Takers of property from a deceased person by will, inheritance or nonprobate transfer, on the other hand, get a big tax break because they're allowed a stepped-up basis for the property they receive. This stepped-up basis is usually the fair market value of the property on the day of the deceased person's death.

Since property usually increases in value, the stepped-up basis is often higher than the carry-over basis. As a result, more taxable capital gain is usually generated by a donee's sale of a gift than by the sale of property received from an owner at death. The example below demonstrates this.

Example: Edith bought some stock in 1988 for $10,000. She makes a will in 1992 with a specific gift giving the stock to Wanda. Edith dies in 1995 and Wanda gets the stock. Its market price then is $20,000, which is also the price at which Wanda sells it. Wanda has no capital gain from the sale because her basis in the stock is the stepped-up basis of $20,000 (its fair market value at Edith's death).

Had Edith made a lifetime gift of the stock to Wanda before her death in 1995, Wanda would have gotten a carry-over basis (the $10,000 cost to Edith), which would have resulted in $10,000 of capital gain when she sold the stock in 1995.

From these examples, it's plain that the interests of a donor and donee may clash over capital gains. Donors like to give gifts of property escalating in value, to reduce their estates for tax or probate reasons. But this same property often has a low carry-over basis yielding high capital gain when sold by the donee. For their part, donees may prefer to get the property by will, inheritance or nonprobate transfer, rather than by gift. That way, the recipient gets a stepped-up basis and faces less capital gain at sale.

These conflicting interests must be reconciled by a donor. In many cases, as in the example above, the capital gains might not be large enough to discourage the gift. But in other cases, the capital gains problem can be enormous. This is often true for property that has been in the family for years.

> *Example*: George has a farm that has been handed down in his family for generations. The carry-over basis for this property is very low, but its fair market value is high. George decides that it would be better to transfer this farm by will rather than gift. With this arrangement, the basis of the farm will be stepped up to fair market value at his death, producing smaller capital gain if the farm is ever sold later.

Gifts of personal residences used to create similar capital gains for donees. But the Taxpayer Relief Act of 1997 has eliminated those worries for all but the rich. For gain on the sale of a principal residence, the 1997 act provides two capital gain exemptions: 1) $250,000 exemption for single persons 2) $500,000 exemption for married couples filing jointly. These exemptions can be claimed once every two years.

Making Gifts

Types of Gifts

There are three ways to make gifts: 1) outright 2) under the Uniform Transfers to Minors Act (UTMA) 3) in trust. An outright gift takes effect immediately and gives the donee complete control of the item. Thus, it has all the practical and tax advantages of a gift.

An UTMA gift is a special trust-like gift to donees who are minors (under age 18). It's a little more complicated than an outright gift, but it too is a complete gift with all the characteristics of a gift.

A gift in trust is a much more complicated affair because a trust, with a trustee, must be created to hold the gift. Depending on how the trust is organized, the gift to the trust may or may not be a complete gift. Because of the complexities of gifts in trust, this book doesn't deal with them. If you want to make one, see a lawyer or get one of the many self-help trust books on the market.

What Can Be Given?

Only property can be given as a gift. Tax law rules out gifts of services, presumably because of the difficulty of putting a value on services.

Any type of real or personal property can be given in outright gifts. Gifts of personal property may include so-called intangible personal property, such as term life insurance, patents, copyrights, trademarks and royalties. Interestingly, tax law allows you to give intangible assets like as life insurance or royalties, even though they represent the right to potential future income or benefits and have no current value. The cancellation or discounting of debts for the benefit of debtors can qualify as gifts since the donor-creditor is giving the money owed back to the debtor. Interest-free or below-market loans may be gifts because these are gifts of the use of money.

Who Can Be a Donor?

You may only give property you own. If you want to give joint property, you can give your fractional interest in the property. Or you can convince the other co-owners to join in the gift and give the joint property away completely.

Minors can't give property personally because the law assumes that they cannot form the intent to give. The same rule applies to mentally incapacitated adults. But with them, fiduciaries can sometimes "substitute their judgment" for the defective judgment of incapacitated people, and make gifts on their behalf. Court-appointed conservators can make gifts of up to 20% of the annual income of an incapacitated person's estate. Agents for incapacitated persons, acting under durable powers of attorney, can make even larger gifts, if they're justifiable.

Who Can Be a Donee?

Any living person may be the donee of a gift. Any organization with a formal legal identity can also be a donee. This might include charities, religious and service organizations, schools, foundations, governments, business and nonprofit organizations, fraternal associations and political parties. Like will gifts, animals cannot receive gifts directly.

You can have multiple donees of a gift when you create joint property. What's more, you can be one of the joint donees. See Chapter 5 for more about the creation of several types of joint property.

You can make small outright gifts to minor donees without much fuss. Minors can easily manage small gifts, especially of cash or near-cash. In fact, financial institutions have special bank accounts and U.S. savings bond options for minors. Giving larger gifts to minors is more difficult. Michigan law says that when a minor possesses any real property or personal property worth more than $5,000 annually, the minor must usually have a conservator to manage the property. Thus, a donor considering a large gift to a minor must make it to the minor-donee's conservator or withhold the gift until appointment of a conservator for the minor.

The appointment of a conservator for a minor requires a court hearing, which is expensive and time-consuming. Luckily, there are alternatives. You can make a large gift to a minor in trust, although this book doesn't have information on this method of giving. Better yet, you can make an UTMA gift to the minor, of virtually any kind of property, in any amount. There is complete information and instructions for UTMA gifts at the end of this chapter.

Many of these rules also apply to gifts to mentally incapacitated adults. Small gifts can be made directly to them; large gifts must go to a fiduciary for their benefit.

Making Outright Gifts

There are several methods of giving real property and items of personal property. In each case, the gift must satisfy the three elements of a gift: intent to give, delivery and acceptance. The intent element is fulfilled by providing a deed, document of title, or receipt covering the gift. The gift must also be transferred—for real or in symbolic terms—to the donee. Transfer satisfies the delivery and acceptance elements.

Real Property

To give real property, you need a deed. There are two basic types of deeds: 1) warranty deed, which contains a promise that the owner has full legal title to the property 2) quit claim deed conveying whatever interest the owner has in the property. For gifts of real property, a quit claim deed is normally used, since the transfer is gratuitous.

Quit claim deeds are easy to prepare. Lawyers and realtors charge modest fees, usually around $25-50, for deed preparation. You can also make one yourself. There are quit claim deeds in the forms section of this book. At the end of this chapter, there's a sample deed for a gift of real property to one donee. If you want to make a gift of real property to two or more persons in joint ownership, see Chapter 5 for more information, instructions and a sample form.

In a quit claim deed, it's customary to say that the deed is given for one dollar, although the donor-grantor never actually gives the token dollar to the donee-grantee. As with all deeds, only the grantor (donor) signs the deed; the grantee (donee) doesn't sign. The donor must sign before two witnesses and a notary public, who must then sign their names in the spaces above their typed or printed names. The donor should also say at the bottom that s/he drafted the deed. Doing all these things puts the deed in recordable form, so the register of deeds will accept the deed for recording.

The deed must be delivered to the donee. Delivery is the symbolic way of transferring real property, which cannot be moved physically. When the donee accepts the deed, all the elements of a gift are present and the gift is complete.

After acceptance, the donee should record the deed in the office of the register of deeds for the county where the property is located. There is a recording fee due of around $9, but no transfer tax because gifts are exempt from the transfer tax. Later, the deed will be returned to the donee in the mail at the address indicated at the bottom of the deed.

Undelivered Deeds

In the past, people sometimes used undelivered deeds of real property as a substitute for a will. In this technique, a donor deeded property to a donee and kept the deed (or had a third party hold it) until the donor died. Then the deed was delivered to the donee.

Withholding delivery of deeds may seem like a neat way of getting the best part of a will (transfer of property effective at death), while avoiding the main disadvantage of a gift (loss of control of the property). The reality is that undelivered deeds are risky. Since they lack the delivery and acceptance elements of true gifts, undelivered deeds are often regarded as incomplete gifts by courts. The IRS shares this view and denies them the tax benefits of true gifts. As a result, you should never attempt to use undelivered deeds as a will substitute.

Personal Property

You can give personal property by transferring: 1) any document of title, and 2) possession of the property to the donee. For untitled property, simple transfer of possession is enough, although it's wise to use some sort of written receipt to showing that the transfer was a gift.

Bank Accounts

Gifts of bank accounts pose special problems because these don't always qualify as complete gifts. Ordinarily, when you put money in a bank account in a donee's name (in the donee's name only, jointly with the donor or jointly with other donees), no complete gift takes place until the donee withdraws money from the account. Then there is a complete gift only to the extent of the withdrawal. Otherwise, the money left in the bank account is an incomplete gift which remains the property of the donor.

Because of that problem, you may want to avoid bank account gifts entirely. Instead, withdraw the money from the bank account and give it to the donee, who can then open his/her own bank account. On the other hand, the creation of some joint accounts by gift can be an effective property management tool. See the next chapter for details.

Stocks

The form of stock ownership determines the method of giving corporate stock. The most popular form of ownership, particularly among investors with small amounts of stock, is ownership in the stockowner's name. With that form of ownership, the stock is registered in the owner's name and s/he has possession of the stock certificate. The owner can give the stock by either of two methods.

- The owner-donor can have the stock reissued in the donee's name, followed by delivery of the new stock certificate to the donee. The gift is complete on the day the stock is reissued, and the value of the stock on this day is the value for gift tax purposes.

- The donor can endorse the stock certificate to the donee and deliver it to the donee or his/her agent. Then it's the responsibility of the donee to apply for a new certificate in his/her name. The gift is complete when the endorsed certificate is delivered to the donee or his/her agent, and the gift tax value of the stock is the value on this day.

If you choose the first method, you can have the stock reissued through a broker or directly from the stock's transfer agent. Any registered broker can handle the reissue, although the broker may charge a fee. To avoid the fee, you can apply to the stock's transfer agent, which should be named on the back of the stock certificate. Corporations often designate banks or trust companies as their transfer agents. But some corporations, especially smaller ones, handle stock transfers themselves. Either way, follow the transfer instructions on the back of the stock certificate. Typically, you must endorse the old certificate to the donee and send it to the transfer agent. Sometimes your signature must be guaranteed by a bank.

Investors trading large blocs of stock often set up custodial accounts at a bank (known as a nominee account) or with stockbrokers (called a street account). This creates an agency between the stockowner-principal and the bank- or broker-agent. The stock is owned by the principal, but it's registered in the name of the bank or broker, which controls the stock certificate. This arrangement permits quick trading of the stock by the bank or stockbroker, on the owner's behalf, as market conditions dictate.

For gifts of stock in nominee or street accounts, the donor should give written directions to the bank or brokerage firm to have the stock reissued in the donee's name. The new stock certificate should then be delivered to the donee. The gift is complete and valued on the day the stock is reissued in the name of the donee.

Bonds

Bonds are debt instruments issued by corporations or the government which pay interest, principal or both until maturity. One popular type of bond is the savings bond issued by the U.S. government in two forms: series EE and series HH.* Series EE bonds are purchased at a discount and are redeemable at face value when they mature. Series HH bonds are bought at face value and pay interest until maturity.

You can give a bond outright to a donee by having the bond reissued in

---

* Series EE and HH bonds have replaced the previous series E and H bonds, although the older bonds are still in circulation. The terms of each set of bonds are similar.

the donee's name and delivering it to him/her.* As with stock, contact the bond's transfer agent for a reissue. Banks serve as the transfer agents for U.S. savings bonds; corporate bonds may have their own transfer agents. The gift of a bond is complete when the bond is reissued in the name of the donee. The value on the day of reissue is the value for gift tax purposes.

You can also give a bond in an indirect, trust-like way if the bond has a pay-on-death (POD) option. By making a POD endorsement on the bond, the donor-bondowner retains the bond during his/her lifetime. But at death, the bond goes to the donee-endorsee without passing through the donor's probate estate. This arrangement is akin to a simple living trust for the bond.

Keep in mind that a POD endorsement of a bond is an incomplete gift because the delivery and acceptance elements are missing. As a result, interest the POD bond earns is taxed to the donor during his/her lifetime. And although a POD bond isn't part of the donor's probate estate, it's subject to estate taxation.

Life Insurance

When you designate a beneficiary of your life insurance, you only decide who receives the insurance proceeds after your death. A beneficiary designation alone doesn't affect ownership of the insurance, and isn't the same as a gift of the life insurance policy to the beneficiary. If you want to give life insurance—and there are often good reasons to do so—you must take the following steps to make the gift:

- Transfer all "incidents of ownership"** of the life insurance policy to the donee. Life insurance companies, agents or employee benefits offices (for employer-provided group term life insurance)*** can furnish the necessary transfer of ownership forms. Transfer of ownership isn't always the same as assignment of life insurance, so make sure you get the correct transfer of ownership forms.

- When you transfer ownership, designate the donee as beneficiary of the policy on the beneficiary designation form (unless the donee is the beneficiary already). This gives the donee complete control of the insurance.

- After the transfer, have the donee pay all the insurance premiums. If the donee can't afford the premium payments, you may give separate gifts of money to the donee for this purpose, but the donee must make the payments personally to the insurer.

A gift of life insurance can produce gift tax, unless the gift is covered

---

* Sometimes bonds are held in bearer form, payable to whomever possesses them. Bearer bonds are like cash, and can be given by delivery alone.

** See Chapter 6 for a list of the incidents of ownership of life insurance.

*** Some employer-provided group term life insurance policies cannot be transferred by employee-insureds.

by a gift tax exemption (annual exclusion, marital deduction, etc.). Before you can apply these exemptions, you must know the gift tax value of the life insurance. This value is different for term and whole life insurance.

- Term life insurance, which has no cash value until the insured dies, has a small gift tax value. The value is the amount of the premium for the year when the gift is made.

- Whole life insurance is valued at either the cost or replacement value:
  - If the policy still requires payment of premiums, the value is the "interpolated terminal reserve value," plus any unearned premiums on the date of the gift. The interpolated terminal reserve value is usually close to the policy's cash surrender value. But it's less if you have borrowed against the policy.
  - If the policy is paid up, the value is the replacement cost, which is the cost of buying a similar policy for the donor-insured at time of the gift. This value is different from the cash surrender value of the policy.

If you ask, most insurance companies are happy to provide the gift tax value of life insurance to you. Some companies will also provide a valuation form which you can attach to the gift tax return if the gift is taxable.

There are good tax reasons for giving life insurance. Life insurance often has a low gift tax value. This is especially true of the term variety. At the same time, the estate tax value of life insurance, the face amount (amount of proceeds payable at death), is usually high. Thus, a gift of life insurance can make a big reduction in the size of your estate, with little or no gift taxation.

Example: Edith buys a $100,000 term life insurance policy with her children as beneficiaries. If she were to give the policy to the children, the value of the gift is small, just the amount of the annual premium during the year of the gift. The gift is easily covered by Edith's annual exclusion for the children. Yet if Edith owned the policy at death, the full $100,000 of the term insurance is included in her estate for estate tax purposes.

Because the potential estate tax savings are so large, the tax law has a special rule to prevent last-minute gifts of life insurance. The law assumes that all gifts of life insurance within three years of the policy-owner's death are motivated by estate tax avoidance reasons, and automatically includes the face amount of the insurance in the policyowner's taxable estate. Thus, it's smart to give away life insurance early in life, before the onset of a final illness.

Life Insurance Trusts

Besides outright gifts of life insurance, it's also possible to make gifts of life insurance in living trusts. The net effect is the same with either type of gift: The life insurance is removed from the policyowner's estate when estate tax is figured. But a gift in trust offers better disposition and management options. This flexibility can be important when the donee is young and unable to pay the policy premiums personally. If you want to look into a life insurance trust, contact an attorney, accountant or financial planner for help.

Motor Vehicles

It's easy to give motor vehicles, such as automobiles, watercraft, aircraft and recreational vehicles, which have titles issued by the Michigan Secretary of State.

The donor can go to a secretary of state office and ask to transfer the motor vehicle to the donee. The title transfer is done by computer, and a new certificate of title is generated for the donee. Or the donor can transfer title on paper using the motor vehicle's certificate of title. The donor should endorse the old title to the donee. The donee can then go to a secretary of state office and get a new title, in his/her name.

Either way, a fee is charged for the new title, but no sales tax is due if the transfer is between certain family members (the clerk can explain the intra-family sales tax exemption).

Miscellaneous Personal Property

You can also give miscellaneous personal property which doesn't have documents of title. For cash or near-cash property, such as certificates of deposit, delivering the item to the donee is sufficient. Checks and notes can be given by endorsement and delivery of the instruments to the donee. The gift is technically incomplete until the instrument is negotiated and paid by the bank. You can give a debt to the debtor-donee by cancellation of the debt. A notation should appear on the debt instrument (promissory note, land contract, etc.) itself stating that the debt is canceled.

Other untitled personal property, such as jewelry, household and personal goods, can be given by simply delivering the item to the donee. With these gifts, the intent-to-give element is implied in the circumstances of the gift.

But to remove any doubt about intent, you may want to prepare a written gift receipt. You can purchase receipt forms at an office supply store, or make one yourself. The form of the receipt isn't really important. What matters is that the receipt says that the transfer is a gift and contains an accurate description of the gift item and names the donor and donee. Preparing a document such as this might seem like a lot of trouble, but it identifies the transfer as a gift rather than a sale, loan, lease or storage arrangement.

Give the gift receipt to the donee during delivery of the gift. Also, have the donee sign the receipt to establish delivery and completion of the gift.

167

Making UTMA Gifts

For years, it's been possible to make special trust-life gifts of money, insurance and securities to minors under Michigan's Uniform Gifts to Minors Act (UGMA). In 1998, Michigan replaced the UGMA with the broader Uniform Transfers to Minors Act (UTMA), which allows gifts of all kinds of property to minors. The UTMA also permits UTMA gifts in wills (covered separately in Chapter 2, on pages 53 and 93) and during distribution of probate and nonprobate property, which the UGMA never did.

An UTMA gift must be made in writing, using a special UTMA designation. The designation satisfies the intent-to-give element of gifts. Unlike other gifts, an UTMA gift isn't transferred from the donor to the donee-minor. Instead, a third person, the custodian, receives the gift and holds it for the donee-minor until maturity.

The absence of a delivery and acceptance would normally jeopardize an UTMA gift, as it does for some gifts in trust. But unlike some trust gifts, where the trustee holds legal title to the trust property, an UTMA donee actually owns the gift. Legal title is considered enough control to excuse strict delivery and acceptance requirements.

Thus, an UTMA gift is a complete gift with all the benefits of a gift. After an UTMA gift is made, the property is removed from the donor's probate and taxable estates. All available gift tax exemptions can be used to cover the gift. And in most cases, any income the UTMA gift produces is taxed to the donee-minor, not the donor.

As you can see, UTMA gifts benefit both donors and donees. UTMA gifts are especially useful for valuable gifts. Recall that a gift to a minor of any real property or personal property worth more than $5,000 annually requires appointment of a conservator for the minor. You can avoid the appointment by making such gifts under the UTMA, because the custodian takes the place of a conservator.

After an UTMA gift is made, the gift becomes custodial property held by the custodian for the minor's benefit. The UTMA gives custodians broad powers over property, similar to those a property-owner has over his/her own property. Among other things, the UTMA says that the custodian shall "collect, hold, manage, invest, and reinvest custodial property." Thus, a custodian can sell the custodial property and reinvest in new property, but the new property remains custodial property.

An UTMA custodian is a fiduciary, like a personal representative, guardian, conservator, or trustee, with the normal fiduciary duties. The custodian must manage the custodial property prudently, and keep it separate from his/her own property. The custodian must also maintain records about the property and make these available to the minor, his/her guardian, or conservator on demand. A custodian is entitled to reimbursement for the reasonable expenses of managing the custodial property. These expenses are paid from the custodial property.

During an UTMA custodianship, the custodian can pay custodial property to the minor personally, or to someone else on the minor's behalf, for the use and benefit of the minor. If the minor dies before adulthood, the UTMA says that the custodian shall transfer the custodial property to the minor's estate for distribution to the minor's heirs.

When the minor reaches maturity, the custodian must make a final distribution of the custodial property to the donee. Under the old UGMA, final distribution always happened at age 18. Under the new UTMA, final distribution takes place at age 18, or any other age between 18 and 21. To extend final distribution beyond age 18, you must add the different age to the UTMA designation, as shown in "UTMA Gifts" below.

Selecting a Custodian

Any mentally competent adult is legally eligible to serve as a custodian of an UTMA gift. The act also allows a "trust company" to act as custodian. This is odd because Michigan doesn't have any real trust companies, as states like New York do, which are financial institutions doing trust work exclusively. Perhaps the act means financial institutions with trust powers. If doing business in Michigan, these institutions can serve as personal representatives, conservators and trustees, and maybe UTMA custodians as well.

Whatever the UTMA intended, it's mostly an academic question because the act is really designed for nonprofessional, volunteer custodians, such as family members or friends. However, if none of these individuals is available, then institutional custodians might be necessary.

One thing is clear, there are two categories of people who shouldn't serve as custodians, both for tax reasons. Donors should never name themselves as custodians of their own gifts. A donor-custodian has too much power over the custodial property, making it includable in his/her taxable estate at death. Parents should also avoid serving as custodians for their children because parents can be taxed on income the custodial property earns.

Custodians should have some of the same practical qualities—honesty, suitability, willingness to serve, etc.—that other fiduciaries have. See "Fiduciaries: Practical Qualities" on page 47 for a review of these qualities. A custodian is basically a property manager, like a conservator. Thus, a custodian ought to have the same practical skills as a conservator. These are discussed in "Article 3.2: Guardian and Conservator" on page 59. The UTMA doesn't permit joint or split custodians.

UTMA Gifts

In many ways, an UTMA gift resembles other types of gifts. But there are several special requirements for an UTMA gift:

- the donee must be a minor (under 18) when the gift is made
- a special UTMA transfer designation must be used, like this:

  to [name of custodian] as custodian for [name of minor] under the Michigan Uniform Transfers to Minors Act

If you want to extend final distribution beyond the normal age of 18 (until a maximum of age 21), you must cite the different age in the UTMA transfer designation, as follows:

to [name of custodian] as custodian for [name of minor] until age [21] under the Michigan Uniform Transfers to Minors Act

- the gift must be transferred from the donor to the custodian

Real Property

As with outright gifts, you make UTMA gifts of real property in quit claim deeds (see page 162 for more about making this type of deed). The deed should transfer the property from the donor-grantor to the custodian-grantee. In the grantee section of the deed, normally the second paragraph, there must be an UTMA transfer designation, like this:

to [name of custodian] as custodian for [name of minor] under the Michigan Uniform Transfers to Minors Act (you can also extend the final distribution age up to 21, as in sample designation above)

After the donor signs the deed, it must be delivered to the custodian on behalf of the donee-minor. The custodian should then record the deed with the register of deeds.

Personal Property

For UTMA gifts of personal property, you must add the UTMA designation to any document of title for the property. Many title documents already contain the designation. For example, financial institutions have special deposit agreements with UTMA designations. Life insurance companies can register policies in UTMA form. Stock and bond certificates usually have directions for UTMA registration or endorsement.

For untitled property, the UTMA conveniently provides all-purpose transfer document. There is a sample form at the end of this chapter, and a blank one in the forms section. As with other UTMA transfers, you must cite the names of the donor, custodian, and minor-donee, and describe the property. The donor must date and sign the transfer, and the custodian must date and sign the receipt section.

QUIT CLAIM DEED

GEORGE EDWARD FRISBIE AND MARGO ANN FRISBIE, HUSBAND AND WIFE grantor(s),
of 900 S. WASHINGTON, LAKE CITY, MI 48800
quit claims to WESLEY FRANCIS FRISBIE
of 107 S. MAIN, LAKE CITY, MI 48800 , grantee(s),
the following real property located in the CITY of LAKE CITY
LAKE County, Michigan:

LOT 3 OF MCPHERSON'S ADDITION TO LAKE CITY, MICHIGAN

for the sum of ONE DOLLAR

This deed is exempt from transfer tax under:

Date JAN. 1, 2000

☒ MCL 207.526(a) (gift)
☐ MCL 207.526(i) (transfer of tenancy by the entirety between spouses)
☐ MCL 207.526(q) (creation of joint tenancy when grantor(s) is one of the joint tenants)

Witnesses:

ARCHIE LOUIS SAVAGE
ARCHIE LOUIS SAVAGE

GUY FRANCIS FISH
GUY FRANCIS FISH

State of Michigan

County of ___LAKE___

Grantor(s):

George Edward Frisbie
GEORGE EDWARD FRISBIE

Margo Ann Frisbie
MARGO ANN FRISBIE

This instrument was acknowledged before me on ___JAN 1, 2000___
by GEORGE EDWARD AND MARGO ANN FRISBIE

Guy Francis Fish
GUY FRANCIS FISH Notary Public
___LAKE___ County, Michigan
My commission expires 7-7-02

Prepared by:
GEORGE EDWARD FRISBIE
900 S. WASHINGTON
LAKE CITY, MI 48800

Return recorded deed to grantee, or other:
Send future tax bills to grantee, or other:

TRANSFER UNDER THE MICHIGAN UNIFORM TRANSFERS TO MINORS ACT

I, _GEORGE EDWARD FRISBIE_

(name of transferor or name and representative capacity, if a fiduciary)

transfer to _CHESTER DEAN FRISBIE_

(name of custodian)

as custodian for _WOODROW JAMES FRISBIE_

(name of minor)

[until age _21_]

under the Michigan uniform transfers to minors act, the following:

(insert a description of the custodial property sufficient to identify it).

40 U.S. PEACE SILVER DOLLARS, DATES 1921-35

JAN. 1, 2000
Dated

George Edward Frisbie
(Signature)

CHESTER DEAN FRISBIE

(name of custodian)

acknowledges receipt of the property described above as custodian for the minor named above under the Michigan uniform transfers to minor act.

JAN. 1, 2000
Dated

Chester Dean Frisbie
(Signature of Custodian)

Chapter 5
Joint Property

It may seem strange that one of the most popular forms of property ownership has roots in feudal land law of 500-600 years ago. But that's the story behind joint property. In the feudal system, the king owned most of the land. He gave the land to tenants in exchange for military service. Feudalism favored joint property because it guaranteed the maximum number of tenants on the land, who could supply a ready source of soldiers for the king.

Later, as feudalism disappeared, joint property fell into disrepute. By the 19th century, many states (but not Michigan) had abolished most types of joint property. But during the last 50 years, joint property made a remarkable comeback. It has a number of characteristics—survivorship, probate avoidance and protection from creditors—that appeal to modern lifestyles. Married people in particular began holding more of their real property jointly. Now according to recent estimates, around three-fourths of all marital real property is jointly owned.

Meanwhile, joint property principles have been extended beyond land to personal property. Today, all kinds of personal property, including financial assets, are owned jointly.

Types of Joint Property

Like most states, Michigan recognizes several types of joint property. Most types apply to both real and personal property, although a few exist in real property only.

Except for one type of joint bank account, all joint property gives co-owners equal rights to the property. But when the joint property terminates, there are marked differences in how co-owners' interests are treated. It is here where estate planning opportunities exist.

Joint Tenancy

Joint tenancy (JT) gives co-owners, called joint tenants, equal but undivided interests in property. There may be two joint tenants or many. Regardless of number, each has an equal right to possess and use the whole property.

Even more important, joint tenants have "rights of survivorship" in JT property. When a joint tenant dies in a two-person JT, his/her interest ceases, and the surviving joint tenant takes full 100% ownership of the property. Similarly, when there are several joint tenants, and one dies, the survivors continue to hold the property in JT. This arrangement lasts until only one joint tenant remains. At that point, the lone survivor takes full ownership.

Survivorship happens automatically, by law. As a result, a deceased joint tenant's interest passes to the surviving joint tenant(s), outside of probate, saving the time and expense of probate administration.

Joint tenancies can terminate in ways besides death: 1) an act of one joint tenant 2) the mutual consent of all the joint tenants 3) a court order (after a partition suit by the joint tenants or during a divorce between married joint tenants). With each method, there is a division of the JT property into shares.

Special Joint Tenancy

Michigan is among a handful of states with a special type of JT that cannot be terminated by the act of one joint tenant. This variety of JT will be referred to as a special joint tenancy (SJT). It exists in real property only. SJT is created by using the words "survivorship," "survivor," or any variation of these words, in the deed for the property.

SJT has several negative characteristics. It's inflexible because all joint tenants must agree to termination of the arrangement. At the same time, SJT doesn't offer much more protection from creditors than an ordinary JT. The tax treatment of a SJT is particularly complicated, because of the nature of the property. Technically, the tenants in a SJT hold life estates in the property with mutual rights of full ownership when one joint tenant dies. These interests are difficult to value because the mortality of the joint tenants must be estimated before the values of the life estates and other rights can be determined. All this plays havoc with gift taxes.

For these reasons, this book recommends avoiding SJT. Later, it explains how to avoid creating a SJT by accident while setting up an ordinary JT.

Tenancy by the Entirety

Michigan and about half of the states recognize a special type of JT, between spouses only, called tenancy by the entirety (TE). In most ways, a TE resembles an ordinary JT: The spouses have equal but undivided interests in the property with rights of survivorship.

With rights of survivorship, TE property is nonprobate property, like a JT. But in other ways, a TE resembles a SJT. Neither spouse alone can terminate a TE; both must consent to a termination. A TE also provides extra protection from creditors. A creditor of one spouse cannot get at the TE while it lasts. And if the TE ends with the death of the debtor-spouse, the surviving spouse takes the property free of the creditor's claims. On the other hand, TE property is vulnerable to a creditor when both spouses owe the debt.

Tenancy in Common

A tenancy in common (TC) is a form of joint property where the co-owners, called tenants in common, are like shareholders in the property. When a TC is created, each tenant in common receives a fractional interest in the property. The creator of the TC may assign equal shares, as is usually the case, or the shares may be unequal.

While a TC lasts, the shares of the tenants are submerged. Each tenant has an equal right to use and possess the whole property, as with the other types of joint property. But when the TC terminates, the tenants receive their respective shares of the property. A TC may terminate from: (1) the mutual consent of the tenants 2) a sale 3) a court order.

TC shares are also divided when a tenant in common dies. Unlike other forms of joint property, a TC doesn't have rights of survivorship. Instead, a deceased tenant's share remains his/her property and goes to the tenant's estate, where it passes by will or inheritance. The surviving tenant(s) keep their shares of the TC as their separate property.

Other Types of Joint Property

Community Property

Nine states, mostly in the South and West, have a special type of joint property known as community property (CP). Community property is akin to a TC for spouses, because it gives spouses equal shares of all property acquired during marriage. Both real and personal property can be CP.

Michigan doesn't have CP itself. But it recognizes CP created in CP states and brought here. Thus, spouses may bring personal property held in CP form to Michigan and it remains CP in the state.

Miscellaneous Joint Property

Michigan law permits several special types of joint property in financial assets which don't fit neatly into the other categories of joint ownership:

Convenience account. In Michigan, you may create convenience accounts at financial institutions. While the convenience account is open, the creator-depositor and co-owner both control the account and may withdraw from it. In fact, either co-owner can empty the entire account. But if the creator-depositor dies, the account goes back to his/her estate and passes as probate property; the surviving co-owner gets nothing.

Each type of financial institution in Michigan—bank, savings and loan association and credit union—has its own version of convenience accounts, although they are similar. Frequently, financial institutions have them for savings but not checking accounts, and permit only one co-owner per account.

Totten trust. Michigan has customarily permitted so-called *Totten* trusts in financial accounts. The creator-depositor creates a *Totten* trust by depositing money at a financial institution for himself/herself and as trustee for a co-owner. In a way, a *Totten* trust is the opposite of a convenience account. The creator-depositor keeps complete control of the account during his/her lifetime. But after the depositor's death, any money in the account goes to the co-owner, outside of probate.

Pay-on-death bond. U.S. savings bonds may also be held in a trust-like way, with survivorship rights. By choosing the pay-on-death (POD) option, savings bonds go to a designated beneficiary at the death of the bondowner, bypassing probate.

Joint safe deposit box. Safe deposit boxes may be held jointly. Boxholders don't really own safe deposit boxes; they receive a license to use them for a while. Nevertheless, the license can be held jointly, giving all the boxholders equal access to the box. This comes in handy when a boxholder dies, since the surviving boxholder(s) can get into the box without a court order.

Pay-on-death brokerage account. Stocks and other securities held in custodial accounts at banks (nominee accounts) or with stockbrokers (street accounts) (see "Stocks" on page 163 for a full description of custodial accounts) may also have a POD option. With a POD designation, the original stockowner may control the account during his/her lifetime. But at the stockowner's death, any stock in the account goes directly to the beneficiary, avoiding probate.

Estate Planning with Joint Property

Survivorship Rules

Two of the three main types of joint property—JT and TE—possess rights of survivorship (TC doesn't). As described before, rights of survivorship give surviving joint owners full ownership of the property after the other joint owners' death. Moreover, this transfer happens automatically, by law, outside probate.

No doubt survivorship largely explains the popularity of JT and TE. People use these as probate avoidance devices, which is fine. Nevertheless, you shouldn't put property into joint ownership merely to avoid probate. Joint property has some serious disadvantages, described below, that may offset the benefit of probate avoidance. Besides, Michigan probate isn't as bad as it once was, and doesn't have to be avoided at all cost.

JT and TE do come in handy as probate avoidance devices in several situations. If your probate estate is almost small enough to use one of the small estate procedures, you can convert some solely-owned property into JT or TE, making your estate eligible for the small estate procedure.

Example: George's probate estate consists of an automobile ($20,000) and cottage in northern Michigan ($20,000). If he put the cottage in JT or TE with Margo, his probate estate would be reduced to the automobile alone. A special small estate procedure for motor vehicle transfer is available to transfer the automobile at George's death, avoiding a probate for him.

It's often smart to hold out-of-state real property in JT or TE. If you own solely-owned real property out of state, the property might have to be probated there in a separate proceeding called ancillary probate. An ancillary probate is necessary even when you have a probate in your home state.

To avoid multiple probates, you can put out-of-state real property in JT or TE. Then, when one joint owner dies, it goes to the survivor without an ancillary probate.

Fall 2000

Example: All of Margo's probate property is located in Michigan, except a vacant lot in Florida. By placing the lot in JT or TE with George, she can avoid an ancillary probate in Florida.

When you want to change ownership of real property in another state, consult an attorney or realtor there. State property laws aren't uniform, so the type of joint property you want may not exist in that state. For example, all states recognize JT, but only around half the states have TE.

Besides probate avoidance, joint property can be a source of liquidity for survivors. Thanks to survivorship, the surviving joint owner of financial assets gets the property quickly after the other joint owner dies, without waiting for probate.

Joint property also has important symbolic value. For example, a TE locks the property up in ownership between spouses, giving them a sense

177

of security. Other joint property provides similar psychological benefits for the joint owners.

On the other hand, there are disadvantages of joint ownership, particularly in comparison to a will. The creation of joint property usually spells some loss of control over the property. When you convert solely-owned property into joint property, you make a gift of part of the property to the new co-owner(s). As a result, an irresponsible co-owner can run off with part or even all (in the case of joint bank accounts) of the joint property, and there's nothing the original owner can do about it.

A will, by contrast, allows you to transfer property at death, without losing any lifetime control. In a will, you earmark property for certain takers. But the actual transfer is suspended until death, giving you complete control of the item until then.

A will is also a more flexible way to transfer property. Recall that you can name alternate takers of specific gifts or a residuary estate in a will. This permits you to direct the transfer of property when the takers die unexpectedly. The survivorship rights of JT and TE don't permit such flexibility; survivorship invariably gives the property to the surviving co-owner. This can create havoc when the co-owners die in ways you didn't anticipate.

Example: Edith creates a JT in her house with Shirley because she wants the house to go to her daughter without going through probate. Neither Edith nor Shirley has a will.

Example #1. Shirley dies first. The house goes back to Edith as the surviving joint tenant, frustrating the purpose of the JT.

Example #2. Edith and Shirley die together in an airplane crash. According to Michigan's Uniform Simultaneous Death Act, the house is divided equally between Edith and Shirley because neither survived the other. These half-shares are probated through the women's estates and distributed under the inheritance law. Shirley's daughter Rhonda gets 50% from Shirley and around 13% from Edith through her mother. The rest of the house is split with Edith's other three children.

Example #3. Edith, Shirley and Shirley's new husband Jasper are in an automobile crash. Edith dies first, followed by Shirley a week later, and Jasper a week after that. In this case, the house goes to Shirley first because she is the surviving joint tenant. After her death, one-half of the house goes to Rhonda and one-half to Jasper. When he dies, his one-half share goes to his relatives by inheritance or his will. Thus, Rhonda has to share the house with Jasper's relatives, who are strangers to her.

These examples show the inflexibility of the survivorship rights of JT and TE, and how they can cause bad patterns of distribution. All would have been fine had Edith died first. This would seem likely because she is older with a shorter life expectancy. But you can never be sure of things like that.

Giving the house to Shirley by will would solve many difficulties. By naming alternate takers of the will gift, Edith could direct the house to others if Shirley failed to survive her. This would have also saved unnecessary probate of the house through Shirley's estate in examples #2 and #3.

Joint property should never be viewed as a complete substitute for wills. Many people, especially spouses, think that they can put all their property into JT or TE and forget about wills. This is risky. No matter how careful you are, you almost always leave some solely-owned property, which needs a will to distribute as you want.

Besides, wills do more than just transfer property. You can also appoint fiduciaries, create trusts, and give final directions in a will. Appointment of fiduciaries—particularly guardians and conservators for minor children—is by far the most important incidental purpose of wills. In fact, parents should have wills for this reason alone.

Property Management

Joint property is also popular as a property management device. The plan is that if one co-owner becomes mentally or physically incapacitated, the healthy co-owner can manage the property. Older people often use joint ownership this way.

Example: Edith puts her $10,000 bank account in JT with Shirley. Edith believes that if she becomes incapacitated, Shirley can withdraw from the account to pay her expenses.

This strategy works to an extent. With joint real property, the healthy co-owner can handle routine maintenance of the property. Joint ownership of bank accounts allows the healthy co-owner to manage the account for the incapacitated one. Convenience accounts are particularly good for this purpose.

On the other hand, joint ownership isn't the best way to manage property for incapacitated persons. Joint ownership doesn't give the healthy co-owner any special power to act for the incapacitated co-owner. On the contrary, the incapacitated co-owner must have a legal representative act for him/her with regard to the joint property.

Example: Edith puts her house in JT with Shirley, and then becomes incapacitated. Shirley can maintain the property as co-owner. But Edith must have a legal representative before she and Shirley can sell, mortgage, or refinance the property.

A court could appoint a conservator to manage all of Edith's property, including the house. Or a protective arrangement can be set up through the court to manage just the house. Either way, there is the expense and trouble of going to court for the appointment. Thus, joint ownership of property don't always avoid court-ordered arrangements.

As an alternative, Edith could have kept the house in her name and made a durable power of attorney appointing Shirley or someone else as agent. The agent can have the full power to manage the house (and other property), without court intervention. And because of its durability, the power of attorney lasts during Edith's incapacity.

Except for convenience accounts, durable powers of attorney are always superior to joint property as property management tools. Chapter 9 has more on planning for incapacity with durable powers of attorney.

Protection from Creditors

Neither JT nor TE provides protection from creditors when all joint owners owe the debt jointly. Creditors know this and often demand joint signatures on debts. Then, they can go after any joint property the joint debtors own.

> *Example:* George takes out a car loan at a bank. The bank insists that Margo sign the loan too. If George defaults on the loan, the bank can go after any joint property the couple own because both spouses are liable to the bank.

But sometimes just one co-owner owes a debt. In that case, the creditor can usually reach only the debtor-joint tenant's share of JT property while it lasts. The creditor may even force liquidation of the JT to satisfy the debt. Not all creditors are this aggressive. If they don't do anything directly to collect the debt, and the debtor-joint tenant dies, the surviving joint tenant normally takes the property free and clear of the creditor's claims.

TE offers even more protection from creditors. A TE is locked up tight and creditors cannot get at a debtor-spouse's share of the property during his/her lifetime. And after the debtor's death, the TE property goes to the surviving spouse free of any creditor claims.

In some cases, joint property can increase liability rather than diminish it. It's simply a matter of arithmetic; with joint property there are more owners and hence more people to sue if something goes wrong with the property.

> *Example:* George and Margo buy a second automobile, which Margo drives, and put the vehicle into JT. Margo causes a serious automobile accident and must pay legal damages to the injured person. The damages exceed the no-fault insurance coverage.* Both spouses are liable for the legal damages as joint owners of the automobile.

Legal liability is a particular concern for high-risk property like motor vehicles, aircraft, manufacturing companies or professional practices, which get sued often. For this kind of property, it's best to leave ownership in the name of the owner-operator alone. As a general rule, the person

---

* Ordinarily, Michigan no-fault automobile insurance, which is mandatory, covers liability for personal injuries. But many people have insurance with low liability limits, leaving gaps in coverage and exposing them to personal liability.

who uses the asset the most should own the property by himself/herself. This plan reduces net exposure to liability.

Example: George and Margo buy a second automobile for Margo to drive. Since she is the main operator of the vehicle, she takes title in her name alone. If Margo causes an accident with the car, she alone is liable for any uninsured legal damages. What's more, if George is ever injured while a passenger in the automobile he might be able to sue and obtain damages (some insurance policies prevent co-owners from suing each other).

Taxation of Joint Property

Gift Taxation

The creation or termination of joint property may result in taxable gifts. Luckily, the various gift tax exemptions for other lifetime gifts (see "Taxation of Gifts" on page 153 for more about these) are available to cover gift taxes from joint ownership of property.

Whenever joint property is created or terminated between spouses no gift tax is owed, thanks to unlimited marital gift tax deduction. Joint property between nonspouses is a different matter. When you create joint property with a nonspouse co-owner, and s/he doesn't pay equally for the property, you make a taxable gift to the co-owner. In most cases, the amount of the gift is the fair market value of the fractional interest received by the co-owner in the joint property, minus any contribution s/he made toward acquisition of the property.

Example: Edith contributes $900 and Shirley $100 for the purchase, as joint tenants, of stock worth $1,000. Edith is making a $400 gift to Shirley because Shirley has received a half-interest in the stock, although she paid only a fraction (10%) of the cost. Edith's annual exclusion for Shirley easily exempts this gift from gift taxation.

Example: Edith has a house with a fair market value of $60,000 for which she paid $10,000. She deeds the house to herself, Shirley and Grover, as joint tenants. Edith has made gifts of $20,000 to Shirley and Grover. Edith's $10,000 annual exclusions for the pair exempt half of these gifts from gift taxation, and the rest is covered by her general exemption (although a gift tax return must be filed).

All this can happen in reverse, so taxable gifts can result from the termination of joint property between nonspouses. When joint property is divided among the joint owners, there may be taxable gifts to the extent the owners receive more than their fractional interests in the property. But once again, the various gift tax exemptions can wipe out any potential gift tax.

Incomplete Gifts

As explained in Chapter 4, a gift remaining under the control of the donor is regarded as an incomplete gift. An incomplete gift won't have the tax or other benefits of a complete gift.

The creation of joint property by gift sometimes causes incomplete gifts. This happens most often with certain types of joint property, such as bank accounts and U.S. savings bonds, because the donor retains a lot of control. Gifts of some of these assets, such as *Totten* trust bank accounts, remain incomplete gifts forever. Gifts of other types of bank accounts or savings bonds remain incomplete until the new co-owner takes full control of the property; then the gift is complete.

Estate Taxation

Most joint property (JT, SJT, TE, *Totten* trusts, POD bonds and POD brokerage accounts) is nonprobate property, passing outside of probate. But that doesn't necessarily mean that the property escapes estate taxation. On the contrary, joint property is part of a deceased's taxable estate and subject to estate taxation.

Except for joint property between spouses, the estate taxation of joint property is based on the contributions the joint owners made toward acquisition of the property. This is similar to the gift tax treatment of joint property, with an important difference. For estate tax purposes, the percentage of a joint owner's contribution, not the actual dollar amount, determines the amount of the joint property included in his/her estate. This method accounts for any appreciation in the value of the joint property between creation and termination at death.

> *Example:* Edith and Shirley create a JT in stock worth $1,000. Edith contributes $900 (90%) and Shirley $100 (10%) for the purchase of the stock. Edith dies when the stock is worth $2,000. Based on the percentage of her contribution, Edith's taxable estate must include $1,800 (90%) of the value of the stock.

There is another twist in the estate taxation of joint property. The law assumes that the first joint owner to die made 100% of the contribution toward acquisition of the property. The burden is then on the deceased joint owner's personal representative to prove that the surviving co-owner(s) made a contribution if, in fact, s/he did. If the personal representative doesn't have proof of contribution, 100% of the value of the joint property is included in the estate of the deceased joint owner. Making matters worse, the property will also be fully exposed to estate taxation when the surviving joint owner dies as sole owner of the property.

> *Example:* Edith and Shirley make equal contributions toward a JT in a lot worth $10,000. Edith dies when the property is still worth $10,000. Edith and Shirley were careless with their financial records, so Edith's personal representative cannot prove that Shirley paid half the pur-

chase price. Thus, the full $10,000 value of the lot is included in Edith's taxable estate. If Shirley dies as sole owner of the property, the full $10,000 value of the lot is counted again in Shirley's estate.

All this shows the importance of good record-keeping. With accurate records, you can prove the contributions of the joint owners and avoid double taxation of the joint property. This is one reason why you should always use written documents, showing contribution, when creating joint ownership of property.

Before 1982, estate taxation of joint property between spouses followed the contribution rules outlined above. However, proof of contribution by spouses was notoriously difficult to establish because spouses often use each other's money to buy things. Consequently, in 1982 the contribution rules for spouses were discarded. For all joint property created between spouses after January 1, 1977, 50% of the value of the joint property is included in the estate of the first spouse to die regardless of his/her contribution toward acquisition of property. Pre-1977 joint property between spouses still uses the contribution rules described above.

Income Taxation

If joint property produces income, it's subject to income taxation. Income is taxed to joint owners in two ways: equally or by percentage of their contributions toward acquisition of the property. For most joint property, income is divided equally among the joint owners, and each reports and pays income tax on their share of the income.

Example: George buys rental property and puts it in JT with Woodrow. Rental income from the property is equally divided between George and Woodrow.

The percentage-of-contribution method is used for a few types of joint property: bank accounts, U.S. savings bonds and stock in street accounts. According to this method, income is taxed to the joint owners in proportion to their contribution toward acquisition of the property.

Example: Edith has a bank account with a $10,000 balance. She places it in JT with Shirley. All interest income earned by the account is taxed to Edith because she made a 100% contribution toward creation of the account.

When income is divided among co-owners, there can be beneficial income-splitting. If the new joint owner is in a lower income tax bracket than the original sole owner, the total tax may be lower than had the original owner held the property alone and been taxed on all the income in his/her higher tax bracket.

The income-splitting effects of joint property have been diminished by the Tax Reform Act (TRA) of 1986. The act reduced the number of income tax brackets from a previous 15 to 5, bunching brackets together and leaving less chance for income-splitting. Joint property with children, who are usually in the lowest tax bracket, was once a favorite income-splitting technique. The TRA's so-called kiddie tax curbed this opportunity by taxing most income of under-age-14 children at their parents' top rates. And even before the TRA, spouses got few income-splitting benefits from joint property because were already splitting income by filing joint returns.

Joint Property and Capital Gains

Like gifts, many of the negative income tax effects of joint property don't appear until the property is sold. If the sale produces a profit, the profit is taxable capital gain. "Gifts and Capital Gains" on page 159 explains how capital gain is figured on the basis of property, and describes the different bases for property: cost, carry-over and stepped-up. Joint property can involve all three bases in circumstances that can generate capital gain.

Example: Edith and Shirley have a JT in stock worth $1,000. Edith contributed $900 (90%) and Shirley $100 (10%) toward purchase of the stock. They sell the stock later for $2,000. Each has received a profit of $1,000 (one-half the $2,000 sale price).

Edith's basis is $900 (her cost). She has a capital gain of $100 only. Shirley's basis is $550 ($100 cost basis and $450 carry-over basis from the partial gift of the stock to her). She has a capital gain of $450.

Joint property often begins as a gift, as in the example above. If so, the non- or under-contributing joint owner may have a low carry-over basis in the property. This can produce a big capital gain at sale if the property has appreciated in value.

The same thing can happen when joint property terminates by death and the surviving joint owner sells the property later at a profit. The tax law says that the share of the deceased joint owner included in his/her estate (under the contribution rules described in "Estate Taxation" on page 182) gets a stepped up basis, to fair market value. The remainder of the property not included in the deceased joint owner's estate keeps the surviving joint owner's basis (cost basis or carry-over basis, if a gift).

Example: In a gift, George puts his cottage, which he bought for $10,000, in TE with Margo. George dies when the cottage is worth $50,000. His estate reports $25,000 (50% presumed contribution for spouses) for the cottage. As survivor, Margo gets the cottage and then sells it for $50,000. Her basis in the cottage is $30,000 ($25,000 stepped up basis from George's share and $5,000 carry-over basis from the partial gift of the cottage to her). She has a capital gain of $20,000.

Joint ownership of personal residences used to create similar tax surprises. But these days, the tax law offers generous tax breaks on capital gain from the sale of a personal residence: 1) $250,000 exemption for single taxpayers 2) $500,000 exemption for married taxpayers filing jointly.

Creating Joint Property

Some joint property is created unwittingly. For example, when several people receive property together by will or inheritance, they get it in TC form. But most joint property requires positive steps for creation. Typically, joint property is made when: 1) two or more people acquire property, by sale or gift, together 2) an owner transfers property by gift to himself/herself and others in joint ownership.

Which Property Can be Owned Jointly?

Most types of joint ownership exist in all kinds of real and personal property. But there are several exceptions. The chart below summarizes:

Ownership of Joint Property in Michigan

	Real property	Bank accounts	Stocks	U.S. bonds	Motor vehicles	Misc. property
Joint tenancy (JT)	Yes	Yes	Yes	Yes*	Yes	Yes
Special joint tenancy (SJT)	Yes	No	No	No	No	No
Tenancy by the entirety (TE)	Yes	S&L only**	Yes	No	Yes	Yes
Tenancy in common (TC)	Yes	S&L only**	Yes	No	Yes	Yes
Convenience account	No	Yes	No	No	No	No
***Totten* trust**	No	Yes	No	No	No	No
Pay-on-death	No	No	Yes***	Yes****	No	No

*Called co-ownership

**Account at savings and loan association

***Available if stocks held in a custodial form (in a nominee or street account)

****Called beneficiary form

185

Who Can Own Joint Property?

Only persons may own joint property with survivorship rights. Organizations cannot own such property because they're immortal, and would always survive and take the property after the death of the mortal joint owners. This problem doesn't exist for TC property, which doesn't have rights of survivorship; it may be owned by people and organizations together.

With TE property, the joint owners must be legally married. Otherwise, joint owners don't have to be related, although they often are. There is no residency requirement for joint ownership; nonresidents may own Michigan joint property without restriction.

Incapacitated adults and minor children may own joint property. In fact, joint ownerships are often created with these people for property management purposes. As pointed out earlier, this technique works to a degree. It's true that healthy or adult co-owners may handle routine property management for incapacitated or minor co-owners. But to do more, such as selling, mortgaging, or refinancing the property, formal legal authority is necessary. This may require appointment of a conservator for an incapacitated or minor co-owner.

For this reason, avoid, if possible, owning property with incapacitated adults or minor children. This is especially true when better alternatives are available: durable powers of attorney for incapacitated adults, and trusts or UTMA gifts for minor children.

Making Joint Property

Real Property

You and others may receive real property from the original owner in some form of joint ownership. If by sale, this transfer will probably be carried out by warranty deed. A quit claim deed is normally used for a transfer by gift (see "Real Property" on page 162 for the difference between warranty and quit claim deeds).

Or you may convert your solely-owned real property to joint ownership by conveying the property to yourself and others. Since this kind of transfer is normally a gift, a quit claim deed is the correct means of transfer.

Quit claim deeds are easy to prepare. Lawyers and realtors charge modest fees, usually around $25-50, for deed preparation. You can also make one yourself. There are quit claim deeds in the forms section of this book. At the end of this chapter, there's a sample deed for creation of a joint tenancy with the current sole owner as one of the joint tenants.

For joint ownership, special granting language must be placed in the grantee section of the deed. The grantee section is ordinarily the second paragraph of the deed, where the grantee(s) (recipient) of the property is named. Each form of joint ownership requires a specific grant, which must be cited carefully without modification.

Deed: Joint Tenancy

The following grant create a JT between nonspouses in real property in Michigan:

> Grover Millsaps and Shirley Millsaps, as joint tenants

If the joint tenants are married, another form of grant must be used:

> George Frisbie and Margo Frisbie, as joint tenants and not as tenants by the entirety

A JT has rights of survivorship. But curiously, you mustn't mention "survivorship," "survivor," or any variation of these words in the grant. Because of a peculiarity in Michigan law, mentioning survivorship in a grant of real property creates a SJT, a special type of JT. As explained earlier in this chapter, a SJT has some negative characteristics, which you probably want to avoid. But if you want a SJT between nonspouses,* use this phrasing:

> Grover Millsaps and Shirley Millsaps, as joint tenants with rights of survivorship

Deed: Tenancy by the Entirety

The following grant creates a TE between spouses in real property in Michigan:

> George Frisbie and Margo Frisbie, husband and wife

Deed: Tenancy in Common

The following grant sets up a TC between nonspouses in real property in Michigan:

> Grover Millsaps and Shirley Millsaps, as tenants in common

For TCs between spouses, use:

> George Frisbie and Margo Frisbie, as tenants in common and not as tenants by the entirety

If you make a TC grant like the ones above, without specifying shares, the tenants in common take equal shares. You can assign unequal shares by specifying the shares in the grant.

> Grover Millsaps and Shirley Millsaps, as tenants in common, with Grover Millsaps receiving a 70% share and Shirley Millsaps receiving a 30% share of the property

---

* A TE is the equivalent of a SJT between spouses, so use a TE if you want a SJT between spouses.

After you prepare a deed, it must be executed. The owner-grantor must sign the deed before two witnesses and a notary public. The joint owner-grantee(s) doesn't sign the deed.

The deed must then be delivered to the joint owners. They should record the deed at the register of deeds for the county where the real property is located. A small recording fee must be paid. Transfer tax is also due (from the owner-grantor) if the transfer is a sale. But if the transfer is: 1) a gift 2) a transfer between spouses creating or terminating a tenancy by the entirety 3) from the grantor to himself/herself as one of the grantees, no transfer tax is due. The statutory transfer tax exemption must be cited in the body of the deed. The quit claim deeds in this book have check-boxes to claim these exemptions. After recording, the deed will be returned in the mail to the grantee(s) named at the bottom of the deed.

Personal Property

You can create joint personal property by specifying the type of joint ownership in the documents of title for the property. If the property is untitled, use a written receipt to establish joint ownership.

Bank Accounts

Bank accounts may be held in several types of joint ownership (see the chart on page 185 for a breakdown). Special types of joint ownership, such as convenience accounts and *Totten* trusts, are also available.

You must specify the joint ownership you want in the deposit agreement with the financial institution. Personnel at the institution can explain how to do this and provide the necessary paperwork.

Safe Deposit Boxes

There are good reasons for holding safe deposit boxes jointly. At the death of one boxholder, the survivor can get quick access to the box and remove the contents.* If a box is held alone, the box may be sealed at the boxholder's death, and a court order must be issued to get access. To avoid this, consider renting safe deposit boxes jointly with family or friends. The financial institution can explain the options.

Stocks

For joint ownership of stock, register the stock certificate in the type of joint ownership you want. To add joint owners to stock you own, have the stock reissued in joint ownership form.

You can obtain a new stock certificate through the corporation's transfer agent. Large corporations, with publicly traded stock, often designate banks or other companies as their transfer agents. Small closely-held companies usually act as their own transfer agents.

---

* The contents of a safe deposit box, such as jewelry, stamps and coins, precious metals, etc., are separate from the box itself. Thus, joint control of the box doesn't necessarily mean that the contents are jointly owned.

Some people have stock in custodial accounts, either nominee accounts with banks or street accounts with stock brokerage firms. With a custodial account, the bank or stockbroker has control of the stock and can trade it for the stockowner. You can put these custodial accounts in various types of joint ownership, including POD form, by specifying the type of ownership in the account agreement with the bank or brokerage firm.

Bonds

U.S. savings bonds may be held in just two forms of joint ownership: JT (which bond regulations call co-ownership) and POD form (known as beneficiary form). No more than two persons may co-own savings bonds.

For joint ownership of savings bonds, have the bond registered or reissued in the joint owners' names. Designation of the owners in the disjunctive as "John Jones *or* Mary Smith" creates co-ownership (JT), while listing "John Jones P.O.D. Mary Smith" sets up a beneficiary (POD) arrangement. Financial institutions serve as transfer agents for U.S. savings bonds, and can explain the details and provide the necessary paperwork.

Motor Vehicles

You may place a motor vehicle in joint ownership by specifying the type of joint ownership in the certificate of title to the vehicle. The Michigan Secretary of State can issue or reissue the title in the form of joint ownership you want.

Keep in mind that it's often smart to leave motor vehicles in sole ownership, to avoid extra liability for the joint owners. See page 180 for more about the liability risks of joint ownership.

Miscellaneous Personal Property

It isn't easy to hold personal property, such as household goods or personal effects, in joint ownership. These items usually don't have title documents where you can specify joint ownership. Making matters worse, in Michigan all household goods in a marital home are presumed to be the sole property of the husband. This rule, fair or not, is based on the duty of husbands to support their families.

For joint personal property, you need written evidence of your intent to establish joint ownership. As you give or receive gifts of miscellaneous personal property, use a receipt designating the recipients as joint owners. In the document, designate the joint owners as "joint tenants, with full rights of survivorship" (for JT), "tenants by the entirety" (for TE), or "tenants in common" (for TC).

Remember to specify the amounts the joint owners contribute toward acquisition of the property. This information is vital for gift and estate tax purposes (see "Taxation of Joint Property" on page 181 for more about the importance of documenting contribution for tax preparation).

QUIT CLAIM DEED

MARGO ANN FRISBIE
of 900 S. WASHINGTON, LAKE CITY, MI 48800 , grantor(s),
quit claims to MARGO ANN FRISBIE AND THELMA ALICE MANGROVE, grantee(s),
AS JOINT TENANTS
of 900 S. WASHINGTON AND 101 W. CHERRY, LAKE CITY, MI 48800
the following real property located in the   CITY   of   LAKE CITY
LAKE County, Michigan:

LOT 3 OF MCPHERSON'S ADDITION TO LAKE CITY, MICHIGAN

for the sum of ONE DOLLAR

This deed is exempt from transfer tax under:

- ☐ MCL 207.526(a) (gift)
- ☐ MCL 207.526(i) (transfer of tenancy by the entirety between spouses)
- ☒ MCL 207.526(q) (creation of joint tenancy when grantor(s) is one of the joint tenants)

Date JAN. 1, 2000

Witnesses:

George Edward Frisbie
GEORGE EDWARD FRISBIE

Guy Francis Fish
GUY FRANCIS FISH

Grantor(s):

Margo Ann Frisbie
MARGO ANN FRISBIE

State of Michigan

County of __LAKE__

This instrument was acknowledged before me on JAN. 1, 2000
by __MARGO ANN FRISBIE__

Guy Francis Fish
GUY FRANCIS FISH Notary Public
__LAKE__ County, Michigan
My commission expires __7-7-02__

Prepared by:
MARGO ANN FRISBIE
900 S. WASHINGTON
LAKE CITY, MI 48800

Return recorded deed to grantee, or other:
Send future tax bills to grantee, or other:

Chapter 6 Insurance

Insurance is a fact of life today. Fire insurance is a necessity for home-owners. If you drive an automobile in Michigan, you must by law have no-fault automobile insurance. And with the high cost of medical care, health insurance is a must.

Many people also have the types of insurance described in this chapter: life, disability and long-term care insurance. According to a recent estimate, 154 million Americans have some kind of life insurance. Millions also enjoy disability coverage, either as a benefit of employment or from public programs like social security and worker's compensation. Fewer have long-term care insurance, although it's becoming more popular as the cost of nursing home care rises.

Despite the popularity of insurance, few people have the correct coverage or the right amount. This neglect can have dire effects on your estate plan, where insurance often plays an important role.

Life Insurance

The basics of life insurance are simple enough. You (the insured) obtain an insurance policy from an insurance company (the insurer), covering your life. You pay money (premiums) for the coverage. Then at your death, if the coverage is still in force, the insurer pays money (the insurance proceeds) to a recipient (the beneficiary) you have previously designated.

Types of Life Insurance

The concept of life insurance is simple. What makes life insurance confusing is that it's packaged and sold in so many ways. A lot of this is just marketing, because there are really just two types of life insurance—term and whole life—with many variations.

MORE INFORMATION

About life insurance, obtain:

"What You Should Know About Buying Life Insurance" (#580G), for free, from:

S. James
CIC - OOA
P.O. Box 100
Pueblo, CO 81002
Or call (888) 878-3256

To check on the reliability of insurance companies, obtain at public libraries:

Best's Key Rating Guide, Oldwick, NJ: A.M. Best Co., 1998, or access Best's insurance company ratings at www.ambest.com

About shopping for affordable term insurance, contact:

Quotesmith Corp., offering a free service comparing term products, and acting as an agent for term insurers, at (800) 431-1147 anytime, or www.quotesmith.com

InstantQuote, with data on 184 term insurers at (888) 223-2220, 11-8 weekdays, or www.instantquote.com

Term insurance. Term insurance provides life insurance coverage for a specific period of time, or term. The term might be a few hours, as with airplane flight insurance, or many years, like most term life insurance policies.

Whatever the term, the face amount of the insurance is paid to the beneficiary if the insured dies during the term. If the insured survives the term, the policy expires and s/he gets nothing more than the security of having had insurance for a while. There are many types of term insurance.

¶ *Ordinary term.* Term insurance lasting for a specified period of time, usually 5, 10, 15, or 20 years, and then expiring without further rights.

¶ *Renewable term.* Term insurance with a guaranteed option to renew or extend coverage for an extra term.

¶ *Convertible term.* Term insurance with the right to convert to a cash-value policy, usually without proof of insurability.

¶ *Declining term.* Term insurance where the amount of coverage declines with time or another variable, such as payment of a debt. Private mortgage insurance (PMI) is an example.

Cash-value insurance. Cash-value insurance is permanent insurance lasting for the insured's lifetime. As its name implies, cash-value insurance has a value separate from the insurance. It has an added savings or investment feature building a cash value. The insurer uses some of this value to defray the cost of insurance. The rest is available as cash savings, which the insured can take as a policy loan or by cashing in the policy.

Cash-value insurance comes in a blizzard of varieties, with more being introduced every year. These are some of the more common varieties:

¶ *Whole life insurance.* Whole life insurance guarantees insurance coverage for a lifetime (a "whole life"), usually at a fixed premium. Traditionally the most popular form of cash-value insurance, whole life has been eclipsed by new varieties of cash-value insurance, particularly universal life insurance.

Whole life insurance premiums are normally fixed for the life of the policy. But today this isn't always true, as some whole life policies offer variable premiums:

- *Single-premium whole life.* The premium is a single lump-sum payable when the policy begins.
- *Modified life.* As a way of making the premiums more affordable for younger persons, the premiums begin low and rise later.
- *Limited payment life.* Premiums are concentrated during a portion of the policy period, such as 10 years of a 20-year policy.

¶ *Universal life insurance.* Like whole life, universal life provides permanent coverage for a lifetime. But with universal life, the premiums aren't fixed. On the contrary, you determine the amount of the premium; you can pay as much or as little as you like, within bounds. In some policies, you can even skip premiums for several years. This flexibility comes at a price, since your choice of premiums may affect coverage.

With universal life, the amount of coverage is tied to another factor besides choice of premium: the investment your premiums are placed in. For most policies, the insurer determines that. But with one type of universal life policy, you select the investment:

- *Variable life insurance.* You pick the investment for your premiums from a menu of choices (stocks, bonds, money market funds, etc.). If the investment performs well, you get more insurance coverage and cash-value. The opposite is true if the investment declines.

Social security survivor's benefits. Social security provides a kind of life insurance in the form of survivor's benefits. These benefits are monthly cash payments to your surviving spouse with dependent children, and/or the children themselves until age 18 or 21 if still attending school.

TO OBTAIN

A personal earnings and benefits estimate statement (PEBES), from the Social Security Administration (SSA), showing your eligibility for survivor's and disability benefits, call the SSA at (800) 772-1213 anytime, and ask for a Request for Earnings and Benefits Estimate Statement.

After you complete and return this request form, the SSA will send you a PEBES.

More information about social security survivor's and disability benefits, obtain:

"Social Security: Understanding the Benefits" (#523G) for free, from:

S. James
CIC - OOA
P.O. Box 100
Pueblo, CO 81002
Or call (888) 878-3256

Disability Insurance

Disability insurance replaces income lost when you're out of work because of a disability.* Whether you know it or not, almost everyone has some disability coverage through:

- social security's disability program
- worker's compensation
- employed-provided disability coverage

The trouble is, social security has tough disability standards, making it hard to qualify for benefits. Worker's compensation pays only when the disabling injury is job-related, which most aren't. And employer-provided disability benefits tend to be stingy and short-term. All this shows the need for extra coverage through disability insurance.

Like other forms of insurance, you pay periodic premiums to obtain disability coverage for a specified period of time. If you're disabled during that period, the insurer pays you disability benefits, which are typically fixed monthly payments of money. The disability benefits continue for a specified period of time.

Disability policies have different definitions of disability that trigger payment of benefits. There are two main types of policies:

Any occupation coverage. With this coverage, you must be unable to do *any* work, including the easiest, before coverage begins.

Own occupation coverage. Disability begins when you cannot work at your own occupation, even though you might be able to do other less taxing work.

As with life insurance, these two types of disability policies come in many different flavors. For example, you can obtain policies with automatic cost-of-living adjustments or guaranteed renewal rights, among other options.

Long-Term Care Insurance

When you get sick, ordinary health insurance, such as private insurance or Medicare, should pay for the cost of the acute phase of the illness. Hospitalization, doctor's fees, X-rays, laboratory tests, drugs, etc., are all covered.

But ordinary health insurance may not help when an illness is past the acute phase, and becomes chronic or lingering. With a chronic illness, you may need extended custodial care, or long-term care (LTC), more than skilled

---

* Disability is the same as incapacity, and includes both mental and physical impairments.

medical care. Ordinary health insurance may not cover LTC. For example, Medicare only pays fully for 20 days of LTC after a three-day hospital stay.

There are programs to pay for the cost of LTC. If your chronic illness was caused by an automobile accident, you can get LTC from your Michigan no-fault insurer. The Medicaid program, which mustn't be confused with Medicare, provides LTC for poor people.

Not everyone qualifies for these LTC programs. Most LTC patients have illnesses rather than automobile accident-related injuries. And Medicaid only helps those who are poor or have become poor by spending the bulk of their assets on health care. And even then, the LTC you receive under Medicaid may not be of the highest quality or the kind of care you want (it's usually institutional care, not at-home care).

LTC insurance is one solution to this problem. LTC insurance scarcely existed 20 years ago. But with an aging population, facing rising LTC costs, it's becoming more popular. Many insurers now offer LTC insurance and a few employers even provide it as an employee benefit.

Most LTC insurance excludes coverage for certain conditions. In Michigan, LTC is regulated by the Long-Term Care Insurance Act, and it rules out many exclusions (for example, Alzheimer's disease cannot be excluded), while allowing a few (such as alcoholism or psychological disorders). Coverage for pre-existing conditions is often excluded during a waiting period, as with health insurance.

> ## MORE INFORMATION
>
> About LTC insurance and other long-term care options, obtain:
> *Long-Term Care Planning: A Dollar and Sense Guide*, for $18.50, from:
>
> **U.S Seniors Health Cooperative**
> 409 Third St. S.W.
> Suite 200
> Washington, D.C. 20024
> Or call (800) 637-2604
>
> About LTC coverage, benefits, exclusions, and regulation of LTC insurance in Michigan, contact the organization serving as Michigan LTC ombudsman:
>
> **Citizens for Better Care**
> 6105 S. St. Joseph
> Lansing, MI 48917
> Or call (800) 292-7852
> Or contact the organization at one of its regional offices in Michigan.

Once in effect, LTC insurance often withholds coverage for a specified period of time (30, 60 or 90 days), which acts likes a deductible. Typically, the shorter the disqualification period, the higher the premiums; the longer the disqualification period, the lower the premiums.

After coverage begins, LTC policies pay fixed daily benefits for care. According to Michigan's LTC law, these benefits must continue for a minimum of one year. LTC policies usually limit coverage to a stated period or maximum amount of benefits, although some provide unlimited, lifetime benefits.

Life Insurance and the Estate Plan

More than anything, life insurance replaces the income of a deceased family breadwinner. You can have the insurance proceeds paid to the surviving family members in a lump-sum, trusting them to invest it wisely for the future. Or you can have the proceeds paid in installments, mimicking how the wageearner would have received income.

If you obtain life insurance to replace income, how much should you have? You don't need much unless you have people who are financially dependent on you. In fact, single or older persons should think twice about life insurance, except as a means of providing cash for final expenses (see below).

For those with dependents, financial planners have devised various tests to determine the correct amount of life insurance coverage. Typically, planners use a multiplier, usually five to ten times, of annual earnings. The best test also considers the number of dependents and investments you have. According to this test, the amount of your life insurance coverage should be four times annual pay, plus two times more for each dependent child, minus your investments and retirement benefits.

The trouble is, you may not be able to afford the premiums for the full amount of insurance you need. Whatever you do, don't impoverish yourself for the sake of life insurance. Life insurance may be important, but it isn't worth stinting on material needs.

For affordable life insurance, shop around for the best rates. In most cases, term insurance is less expensive than cash-value insurance, at least for young people. If you want cash-value insurance, consider a modified life policy where the premiums begin low and rise later. Or choose a universal life policy with a good investment option to hold down the premiums.

Another reason for life insurance is to provide liquid (cash or near-cash) assets for survivors or your estate immediately after death. At that time, your survivors might need ready cash for unexpected expenses. Your estate, which may be depleted after your final illness, may also need cash if other assets are in non-liquid form.

Life insurance can ease this liquidity problem. You can normally count on payment of life insurance proceeds, thanks to incontestability clauses in most policies* and state regulation of insurance companies. And if you choose payment of the proceeds in a lump-sum, the money will be promptly paid to your beneficiaries. They can then use the money for their own needs. Or they can advance money to your estate, either by loan or purchase of estate assets, solving its cash-flow problems.

On the other hand, you may not need life insurance for liquidity purposes. Your survivors may be able to get by after your death without extra money. And if you leave cash or near-cash assets, your estate may have enough liquidity. Adding life insurance for liquidity alone would be unnecessary and expensive.

Life insurance can also be a good investment. Term insurance doesn't have investment value, because it's pure insurance without a cash value. But all cash-value policies have investment value to some degree. In whole

---

* Incontestibility clauses stop insurers from reneging on life insurance policies after they have been in effect for a while (two years in Michigan), even though the insurer may have grounds to deny coverage.

life policies, the investment element is often hidden. The insurer quietly invests part of your premiums, and allocates some investment earnings to the cash value. With a universal life policy, the investment is plain; you see the investment value building, and in some policies even get to pick the investment.

Like any investment, cash-value insurance has an element of risk. The investment portion of the policy—whether the insurer or you select it—may not perform as anticipated, giving you a smaller than expected cash value. In fact, cash-value policies seldom perform as well as direct investments. Nevertheless, the policies are good for those who are unable to save on their own, because these act like a forced investment.

Life insurance also enjoys several tax advantages. If you plan well, your life insurance can escape estate taxation, at an enormous potential tax savings. Life insurance also receives favorable income tax treatment, with tax savings possible there as well.

Living Benefits from Life Insurance

Ordinarily, life insurance pays off only when you die, in a death benefit. But sometimes, you can get living benefits from life insurance, in the form of cash payments while you're still alive. These benefits can cover the cost of long-term care (LTC) or uninsured medical expenses.

There are two ways to tap life insurance for living benefits. Some policies permit acceleration of death benefits into the insured's lifetime. Cash-value policies have living benefits most often, but some term policies also have this option. When you buy a new insurance policy, you can often have it added to the policy, without charge or for an extra fee. Sometimes, it's possible to amend an old policy, adding living benefits.

TO OBTAIN
A viatical settlement, contact a viatical association which can give you a list of viatical companies and brokers:
Viatical Association of America, in Washington, D.C., at (800) 842-9811
National Viatical Association, in Waco, TX, at (800) 741-9465

Living benefits are typically paid out when the insured has a serious illness or is terminally ill. At payout, the insured receives a portion of the death benefit (the face amount of the insurance), usually in monthly installments. Insurers seldom allow full payout, imposing a cap on the living benefits. After the insured's death, the beneficiaries gets the remainder of the death benefit in a normal insurance settlement.

Another way to get living benefits is by a so-called viatical settlement. Financial companies and brokers will buy insurance policies, at some fraction of the face amount (usually 60-80%), and give you the money, usually in a lump-sum. Viatical companies prefer to buy policies of terminally ill people, with a short life expectancy.

After the insured dies, the viatical company, which owns the policy, gets the full face amount of the insurance. However, sometimes its possible to sell just part of the policy, holding back some of the death benefit for survivors or for other estate planning purposes. If you are considering a viatical settlement, shop around for the best settlement offer and deal with a reputable company.

The tax law treats living benefits favorably, and doesn't impose income tax on qualifying benefits. The qualification rules, as always, are complicated. Basically, you must have either be terminally ill (diagnosed with an illness expected to be fatal within 24 months), or chronically ill (suffering from a disabling condition which has destroyed the quality of life).

Taxation of Life Insurance

Estate and Gift Taxation

Unless you name yourself or your estate as beneficiary of your life insurance, the insurance proceeds are nonprobate property, passing outside your will and estate. But this doesn't necessarily mean that the proceeds will escape estate taxation. To accomplish this, you must: 1) name a beneficiary other than you or your estate and 2) give up all incidents of ownership over the policy. These rules apply both to insurance you own on your life and insurance you own on the lives of other people.

For tax purposes, beneficiary designations are important. For insurance on your life, you must designate a beneficiary other than you or your estate to avoid estate taxation. What's more, you mustn't make the insurance payable to your personal representative or others with a legal obligation to use the proceeds for estate expenses.* As described above, beneficiaries may help an estate with a liquidity problem by advancing cash to the estate. But this help must be in the form of loans or purchases, not direct transfers of life insurance proceeds.

Life insurance is taxed in your estate, regardless of beneficiary designations, if you owned the policy at your death. In the eyes of the tax law, ownership is a bundle of rights in the policy, called the incidents of ownership, including rights to:

• change the beneficiary
• assign the policy or revoke an assignment
• pledge the policy for a loan
• borrow against the cash surrender value of the policy
• surrender or cancel the policy
• choose the settlement option
• a reversionary interest of more than 5% in the policy (in other words, a greater than 5% chance that, based on life expectancies, you will survive

---

* You can name the personal representative personally as beneficiary, but not in his/her official capacity as personal representative of your estate.

all beneficiaries and your estate will receive the insurance proceeds by default)

Possession of *any* of these incidents of ownership gives the policyholder ownership of the life insurance. Thus, to avoid ownership, you must surrender complete control over the policy.

When you own insurance on your own life, the full amount of the insurance proceeds are included in your estate for tax purposes. If you own a policy on the life of another, who survives you, the tax treatment varies. For a term insurance policy, which has no real value until the insured's death, the taxable amount is zero. But for a cash-value policy, the cash-value of the policy at your death is subject to estate taxation.

As you can see, life insurance can quickly inflate the size of an estate. In fact, many people of modest means find that life insurance is their single largest asset, putting them near or above the $675,000 general exemption level and exposing them to estate taxation.

> *Example:* George and Margo have an estate, minus insurance, worth $400,000. As a policeman, George has good life insurance coverage: $200,000 group term insurance from his employer and another $200,000 term policy through a police association. If George and Margo were to die suddenly, without any estate tax planning, $125,000 of their estate would be taxable and they would owe $31,300 in estate tax.

For insureds in this predicament, a gift of life insurance often makes sense. The gift tax value of life insurance is usually low or nonexistent, while the potential estate tax liability with the insurance in the estate is high. With this in mind, many people give their insurance to others or a trust, reducing their estates below the $675,000 exemption level.

The details of giving life insurance are described in Chapter 4, on page 165. Basically, you give away the insurance without retaining any incidents of ownership over the policy. And then to keep the proceeds out of your taxable estate, the beneficiary must be someone besides you or your estate.

A gift of life insurance should be done sooner rather than later, because the tax law has a special rule making gifts of life insurance within three years of the donor's death ineffective. If you get caught by this rule, the full amount of the insurance proceeds, plus any gift tax paid, are included in your taxable estate. Thus, if you're considering a gift of life insurance, do it while you're healthy and not at the last minute.

Income Taxation

Thanks to the power and influence of the insurance industry, life insurance has historically enjoyed favorable tax treatment by the income tax law. In cash-value policies, income the investment portion generates has not been taxed when earned, withdrawn (in the form of policy loans or surrenders of the policy for cash), or paid in proceeds after death.

After a tax revision in 1988, life insurance lost a few of its tax breaks. Today, some cash-value policies that are more investment than insurance, called endowment policies, have income taxed when earned. Moreover, withdrawals can be taxed if they exceed premiums paid, minus dividends.

All the same, life insurance remains one of the few tax dodges left. In most ordinary cash-value policies, the earnings still accumulate tax free, and no income tax is due on modest lifetime withdrawals or on the proceeds after death. Thus, for most cash-value policies left largely intact until death, no income tax is ever paid on policy earnings.

Estate Planning with Life Insurance

Who Can Own Life Insurance?

Any mentally competent adult can own life insurance. Business organizations can also take out life insurance, and often do when they insure the lives of important executives or employees with so-called "key-man" insurance.

Minors and mentally incapacitated adults, who lack the legal capacity to sign contracts, ordinarily cannot obtain life insurance directly. However, the Michigan insurance code permits minors between the ages of 16-18 to own life insurance just like adults. Younger minors and mentally incapacitated adults must obtain life insurance through their legal representatives, guardians, or conservators.

If you own life insurance on the life of another person, who survives you, the policy is an asset that must be probated in your estate. To avoid this, some life insurance policies allow you to name a contingent owner, who receives ownership of the policy at your death, without going through probate.

> *Example:* Margo obtains a life insurance policy on George's life. She names their children as contingent owners of the policy. Then, if Margo dies before George, the children will receive ownership of the policy, without probating it through Margo's estate.

Whose Life May Be Insured?

Before you can insure someone's life, you must have an insurable interest in the person's life. Simply put, an insurable interest is a personal stake in the insured's life. In Michigan, you have an insurable interest in the lives of the following people:

- yourself
- your spouse
- close relatives
- business partners
- key executives and employees of your business

- persons who provide you with support

The insurable interest requirement exists to prevent criminals from insuring others peoples' lives and then killing them to collect the insurance proceeds. Murder-for-insurance happens even among families and business associates. But there is less risk of such foul play when the insured and the policyowner have family or business ties.

Who Can Be a Beneficiary?

Ordinarily, you can designate whomever you want as beneficiary of life insurance. Some policies require you to name certain classes of people, such as close relatives, but such restrictions are unusual.

Sometimes you may be legally obligated to designate particular beneficiaries. For example, a judgment of divorce or marital agreement, such as a pre- or post-nuptial agreement, may require the designation of certain beneficiaries. Naturally, you must comply with these obligations.

But otherwise, you may designate anyone as beneficiary: yourself, relatives, nonrelatives, a trust, charity, business or nonprofit organization, or any combination of these. If you neglect to designate beneficiaries, the insurance proceeds usually go to your estate, by default, which is seldom wise (see below for the dangers of an estate as beneficiary).

Your beneficiaries may include minor children and mentally incapacitated adults. But special arrangements may be necessary to manage the insurance proceeds for them. Mentally incapacitated adults need a guardian or conservator to manage the proceeds.

Michigan law says that minors may receive insurance proceeds up to $2,000 annually, without special legal protection. The new Uniform Transfers to Minors Act (UTMA) conveniently allows insurers to pay insurance proceeds to a minor's UTMA custodian, avoiding a guardianship or conservatorship. Otherwise, for large insurance payments, the minor will need a conservator to manage the money.

Designate beneficiaries according to what you want to accomplish with the life insurance. If you have coverage for income replacement, designate your dependent survivors (spouse, children, etc.) as beneficiaries. Choose survivors also if you want to use life insurance to add cash to your estate. These survivors can then make insurance proceeds available to your estate by loan or from purchase of estate assets. If you have life insurance for another reason (to benefit a charity or an ex-spouse, fund a buy-out of your share of a business by your business partners, etc.), choose the correct beneficiary.

As a rule, avoid naming your estate as beneficiary. This designation exposes the insurance proceeds to probate and possible estate taxation, even if you have surrendered ownership of the policy. What's more, your creditors can also get at the proceeds.

On the other hand, a single person, with few or no dependents, might consider making his/her estate the beneficiary of a modest life insurance policy. If the purpose of the policy is to provide cash for payment of final expenses, the insurance proceeds can create or supplement the estate to pay these expenses, without a big probate.

Beneficiary Designations

You should designate, by name, primary and secondary beneficiaries of your life insurance. The primary beneficiary is first in line to receive the insurance proceeds. But if s/he fails to survive the insured, the secondary beneficiary becomes the recipient.

Or you can go a step further and define beneficiaries by class, the percentage shares they get, or the distribution of deceased beneficiaries' shares. Most insurers permit such designations.

Example: George designates Margo as the primary beneficiary of his life insurance. He adds the following secondary beneficiary designation: "the secondary beneficiaries are my children, Thelma Marie Mangrove, Dewey John Frisbie, Woodrow James Frisbie, who shall take the proceeds by representation." By citing representation, George has extended the possible distribution to grandchildren or other descendants if Margo and his children die before he does.

Under Michigan's new estates code, many of the will distribution rules also apply to nonprobate property, such as insurance proceeds and retirement plan death benefits, unless the policy or plan says otherwise. So George's reference to representation in the example above would incorporate the code's representation pattern, unless the insurance policy specified a different one (few do). As you make beneficiary designations using terms like "children," "heirs," "representation," etc., go to the glossary to find out the standard code rules and alternatives to these rules.

To designate beneficiaries, contact your insurance agent for individual insurance or your employee benefits office for employer-provided group coverage. They have forms for the designation and can explain the rules and procedures.

Settlement Options

Most policyowners choose to have the insurance proceeds paid all at once, in a lump sum. But this isn't the only settlement option available. Most insurers also offer one or more installment options. With an installment option, the insurer keeps the proceeds after the insured's death in a trust-like setup, invests the proceeds and ultimately pays the funds to the beneficiaries over a specified period of time.

An installment option can be useful for beneficiaries who aren't good at managing money, such as minor children, incapacitated or developmentally disabled adults. In a way, installment payments are like a simple trust, without the trouble of setting up a trust.

There are several drawbacks to installment payments. The rate of return on the investment of the proceeds may not be competitive. If so, it may be better to take a lump-sum payment and invest the proceeds in a trust or other investment at competitive rates. Installment payments may also produce extra income taxes. No income tax is due on a lump-sum payment. But with installment payments, income taxes must be paid on the income earned by the invested proceeds.

As with beneficiary designations, choose a settlement option according to the purpose of the life insurance. If you want income replacement, consider an installment option. But if you want the insurance to provide liquidity, a lump-sum option is the natural choice.

Choose your settlement option when you designate beneficiaries. Your insurance agent or employee benefits office can explain the options available and provide the necessary paperwork.

Estate Planning with Disability Insurance

Disability insurance is income insurance, covering the loss of earnings from a disability. Thus, only working people, with incomes, need disability insurance and are insurable. Those who aren't steadily employed—the young, homemakers, retirees—aren't normally eligible for disability insurance.

Employers often provide group disability insurance as an employee benefit. Frequently, only short-term coverage is provided, although employees may have the option of picking up long-term coverage at minimal cost.

Self-employed people may have difficulty getting disability coverage, or paying for the $2,000-4,000 annual cost of the premiums. Home-based workers may have trouble getting disability insurance because of the blurry line between home and work. Jobs requiring physical labor, such as farming or construction, may rule out coverage because of the high risk of injury. White-collar workers are the most insurable, at the lowest rates.

Disability insurance policies typically provide fixed monthly benefits, such as $1,000-3,000 per month. You may wish to obtain maximum coverage, replacing 100% of your monthly income. Insurers seldom offer that, figuring that complete coverage gives you scant incentive to resume working after an injury. Instead, they normally insure a fraction of your income, typically a maximum of 60-70% for middle-income people and 30-50% for high-income people.

Most insurance experts recommend around 60-70% coverage. This amount should match your pre-disability income after taxes. If you obtain coverage at a particular level, make sure that you increase coverage as your income rises.

Most disabilities are short-lived, with only 10% lasting more than a year. But some can endure for several years or even a lifetime. That's why it's smart to obtain coverage until age 65, when social security retirement and perhaps private retirement benefits are available. You can get shorter-term coverage, at lower premiums. But longer-term coverage is better if the premiums are affordable.

Your disability coverage may also be influenced by income tax treatment of the benefits. Tax law says disability benefits are nontaxable if you paid for the insurance. On the other hand, you are fully taxed on benefits received from employer-provided coverage. As a result, you may consider paying for the disability coverage provided by your employer. Paying for an employee benefit may seem strange, but may pay off in the long run in tax-free benefits.

Estate Planning with Long-Term Care Insurance

MORE INFORMATION

About finding long-term care, contact:

Michigan Office of Services to the Aging
P.O. Box 30676
Lansing, MI 48909

Or call the office's legal hotline at (800) 347-5297

Or contact one of the 14 regional agencies on aging offices, listed in the yellow pages under "Senior Citizens Organizations."

All offices provide information about long-term care for the elderly, from living options to meal services.

Children of Aging Parents
1609 Woodbourne Road
Suite 302A
Levittown, PA 19057

Or call (800) 227-7294

Provides information, support and referrals for elder care.

National Family Caregivers Association
At (800) 896-3650

Assists those providing care to family members.

National Hospice Organization
1901 N. Moore St.
Suite 901
Arlington, VA 22209

Or call (703) 243-5991

Provides information about hospice care.

For information about nursing homes in Michigan, with a handy checklist for choosing a nursing home, obtain:

Consumer Guide to Michigan Nursing Homes: A Resource for Residents, Families and Other Consumers of Michigan Long-Term Care Services, Lansing: 1999, available at many public libraries.

With the high cost of health care these days, many people need good LTC coverage for custodial care during a lengthy incapacity. The wealthy can often pay, out of pocket, the $30,000-80,000 annual cost of such care. And the poor have good coverage through Medicaid, with no deductibles and few co-payments.

But middle-income people, who don't have great wealth and don't qualify for Medicaid, can easily exhaust all their assets paying for LTC. One study revealed that half of those admitted to a LTC facility spend all their assets within a year of admission. This shows the importance of LTC insurance for middle-income people.

The best time to buy LTC insurance is during late middle age, before the onset of the chronic diseases of old age. Young people can obtain LTC insurance, but it's an extravagance. People in their 70s and 80s need coverage the most, but by that time the premiums are often too high, or they have pre-existing diseases excluding or delaying coverage. All in all, the best time to get LTC coverage is during your 50s and 60s, preferably before age 65.

LTC insurance seldom pays for the actual cost of care; instead, policies pay a fixed daily benefit, usually $50-200, toward care. Judge whether the daily benefit will cover the cost of care you want. Better LTC policies will adjust the daily benefit for inflation, although inflation-adjustment means higher premiums.

Most LTC policies cover basic or custodial care, not skilled nursing care. Make sure the policy defines basic care fully, and that this coverage is satisfactory. Policies typically cover basic care at an institution, such as a nursing home or hospice. But home care is a popular option, and Michigan law now requires some home-care coverage. The best policies cover care in all kinds of settings, at home, in an assisted-living facility, or at an institution.

No doubt LTC insurance is expensive, but

there are income tax credits easing the expense. Since 1997, employees can deduct all or part of LTC insurance premiums as medical expenses if: 1) they itemize deductions 2) the premiums added to qualified medical expenses exceed 7.5% of adjusted gross income. The maximum amount of the deduction varies with age, and is inflation-adjusted. Different rules apply to the self-employed; they can deduct 60% of their LTC insurance premiums as a business expense (this percentage will rise to 70% in 2002 and 100% thereafter).

Chapter 7
Retirement Benefits

Years ago, a retirement plan included social security and maybe a pension paid by your employer after 30 or 40 years of service. Today's job-hopping employees, by contrast, often have a smorgasbord of retirement benefits. Social security is a constant. But in addition, employees may be able to draw retirement benefits from several past employers, and have multiple retirement plans.

Making sense of all these retirement plan benefits is difficult. At some point, you need to knit them into a coherent plan to support you during retirement. However, that's really a financial planning issue and beyond the scope of this book.

Besides providing retirement income, most retirement plans also provide death benefits. Retirement plan death benefits are paid by the plan when the plan participant dies, to beneficiaries the participant has designated. Thus, like life insurance proceeds, retirement plan death benefits can be an important part of your estate.

Types of Retirement Plans

Retirement planning began with social security and private pensions, but now includes a wide array of benefits. Here are the most common retirement plans:

Social security. If you work for a minimum period of time (ordinarily ten years), you're eligible for social security. Social security retirement benefits are generous (most recipients get far more than they paid in). But the death benefit is stingy: $255 payable to either a surviving spouse or children. This benefit is often applied by the survivors to the cost of the deceased's final disposition or death ceremony.

Employer-provided retirement plans. As a means of attracting and keeping employees, employers often provide retirement plans to employees. Most plans pay death benefits when employees die prematurely. There are two main types of employer-provided plans, with many varieties.

¶ *Defined benefit plan.* In a defined benefit plan, or pension plan, the employer promises to pay stipulated benefits at retirement and death. All the employee really has is the employer's promise of benefits (which is guaranteed by the government); there is no account reserved for the employee. Instead, the employer's retirement contributions are pooled in a common fund, and benefits are drawn from the fund as needed. Benefits are paid according to formulas which are usually based on a combination of the employee's age, years of service, and earnings.

MORE INFORMATION

About the types of retirement plans, benefits, and how they're protected, obtain:

"What You Should Know About Your Pension Rights" (#318G), for .50, from:

R. Woods
CIC - 00A
P.O. Box 100
Pueblo, CO 81002

Or order with a credit card at (888) 878-3256

¶ *Defined contribution plan.* An employee with a defined contribution plan has a separate retirement account set aside for him/her, from which the retirement and death benefits are drawn. The account may be funded with contributions from the employer, employee, or both. The money in the employee's retirement account is invested (usually by the employer), and any investment income is added to the account. Whatever the source, all the money in the account remains the employees' own. There are many different kinds of defined contribution plans.

- *401(k) plan.* The employee earmarks a percentage of his/her pay for the plan, temporarily avoiding income tax on the contribution. The employer often matches the employee's contribution. 401(k) plans are the most popular type of defined contribution plan today.
- *Profit-sharing plan.* The employer has the option of contributing a percentage of annual profits to employees' retirement accounts. Employees seldom contribute to the accounts themselves.
- *Employee stock ownership plan (ESOP).* The employer contributes shares of its stock to employees' ESOP accounts. Sometimes, employees have the right to buy more stock adding to their accounts.
- *Savings or thrift plan.* The employee contributes a percentage of after-tax pay to an account managed by the employer. Because the contributions are taxed, these plans have largely been replaced by 401(k) plans.

Individual retirement plans. You can also create your own retirement plan. Self-employed people or employees in small companies, who don't have employer-provided retirement plans, use individual retirement plans the most. But employees with employer-provided retirement plans can use individual plans to supplement other benefits. Or they can use individual plans to hold employer-provided benefits temporarily, such as during a change in employment.

¶ *Individual retirement arrangement (IRA).* With an IRA, you designate a custodian, usually a financial institution or brokerage firm, to manage the account. You also select the investment: savings account, certificate of deposit, money market fund, etc.

IRAs have annual contribution caps: up to $2,000 annually for an individual, and a maximum of $2,000 each annually for spouses. Since 1998, there are two kinds of IRAs, with different rules about deduction of these contributions from income tax.

- *Traditional IRA.* In a traditional IRA, contributions to the account are tax-deductible, unless the contributor is already covered by a qualified employer-provided retirement plan. For these double-dippers, the IRA income tax deduction is scaled back, and even eliminated at certain income levels (the nondeductible portion may still go into the IRA, or better yet, into a Roth IRA).
- *Roth IRA.* With the new Roth IRA, none of the contributions is tax deductible. But at the other end, none of the distributions is subject to income taxation (since tax has already been paid on the money before it went into the account).

¶ *Simplified employee pension (SEP).* Small companies often balk at setting up retirement plans because of all the paperwork required by federal law. A SEP is an alternative for these companies or for self-employed people. SEPs are really separate IRAs for each employee. The employer and/or employee make contributions to the SEP, and the account is managed for the employee by a custodian, like a regular IRA. While maximum contributions to an IRA are limited, up to 15% of an employee's annual compensation may be transferred to a SEP tax-free.

¶ *Keogh (HR-10) plan.* Self-employed people can contribute a certain percentage of their annual income to a Keogh (HR-10) plan. The income is not taxed during the year of contribution and grows tax-free.

Retirement Benefits and the Estate Plan

In many ways, retirement plan death benefits resemble life insurance proceeds, and can do many of the things insurance does. Retirement plan death benefits can qualify as nonprobate property, skipping the estate of the plan participant along with life insurance proceeds. And like life insurance proceeds, death benefits can provide a pot of money at death, which can be used several ways.

With many retirement plans, death benefits can be paid in installments, spreading the payments over years. Thus, death benefits can replace the income of a deceased family breadwinner. Or you can choose a lump-sum payment, making the benefits available to satisfy the liquidity needs of your estate or survivors.

Like life insurance, retirement plans are tightly regulated by law. In defined benefit plans, the employer is obligated to provide the stipulated death benefit, regardless of how the retirement fund investments fare. Moreover, this promise is backed by a federal agency, the Pension Benefit Guaranty Corporation (PBGC). If the employer goes out of business or reneges on its obligations, the PBGC steps in and covers the retirement benefits up to certain maximums. Thanks to these protections, after your rights in a defined benefit plan vest (see below for more about the concept of vesting), you can count on getting a death benefit.

Defined contribution and individual retirement plans are even more secure. There is no vesting requirement for these plans, so anything in the retirement plan account is yours. Naturally, your account investment may perform poorly, eroding the value of your benefits. But barring total disaster, you are certain to get some amount of death benefit.

Where life insurance proceeds and retirement plan death benefits diverge is their tax treatment. Life insurance enjoys many tax breaks, particularly by the income tax law; retirement plan death benefits receive much less favorable tax treatment.

Taxation of Retirement Benefits

Estate and Gift Taxation

Retirement plan death benefits once got a huge break from estate tax. As recently as 1982, retirement plan death benefits passing outside an estate were completely immune from estate taxation. During 1983-84, the first $100,000 of these benefits were nontaxable. Since 1985, the full amount of benefits is taxable, regardless of how or to whom they are paid.*

As with other assets, the various estate tax exemptions, particularly the marital and general exemptions, can cover retirement plan death benefits. But there are some dangers. The general exemption covers all types of benefits; the marital exemption may not. The marital exemption applies to all lump-sum payouts, but not to every type of installment option. Check with your tax or financial adviser for details.

Gift tax may also be due when you designate certain beneficiaries of

---

* You can still qualify for the pre-1985 tax breaks if you left your employer before January 1, 1985, and didn't change your retirement plan before death.

your retirement plan death benefits. The designation of a beneficiary gives the designee a potential right to the death benefit, which has value. Thus, the designation is a gift in the eyes of the gift tax law.

Typically, married people with modest estates designate spouses as primary beneficiaries (as explained later, this designation is often required by law). The gift tax law says that the marital exemption covers any designation of a spouse. The picture isn't so rosy for other designations. For nonspouse designees, none of the other gift tax exemptions is available to cover the tax. This is another reason to stick with a spouse as primary beneficiary.

Income Taxation

Except for Roth IRA distributions, retirement plan death benefits are subject to full income taxation. Basically, the income tax law regards the death benefits as income that has been postponed from the time it was earned. The day of reckoning comes when the income is distributed in the form of either retirement or death benefits.

It's difficult to generalize about the income taxation of retirement plan death benefits because the tax treatment depends on several variables, including the type of retirement plan, your age, marital status, beneficiary designations, and settlement option choice. The combination of these facts determines the amount of tax.

The choice of a settlement option is probably the most important factor in determining the income tax on retirement plan death benefits. As a result, the settlement option section later in this chapter has more information about the income tax consequences of retirement plan death benefits.

Estate Planning with Retirement Benefits

Who Owns Retirement Benefits?

Before you receive full ownership of retirement plan death benefits, the benefits must vest in you. Vesting is akin to ownership; it simply means that your right to the benefits cannot be taken away from you.

Vesting isn't a problem for your own contributions to an employer-provided or individual retirement plan. These contributions vest immediately since they're your own money.

Vesting takes a little longer for the employer's share of an employer-provided retirement plan. Vesting is normally based on years of service with the employer. Today, most benefits vest with five years of service. Some plans vest according to a special seven-year schedule, with 20% vesting after three years of service and 20% for each year thereafter.

To find out about vesting for an employer-provided plan, refer to the summary plan description (SPD) for the plan. The SPD is a short booklet or pamphlet, written in plain English, explaining the plan, including vesting rules. By law, your employer must distribute SPDs periodically or at your request.

Who May Be a Beneficiary of Retirement Benefits?

You don't have the same freedom to designate beneficiaries of retirement plan death benefits as you do with life insurance beneficiaries. Among the restrictions, the most important are the spouse rights created by the Retirement Equity Act (REA) in 1984. According to the REA, the spouse of a married plan participant must be named as the primary beneficiary of some or all of the death benefits of "qualified" employer-provided retirement plans. However, a spouse can waive this right, allowing the plan participant to designate someone else. Moreover, the REA doesn't apply to individual retirement plans, so owners of these benefits can designate anyone as beneficiary.

Some employer-provided retirement plans also limit the choice of beneficiaries to close relatives, such as spouses and children. The SPD for your plan will describe any restrictions. Your hands may also be tied by a judgment of divorce or marital agreement, such as a pre- or post-nuptial agreement, forcing you to designate certain beneficiaries.

Within those limits, you can designate any person or most trusts as beneficiary of your retirement plan death benefits. As with other assets, minor children and mentally incapacitated adults need special representatives to manage the benefits if they are large.

You can also name your estate as beneficiary. This choice is seldom wise because it exposes the benefits to needless probate and makes them available to creditors. But if the death benefits are modest, and you have few other probate assets, you might want to designate your estate as beneficiary. With this arrangement, the death benefits could create a small estate to pay your final expenses, without a big probate.

Your estate can also become beneficiary by default. Many retirement plans make the estate beneficiary when the plan participant neglects to designate beneficiaries. But some plans avoid a default to the estate by specifying beneficiaries (usually close relatives like a spouse or children), much like the inheritance law does for those dying without wills.

Besides legal restrictions like the REA, your beneficiary designations should be guided by what you want to accomplish with the retirement plan death benefits. If you want to replace income, name your survivors (spouse, children, etc.) as beneficiaries. These individuals are also the logical choices if you want to add liquidity to your estate. As explained in the last chapter, your survivors can take insurance proceeds, or retirement plan death benefits, and make them available to the estate by loan or purchase of estate assets, without passing them through the estate (see "Life Insurance and the Estate Plan" on page 195 for more about this technique).

Beneficiary Designations

Most retirement plans allow you to designate primary and secondary beneficiaries of death benefits. The primary beneficiary receives the benefits, unless s/he fails to survive you. If the primary beneficiary dies prematurely, the benefits go to the secondary beneficiaries.

Beneficiary designation forms are often cramped, with only enough space to designate primary and secondary beneficiaries and their shares. If there's more room, you can make a fuller designation. For example, you might provide for distribution of a deceased children's shares by adopting the representation pattern of distribution. See "Beneficiary Designations" on page 202 about making more complete designations. As mentioned in that section, many of the will distribution rules, such as the definition of terms like "children, "heirs," and "representation," apply to nonprobate property in most cases.

Your employee benefits office will have the beneficiary designation forms for retirement plans provided by your employer. For individual retirement plans, the custodian of the plan, such as a financial institution or brokerage firm, provides the paperwork. Ordinarily, you must stick closely to the form. But some plans allow you to prepare your own beneficiary designation form if the regular one doesn't fit your needs.

Settlement Options

There are two basic settlement options or payout methods for retirement plan death benefits, with several possible sub-choices. Ordinarily, a beneficiary may receive benefits in a lump sum or installments. With the lump-sum option, the beneficiary can take the benefits all at once, in a true lump sum; or sometimes the payment can be rolled over into an IRA. Installments also come in two forms: 1) installment payments for a fixed number of years 2) installments in annuity form, lasting indefinitely for the life of the beneficiary.

Not every plan offers all these settlement options. And some options are restricted to certain beneficiaries. For example, only spouses may take lump-sum payments and roll them over into IRAs. Check with the SPD to see which options are available to you.

There is a new wrinkle for settlement of IRAs. Recently, some IRA custodians, such as banks and brokerage firms, have begun allowing IRA beneficiaries to pass up settlement, leaving the IRA intact, and name their own beneficiaries. This can delay final settlement—and payment of estate and/or income tax—for 10, 20, 30, or more years. Not all custodians permit this, and the IRS has yet to approve the practice.

Naturally, your settlement option choices are shaped by what you want to accomplish with your retirement plan death benefits. If you want immediate income replacement, consider the installment option, in either fixed payment or annuity form. When your beneficiary is a spouse with a good job, you may want to choose a lump-sum payment. That way, the spouse can roll the benefits over into an IRA, and draw on it later. A lump sum also makes sense when you want to use the benefits to provide cash for survivors or your estate.

As you consider the various options, don't forget the impact of income taxes on your choice. As mentioned before, settlement options and income taxes are closely linked, so it's irresponsible to choose a settlement option without regard to possible income taxation of benefits.

Retirement plan benefits are usually untaxed income that must be taxed when received. Thus, if you choose a lump sum, the entire amount will normally be taxed to the beneficiary upon receipt. There are some exceptions. Roth IRAs are created with after-tax money, so no income tax is due when Roth accounts are distributed. And as described above, spouse-beneficiaries can roll over lump sum payments into IRAs, and delay taxation until the IRA is distributed. In addition, lump-sum payments from some employer-provided plans are eligible for special five-year income tax averaging. According to this rule, the lump sum is taxed as if it had been received over five years. By spreading the payments out, the tax bill is usually less. The trouble is, you still have to pay the full tax in the year the lump sum is received, not over the five-year averaging period.

By choosing installment payments, either in fixed or annuity form, the beneficiaries pay income tax on the death benefits as they receive them. This eases the tax burden on the beneficiaries. In addition, there may be a net tax savings if the beneficiaries are in lower income tax brackets when the payments are received.

Chapter 8
Final Matters

Introduction to Final Matters

8A: Final Disposition

    Sample Letter of Instruction and Anatomical Donor Document

8B: Death Ceremony

Introduction to Final Matters

After the death of a loved one, surviving family and friends are seldom in the mood to make important decisions about the deceased. But ready or not, these survivors are quickly confronted with two big decisions:

Final disposition of the body. After death, the body of the deceased must be removed from the place of death, preserved temporarily, and then finally disposed of by:

¶ *Burial.* There are two main forms of burial: 1) earth burial, or interment of the body in the ground 2) entombment where the body is encased in a tomb above ground.

¶ *Cremation.* With cremation, the body is burned at high temperature, leaving a gravelly residue called cremains. The cremains can be disposed of directly (usually by burial or entombment), or they can be reduced further to fine ashes. The ashes can be stored at home in a container, such as an urn, buried, entombed or scattered outdoors.

¶ *Anatomical gift.* A body can be disposed of by giving it away as an anatomical gift. Individual body parts can be given to specified or unspecified recipients, or the whole body can be given to a medical school for medical research and education.

217

¶ *Miscellaneous.* Some people choose exotic final dispositions, such as burial at sea (available to some Navy veterans), mummification, celestial burial (rocketing cremated remains into space orbit, offered by the Texas firm Celestis, and chosen famously a few years ago by Star Trek creator Gene Roddenberry), and even cryonic disposition (freezing the body for possible reanimation later!).

Death ceremony. All societies have ceremonies or rituals marking death. In the United States, the customary ceremonies include:

¶ *Funeral.* A funeral is a death ceremony with the body present. Most funerals take place at commercial funeral homes, but they can also be held at places of worship (churches, synagogues, mosques, etc.).

¶ *Memorial.* A memorial is a death ceremony without the body. Typically, a memorial is held at a place of worship, after final disposition of the body.

¶ *Committal.* A committal is a brief death ceremony during final disposition. For example, a committal is often held graveside during a burial.

The survivors must sort through all these options, and make final decisions about body disposition and death ceremonies. The survivors must act quickly, because these decisions can't wait. This leaves little time for shopping around, to get more information about the various options and prices. In fact, experts say that funerals and burials are probably the largest purchases (an average funeral and burial now exceed $6,000) consumers make in the shortest time, with the least information.

With this in mind, more people are planning for final matters. According to a 1989 survey, a scant 2% of funerals were planned in the late 1970s, 25% in 1989, but now it's estimated that 50% of funerals are planned.

Estate Planning for Final Matters

Planning for final matters has several benefits. By making arrangements ahead of time, you take the pressure off your survivors to make these decisions for you. Your foresight can also prevent family squabbles, since survivors often disagree about final matters.

You have more control over final matters if you plan. You can leave instructions about final disposition and death ceremonies. These instructions aren't legally binding on your survivors, but they provide clear guidance about your wishes. Keeping control over final matters is especially important for those with unusual wishes, or those in nontraditional living arrangements. These people often give formal instructions on final matters, out of fear that their survivors will misinterpret or won't respect their informal wishes.

Planning also helps funeral homes, cemeteries, crematoria, etc., which provide the goods and services for final dispositions and death ceremonies. Before they begin work, providers must know which goods and services to provide. With the correct planning documents, you can give providers the confidence to act without delay.

Planning has another, often forgotten, benefit. As explained later, expenses for final matters are debts of the deceased's estate, which must be paid before property is distributed from the estate. If these expenses are large, they can consume the estate, frustrating your plan of estate distribution. By planning for final matters, you can make sure that the final expenses are reasonable, and won't disturb the rest of your estate plan.

Chapter 8A
Final Disposition

The death of a loved one is an emotionally wrenching experience. But just as the survivors are coping with their grief, they are confronted with the business end of death: what sort of final disposition should the body of the deceased have?

Autopsy

An autopsy may intervene between death and final disposition of the body, delaying disposition a while. An autopsy is the dissection and examination of a body to determine the cause of death and/or the extent of disease.

In a full autopsy, the body is opened and examined. Various organs, tissues and fluids are removed for testing and examination. Some samples may be kept for future reference. Otherwise, the body parts are put back in the body, which is closed and restored to a normal appearance.

All autopsies use similar medical procedures, but there are different kinds of autopsies:

Official autopsy. Conducted by the county medical examiner (formerly known as the coroner under old Michigan law), usually at the county morgue, for a public purpose, at public expense. In Michigan, medical examiners have considerable judgment in performing official autopsies. Examiners may hold autopsies when a death is sudden, unexpected, accidental, violent, or without medical attention within 48 hours of the death. Medical examiners cannot perform official autopsies in other situations, even if asked by the survivors.

Official autopsies are vital for solving crime, explaining mysterious

221

deaths, and controlling disease. As a result, official autopsies don't need the consent of the deceased's survivors, and may go forward after proper notice, despite the survivors' personal or religious objections. Autopsies also come before anatomical gifts.

Hospital autopsy. Performed at a hospital by a staff pathologist, to obtain medical information for the hospital or the deceased's survivors. A hospital may ask for a hospital autopsy to gather medical data or check on the quality of hospital care. A hospital autopsy requires the consent of the deceased's survivors: a surviving spouse, parent, guardian, next of kin, or other lawful custodian of the body.

Private autopsy. Freelance autopsies conducted by pathologists, usually at a funeral home, at the request of survivors. These days, with better diagnostic procedures and fear of medical malpractice, fewer and fewer deaths are autopsied. Hospital autopsies in particular are in decline (only 5% of hospital deaths receive autopsies today compared with 42% in 1965). If the hospital refuses to autopsy, the survivors may pay for a private one, which typically cost around $2,000.

The survivors may want a private autopsy to establish the cause of death or the presence of disease for a civil lawsuit, such as a medical malpractice, wrongful death, or workers' compensation case, or in a dispute with an insurance company. Some survivors get private autopsies just for peace of mind.

MORE INFORMATION

There is at least one Michigan company offering private autopsies:

Autopsy Associates, in Dearborn, at (313) 561-8207

Methods of Final Disposition

With or without an autopsy, the body is ready for final disposition. As described in the introduction to this chapter, there are several ways to dispose of bodies, including some exotic ones like cryonic disposal (freezing the body) or ocean or space burial. Nevertheless, most people choose more down-to-earth methods, such as burial, cremation, anatomical gifts, or some combination of these.

Burial

Burial is interment of a body (or sometimes the remains of a body after cremation or anatomical gifts) in or above the ground. There are two types of burials: earth burial and entombment.

Earth Burial

For Americans, earth burial is by far the most popular method of final disposition, accounting for 75% of all dispositions. In an earth burial, the body is buried in the ground. Ordinarily, a grave-marker, either an upright stone monument or a flat stone or metal plaque, is placed on the ground above the burial marking the grave site.

Entombment

With entombment, the interment is in an above-ground tomb. The body can be placed in its own stand-alone tomb. Or the body may be put in a niche in a mausoleum, which is a building with many tombs.

Places for Burial

A burial—whether earth burial or entombment—must take place either in a cemetery or on private burial grounds.

Cemetery

There are two types of cemeteries: 1) ordinary cemeteries that permit both upright and flat grave-markers 2) memorial gardens or parks featuring natural landscaping with flat markers only. Michigan has around 4,000 cemeteries. Most are nonprofit, operated by federal, state, or local governments. Some religious or fraternal groups have cemeteries. There are also a smaller number of for-profit commercial cemeteries in the state.

> ### MORE INFORMATION
>
> About the location of all known cemeteries in Michigan, obtain these reference books available at most public libraries:
>
> *Michigan Cemetery Atlas,* Lansing: Library of Michigan, 1991, which has county maps showing the location of Michigan cemeteries.
>
> *Michigan Cemetery Sourcebook,* Lansing: Library of Michigan, 1994, the companion volume to the atlas, listing the names and addresses of Michigan cemeteries.

You reserve space in a cemetery by buying a plot from the cemetery. In some ways, a cemetery plot resembles other forms of real property. You own the plot and receive a deed to it. But there are differences. Typically, cemetery deed restrictions stop you from selling the plot, and give the cemetery the right to buy the plot back if you want to get out. As a result, a cemetery plot is a special type of real property, without real market value.*

Cemeteries normally require full payment for a plot before you can use it for burial. With this in mind, people often buy and pay for cemetery plots during their lifetimes. If you've done that, make sure that your survivors know you own the plot. Mention the plot in your letter of instruc-

---

* Since cemetery plots don't have market value, omit them from your inventory of property.

tion to survivors (see "Giving Burial and Cremation Instructions" on page 235 for more about these documents), or keep the deed or other evidence of ownership among your vital papers.

You may already have access to a family cemetery plot and don't know it. Families often purchase larger-than-necessary cemetery plots with enough space for relatives. The deed to the plot should specify which family members are eligible for burial in the plot. Ask your relatives to see if you have a family plot available to you.

Another way to save on cemetery expenses is to bury more than one body in a grave. Most cemeteries allow up to three bodies per grave. This is achieved by stacking the caskets on top of each other in the grave. To do this, cemeteries usually require outer burial containers (see "Other Burial Products and Services" on page 226 for more information) for the caskets, so the grave doesn't settle or collapse. By using a grave more than once, you get maximum use out of a cemetery plot, saving money.

U.S. military veterans have special burial benefits and privileges, courtesy of the Veterans Administration (VA). Almost all veterans, their spouses (and sometime ex-spouses), and dependent children are entitled to burial, with gravestones or grave-markers, in a national cemetery. Spouses and dependent children are buried in the some plot as their veteran-relative. If they predecease the veteran, they can be buried in the national cemetery where the veteran intends to be buried. Burial is free in these national cemeteries, but the government doesn't pay the cost of transporting the body to the cemetery.

Veterans buried in private nonmilitary cemeteries are entitled to government-issued flat grave-marker of bronze, granite, or marble, or an upright gravestone of marble. The government will also pay for inscription on these burial markers.

Extra burial allowances are paid to veterans whose deaths are somehow service-connected. Military retirees, veterans dying from service-related injuries or in VA hospitals, and several categories of disabled veterans can receive burial allowances from $300-1,500. These burial allowances can be used to pay the costs of final disposition, such as a funeral or casket, or a death ceremony, which the government doesn't pay for directly.

For entombment, you can buy a cemetery plot to erect a stand-alone tomb, which serves as both the place for the body and the burial marker.

MORE INFORMATION

About veteran's final disposition benefits, contact:

Funeral directors who usually have information and the forms to apply for benefits.

Or obtain:

"Federal Benefits for Veterans and Dependents" (#112G), by sending a check for $5.00, payable to "Superintendent of Documents," to:

R. Woods
CIC - 00A
P.O. Box 100
Pueblo, CO 81002

Or to order with a credit card, call (888) 878-3256

This publication has a directory of all national cemeteries. Michigan has only one national cemetery:

Ft. Custer National Cemetery
On Dickman Road, in Augusta, west of Battle Creek

Call (616) 731-4164

Also, some counties contribute for veteran's burials and grave-makers. Call your county veteran's affairs office for information.

A single tomb is expensive. A cheaper alternative is a cemetery mausoleum, which is a building with spaces or "niches" for tombs. You buy a niche in a mausoleum like you do a cemetery plot. During burial, the casket is sealed inside the niche and normally a plaque is attached to the front of the niche. The plaque serves as a burial marker which is visible to visitors to the mausoleum.

Selecting a Cemetery

Whether you choose earth burial or entombment, you must find a suitable cemetery. Naturally, you want a cemetery that's clean and well-maintained. Michigan cemetery law requires cemeteries to put 15% of the sales price of plots into trust funds for the maintenance of graves and markers. Nevertheless, some cemeteries neglect this requirement and let their grounds deteriorate. Michigan's Office of Cemetery Regulation keeps records of violators, and these are available to the public.

Affordability is another concern. As a general rule, new cemeteries are cheaper than old ones, which are at or near capacity, because new cemeteries get revenue from selling new plots and don't have to depend solely on maintenance fees. Memorial gardens may also be more economical than ordinary cemeteries. In a memorial garden, with flat grave-markers only, it's easier to mow the grounds, reducing maintenance costs.

As you shop around, ask the cemetery if they charge extra for maintenance. Does it require an outer burial container for every burial, or just in special situations? Does the cemetery permit multiple burials in the same grave? All these factors influence the cost of a cemetery plot.

> ## MORE INFORMATION
>
> About regulation of for-profit cemeteries (public and religious cemeteries are unregulated in Michigan), contact:
>
> **Office of Cemetery Regulation**
> P.O. Box 30004
> Lansing, MI 48907
>
> Or call (517) 241-9246

Private Burial Grounds

Michigan law permits private burial grounds, for the burial of family and descendants. You set up private burial grounds with a deed of trust, recorded in the county register of deeds. The burial grounds, which cannot exceed one acre, are permitted in rural areas only, outside of cities and villages. Township zoning laws must also permit the use.

Despite their low cost, private burial grounds are seldom a good idea. Maintenance is a headache. And what happens if you move? It's possible to dig up graves and have the remains removed, but excavation is expensive. If you leave the graves behind, the burial grounds may diminish the value of the property, because prospective buyers probably won't want graves on the property.

Other Burial Products and Services

No matter which type of burial you choose, or where, the body must be housed in a container before and after interment. If earth burial is chosen, an outer burial container may also be necessary to protect the grave. In an entombment, the tomb itself serves this function.

Before burial, the body must be held in a container. Some people choose low-cost containers like canvas body-bags or cardboard boxes, but most prefer caskets (coffins). Caskets come in many varieties, from inexpensive plain wood or composition-material caskets, to expensive solid-wood or metal caskets (see "Funeral" on page 243 for more about casket choices and costs).

There are few legal requirements for caskets. However, some cemeteries and funeral homes have minimum standards for caskets. For example, in an entombment in a mausoleum a sealed metal casket may be required to prevent the release of odors into the mausoleum as the body decomposes.

Otherwise, the selection of a casket is a matter of personal taste. Contrary to what some casket dealers tell you, no casket will prevent decomposition of the body. Even the most expensive casket, with special seals and gaskets, will admit outside elements, causing decomposition of the body within a year of interment. When you buy a fancy casket, you're getting a nice piece of furniture, but not much more.

Ordinarily, the body is buried in the casket it was stored in before burial. But it's possible to rent an expensive casket during the pre-interment period, such as for a funeral, and then transfer the body to a less expensive burial casket. See "Funeral" on page 243 for more about these rental options.

If you choose earth burial, you may need an outer burial container to protect the grave. There are two types of outer burial containers: grave liner and burial vault. A grave liner, which costs around $300, is a box of concrete slabs enclosing the buried casket. A burial vault, selling for around $500, is a reinforced box of concrete or metal protecting the buried casket.

Outer burial containers aren't required by Michigan law. However, cemeteries usually want them for multiple burials in the same grave, to stabilize the grave. Some cemeteries also require outer burial containers for single-burial graves for the same reason, which is doubtful. Check with the cemetery to find out its outer burial container policy.

In a burial, the cemetery will also charge for opening and closing a grave or tomb. There may also be miscellaneous charges, such as burial permit fees.

Burial Providers

Burial goods and services are available from a number of providers:

Funeral home. In Michigan, funeral homes, also known as mortuaries, may provide all the burial goods and services, except for the cemetery plot. A funeral home can transport the body, preserve it, provide a casket and an outer burial container at the cemetery.

Cemetery. Cemeteries also offer burial-related products. Naturally, cemeteries provide cemetery plots, tombs and outer burial containers. But cemeteries sometimes contract with funeral homes, memorial societies, or direct disposition firms, and offer complete burial packages.

Memorial society. Memorial societies, also known as funeral or burial societies, are cooperative associations* providing low-cost final disposition services to their members. Membership is normally open to anyone, although a few societies are affiliated with fraternal or religious groups. You join a memorial society by paying a nominal membership fee of $20-30. Some societies permit posthumous membership.

Memorial societies seldom handle burials themselves; they contract with funeral homes and cemeteries for burial goods and services. By guaranteeing these providers a high volume of business, memorial societies get discounts on burials that they pass onto their members.

Direct disposition firm. Direct disposition, also known as immediate burial, is probably the cheapest and quickest form of burial. With direct disposition, the body is taken from the place of death in an inexpensive container directly to burial, eliminating extra handling of the body and fancy containers.

Direct disposition firms are usually for-profit companies. But like memorial societies, you often must join them and pay a small membership fee before you're eligible for their services. Some funeral homes, cemeteries, and memorial societies also offer direct disposition.

Private burial. In some states, survivors can handle burials themselves. But in Michigan, care of the dead is tightly regulated. Only licensed funeral specialists may transport bodies and supervise burial. Survivors are allowed to prepare the casket (see "Funeral" in on page 243 for more about building caskets). And as explained before, it's possible to bury on private land.

MORE INFORMATION

About the benefits of memorial societies, and a directory of these societies in Michigan and nationally, write:

Funeral and Memorial Societies of America
P.O. Box 10
Hinesburg, VT 05461

Cremation

In many parts of the world, cremation is the preferred method of final disposition. But cremation was never popular in this country. Many religious groups were hostile to the practice. For example, the Roman Catholic Church condemned cremation until 1961, when the church finally

---

* Some for-profit direct disposition firms call themselves societies. Don't confuse them with true memorial societies, which are nonprofit.

approved the practice. Today, the Catholic Church not only approves of cremation, but it allows cremated remains in church during funeral masses. Some parishes even have memorial gardens for burial of the cremains or ashes.

As religious hostility to cremation has faded, and burials have gotten more expensive, more Americans are choosing cremation. The Cremation Association of North America estimates today that around 25% of all final dispositions in the U.S. are by cremation, and that this share will approach 50% by the end of the decade.

Before cremation, the body must be kept in a container. Almost any container will do: a body-bag, cardboard box, or casket. The container doesn't need to be fancy because the body is usually burned in the container. In fact, casket manufacturers make special cremation caskets, which are easily combustible. By contrast, some burial-type caskets are unfit for cremation, such as metal caskets (which don't burn) or synthetic ones (which emit toxic fumes).

During the cremation, the body and container are burned in an incinerator at a facility called a crematorium. The process normally takes two or three hours. The residue of the burning are 4-8 pounds of gravely material, bone fragments mostly, called cremains.

After cremation, the crematorium will box the cremains, which are odorless and sanitary, for final disposal. The cremains can be buried in an ordinary cemetery or in the cemetery-like gardens crematoria often maintain. Some churches also have special memorial gardens for burial of cremains. There may be a charge of $100-300 for burial, which often includes a permanent marker or plaque.

Cemeteries, crematoria and even some churches may have special buildings resembling mausoleums, called columbaria, with niches for above-ground storage of cremains in urns or other containers. The cost of entombment in a columbarium is usually $500–1,000.

With the popularity of cremation, national military cemeteries have added columbaria. Veterans, their spouses, and dependents eligible for free burial in a national cemetery are also entitled to have their cremains entombed in one of these columbaria, without charge. See "Cemetery" on page 223 for more about veterans' final disposition benefits. The government will also pay for veterans' niche-markers with an inscription, as it does for burial markers, at a military or nonmilitary cemetery.

On request, crematoria will reduce cremains to powdery ashes. The ashes can be disposed of in the ways described above (earth burial or entombment in a columbarium), or they may be stored in an urn or other container at home.

MORE INFORMATION

About cremation, ask for a free pamphlet from:

Cremation Association of North America
401 N. Michigan Ave.
Chicago, IL 60611

Or call (312) 644-6610

The association can also make referrals to cremation providers in your area.

Ashes may also be scattered outdoors. Cemeteries, crematoria, and even some churches (exception: the Roman Catholic Church which prefers burial or entombment of cremated remains, and discourages scattering) have designated scattering grounds for this purpose. You can also scatter on your own property or someone else's with permission. Technically, scattering ashes in a public place is littering. But no one should mind if the scattering is done quietly in an uninhabited area.

Cremation Providers

In Michigan, cremations must be carried out in licensed crematoria. However, cremations are available from several providers:

Crematorium. In the past, crematoria marketed their services through funeral homes and memorial societies, and seldom dealt with the general public. Today, crematoria sell directly to the public. In fact, some offer complete final disposition packages, from pick-up of the body at the place of death, a death ceremony, followed by cremation and final disposal of the cremains.

Funeral home. Funeral homes can also arrange for cremation services.

Memorial society. Memorial societies once specialized in cremations, and were the primary access to this form of disposition. Nowadays, these societies still provide cremation services as well as other burial options.

Direct disposition firm. Like memorial societies, direct disposition firms offer both cremations and burials.

Anatomical Gifts

Another way to dispose of a body is by anatomical gift, where the body is used by others for medical or scientific purposes. There are two types of anatomical gifts: organ/tissue donation and gift of body.

Organ/Tissue Donation

Everybody is familiar with donation of vital organs like the heart, kidney, liver, etc. But you may not know about donation of other tissues, such as skin, bone, cartilage, etc. In all, around 25 different body parts may be given in organ/tissue donations for use by others (see "What Can Be Given in an Anatomical Gift?" on page 234 for a complete list).

MORE INFORMATION

About organ and tissue donations, contact:

Gift of Life
2203 Platt Road
Ann Arbor, MI 48104
Or call (800) 482-4881

Gift of Body

It's also possible to give whole bodies to medical schools. The schools use the bodies for medical research and education, particularly anatomy instruction. Michigan's three medical schools have donation programs accepting gifts of bodies.

Estate Planning with Anatomical Gifts

Anatomical gifts have several advantages. Needless to say, they provide enormous benefits to the living. Organ/tissue donations are the primary source of organ and tissue transplants, saving or improving the lives of many desperately ill people (at last count, around 2,600 Michiganians are waiting anxiously for organs). Organ/tissue donations and gifts of bodies also promote medical research and education.

From a donor's point of view, anatomical gifts can be an inexpensive method of final disposition. With a gift of body, the donor's estate may have to pay for transportation of the body to the donee-medical school (some schools provide free local pick-up of bodies). On the other hand, medical schools normally pay all costs of final disposition after they are finished with donated bodies.

There are fewer savings with an organ/tissue donation. Organ/tissue donors are never charged for the cost of removing the organs. But after the donation, the donor's estate is responsible for final disposition of the remains (by burial, cremation, etc.), as with any death. Thus, an organ/tissue donation is cost-neutral to the donor; it doesn't save money or increase the cost of final disposition.*

You can make either type of anatomical gift, or both kinds. If you make both, it might not be possible to honor both because carrying out one type of anatomical gift can spoil the body for the other type of gift. For example, if you make an organ donation, a medical school will usually reject a gift of a body with missing organs.** And naturally, after a body has been donated and used by a medical school, it's too late for organ donations.

What happens when you make both types of anatomical gifts? Ordinarily, the donee will accept the organ donation and disregard the gift

---

MORE INFORMATION

About gifts of bodies, contact Michigan's three medical schools:

Department of Anatomy, **Michigan State University**, E. Lansing, MI 48824, (517) 353-5394

Department of Anatomy and Cell Biology, 3626 Medical Science II Bldg., **The University of Michigan Medical School**, Ann Arbor, MI 48109, (734) 764-4359

Department of Anatomy, **Wayne State University Medical School**, 540 E. Canfield, Detroit, MI 48201, (313) 577-1188

---

* A donor cannot profit from an organ/tissue donation either, because in the U.S. it's illegal to sell organs and most other body parts.

**Some medical schools accept bodies after removal of small body parts, such as corneas or eyes.

of body. The reasoning is that organs are needed more than bodies, so the organ donation is preferred.

If you make an anatomical gift, you should also have a plan of *final* disposition. With an organ donation, the standby plan is necessary because the post-donation remains of the body must be disposed of by burial or cremation.

When a medical school accepts a gift of body, it assumes responsibility for final disposition. Most schools cremate the bodies and bury the cremains in local cemeteries. At the survivors' request, medical schools will cremate and release the cremains or ashes to the survivors.

However, medical schools reserve the right to reject gifts of bodies. Schools reject bodies that are damaged, infected with contagious disease or incorrectly preserved. They also reject bodies when they have a surplus. As a result, you should always have a backup plan of final disposition when you make a gift of body.

Anatomical Gifts in Michigan

Anatomical gifts may seem like the latest in a series of modern medical miracles. But in fact, anatomical gifts are nothing new. Body parts such as skin and teeth have been removed and transplanted for centuries. The right to give a body for medical science was established by England's landmark Anatomy Act of 1832. Before long, many American states, including Michigan, adopted similar anatomy laws.

The modern era of anatomical gifts began with the successful transplantation of eye corneas around 50 years ago. In 1947, California adopted the first comprehensive anatomical gift law, regulating gifts of all kinds of body parts and whole bodies.

As organ and tissue transplantation grew, a uniform anatomical gift law, the Uniform Anatomical Gift Act (UAGA), was developed in 1968. Since then, every state and the District of Columbia have adopted the UAGA in some form. Michigan enacted the UAGA in 1969, and it's now part of the state public health code.

The foundation of the UAGA is consent. Either the deceased donor before death, or the donor's survivors after death, must consent to the anatomical gift. Without actual consent, no gift is possible.

Other countries have a different system, in which dead bodies are treated more like a public resource for the living. In many European countries, donors' consent for anatomical gifts is implied, and body parts may be removed unless the donor or survivors prohibit the removal.

Michigan's UAGA requires actual consent of the donor or survivors for anatomical gifts, with two exceptions. In Michigan, corneas and pituitary glands may be removed during official autopsies, after notice to the survivors, unless the donor or survivors forbid removal. The reasoning is that these small body parts, which are often ruined during an autopsy, can be removed unnoticeably. Thus, consent for the removal is unnecessary.

Who Can Be a Donor of an Anatomical Gift?

Direct Donation

Michigan's UAGA says that you must be at least 18 years of age to make an anatomical gift. There isn't a maximum age, either by law or for practical reasons. You're almost never too old to make anatomical gifts, and even elderly people have become anatomical donors.

The UAGA requires a sound mind for anatomical donors, which is the same mental capacity for a will. In the context of anatomical gifts, soundness of mind means that you understand the legal significance of the anatomical gift. In other words, you know what the gift is, what it does and whom it benefits.

Donation by Family Consent

If you don't make anatomical gifts yourself during your lifetime, your survivors can make such gifts for you. Except when forbidden by the donor or a close relative/legal representative of the donor, your survivors may consent to any anatomical gifts immediately before or after your death. The UAGA gives the following persons the right of consent, in the order listed below:

- spouse
- adult child
- either parent
- adult brother or sister
- guardian of the deceased
- any person authorized to dispose of the body

You may veto a potential anatomical gift by notifying survivors that you object to such a gift. To avoid any doubt about your wishes, the notice should be written. It's possible to put the notice in your will; but the will may not be read until well after your death, which is too late for an anatomical gift. A better place for the notice is a letter of instruction, because this document will be in the hands of your survivors at death.

Survivors may also veto anatomical gifts. When someone or some class of persons have priority to make an anatomical gift, the person with priority, any member of the priority class, or anyone with higher priority, may veto a proposed anatomical gift.

Example: George dies without having said anything about anatomical gifts. Margo doesn't want to donate any of his organs; their adult children do. As surviving spouse, Margo has priority to decide, and her veto outweighs the children's consent.

Survivors actually receive greater veto rights than the law allows. According to the Michigan Attorney General's interpretation of the UAGA, a deceased's anatomical gift is legally binding, and shouldn't be canceled by survivors. Despite this ruling, hospitals routinely seek the consent of survivors before they carry out anatomical gifts. And if the survivors voice objections to the deceased's gift, hospitals usually cancel the gift.

In some ways, this survivors' consent policy is regrettable because it makes anatomical gifts more difficult to carry out, resulting in fewer gifts. But hospitals reason that, if anatomical gifts are enforced against survivors' wishes, the ill-will and bad publicity would discourage future anatomical donations. As a result, most hospitals insist on survivors' consent.

Who Can Be a Donee of an Anatomical Gift?

The UAGA says that any individual in need of organs or tissues for therapy or transplant may receive anatomical gifts. In addition, doctors and many medical institutions (hospitals; organ and tissue banks; medical, dental, nursing, veterinary and optometry schools) can receive anatomical gifts for science, therapy or transplantation.

You may make anatomical gifts to a specific donee or without naming a donee. If you don't designate a donee, or your specified donee can't accept the gift, medical staff will accept the gift and find a suitable donee through the national organ allocation system (described below).

The allocation of anatomical gifts for transplantation has been controversial. When celebrities like David Crosby and Mickey Mantle received liver transplants, some accused the organ allocation system of giving them special treatment. Those involved denied any favoritism.

Here's how the organ allocation system is supposed to work. A potential donee's medical condition (age, physical health, etc.) and biological characteristics (blood type, tissue type, etc.) are recorded, and the donee is placed in a national pool with similar donees. The donees aren't ranked while they're in the donee pool.

When an organ becomes available, donor and donee must be matched. In Michigan, the matching is made by the Transplantation Society of Michigan (also known as Gift of Life), in Ann Arbor, which belongs to the national organ allocation system operated by the United Network for Organ Sharing (UNOS) in Richmond, Virginia. During matching, the donees are ranked (for the first time) by their medical compatibility with the donor and nonmedical factors, such as geographical distance from the donor. The organ is assigned according to this ranking.

The allocation of tissues is more straightforward. Tissues can be treated to prevent rejection by donees, and stored for a long time. As a result, tissues can be banked and used as needed by donees, without complicated matching.

Donees are entitled to reject anatomical gifts, and sometimes do. Donees turn down gifts of organs or tissues when they are old, damaged, diseased, or for nonmedical reasons. And as mentioned before, medical schools reject gifts of bodies when they are damaged, diseased, incorrectly preserved, or when the schools have a surplus of bodies.

What Can Be Given in an Anatomical Gift?

The UAGA allows the donation of any body part or a whole body. Organ donations grab most of the attention, with good reason. The donation and transplantation of vital organs such as a heart, kidney, liver, pancreas, spleen, stomach, small and large intestine, bowel and lung, save lives, often in a dramatic way.

But gifts of other body parts are equally important. For every organ donation-transplant, there are 250 donation-transplants of ordinary tissues like blood, skin, bone, bone marrow, tendon, ligament, cartilage, fascia, vein, heart valve, teeth, middle ear, eye and cornea. These gifts of flesh and bone aren't always noticed, but they bring about vast improvements in the quality of lives of donees.

In addition, gifts of whole bodies are vital to medical research and education. Bodies are used by medical schools and laboratories for experimentation and research. Schools also use bodies for medical education, particularly anatomy instruction, for doctors, dentists, nurses, veterinarians, optometrists, physical therapists and medical technologists.

When you make an anatomical gift, you may specify in the donor document which body parts you want to give. Or you can give them all and let the donee decide which ones to take.

When Does an Anatomical Gift Take Effect?

All anatomical gifts under the UAGA take effect after the donor's death. Thus, there's never any danger that body parts will be removed while you're still alive. Likewise, an anatomical gift won't hasten your death, because a doctor must certify your death before the gift may begin. As extra protection, the doctor certifying death must not participate in the anatomical gift.

In fact, living people do make anatomical gifts of renewable body parts (blood, bone marrow, and sperm), spare ones (kidney), or even parts of vital ones (liver, lung, and pancreas). But gifts by living donors aren't covered by the UAGA and are beyond the scope of this book.

Final Disposition Instructions

If you don't plan for the final disposition of your body, your survivors control the disposition. They must decide according to your wishes, their own tastes and the public interest. The actual disposition decisions are made by the following persons, in the order listed below:

- spouse
- next of kin
- personal representative

Leaving final disposition entirely to your survivors, without any guidance from you, has risks. The survivors may be uncertain or confused about your wishes and choose something inappropriate. The survivors themselves may disagree about final disposition, and feud over the decision. And finally, the survivors might choose a final disposition the estate can't afford. Such extravagance can deplete the estate, playing havoc with estate distribution and/or saddling the survivors with the bill.

You can avoid these problems by planning your final disposition. For a burial or cremation, you can give directions in a so-called letter of instruction. You can make an anatomical gift—of body parts or the whole body—by preparing an anatomical donor document.

Giving Burial and Cremation Instructions

Letter of Instruction

Years ago, it was customary to put final disposition instructions in wills. The trouble is, a will isn't always available at death, so the instructions often go unheeded. As an alternative, the letter of instruction was developed. This is an informal document with final disposition instructions, death ceremony instructions, and post-mortem information, which is readily available at death.

In a letter of instruction, you can give directives about any part of your final disposition. You can begin by choosing either a burial or cremation. You can then request a particular type of burial or cremation, adding as much detail as you like.

No matter where you make them—in a will, letter of instruction, or someplace else—final disposition instructions are never legally binding on survivors. If they fail to follow the instructions, they cannot be ordered by a court to carry them out or be held liable for neglecting them.

Michigan law is contradictory on final disposition instructions. One law seems to give the deceased the right to control final disposition (through the personal representative) , but the wording of the law is fuzzy and not very forceful. Another law empowers the deceased's survivors. Funeral operators, who have always been cool toward final disposition instructions (because deceaseds often choose cremation over funeral/burial), rely on the second law and typically go to survivors for final disposition consent. For example, if the deceased left written instructions for cremation, but his survivors wanted burial, funeral homes would bury.

If final disposition instructions aren't enforceable, why go to the trouble of making them? There are several benefits. Final disposition instructions provide clear guidance to survivors about your wishes, allowing them to choose what you want. At the same time, it's still wise to tell your close relatives about your wishes, as reinforcement of the written instructions.

Final disposition instructions also help burial or cremation providers. Providers must be careful to act properly, because some final dispositions are irreversible (for example, after direct disposition by cremation, it's too late for a funeral and burial). There are also strict liability rules for mishandling corpses. As a result, having written instructions from the deceased, which jibe with survivors' consent, allows the provider to act confidently, without delay.

There isn't a prescribed letter of instruction form, as there are for other vital documents like wills. Financial institutions, insurance companies, and funeral homes distribute their own letter of instruction forms. A letter of instruction is also included in the forms section of this book.

The letter of instruction has several sections, including one for final disposition instructions. You can state your instructions in as much detail as you want. Don't try to manage every last detail because it's difficult to anticipate everything about final disposition. For example, you might ask for burial in a particular cemetery, but then move far away, making the request impractical.

As a general rule of final disposition planning, add more detail the nearer to death you are. Young people and those in good health should leave only general instructions; older or infirm persons can explain more fully.

A letter of instruction is an informal document, which doesn't need to be witnessed or notarized. You should, however, sign and date the form after completion.

After You Make a Letter of Instruction

More than other estate planning documents, a letter of instruction must be accessible after your death. Since final disposition begins immediately after death, the instructions must also be available then to guide the disposition.

As explained above, a letter of instruction can be followed by any of your survivors. But the appointed personal representative is usually the one who carries out the instructions. Thus, the personal representative should have the letter of instruction after death.

With this in mind, give the original letter of instruction to your first-choice personal representative. Copies should go to the second choice and close relatives likely to be around at your death. Also keep a copy among your vital papers.

Amending or Revoking a Letter of Instruction

It's easy for a letter of instruction to become outdated. Your final disposition wishes may change, or may no longer be affordable or feasible. Moving far away often has a big impact on final disposition instructions, because they are often tied to a particular location (cemetery, church, funeral home, etc.).

You can amend your letter of instruction by removing old material and/or adding new material. Unlike other estate planning documents, a letter of instruction is an informal document and can be amended that way. If amendments are extensive, leaving a messy document, make a whole new letter. If you do, destroy the old one and all copies.

Making Anatomical Gifts

The UAGA authorizes two means for making anatomical gifts directly: will and "donor document." You can also pave the way for a post-mortem donation by your surviving family, by informing them of your approval of anatomical gifts.

Will

The UAGA permits anatomical gifts by will, but really a will is a bad place for the gift. Dead bodies spoil quickly, so time is of the essence for an anatomical gift. A will is often unavailable at death, making it an ineffective way of making anatomical gifts directly.

Donor Document

The best method for making anatomical gifts is in a separate donor document, which is readily available at death. This book has a full-size anatomical donor document in the forms section that you can use for anatomical gifts.

Donor documents are also available in reduced-size versions, which you can carry everywhere. Many organ donor agencies provide wallet-size donor documents. The Michigan Secretary of State used to provide an anatomical gift sticker attachable to the backs of driver's licenses, which was a valid donor document. The new Michigan driver's licenses have printed anatomical gift directions. These aren't valid donor documents (they omit required signing, dating and witnessing information), but they are useful for showing approval of an anatomical gift (see "Family Consent" on page 239 for more about making gifts post-mortem through your survivors).

Whichever donor document you choose, complete the form, selecting which body parts you want to give. In most documents, you may give all body parts, specific body parts, or the whole body (see "What Can Be Given in an Anatomical Gift?" on page 234 for more about these options).

You may also designate a donee. For organ donations, most people don't designate donees, leaving it to attending doctors to decide. With a gift of body, a specific medical school is usually designated as donee (see "Who Can Be a Donee of an Anatomical Gift?" on page 233 for more about the selection of donees).

To finish the anatomical gift, date and sign the donor document before two witnesses. The UAGA doesn't disqualify anyone from serving as witness. Nevertheless, it's a good idea to use mentally capable adults only. If possible, avoid having a designated donee, attending doctors, or anyone else with a direct stake in the anatomical gift, act as witness.

If you're physically (but not mentally) unable to sign the donor document, the UAGA permits signature by proxy. A proxy is someone who does something for you, at your direction. For a proxy signature, ask the proxy, in the presence of the witnesses, to sign the donor document for you. The proxy then signs as follows:

George Edward Frisbie, by Archie Louis Savage, in his presence and at his direction

After witnessing the donor's signature, the witnesses must sign their names on the donor document. The donor should also date the document during signing.

Donor Documents for Gifts of Bodies

A different donation procedure is used for a gift of a whole body to a specific medical school. Medical schools usually require special gift of body forms. These forms contain donation information, transportation and preservation instructions, and consents to release medical records (so the medical school has full information about the donor's medical history).

For a gift of body, complete the medical school's gift of body form and a donor document, which makes the gift legally binding. As a convenience, schools often provide a combined gift of body and donor document form. The medical school may also furnish brochures and other materials about carrying out the gift of body at the time of death.

After You Make an Anatomical Gift

After you make a direct anatomical gift, preferably in a donor document rather than a will, tell your family about the gift. Notice signals the importance you attach to the gift. Knowing this, your survivors are more like likely to consent to the gift after your death.

Another way to give notice is by enrolling in the Michigan Organ and Tissue Donor Registry. This is a confidential database of Michigan residents who have expressed a desire to make anatomical gifts. Hospitals have around-the-clock access to the registry, and can check it quickly after death for approval of an anatomical gift. Your survivors will be informed of your enrollment in the registry, encouraging them to consent to the gift.

You can also put your family on notice by making your donor document accessible after your death. If you made an anatomical gift in a full-size donor document, store the document with your advance directive or other vital documents you keep at home or with your doctor. During your final illness, the donor document can be added to your medical record, and be ready for use. With a reduced-size donor document, simply carry the document with you at all times in your wallet or pocketbook.

One other person should get notice of your anatomical gift: the donee, if you specified one. At minimum, tell the donee that you have made the gift. As described before, medical schools like prior notice because they often need extra forms for whole body gifts. You may also decide to distribute a copy of the donor document to the donee. However, distribution makes amendment or revocation of the document more complicated, as explained below.

Amending or Revoking an Anatomical Gift

Your anatomical gift can become outdated for a number of reasons. You might change your mind about which body parts you want to give, or want to change donees. You may move away, making a gift to a local donee impractical.

If your anatomical gift is outdated, for whatever reason, it needs amendment. Don't try to amend the donor document by adding new material or removing old material. After a donor document is signed, dated, and witnessed, it's complete and mustn't be altered. The best amendment procedure is simply making a new donor document. Afterward, revoke the previous document as described below.

You may decide an anatomical gift needs revocation instead of amendment. The UAGA provides several methods of revocation. If you have delivered the donor document to a specified donee, you may revoke by:

- execution and delivery to the donee of a signed revocation statement
- an oral revocation uttered in the presence of two witnesses and communicated to the donee
- a revocation statement made during a terminal illness or injury, addressed to an attending doctor and communicated to the donee
- a signed revocation on your person or among your effects

> ### TO JOIN
>
> Michigan's Organ and Tissue Donor Registry, contact:
>
> **Gift of Life**
> 2203 Platt Road
> Ann Arbor, MI 48104
>
> Or call (800) 482-4881
>
> Gift of Life provides organ/tissue donor registry enrollment cards.
>
> Any **Michigan Secretary of State** branch office, which also distributes donor registry enrollment cards, and has organ/tissue donation consent stickers which you can attach to the back of your driver's license.

If the donor document hasn't been delivered to the donee, you may revoke by any of the ways listed above. Or you can revoke by destroying or mutilating the donor document.

Family Consent

You can also rely on your family to make an anatomical gift for you. Unlike making a gift directly in a donor document, this method isn't legally binding. But as explained before, hospitals seek survivors' consent for all anatomical gifts anyway, with or without a donor document. Thus, your survivors will normally get a chance to make the gift for you.

The important thing is to signal your wish to make an anatomical gift to family during your lifetime. With this information, your survivors are more likely to consent to the anatomical gift you want to make.

You can communicate your wish orally to your family, which is fine. But it's better to put the wish in writing, especially if it's going to be controversial. A donor document is a good place for this, which also has the advantage of legal authority. But you can also put the wish in other vital documents, accessible at death, such as a letter of instruction. The letter of instruction in this book has a place to state an anatomical gift preference.

Another way to show approval of an anatomical gift is by enrollment in the Michigan Organ and Tissue Donor Registry, described above. The registry was set up specifically for this purpose, and is the most efficient way of giving notice to medical staff and family about your desire to make an anatomical gift.

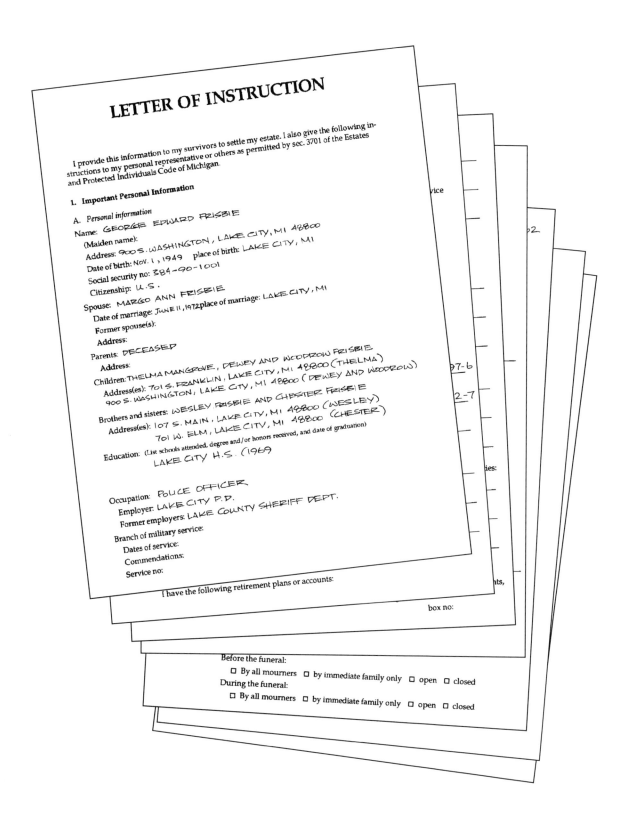

LETTER OF INSTRUCTION

I provide this information to my survivors to settle my estate. I also give the following instructions to my personal representative or others as permitted by sec. 3701 of the Estates and Protected Individuals Code of Michigan.

1. Important Personal Information

A. *Personal information*

Name: GEORGE EDWARD FRISBIE

(Maiden name):

Address: 900 S. WASHINGTON, LAKE CITY, MI 48800

Date of birth: Nov. 1, 1949   place of birth: LAKE CITY, MI

Social security no: 384-90-1001

Citizenship: U.S.

Spouse: MARGO ANN FRISBIE

Date of marriage: JUNE 11, 1972 place of marriage: LAKE CITY, MI

Former spouse(s):

Address:

Parents: DECEASED

Address:

Children: THELMA MANGROVE, DEWEY AND WOODROW FRISBIE

Address(es): 701 S. FRANKLIN, LAKE CITY, MI 48800 (THELMA)

900 S. WASHINGTON, LAKE CITY, MI 48800 (DEWEY AND WOODROW)

Brothers and sisters: WESLEY FRISBIE AND CHESTER FRISBIE

Address(es): 107 S. MAIN, LAKE CITY, MI 48800 (WESLEY)

701 W. ELM, LAKE CITY, MI 48800 (CHESTER)

Education: (List schools attended, degree and/or honors received, and date of graduation)

LAKE CITY H.S. (1969

Occupation: POLICE OFFICER

Employer: LAKE CITY P.D.

Former employers: LAKE COUNTY SHERIFF DEPT.

Branch of military service:

Dates of service:

Commendations:

Service no:

I have the following retirement plans or accounts:

box no:

Before the funeral:
  ☐ By all mourners ☐ by immediate family only ☐ open ☐ closed
During the funeral:
  ☐ By all mourners ☐ by immediate family only ☐ open ☐ closed

ANATOMICAL DONOR DOCUMENT

_____GEORGE EDWARD FRISBIE_____
Print or type name of donor

In the hope that I may help others, I hereby make this anatomical gift if medically acceptable, to take effect upon my death. The words and marks below indicate my desires.

I give:

(a) _X_ any need organs or physical parts

(b) ____ only the following organs or physical parts

_____
Specify organ(s) or physical part(s)

For the purposes of transplantation, therapy, medical research or education:

(c) ____ my body for anatomical study if needed.

Limitations or special wishes, if any: _____

Signed by the donor and the following 2 witnesses in the presence of each other:

_____George Edward Frisbie_____
Signature of donor

_____Nov. 1, 1951_____
Date of birth of donor

_____JAN. 1, 2000_____
Date signed

_____LAKE CITY, MI_____
City and state

_____Margo Ann Frisbie_____
Witness

_____Archie Louis Savage_____
Witness

Chapter 8B
Death Ceremony

Human societies have an incredible variety of customs and rituals. But one thing is constant: All societies treat death with reverence, and have death ceremonies paying respect to the recently deceased. The United States is no different. As a culturally diverse country, America has an enormous variety of ceremonies, such as the Irish wake or Jewish shiva. But three types of death ceremonies prevail: funeral, memorial, and committal.

Funeral

A funeral is a death ceremony held in the presence of the body. The body may be displayed openly or covered in a container. The presence of the body defines a funeral; the body also makes the ceremony more complicated. In fact, a traditional American funeral is carefully choreographed, requiring a number of goods and services:

Transportation of the body. The body must be transported from the place of death to the funeral, and then to the place of final disposition.

Restoration and preservation of the body. If the body is going to be viewed, it must be restored to a presentable appearance. The body is dressed in nice clothes (which the survivors can provide), and cosmetics may be applied. Restoration requires extra effort when the body has been damaged before death or been autopsied.

A funeral adds time between death and final disposition. During this time, the body must be preserved. There are three preservation options:

¶ *Embalming.* With embalming, body fluids are drained from the body and replaced with a preservative, usually formaldehyde. The preservative keeps the body fresh for several days. A special extra-strong preservative is used for gifts of bodies to medical schools, preserving the body for months or even years.

Contrary to what many people believe, embalming is not legally required. When a body is shipped long-distance, embalming may be necessary for preservation. According to the Federal Trade Commission's funeral rule (see below), the funeral director must always obtain consent for embalming.

¶ *Refrigeration.* As an alternative to embalming, the body can be preserved a while by refrigeration. This method is much cheaper than embalming. However, a refrigerated body won't stay fresh as long as an embalmed one, and may not be suitable for every type of viewing.

¶ *Cooling with ice.* Another option is cooling the body with dry ice in a sealed casket. This technique is used most often during interstate shipment of bodies.

Container for the body. During the funeral, the body must be kept in a container. A casket, or coffin, is the customary choice, particularly if the body is going to be viewed.

Caskets come in three main varieties: 1) wood 2) metal (with or without seals) 3) synthetic (plastic or fiberglass). Wooden caskets are both the cheapest and most expensive. Plain wood or composition-material caskets cost as little as a few hundred dollars, while solid-wood ones can be as much as $15,000-20,000. Metal and synthetic caskets fall within that price range. In most funerals, the casket is the single most expensive item, averaging around $2,000, and accounting for around half the cost of the total funeral package.

Critics of the funeral industry complain that funeral operators often make most of their profits from casket sales by marking them up as much as 500%. Funeral operators deny this and say they have affordable caskets at competitive prices.

It's true, funeral operators have competition from a new breed of discount casket sellers, which offer caskets directly to consumers. Michigan

---

MORE INFORMATION

About low-cost burial products and services, obtain:

Dealing Creatively with Death: A Manual of Death Education and Simple Burial, Ernest Morgan, Burnsville, NC: Cello Press, 1988.

Caring for Your Own Dead: A Complete Guide for Those Who Wish to Handle Funeral Arrangements Themselves as a Final Act of Love, Lisa Carlson, Hinesburg, VT: Upper Access Publishers, 1987.

Carlson also operates **Funeral Consumers Alliance**, a consumer's group, at (800) 765-0107, or www.funerals.org.

Michigan has several discount-casket sellers, and there are other national outfits selling on the Internet:

Affordable Casket
18829 Eureka Road
Southgate, MI 48192

Or call (734) 281-7450

Smart Choices
30701 Dequindre
Madison Heights, MI 48071

Or call (248) 616-0800

Direct Casket
At www.directcasket.com

Web Caskets
At www.webcaskets.com

For a do-it-yourself kit for building a casket ($499), contact www.buildacasket.com

has several of these, and there are more national outfits, many selling over the Internet. If you buy from these companies, the funeral home must accept the casket, without tacking on a casket-handling fee, thanks to the FTC funeral rule described on page 246.

Another way to save is by renting a casket. You can rent a fancy casket, and then use a cheaper one for final disposition. Another option is a catafalque, which is a sort of double casket. The fancy outer casket has a trapdoor in which a low-cost synthetic inner liner is inserted. The body is kept inside the casket during the funeral. Afterward, the body and liner are removed for disposal, and the outer casket is reused.

For the budget-minded, casket plans and kits are available for building your own casket. If you choose this option, make sure that the casket is built solidly, or funeral homes or cemeteries may reject it.

Viewing the body. In many funerals, the body is viewed by mourners in what is known as an open-casket funeral. Viewing advocates (who include most funeral directors) argue that viewing the body forces survivors to come to grips with the death, allowing them to overcome grief. Opponents find viewing creepy and usually choose a closed-casket funeral.

A viewing is a matter of personal taste, because almost any body can be restored for viewing. Even bodies damaged by disease, trauma or autopsy, or those with missing organs after organ donations, can be restored to an acceptable appearance.

If you want a viewing, decide whether the viewing should take place before, during, or after the funeral, or at all these times. Typically, the viewing is open to all mourners, but some viewings are reserved for the immediate family only. Whatever you choose, keep in mind that the funeral home must make special arrangements for viewings and provide staff to attend them, adding to the cost of the funeral.

Funeral service. A funeral service, which may be religious or secular, is a ritual marking death. Typically, a speaker makes some personal remarks about the deceased. There may also be music or another type of program during the service.

A funeral service may be held at a funeral home or a place of worship. If the funeral is at a funeral home, there is a charge for use of the home, plus fees for ushers, pallbearers, music, handling flowers, prayer cards, and a gratuity for any religious leader speaking at the service.

One thing available without charge to many veterans is an American flag for draping on a casket during a funeral. After the funeral, the flag is given to the deceased's next of kin or close associate. These burial flags are available at regional VA offices, national cemeteries, or post offices.

Miscellaneous services. Funeral providers often perform other funeral-related services, such as preparation of death notices and obituaries, ordering death certificates, and applying for death benefits.

Funeral Providers

As with final disposition goods and services, funerals are available from several providers:

Funeral home. Funeral homes are by far the largest providers of funerals. There are over 20,000 funeral homes in the U.S. These are typically small owner-operated businesses. But many small funeral homes are being swallowed up by large chains, like Service Corporation International, which owns around 3,800 funeral homes and 300 cemeteries all over the world.

In Michigan, funeral directors are licensed by the Mortuary Science Board, within the Department of Consumer and Industry Services. Since 1984, the funeral industry has also been regulated by the Federal Trade Commission (FTC), under its so-called funeral rule.* The rule requires funeral providers to furnish full and accurate price information before and after purchases. The rule also prohibits deceptive funeral practices, such as providing inaccurate funeral information, tying funeral purchases to each other (such as requiring purchase of casket to receive funeral services), and embalming unnecessarily or without consent.

Memorial society. Memorial societies specialize in offering budget final dispositions. Many also provide funeral goods and services. Memorial societies don't provide funeral products themselves; they contract with funeral homes, which agree to offer low-cost products to society members.

Cemetery. Like memorial societies, cemeteries contract with funeral homes for funeral goods and services, and then provide funeral packages to customers.

Do-it-yourself funeral. Michigan law doesn't give a deceased's survivors much opportunity to hold a funeral without professional help. For example, only licensed funeral directors (or those acting under their control) may transport bodies and obtain burial permits. However, the survivors can organize a funeral service and take care of details that don't require professional supervision.

> ## MORE INFORMATION
>
> About state regulation of the funeral industry, contact:
>
> **Mortuary Science Board**
> At (517) 241-9258
>
> About the federal funeral rule, obtain:
>
> "Funerals: A Consumer Guide" (#362G) for .50, from:
>
> **R. Woods**
> CIC - 00A
> P.O. Box 100
> Pueblo, CO 81002
>
> Or to order with a credit card, call (888) 787-3256
>
> About the benefits of memorial societies, and a directory of these societies in Michigan and nationally, write:
>
> **Funeral and Memorial Societies of America**
> P.O. Box 10
> Hinesburg, VT 05461

---

* Despite its name, the funeral rule covers more than just funerals and funeral homes. The rule applies to anyone, including cemeteries and crematoria, providing both final disposition goods/services and death ceremony services.

Paying for a Funeral

Unless you arrange for prepayment, your funeral bill* is a debt of your estate. During probate, payment of the bill has priority. The estates code says that the bill shall be paid from the estate before payment of all other debts, except the probate costs themselves.

Whenever possible, try to keep the funeral bill as an estate debt, and have money in the estate to pay the bill. For reasons explained later (see "Giving Instructions for Death Ceremonies" below), the person appointed as personal representative in the will should make the funeral arrangements. The appointee should sign the funeral contract in a representative capacity, as follows:

Margo Frisbie, as appointed personal representative for the estate of George Frisbie

By signing this way, instead of personally, the funeral bill remains a debt of the estate. What's more, the personal representative won't be personally liable for the bill if the estate can't pay.

Naturally, funeral directors are aware of this risk, and often ask the personal representative or other survivors to cosign the funeral contract, guaranteeing payment. No one is legally obliged to cosign a funeral bill. But if survivors do cosign, they must realize that they are personally liable for the bill, so there is no misunderstanding later.

Luckily, cosigners have some protection from liability. As mentioned before, payment of a funeral bill (or the claim of someone who has paid it) has top priority during probate. Thus, cosigners are apt to get something back, if only partial reimbursement. In addition, funeral bill payers have special rights during distribution of small estates.

All these problems can be avoided by having liquid (cash or near-cash) assets in the estate for payment of the funeral bill. You can simply leave an estate with sufficient liquid assets to pay the bill. Or you can use life insurance or retirement plan death benefits for this purpose (see "Life Insurance and the Estate Plan" on page 195 for more about this technique). Special benefits, such as veterans, social security, and worker's compensation death benefits, are also available to pay a funeral bill.

Prepayment of funeral expenses is another option. Cemeteries developed prepaid or "preneed" funeral and burial plans in the 1970s, and then funeral homes began pushing them. This sales effort has paid off, as an estimated 25% of people now have some sort of prepaid funeral plan.

Prepayment plans provide a funeral (and/or final disposition) package, with a means of paying for the package at the time of death. The most popular payment methods are trusts and life insurance policies. Typically, the plan participant sets aside money in a trust or life insurance policy equal to the cost of the funeral package. At the participant's death, the

---

* The costs of final disposition are treated the same as the funeral bill, so information in this section also applies to final disposition expenses.

MORE INFORMATION

Michigan's Prepaid Funeral Contract Funding Act regulates prepayment contracts through the:

Funeral Prepaid Contract Office
P.O. Box 30004
Lansing, MI 48907
Or call (517) 241-9236

trust or life insurance proceeds are paid to the funeral home, covering the cost of the funeral.

Like any investment, there are good prepayment plans and bad ones. Some financial experts believe that you are better off avoiding these entirely, and recommend investing money earmarked for a funeral yourself. On the other hand, Americans are not very good savers, and many need the discipline that a formal contract like a prepayment plan imposes.

If you choose prepayment, look for a plan that offers inflation protection (against increases in the cost of the funeral), portability (the right to transfer the plan to the place of death, if you move), with some cancellation rights should you change your funeral plans.

Memorial

A memorial is a death ceremony without the body. The ceremony, which may be religious or secular, is usually devoted to remembering the deceased, with a eulogy or other personal remarks. There may also be music or another kind of program.

A memorial is customarily held after final disposition of the body, usually within a week or so after death. A memorial may be held along with a funeral, or it may replace the funeral and be the primary death ceremony. In fact, as families and friends become more far-flung, making funerals difficult to organize on short notice, memorials are replacing more and more funerals.

Memorial Providers

A memorial may be organized by a funeral home, a memorial society, or the survivors themselves. Since the body isn't present, the need for a professional organizer like a funeral home or memorial society is less. Thus, the survivors may assume the responsibility of holding a memorial at a place of worship or somewhere else. Nevertheless, funeral homes and memorial societies offer memorial services for a fee.

Committal

A committal is a death ceremony during final disposition of the body. A committal is usually brief, and often religious in nature. Examples include a graveside ceremony during burial of a body and rites during burial or scattering of cremated remains.

A committal often complements a funeral or other death ceremonies. If so, it may be organized by a funeral home, a memorial society, or whoever else is handling the main death ceremony, and be included in the total package.

Survivors of veterans sometimes want to have a military honor guard, with riflemen or a bugler, at committals. Local military bases or veterans groups used to provide volunteers for these honors.

> ### TO OBTAIN
>
> A military honor guard for the committal of eligible veterans, contact funeral directors who have access to a toll-free telephone number at the Department of Defense, which assigns the honor guard.

But a new federal law provides military honors at committals of eligible veterans, which include: 1) a two-man honor guard, one of whom must be a member of the deceased's service branch 2) folding and presentation of the American flag draped on the casket to the next of kin or a close associate of the deceased 3) live or recorded performance of "Taps."

Giving Instructions for Death Ceremonies

Death ceremonies are closely linked to final disposition of the deceased's body. The two may overlap, such as a committal during a burial. The choice of a method of final disposition may also influence the death ceremony. For example, direct disposition, where the body is disposed of quickly after death, may not leave time for a funeral.

There are other links between death ceremonies and final disposition. As described in "Final Disposition Instructions" on page 234, there are rules to determine which survivors decide about final disposition, with or without instructions from the deceased.

Many of these rules also apply to death ceremonies. Your survivors (spouse, next of kin, personal representative) have the authority to decide on death ceremonies according to your wishes, their own tastes and the public interest. You have the right to give death ceremony instructions. These instructions aren't legally binding on your survivors, but they are beneficial in providing guidance to survivors and death ceremony providers alike.

Letter of Instruction

In older wills, you sometimes encounter funeral instructions. But wills are a bad place for death ceremony instructions because wills are often unavailable during the death ceremony. The best place for death ceremony instructions is a letter of instruction. This is an informal document, with final disposition instructions, death ceremony instructions, and other important postmortem information, which is readily available at death.

In a letter of instruction, you can give directions about any part of the death ceremonies. You may request a funeral, memorial, committal, some combination of these, or something else. You can specify the form the death ceremonies take. Or you can forbid things. For example, some people consider viewing the body in an open-casket funeral distasteful, and may prohibit this.

When you give death ceremony instructions, keep in mind the difficulty of giving detailed instructions far in advance of death. Detailed instructions may become outdated with time. As a general rule, add more detail the older and/or sicker you are. Young people or those in good health should limit themselves to general instructions.

Your death ceremony instructions should also be coordinated with your final disposition instructions within the letter of instruction. As explained before, both issues are tied together, and the choice of a method of final disposition may affect the death ceremony. Make sure they are compatible.

See "Giving Burial and Cremation Instructions" on page 235 for complete information about preparing, distributing, amending and revoking letters of instruction.

Chapter 9 Durable Power of Attorney

As mentioned in Chapter 1, incapacity—whether mental or physical—is a greater threat than death for everyone, even the elderly. When incapacity strikes, the victim typically needs help managing financial affairs and making health care decisions.

Despite the gravity of the problem, the law offered few satisfactory financial management options. Conservatorships, protective arrangements, representative payeeships, etc., (see below for a complete list), were available. Yet most of these devices required expensive and time-consuming court procedures or had other drawbacks.

One promising alternative was a power of attorney. A power of attorney is based on the legal concept of agency. In an agency, a person known as the principal, appoints another, the agent or attorney,* to act on his/her behalf. A power of attorney is a document creating or confirming an agency.

Estate planners quickly grasped that a power of attorney could be used to appoint an agent to manage one's financial affairs after incapacity. The trouble was, agencies normally ceased with the onset of mental incapacity, since the law assumed that a mentally incapacitated principal couldn't supervise an agent. Thus, an estate planning power of attorney would often fail exactly when it was needed the most.

Many European countries also had powers of attorney, but with an important difference. In these countries, a principal could make a power

---

* An agent is the same as an attorney (technically an attorney-in-fact). An attorney-at-law is simply one type of agent, who is also a lawyer and does legal work for the principal.

durable, so that it lasted during the principal's incapacity. Virginia was the first state to borrow the durability idea from Europe, followed by all the other states. Michigan enacted its first durable power of attorney law in 1976. It was replaced by a more comprehensive law in 1979, which remains in effect today.

Types of Durable Powers of Attorney

There are many types of durable and nondurable powers of attorney in Michigan. For example, people often use limited-purpose powers of attorney in real estate transactions. Michigan also has a special power of attorney for health care, called a patient advocate designation (PAD), which is covered extensively in the next chapter.

But for financial management, there are two main kinds of durable powers of attorney (DPAs): immediate and springing. Both powers are durable. Each may give broad powers to the agent to manage the financial affairs of the principal. But there is an important difference when the powers take effect.

Immediate power of attorney. An immediate DPA is effective immediately, when you sign it. The agent's powers begin at signing and s/he can make financial decisions for you then. An immediate DPA is designed for someone who needs financial management help right away or in the near future.

> *Example:* Margo's mother has broken her hip and become frail. She's having trouble managing her property, so she makes an immediate DPA.

> *Example:* George is a member of the National Guard, and his unit is called into active duty for an indefinite period of time. He makes an immediate DPA before his unit leaves.

> *Example:* Grover knows that he will be incapacitated for a while after major surgery. He makes an immediate DPA before entering the hospital.

Springing power of attorney. A springing DPA doesn't give the agent any power unless and until the principal becomes incapacitated. At that point, the DPA springs into effect, activating the agent's powers. The trigger for a springing DPA is the incapacity or disability* of the principal, when the principal is unable to manage his/her personal affairs. Disability is an informal concept, which a doctor can certify without a court order.

---

* Michigan's power of attorney law uses "disability" while this book prefers "incapacity," but the two terms are basically the same. However, the power of attorney forms in this book use disability to keep in step with the law.

> *Example:* George and Margo are in good health, but they worry about incapacity as they get older. They make springing DPAs now, naming each other as agent. Later, George has a serious stroke. His doctor certifies that he is disabled, and his DPA goes into effect with Margo as agent.

Estate Planning with a Durable Power of Attorney

Besides powers of attorney, there are other ways to manage the financial affairs of an incapacitated person. Some of these are court-ordered and some are private, out-of-court arrangements.

Conservatorship. A court can appoint a conservator to manage the financial affairs of an incapacitated person. The conservator takes full or partial control of the person's property and manages it under court supervision.

Protective arrangement. Instead of a full-fledged conservatorship, a court can set up a protective arrangement for an incapacitated person. The protective arrangement handles only one or two tasks for the person, leaving him/her responsible for the rest of his/her affairs.

Representative payeeship. Several state and federal public benefit programs allow payment of benefits to a representative payee, who manages the money for the benefit of an incapacitated beneficiary. The following programs have representative payee arrangements for their benefits: 1) Civil Service (federal) 2) Veterans Administration 3) Railroad Retirement Board 4) Social Security Administration 5) Michigan Family Independence Agency.

Living trust. You can create a living (*inter vivos*) trust, put all your property in the trust, and name yourself as sole beneficiary. If you become incapacitated later, a trustee can take over and manage the trust property for you as beneficiary. This arrangement is akin to a conservatorship, but without court intervention.

Joint ownership of property. Owning property jointly offers some protection from incapacity. If a joint owner becomes incapacitated, the healthy joint owner(s) can manage the property while the joint property lasts.

Miscellaneous. Financial institutions offer services such as direct deposit of checks and automatic bill-paying which incapacitated people can use for financial management purposes.

This is an impressive list. But compared to DPAs, all the listed items fall short.

Conservatorships and protective arrangements must be set up by court order. With a court in the picture, there are inevitable costs of time, money and loss of privacy. A DPA, by contrast, is a private arrangement between you and your agent. As such, it's easy and cheap to create. A DPA also guarantees maximum privacy, since there's nothing to file with a court or other public agency.

Many of the other devices spell a loss of control over your financial affairs. In a conservatorship or protective arrangement, the court takes firm control of your financial affairs by appointing a legal representative for you and supervising his/her activities. In fact, it's often said that a conservatorship with a guardianship (the two often go together) is the most severe loss of personal rights allowed by law; even imprisoned criminals keep more rights!

Joint property and a living trust also result in a loss of control, but in a more subtle way. With both devices, you give up some ownership of your property for the sake of security. The loss of control with joint property is plain: You must now share property you once owned yourself. Your new co-owners can now exert control over the property, and may even sell it. In a living trust, the transfer of property to the trust is mostly a paper transaction, allowing you to keep more control. Even so, you must surrender legal ownership of all trust property.

In a DPA, you retain far more control over your financial affairs, without a loss of security. To begin with, you get to handpick your agent and the substitute who steps in if the first choice is unable to serve. The law of agency imposes a number of fiduciary duties (duties of loyalty, obedience, to account for funds, etc.), guaranteeing that the agent acts in your best interests. (Many of these duties also apply to conservators and trustees, who like agents are also fiduciaries.)

With a DPA, you can regulate the agent's power, giving him/her as much power as you're comfortable with, but no more. You also have ultimate control over the agent since a DPA is revocable at any time. If you're ever dissatisfied with the agent, you can appoint a new agent or simply cancel the whole arrangement.

And above all, you never lose ownership of your property with a DPA. No matter how long the power of attorney lasts, or how much power you give your agent, you keep full ownership of all your property.

Few of the other devices match the scope of a DPA. A protective arrangement is normally a temporary remedy, good for solving one problem. A representative payeeship covers a single benefit program. Joint ownership provides limited protection for the joint property only.

All in all, when you consider informality, privacy, degree of control and scope, DPAs are the best choice for planning against incapacity.

Although DPAs are easy to make, there some firm rules about who can become a principal and make one, and who can serve as agent.

Who Can Be a Principal?

Age and Mental Capacity

Either adults (persons 18 years of age or older) or minors (persons under the age of 18) may become principals and make DPAs. Regardless of age, a principal must have the proper mental capacity to make a power of attorney. The principal must be able to give consent to having an agent act for him/her. This is a very low threshold of competency, lower than the mental capacity to sign a contract or the sound mind required for a will.

You must have mental capacity at the moment you make your power of attorney. Spells of incapacity before or after execution of a power of attorney aren't significant.

Example: George suffers a serious stroke. For several days he is confined to an intensive care ward where he is under heavy sedation and semi-conscious. He recovers his senses and makes a DPA. Before long, George has another stroke and becomes physically and mentally incapacitated. Despite his spells of incapacity, the power of attorney is valid because it was made during a period of mental capacity.

Undue Influence, Duress and Fraud

Besides mental capacity, you must make your DPA free of undue influence, duress and fraud. A power of attorney is a voluntary arrangement. If someone has influenced you to the extent the power of attorney is not your free choice, undue influence exists. Undue influence usually comes from those you trust, such as relatives, friends or advisers. Duress is like undue influence, but with duress you are actually forced (usually by physical force or the threat of it) to make the power of attorney. A fraudulent power of attorney is one based on a misrepresentation (falsification) of a fact that you relied on in making the instrument. A DPA tainted by undue influence, duress or fraud is normally invalid.

Residence

You should be a resident of Michigan when you make a Michigan DPA. The residency requirements for powers of attorney are murky. But to be on the safe side, it's best to be a resident of the state where you make a power of attorney.

After you make a Michigan DPA, it should be accepted out of state. States typically recognize out-of-state documents if they are legal in the states where they were made. To increase acceptance in another state, the power of attorney itself has a provision authorizing out-of-state use.

Nevertheless, it still may be necessary to make a new DPA when you move out of state. As mentioned earlier, all states now have DPA laws, but they differ a great deal. For example, not every state permits springing powers of attorney, and you might have difficulty using one in another state. Whenever you move to another state, it's smart to review your DPA and see whether it satisfies local law. If not, you shouldn't hesitate to make a new DPA in that state.

Who Can Be an Agent?

There are few restrictions on who can serve as agent under a power of attorney. As a matter of fact, almost any person or organization is legally eligible to become an agent.

Despite this flexibility, the DPA in this book isn't designed to have an organization as agent. For one thing, the DPA gives agents very broad powers. You might be uncomfortable about giving a bank or other organization that much power. And organizations themselves may hesitate at serving as agent under the power of attorney. Agents can be compensated for the work they do. But the DPA in this book withholds compensation (except reimbursement for out-of-pocket expenses) to conserve your property. This fact alone would probably discourage most organizations from serving as your agent.

There is one kind of organization that might make a suitable agent: a qualified nonprofit corporation, such as a religious, charitable or social welfare organization. You can usually trust these organizations to exercise the broad powers the DPA gives. And as not-for-profits, with independent sources of funding, these organizations don't mind serving without compensation.

Practically anybody can become an agent. It's even possible for minors or mentally incapacitated persons to serve as agents. Needless to say, these individuals are poor choices since they usually lack the maturity or judgment to handle financial matters. Thus, limit your choice to mentally capable adults. As you make your selection, look for these practical qualities:

Financial decision-making. Since your agent will be managing your financial affairs, the agent must be able to make sound financial decisions for you.

¶ *Honesty.* Above all else, your agent must be honest. An agent handles your finances with little supervision. A dishonest agent can do considerable harm before detection and removal, making honesty a necessity.

¶ *Good financial judgment.* In most cases, good financial judgment simply means common sense. But if your financial affairs are difficult to manage, special skills might be necessary. For example, if you own a small business, your agent must know how to manage it.

Capacity to help. Your agent must have the time and inclination to give close attention to your financial affairs.

¶ *Commitment.* Like other agencies, a DPA agency is strictly voluntary; the agent can refuse to serve, or quit anytime after beginning to serve. To prevent this, always ask agent-candidates whether they are willing to serve before you appoint them. By getting prior consent, you reduce the chance they will fail to serve later.

¶ *Health and stability.* Some candidates, such as older people, may seem like good choices now, but will they be around when you need them?

Location. Michigan law doesn't disqualify nonresident agents, so your agent can be someone who lives outside Michigan. Nevertheless, a DPA gives your agent many duties, which a nonresident might have difficulty carrying out from far away. As a result, it's usually better to stick with someone who lives near you in Michigan.

Combining agent and patient advocate role. When you're making a health care power of attorney (a patient advocate designation (PAD) in Michigan) along with a DPA, consider selecting the same person as patient advocate (in the PAD) and agent (in the DPA). If you name different persons, the patient advocate must apply constantly to the agent for money to pay for your health care. By naming the same person as patient advocate and agent, the patient advocate can make health care decisions and pay for the care. On the other hand, you might not like such coziness, and may want to divide these responsibilities between two people.

As you select your agent, don't forget your spouse or other relatives. Spouses often make excellent agents since they're usually honest, willing and available. Your spouse may also be a suitable choice because s/he may have a stake in managing your affairs. The spouse usually stands to get the bulk of your property after death through inheritance or your will. S/he may already be a co-owner of much of that property if you have joint property, as most spouses do. All this gives your spouse the incentive to manage your financial affairs well. Other relatives may share similar qualifications and incentives.

Spouses and relatives may also be willing to serve as agents without compensation. As mentioned above, the DPA in this book doesn't pay agents, except reimbursement of out-of-pocket expenses. This lack of compensation could discourage nonrelatives from serving as your agent. Yet it shouldn't bother your spouse or other relatives, who will usually act without compensation.

Your relatives also have an edge when it comes to tax matters. The Internal Revenue Service (IRS) has its own rules about powers of attorney, and who can use them for federal tax purposes (see "Other Power of

Attorney Forms" on page 263 for more about this). According to IRS rules, your agent must be either a professional (lawyer, certified public accountant, etc.) or a relative (spouse, parent, child, brother or sister) before s/he can handle your federal tax matters. This restriction may be another reason to select a spouse or other close relative as your agent.

Despite the advantages of selecting relatives as agents, be careful when you appoint them because your relatives may exert influence as you make a DPA. If this influence becomes excessive, the power of attorney could be marred by undue influence. It's interesting to note that very few court decisions regarding powers of attorney have been reported. But the ones that have often concern undue influence—usually from close relatives.

After you review your candidates, select two agents: a first choice and a successor. The first choice will probably become your agent. But if the first choice fails to serve, the successor can take over. In that case, the successor agent receives all the powers the first choice would have had.

One thing you can't do with the DPA in this book is appoint a group of agents to act collectively. Collective agencies take several guises, including joint or split agencies. With a joint agency, two or more co-agents share the powers given in the power of attorney. In a split agency, the co-agents are assigned separate powers or duties which they perform independently of each other.

Collective agencies are legally permissible, but they can be more trouble than they are worth. When one agent is unable or unwilling to serve, there may be doubt about whether the other(s) can act without him/her. Worst of all, co-agents may disagree about decisions. Sometimes these kinds of problems can wind up in court, which is the very thing a power of attorney is designed to avoid.

Making a Durable Power of Attorney

For many, making a DPA is unpleasant because it confronts them with the possibility of physical or mental incapacity. Maybe that's why some people delay making powers of attorney until they are close to mental incapacity or actually suffering from physical incapacity.

If you wait that long, you may have to rely on friends or relatives to help you make your DPA. There isn't anything necessarily wrong with relatives or others helping out, but there are risks. If there are doubts about your mental capacity, these must be answered because you must have mental capacity to make a power of attorney.

Your relatives can assist you while you make your DPA—by providing the forms and information to fill them out—but the instrument must be entirely your own. You must want to make the power of attorney and choose all its provisions. Otherwise, the power of attorney could be tainted by undue influence, duress, or fraud.

When you make your DPA, complete the form by printing or typing. If you print, use a pen, instead of a pencil, to make a permanent document.

This prevents someone from altering the document later.

Begin with the introductory paragraph of the DPA, and insert your name and address as the principal. Place the name and address of your agent in paragraph #1. Just below that, put the name and address of the successor agent.

In paragraph #2, you must chose which type of DPA you want: 1) an immediate DPA effective right away 2) a springing DPA which lies dormant until you become incapacitated (disabled). Place your initials on the line in #2A to choose an immediate DPA; do the same in #2B for a springing DPA.

If you make a springing DPA, you can name a particular physician, such as your personal physician, to determine your incapacity (disability). To designate a physician, insert the physician's name on the line below paragraph #2B.

Most people want their agents to handle all financial affairs, so paragraph #3 of the DPA gives agents broad financial powers. You can modify these standard powers to fit your own situation. Subparagraph #3(n) has a space to add extra powers. Or you can limit the agent's powers in several ways. If you want to take away any of the standard powers given in subparagraphs #3(a)-(m), simply strike out the subparagraph containing the power you wish to remove. Paragraph #4 places some standard restrictions on the agent's powers, but you can add others at the end of this paragraph.

Executing a Durable Power of Attorney

Michigan law has few execution requirements for DPAs. Nevertheless, putting the power of attorney in official-like form aids acceptance of the document by third parties, which is important. At a minimum, you should do the following to execute the DPA:

Dating.   When you sign the power of attorney, insert the date in the space provided.

Signing.   You must sign the power of attorney near the end, above the line marked "principal." If you are unable to sign easily because of a physical problem, you can scrawl your signature or even use a mark, such as an X. Your agent doesn't have to sign the power of attorney anywhere to show that s/he accepts your appointment. Instead, the agent accepts by exercising the powers you have given.

Witnessing.   As you sign, your signature should be witnessed by two mentally capable adults. Whenever possible, your agent shouldn't serve as a witness because his/her presence might create a suspicion of undue influence, duress or fraud. After witnessing, the two witnesses must sign their names in the spaces provided.

Transferring Real Property

Dating, signing and witnessing your DPA should be enough for the management of personal property. But if you want your agent to be able to transfer* real property, you must do two extra things to your DPA: 1) add legal descriptions of your real property 2) put the power of attorney in recordable form so a register of deeds will accept the document for recording.

By including legal descriptions of real property in your DPA, the document shows that your agent has the power to transfer that particular property for you. And later, after the power of attorney is recorded by the register of deeds, there will be a public record of this fact. Title insurance companies in particular require such proof in order to insure title to the property. Without title insurance, your agent probably won't be able to transfer the property.

Everybody knows the street address of their real property, but they might not be familiar with the legal description. A legal description is the official description appearing in deeds, land contracts, mortgages, abstracts of title, title insurance policies, etc. Legal descriptions of urban property are often quite brief. In rural areas, legal descriptions are apt to be longer, often filling up a half-page or more.

It's possible to put these legal descriptions inside a power of attorney itself. But this would be difficult when the descriptions are long. Besides, you would have to revise your power of attorney constantly to add and remove legal descriptions as you buy and sell property.

Instead, the DPA permits the attachment of legal descriptions. Subparagraph #3(a) authorizes attachments, and special attachment forms are included in the form section of this book. To use this method, insert the legal descriptions of all the real property you own on an attachment and staple it to DPA. Your agent will then be able to transfer any of this property later.

As you acquire new property, add the legal descriptions of the new property to the attachment. Conversely, if you dispose of property described in the attachment, simply strike it out. The DPA permits this sort of revision, saying that attachments "may be revised from time to time."

In preparing an attachment, don't try to recopy a legal description onto the attachment, unless it's very brief. Legal descriptions are notoriously difficult to copy, and you don't want to make mistakes. An easier way is to use a cut-and-paste method. Photocopy the legal description from a document, such as a deed, land contract, mortgage, abstract of title, title insurance policy, etc., containing an accurate legal description of the property. Cut out the photocopied legal description and paste it onto the attachment (if you have several, do the same for each one). Then make a final photocopy of the pasted-up attachment and use this as the attachment to your durable power of attorney. If you can't fit all the legal descriptions into one attachment, add extras as needed.

---

* Transfer includes selling, conveying (deeding), giving, mortgaging, optioning, or other disposition of property.

After you prepare the attachment, put your DPA in recordable form so a register of deeds will accept it for recording. To be recordable in Michigan, a power of attorney must satisfy the following requirements:

Dating. When you sign the power of attorney, insert the date in the space provided.

Signing. You must sign the power of attorney near the end, above the line marked "principal." If you are unable to sign easily because of a physical problem, you can scrawl your signature or even use a mark such as an X. Your agent doesn't have to sign the power of attorney anywhere to show that s/he accepts your appointment. Instead, the agent accepts by exercising the powers you have given.

Witnessing. As you sign, your signature must be witnessed by two mentally capable adults. Whenever possible, your agent shouldn't serve as a witness because his/her presence might create a suspicion of undue influence, duress or fraud. After witnessing, the two witnesses must sign their names in the spaces provided.

Notarizing. After you sign, the power of attorney must be notarized. The notary public (who, incidentally, can also serve as one of the witnesses) will have you: 1) identify yourself and your signature 2) acknowledge that you signed voluntarily and without duress. The notary will then complete the acknowledgment section. If you plan to use the power of attorney out of state, you should also have the notary affix a seal or certificate to the document, since this aids out-of-state acceptance.

Miscellaneous. The power of attorney must also satisfy a few other recording requirements. The addresses of you and your agent must appear in the document, so don't forget to include them in the introductory paragraph. The person who prepared the power of attorney (you or possibly someone else) must be identified by name and address in the space below the prepared-by-notation. And the names of you, the witnesses and notary public must be typed or printed below their signatures in exactly the same form as the signatures appear.

All recorded documents must have a 2 ½" blank space at the top of the document for insertion of official information. That's why the DPA in this book has a large top margin. Below this margin, the first printed line must identify the nature of the document, in this case a durable power of attorney.

After you put your durable power of attorney in recordable form, it's ready for recording with the register of deeds whenever your agent transfers real property. During a transfer, the instrument can be recorded with the register of deeds of the county where the property is located. A recording fee will be charged according to the number of pages in the document. You should also give the register of deeds a note indicating where you want it returned after recording.

Using a Durable Power of Attorney

A DPA is only as good as its acceptance by third parties—financial institutions, government agencies, real estate agents, retirement plans, insurance companies, etc.—dealing with the agent. Without their acceptance, the power of attorney is worthless.

The DPA tries to aid acceptance in several ways. Paragraph #6 says that third parties can rely on the power of attorney, generally without liability. Putting the power of attorney in official-like or recordable form also helps. But you can increase acceptability of the instrument even more by distributing copies to third parties. That way, the third parties will be familiar with the power of attorney before your agent uses it.

If you have made an immediate DPA, distribute copies to some third parties without delay. Make several photocopies of the document and give them to third parties your agent is likely to deal with. They can keep the copies for their records as proof that the agent can act for you.

With a springing DPA, the method of distribution is different. The power of attorney may be dormant for years, so distribute it to few third parties now. The physician who certifies your disability (incapacity) should get a copy. Otherwise, store the original DPA in a safe place, with your vital papers at home or in a safe deposit box at a financial institution.*

Later, if you become disabled, the springing DPA can be removed from storage and the physician can complete the physician's statement certifying your disability. Then, the document can be photocopied and distributed to the third parties your agent will deal with.

Besides third parties, your agent should get a copy of the durable power of attorney. In most cases, the agent can use copies of the power of attorney. Paragraph #7 says that photocopies of the documents have the same legal authority as the original. Thanks to this provision, you should be able to keep the original document while the agent uses photocopies.

Nevertheless, there may be situations in which your agent needs the original DPA. Some third parties might not deal with the agent unless s/he has the original. Likewise, the agent will need the original power of attorney during the transfer of real property because the register of deeds requires original documents for recording. In either case, you shouldn't hesitate to give the original power of attorney to your agent whenever necessary.

However you distribute your DPA, don't put too many copies into circulation. As explained later, when you revoke the power of attorney, you must give notice of this fact to all third parties who have dealt with your agent. You should also follow up the revocation by retrieving and destroying any copies of the power of attorney third parties have. All this may be

---

* If you use a safe deposit box, make sure that others have access to the box. For this reason, you may want to lease the box jointly with your spouse or others. See "Safe Deposit Boxes" on page 188 for more about joint boxes.

difficult if you have distributed the power of attorney widely. Thus, it's better to distribute your DPA to only a few key third parties.

Other Power of Attorney Forms

Despite all you have done to make your DPA acceptable, you may still encounter third parties who stubbornly refuse to accept the instrument.

Years ago, when Michigan's durable power of attorney law was new, financial institutions often rejected other powers of attorney in favor of their own forms. But as they have become familiar with the law, most financial institutions now accept other forms without hesitation. If they don't, use their form to give your agent the power to conduct business with them.

> **TO OBTAIN**
>
> The IRS power of attorney form, ask for Power of Attorney and Declaration of Representative (Form 2848), and explanatory pamphlet, "Practice Before the IRS and Power of Attorney" (Pub. 947), at any IRS office, or call the IRS forms center at (800) 827-3676.

The IRS also has its own power of attorney form for federal tax matters: the Power of Attorney and Declaration of Representative (Form 2848). You can use other powers of attorney, but they must satisfy IRS requirements. According to IRS rules, a power of attorney must give the agent powers to deal with specific taxes (estate, gift, income, etc.), and returns (706, 709, 1040, etc.), for particular tax periods (which cannot exceed three years in the future). And even when your power of attorney follows these rules, you must still file a Power of Attorney and Declaration of Representative, with the Declaration of Representative section completed, to show that your agent is qualified to act.*

With this in mind, it's usually easier to use the IRS form than adapt other powers of attorney to IRS requirements. The IRS form with instructions is included in the forms section of this book. If you're able, you can prepare the Power of Attorney section yourself, have your agent complete the Declaration of Representative section, and use this as your power of attorney for federal tax purposes.

But if you've become incapacitated, your agent can use the broad tax powers given in subparagraph #3(g) of the DPA to make a Power of Attorney and Declaration of Representative for you. The agent must complete both sections of the form. Then the agent must file the form with the IRS along with two attachments: 1) a copy of your durable power of attorney 2) a statement from the agent (signed under penalty of perjury) that the power of attorney is valid under Michigan law.

Like the IRS, the Michigan Department of Treasury has its own power of attorney form for state tax matters: Power of Attorney Authorization (Form 151). State rules are more liberal than federal ones, and the state will accept any valid durable power of attorney with tax powers.

---

* As mentioned in "Who Can Be an Agent?" on page 256, the IRS limits the choice of agents to professionals or close relatives (spouse, parent, child, brother or sister).

Terminating a Durable Power of Attorney

Because powers of attorney are voluntary arrangements, you may revoke your DPA, and end the powers of your agent, anytime you wish. But just as you need mental capacity to make a power of attorney, you must have mental capacity to revoke it. If you have become mentally incapacitated, you cannot revoke the power of attorney. Instead, a court must appoint a conservator for you, and the conservator can revoke the power of attorney on your behalf.

> *Example:* George makes a DPA appointing his friend Stanley as his agent. Later, he becomes mentally incapacitated and Stanley begins using the power of attorney. George's family believes that Stanley is abusing the power of attorney and squandering his property. They want to have the power of attorney revoked. But to do this, they have to petition a court and get a conservator appointed for George. His conservator can then revoke the power of attorney for him.

As long as you remain mentally capable, revoking your DPA is easy. The best way to revoke is in writing, using the revocation of power of attorney contained in the forms section of this book.

Ordinarily, you can just prepare, date and sign the revocation of power of attorney (it doesn't need to be witnessed or notarized). You may have to do more if you recorded your DPA with the register of deeds. Michigan law says that a recorded power of attorney isn't revoked until the revocation is also recorded.

When you want to revoke a recorded DPA, prepare a revocation of power of attorney (the information about when and where your power of attorney was recorded will be stamped on the document). You must also put the revocation in recordable form (see "Making a Durable Power of Attorney" on page 258 for a list of recording requirements). Afterward, record the revocation of power of attorney in the register of deeds office where your DPA was recorded.

Whenever you revoke a DPA, it's vital to give notice of the revocation to your agent and any third parties with whom your agent has dealt. Until this notice, your agent can sometimes still deal with these third parties. Therefore, give notice of revocation immediately after revocation.

To give the agent notice, deliver a copy of the revocation of power of attorney to the agent personally. If that's inconvenient, send a copy of the revocation to the agent by certified mail, return receipt requested. The receipt proves that the agent got the revocation. Likewise, deliver or send copies of the revocation to the third parties who have dealt with the agent.

After you revoke your DPA, destroy the original document and as many copies as you can get back from third parties (but keep a copy marked "canceled" for your records). Destroying the power of attorney leaves absolutely no doubt that you intend to revoke the instrument. Destruction also makes it impossible for someone to get the document and attempt to exercise it against your will.

Another way to revoke your DPA is to make a new one. The introductory paragraph says that, by making the instrument, you intend to revoke any DPA you have made. Thanks to this provision, the last DPA you make is the one that's effective. Nevertheless, it's also a good idea to destroy any prior DPAs (and all copies except yours) for the reasons described above.

Besides revocation, there are several other ways a DPA can terminate:

Death. The power of attorney ends around the time of your death. The power of attorney can actually survive you a while, because it remains in effect until your agent and/or third parties find out about your death. But when they do, the power of attorney ends immediately.

Recovery from disability. If you made a springing DPA, which went into effect during your disability (incapacity), your recovery from disability terminates it. According to paragraph #2, a physician can certify recovery in the same manner your initial disability was certified.* This certification ends the power of attorney immediately.

Loss of agents. The power of attorney terminates when your agent dies or quits, and the successor agent is also unable to serve.

Expiration. A power of attorney can expire on a particular date or after a specified period of time. Neither power of attorney in this book has an expiration provision because you can seldom foresee how long you will need the power of attorney.

Revising a Durable Power of Attorney

After you make your DPA, review it periodically to see whether revision is necessary. For example, you may want to change some of the powers given to your agent. You may even want to change agents.

You will almost certainly want to appoint a new agent when your spouse is your agent, and you have divorced, had your marriage annulled or are legally separated. Michigan's health care power of attorney law says that these events automatically revoke appointment of a spouse as agent under a patient advocate designation (PAD). But Michigan law doesn't do the same for DPAs. So unless you want your ex-spouse to remain as your agent, you must revise the DPA yourself.

When you want to revise, don't make revisions by scratching out parts of the power of attorney and/or writing in new ones. After a DPA has been made, it's complete and shouldn't be altered. There are ways to amend the instrument, but amendment is a lot of bother. The best way to revise your DPA is to start over and make a new one.

---

* When a physician certifies your recovery from disability, s/he must make the certification in a separate document because the DPA's physician's statement doesn't have space for the certification.

DURABLE POWER OF ATTORNEY

I _GEORGE EDWARD FRISBIE_____ the principal

of _900 S. WASHINGTON, LAKE CITY, MI 48800_____

make this power of attorney according to sections 5501-5505 of the Estates and Protected Individuals Code of Michigan. I also revoke prior powers of attorney I have made dealing with my financial affairs as described below.

1. Appointment of Agent. I appoint as my agent

_MARGO ANN FRISBIE_____

of _900 S. WASHINGTON, LAKE CITY, MI 48800_____

If that person fails, for any reason, to serve as my agent, I appoint as successor agent _CHESTER DEAN FRISBIE_____

of _701 W. ELM, LAKE CITY, MI 48800_____

2. Duration. Choose one of the following sections (A or B), by writing your initials before your choice.

A. _____ (*Immediate powers*) This power of attorney shall take effect when I sign it. The power of attorney shall not be affected by my disability.

B. _GEF_ (*Springing powers*) This power of attorney shall take effect upon my disability. For the purpose of this power of attorney, I shall be disabled when I am unable to manage my own affairs. This determination shall be made, in writing, by a physician.

If possible, the physician determining my disability, or recovery from disability, shall be _DR. DAVID L. JOHNSON_____

This power of attorney shall be suspended when I recover from disability. I shall be recovered from disability when a physician determines, in writing, that I am able to mange my own affairs again.

(i) *Government benefits.* Apply for and receive any government benefits, including social security, that I am eligible for; receive and cash or deposit any benefit check or draft.

(j) *Legal and administrative proceedings.* Begin, continue, defend, appeal, or settle any legal or administrative proceedings involving me or my property.

Guy Francis Fish
GUY FRANCIS FISH Notary Public

_LAKE_____ County, Michigan
My commission expires _7-7-02_

Prepared by: GEORGE EDWARD FRISBIE
900 S. WASHINGTON
LAKE CITY, MI 48800

REVOCATION OF POWER OF ATTORNEY

I GEORGE EDWARD FRISBIE _____ the principal

of 900 S. WASHINGTON, LAKE CITY, MI 48800 _____

revoke my power of attorney dated JAN. 1, 2000 _____ [and recorded

on JAN. 2, 2000 _____ at Liber 101 Page 59 ____ in the office of the

Register of Deeds, LAKE _____ County, Michigan], and all the powers

given to my agent MARGO ANN FRISBIE _____

in this power of attorney.

JUNE 1, 2000
Date

George Edward Frisbie
GEORGE EDWARD FRISBIE
Principal

Witnesses:

Archie Louis Savage
ARCHIE LOUIS SAVAGE

Guy Francis Fish
GUY FRANCIS FISH

State of Michigan

County of LAKE _____

This instrument was acknowledged before me on JUNE 1, 2000 _____

by GEORGE EDWARD FRISBIE _____

Guy Francis Fish
GUY FRANCIS FISH
Notary Public

LAKE _____ County, Michigan

My commission expires 7-7-02 _____

Prepared by: GEORGE EDWARD FRISBIE
900 S. WASHINGTON
LAKE CITY, MI 48800

Chapter 10
Advance Directives

Introduction to Advance Directives

10A: Living Will

Sample Living Will, Revocation of Advance Directive, and Do-Not-Resuscitate Order

10B: Patient Advocate Designation

Sample Patient Advocate Designation and Affidavit in Support of Patient Advocate Designation

Introduction to Advance Directives

You're suddenly struck with a severe mental or physical illness, leaving you incapacitated. Luckily, you made a durable power of attorney (DPA), so there's an agent ready to handle your financial affairs. But the DPA only solves half your problems. Besides financial management, you may need help making health care decisions, which might even include terminating life-sustaining treatment.* A durable power of attorney doesn't fix this problem.

As serious as the problem is, the law has offered few satisfactory solutions to health care decision-making for incapacitated people. The customary options were:

Guardianship. When a person becomes incapacitated, a court can appoint someone to make health care decisions for him/her. In Michigan, these appointees are called guardians.

Family consent. Patients are supposed to consent to all medical treatment they receive either personally or through their guardians. Nevertheless, this requirement has often been skirted, as patients' families and doctors made medical decisions for patients informally, without any real legal authority.

By the 1970s, the inadequacy of these options was plain. This decade saw several sensational right-to-die cases, like the Karen Ann Quinlan case in New Jersey, in which incapacitated patients sought termination of life-

---

* Following the example of a 1983 presidential commission on end-of-life issues, this book uses the phrase "life-sustaining" to describe medical treatment that extends the lives of hopelessly ill patients. "Terminating" means either withholding such treatment or withdrawing treatment already begun.

sustaining treatment. Cases like Quinlan's revealed, in stark terms, the limitations of guardianship and family consent.

Like a conservatorship, a guardianship requires a court appointment. There are costs of time and money of going to court for the appointment, not to mention the intrusion a court case brings. After the appointment, the guardian remains under the control of the court, and must report to the court periodically. All this supervision is for a good reason, but many guardians find it bothersome.

Family consent also has flaws. The method works only when the patient's family and doctors agree on treatment. If they disagree, it's worthless. Moreover, the legal foundation for family consent is a little shaky in Michigan. Other states have family consent laws giving family members consent powers. Michigan hasn't adopted such a law yet. A few Michigan courts have condoned family consent, especially between spouses. But until a law is adopted, the method poses liability risks for family members and doctors alike.

Advance Directives

In the aftermath of the Quinlan case, people searched for alternatives to guardianship and family consent. The most promising idea was so-called advance directives. These are instructions, usually written but sometimes oral, given by a person before incapacity, providing guidance about future health care.

Advance directives come in two main varieties: living will and health care power of attorney. Both directives can deal with virtually any health care decision, including termination of life-sustaining treatment. Yet there is a subtle but important difference between the two instruments.

A living will gives instructions directly to medical caregivers (family, doctors, nurses, hospitals, etc.). In a way, a living will is the patient speaking to the caregivers, telling them what or what not to do. In a health care power of attorney, the patient makes health care decisions indirectly, through an agency. The patient appoints an agent and gives him/her health care powers. The agent uses these powers to make health care decisions for the patient.

In most states, the acceptance of advance directives went smoothly. For example, in 1976, while the Quinlan case was still in court, California adopted a living will law without much fuss, and then added a health care power of attorney law a few years later. During the next few years, most other states followed California's example and adopted their own advance directive laws.*

* There is enormous variety among advance directive laws, especially in terminology. Living wills go by the names of "directives," "declarations," and "terminal care documents," while health care powers of attorney are sometimes called "patient advocate," "proxy," or "surrogate" designations.

In Michigan, by contrast, the debate over advance directives was long and bitter. This experience explains why Michigan was one of the last states to pass an advance directive law, and also accounts for the peculiar form of advance directives in the state.

The first advance directive proposal, in the form of a health care power of attorney bill, was introduced in the Michigan Legislature in 1977. The proposal quickly drew fire from right-to-life and religious groups opposed to the concept of advance directives. During the next 13 years, a health care power of attorney bill was reintroduced in every legislative session and failed every time.

Meanwhile, living will advocates began pushing for a living will law in Michigan. One of the first such groups was the Living Will Association of Washtenaw, which later became the Michigan Medical Self-Determination Association. It sponsored living will bills in 1986 and later legislative sessions, but they met the same fate as the health care power of attorney proposals.

As 1990 began, almost every state except Michigan had some type of advance directive law. That would change by the end of the year, after a nudge from the U.S. Congress and a push from a retired Royal Oak doctor named Jack Kevorkian.

The federal government was alarmed about the growing costs of medical care for the terminally ill, and viewed advance directives as a way to curb these costs. In October 1990, Congress passed the Patient Self-Determination Act (PSDA). The act required all health care providers receiving federal funds, such as hospitals, nursing homes, and hospices, to advise patients of their rights to make advance directives under state law, or risk losing federal funds. The PSDA didn't force holdout states like Michigan to adopt advance directive laws, but the act had the effect of encouraging these laws.

Meanwhile, Dr. Jack Kevorkian almost single-handedly refocused public attention on the right-to-die issue in Michigan. Kevorkian had been on the fringes of the euthanasia movement* since the 1980s. Convinced that dying was a medical rather than legal issue, Kevorkian took matters into his own hands by helping hopelessly ill patients commit suicide. He participated in the first such suicide in June 1990, followed by many more later.

Encouraged by the PSDA and prodded by Kevorkian's outspoken tactics, Michigan lawmakers were forced to do something about advance directives. In late 1990, they hastily passed a health care power of attorney law, preferring that type of advance directive over living wills. Michigan's health care power of attorney, which is known as a patient advocate designation (PAD), allows a principal, or patient, to appoint an agent, or

---

* Euthanasia means good or merciful death. It's a general term covering a wide range of end-of-life decisions, from termination of life-sustaining treatment to various forms of suicide and even homicide.

patient advocate, with full health care powers, including the authority to terminate life-sustaining treatment.

Like the legislature, Michigan appeals courts shied away from the right-to-die issue for as long as possible. While the high courts in California, Florida and New Jersey had bravely confronted the issue in the 1970s, Michigan appeals courts avoided it.

At last, beginning in 1992, Michigan appeals courts issued their first right-to-die decisions. In these cases, the courts recognized that every adult had a right to control their health care, including termination of life-sustaining treatment. Although none of the cases dealt with advance directives directly, the courts approved of these devices. The approval extended to living wills, which have not yet been adopted by the legislature. Thus, thanks to these decisions, it's clear that you can make a legally-binding living will in Michigan, even without a statute authorizing the instrument.

Making up for lost time, the Michigan Legislature has added other end-of-life laws recently. In 1996, lawmakers passed the Dignified Death Act, which requires medical caregivers to inform terminally ill patients, or their surrogates, about: 1) the nature of their illness, and the risks and benefits of various treatments 2) their right to make PADs and end-of-life decisions 3) availability of palliative care, including hospice services and pain management.

Around the same time, the legislature passed a detailed law about one kind of advance directive: do-not-resuscitate (DNR) orders withholding cardiopulmonary resuscitation (CPR), which is customarily given to dying patients. Under the Do-Not-Resuscitate Procedure Act, you can give a DNR order forbidding CPR after cardiopulmonary arrest when all vital signs have ceased. The DNR order, which can be written, or both written and inscribed on a medical-alert bracelet, must be respected by emergency medical service (EMS) workers coming to your aid outside of a health care facility.

In 1999, the legislature passed several laws for alleviation of pain for chronically ill patients. The laws make it clear that patients suffering from intractable pain can receive controlled substances, such as morphine, as painkillers. The laws also encourage medical caregivers to learn more about pain management, and provide this information to their patients.

Choosing an Advance Directive

How do you choose which advance directive is best for you? Sometimes you have no choice. If you don't have any close relatives or friends, you have no one to name as patient advocate in a PAD. Under these circumstances, you must make a living will. Likewise, if you want an advance directive, but don't have preferences about your health care, you should make a PAD and leave it to the patient advocate to make decisions. Nevertheless, most people can make either type of directive, and must choose between them.

Each instrument has pluses and minuses. The advantage of a living will is its directness; you give instructions to medical caregivers without anyone in between. Unlike a PAD, you don't have to worry about choosing a patient advocate and wonder if s/he will carry out your wishes.

But the direct nature of a living will also creates a problem. Since the document itself is the only guide to medical treatment, you must give complete and specific instructions in the living will. You must envision possible medical problems and leave detailed instructions about treatment. All this is difficult, particularly if you are healthy when you make the instrument. Moreover, the specific instructions in a living will can easily become obsolete if you change your mind about treatment, or medical science or technology changes. Naturally, you can revise or even revoke the instrument, but not everyone gets around to doing that.

> ## MORE INFORMATION
>
> About end-of-life issues and advance directives, contact the oldest right-to-die organization in the U.S.:
>
> **Choice in Dying**
> *Headquarters:*
> 1035 30th St. N.W.
> Washington, D.C. 20016
> Or call (800) 989-9455
> *Program office:*
> 475 Riverside Dr.
> Room 1872
> New York, NY 10115
> Or call (212) 870-2003

Another problem with living wills in Michigan is that they exist by common law, without an authorizing statute. The common law nature of living wills doesn't affect their legality; they're as valid as PADs. But without a statute for guidance, there are vagaries about the form, preparation, and revocation of living wills.

A PAD avoids the problem of anticipating medical problems by delaying health care decision-making until onset of illness. You appoint a patient advocate with authority to make health care decisions for you. The advocate makes the necessary decisions after you become incapacitated, with full knowledge of your medical condition and the state of medical technology at the time.

Unlike a living will, a PAD is authorized by statute. In fact, the PAD law has detailed requirements about eligibility, form, making and revocation. This makes PADs easier to make, enforce and revoke.

On the other hand, in a PAD you must rely on the patient advocate to make health care decisions for you. You have protection by picking a trustworthy patient advocate. And there are also legal safeguards, since your advocate is an agent with fiduciary duties (see page "Estate Planning with a Durable Power of Attorney" on page 253 for a description of these duties). Even so, a PAD puts a middleman between you and your medical caregivers, which some people dislike.

Luckily, living wills and health care powers of attorney can be combined. By combining the two devices, you get the advantages of each, with few of the disadvantages.

If you look closely, you'll see that Michigan's PAD is a combined form. The PAD is primarily a power of attorney, but it permits the addition of living will-like instructions. Thus, the PAD is a health care power of attorney and a living will rolled into one instrument. Because you get both devices in one form, the PAD is usually the best advance directive for most people.

Whichever advance directive you choose, this book has instructions for making both types of instruments. Chapter 10A has information on living wills, and Chapter 10B deals with PADs. The blank forms for each are in the forms section of the book.

Chapter 10A
Living Will

As explained in the introduction to this chapter, Michigan living wills are authorized by common law, instead of statute. This doesn't make them any less legal or binding. But without a statute, there aren't specific guidelines for making living wills. Nevertheless, there are detailed rules about making other vital documents, such as contracts and regular wills. Many of these rules can be applied to living wills.

Who Can Make a Living Will?

Mental Capacity

Before you make an important legal document, you must have the proper mental capacity. Following the examples of ordinary wills and the PAD, the living will requires a sound mind. Courts have interpreted this to mean awareness of the legal significance of a document. In other words, you have a sound mind to make a living will when you know what the instrument is and what it does.

Living wills are sometimes made by people who are already ill and having spells of mental incapacity. A person like that may make a living will if it's made during a period of capacity, when his/her mind is sound. A later mental incapacity won't affect the will.

Example: George suffers a stroke. For several days he is confined to an intensive care ward where he is under heavy sedation and semi-conscious. He recovers his senses and makes a living will. Before long, George has another stroke and becomes mentally and physically incapacitated. Despite his spells of incapacity, the living will is valid because it was made during a period of mental capacity.

Undue Influence, Duress and Fraud

Besides mental capacity, you must make your living will free of undue influence, duress and fraud. As its name implies, a living will must be the product of your own will. If someone has influenced you to the extent the instrument is not a free choice, undue influence exists. Undue influence usually comes from those you trust, such as relatives, friends or advisers.

Duress is like undue influence, but with duress you are actually forced (usually by physical force or the threat of it) to make the living will. A fraudulent living will is based on a misrepresentation (falsification) of a fact that you relied on in making the instrument. A living will tainted by undue influence, duress or fraud is normally invalid.

Age

You need a degree of maturity and good judgment to handle your legal and business affairs. That's why the law says that you must be an adult (a person 18 years of age or older) before you can make a regular will or enter into contracts. It's also why minors (persons under 18) are unable to make these vital documents.

One might assume that those rules also apply to living wills, reserving them for adults only. That might not be true. Some states recognize the mature minor rule and allow older minors to make living wills. In one of the leading Michigan right-to-die cases, the Court of Appeals endorsed the mature minor concept, although it didn't say who is a mature minor. Whatever the rule, the issue is mostly academic because minors are seldom interested in making living wills.

Residence

You should be a Michigan resident when you make a Michigan living will. Michigan law is inconsistent on residency requirements for making vital documents. Nonresidents cannot make wills, but can make contracts in the state. It's hard to say what the rule is for living wills. But one thing is clear: Michigan residents can make them. So to be on the safe side, make sure you are a resident of Michigan before you make a living will in this state.

After you make a Michigan living will, it should be accepted out of state. With the mobility of people these days, out-of-state enforceability of vital documents is a worry. Luckily, many states have reciprocity provisions in their advance directive laws, recognizing out-of-state instruments. Thanks to these provisions, if a living will is valid in the state where it was made, it's valid elsewhere. Nevertheless, if you move permanently to another state, it's a good idea to make a new living will in the state where you live.

Making a Living Will

Ordinarily, during an illness you tell your medical caregivers what kind of treatment you want. This is the right of informed consent. But if you're incapacitated, you won't be able to give these instructions. A living will is a way to leave health care instructions ahead of time, before incapacity strikes. Then afterward, the instrument goes into effect and directs your health care.

What sort of instructions can you leave in a living will? Many people believe that a living will is good for just one thing: terminating life-sustaining treatment. That's incorrect. The fact is, you can give virtually any type of health care instruction in a living will

You may decide, as many people do, on termination of life-sustaining treatment in your living will. But it's also possible to ask for the opposite, so-called aggressive care* so you continue to receive life-sustaining treatment until your condition is utterly hopeless. You can also use your living will to give directions about more practical things, such as which doctor or hospital you want.

Life-Sustaining Treatment

When it comes to life-sustaining treatment for hopelessly ill patients,** the living will in this book offers two main choices: 1) aggressive care, in which treatment is continued 2) termination of treatment. You may choose between these options in section 2A. If you select termination of life-sustaining treatment, three subchoices are available allowing you to specify the level of incapacity at which the treatment must stop. You may choose one or more of these subchoices.

"Aggressive Care"

One problem with many living will forms is that they assume everyone wants to terminate life-sustaining treatment in the face of a hopeless illness. While many people do, not everyone does. On the contrary, some people want aggressive care.

In the living will, select choice #2A(1) to get aggressive care. Then, no matter how desperate your condition is, you will continue to receive life-sustaining treatment. The only restriction is that the treatment must be medically appropriate. This reaffirms the right of medical caregivers to withdraw medically futile or wasteful treatment.

---

* Some experts dislike the phrase "aggressive care" because it incorrectly implies that those who don't choose this option want a less active form of treatment. But like it or not, the phrase has stuck.

** As used in this book, "hopelessly ill" includes chronic diseases and conditions that are either terminal (fatal) or nonterminal (nonfatal), but which destroy the quality of life.

Terminating Life-Sustaining Treatment

Many people make living wills for one purpose: termination of life-sustaining treatment when their condition is terminal or hopeless. You can choose this option in choice #2A(2). You may then specify the level(s) of incapacity for termination in #2A(2)(a),(b), and (c). To amplify these subchoices, you may give examples of the conditions you find intolerable.

After California adopted its landmark living will in 1976, many states quickly passed similar laws, which are still in force. The trouble with these early living will laws is that they usually permit termination of life-sustaining treatment only when a patient's condition is terminal. But many hopelessly ill people also want to terminate life-sustaining treatment in nonterminal situations. They cannot benefit from these first-generation living will laws. Moreover, the early laws often fail to define "terminal" satisfactorily, creating doubt about when treatment can be discontinued.

These restrictions don't apply to Michigan living wills. In a Michigan living will, you can request termination of life-sustaining treatment in either terminal or nonterminal situations. What's more, you can define what terminal is. Here's how you take full advantage of the flexibility of Michigan's living will.

After you select choice #2A(2), you may specify the circumstances in which life-sustaining treatment is terminated. The living will provides for termination at three levels of incapacity:

Terminal condition. #2A(2)(a) describes a fatal condition where death will happen quickly or fairly soon. Examples include untreatable cancer, AIDS or end-stage diseases of the heart, lung, kidney or brain. There are degrees of terminal illness. A terminal patient may be on his/her deathbed, or the patient may be expected to live for weeks or even months. #2A(2)(a) allows you to spell out the severity of terminal illness at which life-sustaining treatment is terminated.

Permanent unconsciousness. #2A(2)(b) is when a patient has lost most or all senses (sight, hearing, touch, etc.), and cannot interact with the outside world. Examples include a coma (where the patient is senseless and appears to be in a deep sleep), and a so-called permanently vegetative state (where the patient is in a sleep-like state but still may able to respond to some stimuli, such as light or touch). When people say they don't want to become a vegetable, they mean a permanently unconscious condition as described in #2A(2)(b).

Chronic disease. In #2A(2)(c)), the patient has a chronic mental or physical disease, causing a severe loss of quality of life (where the burdens of life outweigh the benefits). Patients with advanced Alzheimer's disease, severe kidney disease or diabetes, or those in nursing homes fed by tubes may fall into this category.

These scenarios describe various degrees of incapacity. As a terminal condition, #2A(2)(a) is naturally the most serious. #2A(2)(b) and (c) may be terminal or nonterminal, and are slightly less serious. Nevertheless, many people would still prefer death over permanent unconsciousness or chronic disease as described in (b) and (c).

To give full meaning to choice #2A(2), which directs termination of life-sustaining treatment, you may choose as many subchoices as you wish. If you want to terminate life-sustaining treatment in terminal situations only, choose just #2A(2)(a). Add (b) and/or (c), as appropriate, if you want to terminate treatment in nonterminal cases as well.

Example: George has always been an active person who enjoys physical activities. His greatest fear is incapacity where he cannot be active. George makes a living will and chooses #2A(2), plus subchoices (a), (b), and (c). With this selection, his life-sustaining treatment will be terminated at various levels of incapacity, from a terminal condition ((a)) to nonterminal cases ((b) and (c)).

If you choose #2A(2)(c), you can provide more detail for your choice in the spaces provided. This isn't absolutely necessary. But you may have some firm views on treatment you want respected.

Example: Like her father, Edith has diabetes. As her father struggled with the final stages of the disease, he developed circulatory problems and had a leg amputated. Edith doesn't want to go through an amputation. She makes a living will choosing #2A(2) and subchoices (a), (b), and (c). She also adds an instruction in the space below subchoice (c) that she doesn't want amputation of limbs during treatment for diabetes.

Limits on Terminating Life-Sustaining Treatment

Whether you realize it or not, #2A(2)(a), (b), and (c) provide for types of passive euthanasia. Passive euthanasia is a way of hastening death by taking away treatment. Some people shy away from the concept of euthanasia. But the fact is, these days passive euthanasia is well-accepted and uncontroversial.

---

* Because it covers a wide range of end-of-life decisions—some controversial—euthanasia suffers from a bad reputation. That's why many advance directive laws try to disguise the fact that they're authorizing passive euthanasia by calling it something else, such as death with dignity or natural death. Whatever the packaging, they all provide for some form of passive euthanasia.

The picture is far different for active euthanasia, where death is hastened by active means, such as fatal injection or drug dosage. Active euthanasia, which includes assisted suicide, is highly controversial, especially in Michigan. In response to Dr. Jack Kevorkian's assisted suicide campaign, Michigan adopted a temporary ban on assisting suicide in 1993. That law later expired, but a new permanent ban was re-enacted in 1998, making assisting suicide a felony. As a result, it's doubtful you can ask for active euthanasia or that your medical caregivers would provide it.

Do-Not-Resuscitate Orders

When a person goes into cardiac or pulmonary arrest, CPR can be given to restart the heart and lungs, restoring circulation of blood and preventing damage to the brain or other organs. CPR includes several therapies, including mouth-to-mouth resuscitation, administration of vasoactive drugs, tracheotomy with intubation, mechanical ventilation, and electric defibrillation. Some of these procedures are gentle and nonintrusive, such as mouth-to-mouth resuscitation; others, like defibrillation, can be violent, causing broken ribs or other trauma.

> ### MORE INFORMATION
>
> About passive and active voluntary euthanasia, contact:
>
> **Hemlock Society USA**
> P.O. Box 10180
> Denver, CO 80250
>
> Or call (800) 247-7421
>
> **Hemlock Society of Michigan**
> 902 Sunset Road
> Ann Arbor, MI 48103
>
> Or call (734) 663-1627
>
> For practical information about euthanasia, obtain:
>
> *Final Exit: The Practicalities of Self-Deliverance and Assisted Suicide for the Dying,* Derek Humphry, Secaucus, NJ: Hemlock Society, 1991.

These days, CPR is given to almost every patient in cardiopulmonary arrest, whether a hospital in-patient or someone aided by emergency medical service (EMS) workers at home or in a public place. Some hopelessly ill patient would prefer to forego CPR, welcoming the chance to die and fearing the trauma of the procedure. To opt out of CPR, you must give a do-not-resuscitate (DNR) order to your medical caregivers.

CPR is really just one kind of life-sustaining treatment, and a DNR order is merely an advance directive about CPR. Ordinarily, these things could be dealt with in the main advance directive. The problem is, people are often stricken outside of health care facilities, and are treated by EMS workers who don't have immediate access to the advance directive, or the time to read it even it were available.

Michigan law allows you to issue a DNR order rejecting CPR. The order is legally binding on doctors, nurses, respiratory therapists, various EMS workers, and other "medical first responders" coming to your aid outside a hospital or other health care facility (nursing home or state mental health facility). During an emergency, these caregivers must determine if you have any vital signs (pulse or respiration). If all vital signs have stopped, and the caregiver finds that you have a written DNR order and/or a DNR bracelet, the caregiver must not administer CPR.

Why does a DNR order stop at the hospital door? As it happens, blanket DNR orders can create problems in a hospital setting, particularly during surgery. The anesthesia for surgery invariably depresses the cardiopulmonary system of the patient, making some degree of resuscitation necessary for recovery. A DNR order might be interpreted to prevent revival of the patient and make the surgery fatal.

If you want to give a hospital DNR order, for a nonsurgical situation, put it in your advance directive, perhaps in paragraph #2B of your living will, as described below. For example, you might give a DNR order only after cardiopulmonary arrest during hospitalization, except while diagnostic or surgical procedures are being performed. Your doctor can advise you about the correct wording for a hospital DNR order.

Making Do-Not-Resuscitate Orders

Michigan's DNR law says that you or your patient advocate can give a DNR order rejecting CPR outside a health care facility (hospital, nursing home, or state mental health facility). The order can be written only, or both written and inscribed on a medical-alert bracelet.

Actually, there are two kinds of DNR orders: 1) general order 2) religious order. The general order is given for medical and/or personal reasons, after consultation with your attending doctor, who must also sign the order. The religious order is for members of churches or religious denominations practicing faith-healing. The religious order is executed by the patient or patient advocate alone, without participation of a doctor.

Both types of DNR orders are included in the forms section of this book, and there is a sample general order at the end of this chapter. You must be 18 or older and of sound mind to make one. You sign the order as the "declarant," although signing by proxy (agent) is permissible if you are physically unable to sign (see the sample proxy signature in "Executing a Living Will" on page 285, about how to sign by proxy and the correct form of a proxy signature).

The general order requires your doctor's signature. Each order must be witnessed by two adults, at least one of whom is not the declarant's spouse, parent, child, grandchild, sibling, or presumptive heir. The witnesses must also sign the order.

After execution of a written DNR order, the declarant-patient or a designee can attach a DNR bracelet to the declarant's wrist. The bracelet must be inscribed with, "DO-NOT-RESUSCITATE ORDER," the declarant's name and address, and the name, address, and telephone number of the declarant's attending doctor. Your medical caregivers can help you get a DNR bracelet, with this information.

Using Do-Not-Resuscitate Orders

The DNR law says that you must keep the original DNR order at home, where it will be available to EMS personnel. Some people tack the order on the door of their bedroom, for nighttime emergencies. If you got a DNR bracelet, you should wear it everywhere. For a general DNR order, the doctor who consulted with you must receive a copy of the executed order and put it in your permanent medical record.

If you want to revoke a DNR order, you or your patient advocate can revoke by any means showing an intent to revoke: 1) written revocation (by separate revocation document or by defacing the DNR order) 2) oral revocation (which must be recorded in writing by a witness and signed by the witness) 3) physical revocation, such as by destruction of the order and/or bracelet. After any kind of revocation, the original DNR order and all copies should be destroyed. Also, the bracelet must be removed immediately from the declarant's wrist.

Additional Written Instructions

In paragraph #2B, you may add any general instructions about health care you wish. For example, you may want treatment from a particular doctor, hospital or nursing home. This is the place for these practical instructions.

It's particularly important to give instructions about out-of-the-ordinary treatments. Otherwise, you will probably get customary treatment, which may be contrary to your personal views or religious beliefs.

Example: Eugene joins the Jehovah's Witnesses church, which has a firm ban on blood transfusions. Eugene makes a living will and forbids blood transfusions under any circumstances in paragraph #2B.

Oral Instructions

Paragraph #2 permits giving oral health care instructions to those responsibile for your health care, such as your family and medical caregivers. Needless to say, there are risks with this method. Your instructions may get garbled or misinterpreted. Or those around you may choose to ignore them. That's why you should put all specific instructions in writing in the living will.

Nevertheless, there is a place for oral instructions. Oral instructions are a good way to transmit the big picture to your family and medical caregivers. Use them to describe your hopes, fears, personal or religious values, or philosophy of life. All this information provides a context for the specific written instructions you leave inside the living will.

If those responsible for your health care know you well, they may be familiar with this information. But it never hurts to go over it again.

Executing a Living Will

As with other advance directives, many people avoid making living wills because they deal with unpleasant subjects like sickness, incapacity, and death. These people often wait until the last minute, when they are close to mental incapacity or actually suffering from a physical incapacity, before they make living wills.

If you wait that long, you may need friends or relatives to help you with your living will. That's fine, as long as you still have the mental capacity to make the instrument. Your friends or relatives can assist you while you make the living will—by providing the form or information to fill it out—but the instrument must be your own choice. Otherwise, the living will could be tainted by undue influence, duress or fraud.

Complete the living will form by printing or typing. If you print, use a pen, instead of a pencil, to make a permanent document. This protects the document from alteration. It also helps convince others that the living will is authentic.

As a common law instrument, Michigan's living will doesn't have any formal requirements, as a PAD does. The living will doesn't require notarization, as some durable powers of attorney do. Nevertheless, you should do the following to put the document in official-like form:

Dating.   You must date the living will when you sign it.

Signing.   The living will must be signed in paragraph #6. If you are physically (but not mentally) unable to sign, you can scrawl your signature or even use a mark, such as an X. The living will also allows a proxy signature. If you are too weak to sign, you can authorize a proxy or substitute to sign for you. You should give the proxy this authority in front of the witnesses, either verbally or by a nonverbal sign. The proxy should then sign the living will as follows:

George Edward Frisbie by Archie Louis Savage, in his presence and at his direction

Witnessing.   Your signature should also be witnessed by at least two witnesses. The witnesses must watch you as you sign the living will. Immediately afterward, they should read paragraph #7, and then sign their names in the spaces below the paragraph. The witnesses should also print their names and addresses below their signatures.

No one is legally disqualified from serving as a witness to a living will. But to avoid any hint of undue influence or duress, the following people shouldn't serve:

• spouse
• close relatives (parents, children, siblings, etc.)
• presumptive heirs (people who would inherit from you if you died without a will)
• known devisee (person designated to take property in your will)
• doctor and other medical caregivers

After You Make a Living Will

At a time when more people than ever are making advance directives, there are disturbing reports that these instruments aren't always followed.

285

A recent survey by the Department of Health and Human Services found that 40% of patients with advance directives didn't put them in their medical records, where doctors could find them.

The problem is probably worse for living wills because they don't have a natural enforcer. In a DPA or other health care power of attorney, the patient advocate-agent often assumes responsibility for enforcing the instrument. A living will itself doesn't have anyone to do that, although family and friends may act as informal enforcers.

All this emphasizes how important it is to distribute your living will. By distributing the instrument, you guarantee it will be recognized and accepted by your medical caregivers.

The method of distribution depends on whether you intend to use your living will now or later. If you are going to use the living will soon, distribute photocopies of the document to your doctors, HMO, hospital, hospice, nursing home, etc., without delay. Make sure that the living will is placed in your medical record or file, so it will be ready to use.

On the other hand, you may be making a living will while healthy, as a long-term planning device. If so, store the original living will in a safe place, with your vital papers at home or in a safe deposit box at a financial institution.* Also give a photocopy to your personal doctor. And you may want to give extra copies to close family or friends.

Using a Living Will

A living will doesn't do anything until you become incapacitated. The test for incapacity is inability to make your own health care decisions. This demands a serious degree of incapacity, since you must be gravely ill to be unable to participate in medical decision-making.

Your attending physician and another physician or licensed psychologist certify your incapacity informally, avoiding the time and trouble of going to court. If it's convenient, they can make this certification in the doctors' statement in the living will, or use another form. Either way, the doctors must state that they have examined you and, in their opinion, you're unable to participate in medical treatment decisions. After the certification, the living will goes into effect and guides your health care.

Terminating a Living Will

A living will asks you to make vital decisions about health care in advance. This creates a risk that you may change your mind later and no longer want what you said in your living will. As a result, there must be ways to revoke or revise your living will.

---

* If you use a safe deposit box, make sure that others have access to the box. For this reason, you may want to lease the box jointly with your spouse or others.

The living will in this book makes revocation as easy as possible. It says that you can revoke the living will "any time," regardless of mental capacity. This is important because normally you must have full mental capacity to revoke vital documents like contracts and regular wills. But this is impractical with a living will, since it doesn't become effective until incapacity. Thus, you must be able to revoke it after the onset of mental incapacity whenever you change your mind about your health care treatment.

You may also decide to revoke during a physical incapacity, when you are unable to speak or move. Therefore, the living will allows you to revoke "by any manner." This might include a gesture, such as nodding your head in answer to a question by others about whether you want to revoke.

The best way to revoke your living will is in writing. You can use the revocation of advance directive included in the forms section of this book. After you complete the revocation, give copies to your doctors and others who have copies of your living will. Above all, make sure a copy of the revocation is placed in your medical record. Then, ask for return of all copies of the revoked living will and destroy them.

Another way to revoke is by making a new living will. Notice the first paragraph of the form says that it revokes all prior living wills. Thanks to this provision, you revoke previous living wills by making a new one. Even so, it's a good idea to destroy any prior living wills and all copies after making a new one.

Finally, a living will ends immediately at death. A living will takes care of lifetime health care only; it cannot deal with anything after death. You need other documents to handle property distribution after death (regular will), final matters (letter of instruction), or anatomical gift (anatomical donor document).

Revising a Living Will

After you make your living will, review it periodically, perhaps every year or two, to see if revision is necessary. A living will can become easily outdated if you change your mind about health care. Advances in medicine may also make it obsolete.

When you want to revise, don't try to make revisions by crossing out old material and/or adding new material. After a living will is dated, signed, and witnessed, it's complete and mustn't be altered. There are ways to amend the document, but amendment is a lot of trouble. Instead, the best way to revise is to make a new living will.

LIVING WILL

I _GEORGE EDWARD FRISBIE_

LAKE CITY, MI

of _____

give the following instructions for my future health care. I also revoke prior
living wills I have made.

1. Duration. This living will shall take effect when I am unable to make
my own health care decisions. That determination shall be made, in writing, by
my attending physician and another physician or licensed psychologist who has
examined me.

2. Health Care Instructions. Those responsible for my health care shall
provide such care as instructed by me orally or in writing below.

A. Life-Sustaining Treatment.

Sign *one* (1 or 2) of the following two statements with which you agree:

(1) I direct that all medically appropriate treatment be provided to
sustain my life, regardless of my mental or physical mental condition.

_____
Signature

(2) There are circumstances in which I do not want my life to be prolonged by further medical treatment. In these circumstances, life-sustaining
treatment shall not be initiated, and if it has been, it must discontinued. I
recognize that these decisions could or would allow me to die. In the following section, I specify the circumstances in which I choose to terminate life-sustaining treatment.

George Edward Frisbie
Signature

If you have signed statement (2), initial each of the statements (a,b,c) with
which you agree:

(a) _GEF_ I realize that someday I may be diagnosed with an incurable and
irreversible illness, disease, or condition. If this occurs, and my attending
physician and at least one additional physician who has personally examined
me determine that my condition is *terminal*, I direct that life-sustaining treatment that would artificially prolong my death be withheld or withdrawn. I
also direct that I receive all medically appropriate care to make me comfortable and relieve pain.

To me, terminal condition means that my physicians have determined that:
(Initial one choice)

____ I will die within a few days

____ I will die within a few weeks

3. Revocation. I may revoke this living will anytime, regardless of my
mental capacity, by any means I am able to show an intent to revoke.

City   MI   48800
              State Zip

Doctors' Statement

I _____

of _____

am the patient's attending physician.

DO-NOT-RESUSCITATE ORDER
(General)

I have discussed my health status with my physician,

DR. DAVID L. JOHNSON

I request that in the event my heart and breathing should stop, no person shall attempt to resuscitate me. This order is effective until it is revoked by me.

Being of sound mind, I voluntarily execute this order, and I understand its full import.

George Edward Frisbie
(Declarant's signature)

GEORGE EDWARD FRISBIE
(Type or print declarant's full name)

JUNE 1, 2000
(Date)

_____
(Signature of person who signed for declarant, if applicable)

_____
(Type or print full name)

_____
(Date)

Dr. David L. Johnson
(Physician's signature)

DAVID L. JOHNSON
(Type or print physician's full name)

JUNE 1, 2000
(Date)

Attestation of Witnesses

The individual who has executed this order appears to be of sound mind, and under no duress, fraud, or undue influence. Upon executing this order, the individual has (has not) received an identification bracelet.

Archie Louis Savage
(Witness signature)

ARCHIE LOUIS SAVAGE
(Type or print witness' name)

JUNE 1, 2000
(Date)

Guy Francis Fish
(Witness signature)

GUY FRANCIS FISH
(Type or print witness' name)

JUNE 1, 2000
(Date)

THIS FORM WAS PREPARED PURSUANT TO, AND IS IN COMPLIANCE WITH, THE MICHIGAN DO-NOT-RESUSCITATE PROCEDURE ACT

REVOCATION OF
ADVANCE DIRECTIVE

I _GEORGE EDWARD FRISBIE_

of _LAKE CITY, MI_

have made the following advance directive: ☒ living will ☐ designation of
patient advocate ☐ do-not-resuscitate order; dated _JAN. 1, 2000_

I revoke this instrument, effective immediately.

JUNE 1, 2000
Date

George Edward Frisbie

RECORD OF NONWRITTEN REVOCATION

I _____

of _____

witnessed _____

revoke the advance directive described above by doing: (Describe oral or nonverbal
revocation in space below)

_____
Date

_____
Witness

Chapter 10B Patient Advocate Designation

As explained in the introduction to this chapter, Michigan's patient advocate designation (PAD) is a health care power of attorney, creating an agency. In a PAD, the principal, known as the patient, gives health care powers to the agent, or patient advocate. The patient advocate exercises these powers on behalf of the patient after s/he becomes incapacitated and can no longer make health care decisions for himself/herself.

Michigan's PAD law has detailed requirements for eligibility, form, making, and revocation. All these rules must be followed to have an enforceable instrument.

Who Can Make a Patient Advocate Designation?

Mental Capacity

The PAD law says that you must have a sound mind to make a designation. Courts have interpreted this as awareness of the legal significance of the document. In other words, you have a sound mind to make a PAD when you know what the instrument is and what it does.

PADs are sometimes made by people who are already ill and suffering from spells of mental incapacity. A person like that may make a PAD during a period of capacity, when his/her mind is sound. A later mental incapacity won't affect the PAD.

Example: George suffers a stroke. For several days he is confined to an intensive care ward where he is under heavy sedation and semi-conscious. He recovers his senses and makes a PAD. Before long, George has another stroke and becomes mentally and physically incapacitated. Despite his spells of incapacity, the PAD is valid because it was made during a period of mental capacity.

Undue Influence, Duress and Fraud

Besides mental capacity, you must make your PAD free of undue influence, duress and fraud. A PAD must be the product of your own will. If someone has influenced you to the extent the instrument is not a free choice, undue influence exists. Undue influence usually comes from those you trust, such as relatives, friends or advisers. Duress is like undue influence, but with duress you are actually forced (usually by physical force or the threat of it) to make the PAD. A fraudulent designation is based on a misrepresentation (falsification) of a fact that you relied on in making the instrument. A PAD tainted by undue influence, duress or fraud is normally invalid.

Age

The PAD law says you must be 18 years of age or older to make a designation. This rules out the possibility of older minors making PADs under the mature minor rule, as they might with living wills.

Residence

For all its detail, the PAD law doesn't say whether you must be a Michigan resident to make a designation. The residency rules for other vital documents don't provide much help either, because they are inconsistent (nonresidents cannot make Michigan wills, but can make contracts). But one thing is clear: Michigan residents can make PADs. So to be on the safe side, make sure you are a Michigan resident when you make a PAD.

After you make a PAD, it should be accepted out of state. With the mobility of people these days, out-of-state enforceability of vital documents is a worry. Luckily, most states have reciprocity provisions in their advance directive laws, recognizing out-of-state instruments. Thanks to these provisions, a Michigan PAD should be valid in other states. Nevertheless, if you move to another state, it's a good idea to make a new health care power of attorney in that state.

Who Can Be a Patient Advocate?

Legal Eligibility

The PAD law says that a patient advocate must be a "person who is 18 years of age or older." Thus, the patient advocate must be an adult. By imposing an age requirement, the law also implies that the patient advocate must be a person who is a human being, not an organization.* This makes sense, because few organizations are able to exercise the intimate kind of powers a PAD grants.

---

* In legal parlance, "person" is ambiguous because it includes both human beings and organizations.

Practical Qualities

As you can see, almost any adult is legally eligible to serve as patient advocate. But for practical reasons, some people make better advocates than others. When you select your patient advocate, look for the following practical qualities:

Decision-making. Above all else, your patient advocate must have the ability to make sound health care decisions for you—and the firmness to carry these out.

¶ *Good judgment.* The PAD law doesn't mention mental capacity as a requirement for a patient advocate. But naturally, your advocate must be mentally capable because of the important decisions s/he makes for you.

Beyond this, the advocate should have the maturity and experience to make sound decisions, in often complicated areas. The patient advocate doesn't have to possess any special medical knowledge or expertise; common sense should be enough.

¶ *Firmness.* Your patient advocate must have the strength of will to make often wrenching health care decisions for you. Many of these are routine. But someday s/he may have to make life-or-death decisions for you. Likewise, you need someone who is strong enough to represent your interests at all times, and won't be bullied by family members or medical staff into bad decisions.

Capacity for help. Your patient advocate doesn't have to provide hands-on care (unless s/he wants to), but s/he must be available when needed to make critical decisions for you.

¶ *Commitment.* A patient advocate is a strictly volunteer position, and the advocate can quit anytime. Find out the level of commitment by asking candidates whether they are up to the task. Even if they say "yes," judge how realistic this is.

¶ *Health and stability.* Some candidates, like older people, may seem like good candidates now, but will they have sufficient health and longevity to help you perhaps many years in the future?

Location. The PAD law doesn't disqualify nonresident patient advocates, so your advocate can be someone who lives outside Michigan. Nevertheless, a PAD gives your patient advocate many responsibilities. A nonresident advocate might have difficulty carrying them out from far away. As a result, it's better to stick with someone who lives near you in Michigan.

Combining patient advocate and agent. When you're making a durable power of attorney along with your PAD, consider selecting the same person as agent (in the durable power of attorney) and patient advocate (in the PAD). If you name different persons, the patient advocate must apply constantly to the agent for funds for your health care. By combining the two roles in one person, the advocate can make health care decisions and pay for the care. On the other hand, you might not like such coziness, and may choose to divide these responsibilities between two people.

As you select your patient advocate, don't forget your spouse or other relatives. Spouses often make excellent patient advocates because they usually have good judgment, and are suitable, willing and available.

Other relatives may share these qualifications. Maybe that's why most people prefer to have relatives make tough health care decisions for them. According to a Harris poll, when asked whom they want to make important medical decisions for them, 57% of the respondents said "a family member," 31% "my doctor," 2% "a close friend," 2% "a lawyer," 6% "my doctor and family [or a] friend."

Spouses and other relatives may also be willing to serve as patient advocate without compensation. Ordinarily, agents can be compensated for the work they do. However, the PAD law forbids paying patient advocates anything except reimbursement for out-of-pocket expenses. This lack of compensation could discourage nonrelatives or friends from serving as your patient advocate. Yet it shouldn't bother your spouse or other relatives, who usually will serve without compensation.

Despite the advantages of selecting relatives as patient advocates, be cautious when you appoint them. Your relatives usually take your property after death, creating a possible conflict of interest during your final illness. Relatives want you to get well, yet they won't get anything from your estate until you die. This conflict can influence the health care decisions patient advocates make.

"Emotional" conflicts of interest may also exist between relatives. For example, a child who has been estranged from a parent may want to prolong the life of the parent needlessly to make up for previous neglect. If you suspect that these conflicts of interest might influence the judgment of a relative, don't appoint that person as your patient advocate.

Another person who may have a conflict of interest is your doctor. If you name your doctor as patient advocate, the doctor will make health care decisions for you and then carry them out, with minimal supervision. This situation has the potential for abuse. That's why advance directive laws in many states bar doctors from serving as health care agents/advocates. Michigan's PAD law doesn't do that. Nevertheless, it's probably wise to avoid naming a doctor as patient advocate. In fact, few doctors will want to act in that role anyway.

After you review your candidates, select two patient advocates: a first choice and a successor. The first choice will probably become your patient advocate. But if the first choice fails to serve, the successor can take over. In that case, the successor patient advocate receives all the health care powers the first choice would have had.

The PAD in this book doesn't permit appointment of several patient advocates to act collectively. Collective advocacies take several guises, including appointment of joint or split advocates. With joint advocates, two or more co-advocates share the powers given in the PAD. In the case of split patient advocates, the co-advocates are assigned separate powers or duties which they perform independently of each other.

It's legally permissible to appoint multiple patient advocates. But making critical health care decisions by committee creates problems. When one advocate is unable or unwilling to serve, there may be doubt about whether the other(s) can act without him/her. Worst of all, co-advocates may disagree about decisions. Sometimes these kinds of problems can wind up in court, which is the very thing a PAD is designed to avoid.

Making a Patient Advocate Designation

Ordinarily, during an illness you tell your medical caregivers what kind of treatment you want. This is the right of informed consent. But if you're also incapacitated, you won't be able to make these decisions. A PAD is a way to appoint someone to make health care decisions for you. The instrument lies dormant until you become incapacitated. Then it goes into effect and gives your patient advocate powers to make health care decisions.

But there's more. As explained in the introduction to this chapter, Michigan's PAD is really a combined health care power of attorney and living will. In a PAD, you can appoint a patient advocate (health care power of attorney) and also leave health care instructions (living will). So if you like, you can give specific instructions about your health care treatment, which your patient advocate must follow.

Assignment of Basic Health Care Powers

With or without specific instructions, the patient advocate automatically receives several basic health care powers. These powers are described in paragraph #3. They include powers to: 1) look after your "care" and "custody" by providing for physical needs like food, clothing, and shelter 2) make ordinary medical treatment decisions for you. For emphasis, several important medical treatment powers are spelled out in subparagraphs #3(a)-(d). By possessing these basic health care powers, your patient advocate should be able to provide for your physical well-being.

Life-Sustaining Treatment

If you decide to give health care instructions to your patient advocate, you may direct any part of your health care. You may decide, as many people do, on termination of life-sustaining treatment. But it's also possible to ask for the opposite: so-called aggressive care* so you continue to receive life-sustaining treatment until your condition is utterly hopeless. You can also use your PAD to give directions about more practical things, such as which doctor or hospital you want.

When it comes to life-sustaining treatment for hopelessly ill patients,** the PAD offers two main choices: 1) aggressive care, in which treatment is continued 2) termination of treatment. You may choose between these options. If you select termination of life-sustaining treatment, three sub-choices are available allowing you to specify the level of incapacity at which the treatment must stop. You may choose one or more of these subchoices.

"Aggressive Care"

One problem with many advance directive forms is that they assume everyone wants to terminate life-sustaining treatment in the face of terminal or hopeless illness. While many people do, not everyone does. On the contrary, some people want aggressive care.

In the PAD, select choice #4A(1) to get aggressive care. Then, no matter how desperate your condition is, you will continue to receive life-sustaining treatment. The only restriction is that the treatment must be "medically appropriate." This reaffirms the right of medical caregivers to withdraw medically futile or wasteful treatment.

Terminating Life-Sustaining Treatment

Many people make PADs for one purpose: termination of life-sustaining treatment when their condition is terminal or hopeless. You can choose this option in choice #4A(2). You may then specify the level(s) of incapacity for termination in #4A(2)(a),(b), and (c). To amplify these subchoices, you may give examples of the conditions you find intolerable.

After California adopted its landmark living will in 1976, many states quickly passed similar laws, which are still in force. The trouble with these early advance directive laws is that they usually permit termination of life-sustaining treatment only when a patient's condition is terminal. But many hopelessly ill people also want to terminate life-sustaining treatment in nonterminal situations. They cannot benefit from these first-gen-

---

* Some experts dislike the phrase "aggressive care" because it incorrectly implies that those who don't choose this option want a less active form of treatment. But like it or not, the phrase has stuck.

** As used in this book, "hopelessly ill" includes chronic diseases and conditions that are either terminal (fatal) or nonterminal (nonfatal), but which destroy the quality of life.

eration advance directive laws. Moreover, the early laws often fail to define "terminal" satisfactorily, creating doubt about when treatment can be discontinued.

These restrictions don't apply to Michigan's PAD. In a Michigan PAD, you can request termination of life-sustaining treatment in either terminal or nonterminal situations. What's more, you can define what terminal is. Here's how you take full advantage of the flexibility of Michigan's PAD.

After you select choice #4A(2), you may specify the circumstances in which life-sustaining treatment is terminated. The PAD provides for termination at three levels of incapacity:

Terminal condition. #4A(2)(a) describes a fatal condition where death will happen quickly or fairly soon. Examples include untreatable cancer, AIDS or end-stage diseases of the heart, lung, kidney or brain. There are degrees of terminal illness. A terminal patient may be on his/her deathbed, or s/he may be expected to live for weeks or even months. #4A2(a) allows you to spell out the severity of terminal illness at which life-sustaining treatment is terminated.

Permanent unconsciousness. #4A(2)(b) is when a patient has lost most or all senses (sight, hearing, touch, etc.), and cannot interact with the outside world. Examples include a coma (where the patient is senseless and appears to be in a deep sleep) and a so-called permanently vegetative state (where the patient is in a sleep-like state but still may able to respond to some stimuli, such as light or touch). When people say they don't want to become a vegetable, they mean a permanently unconscious condition as described in#4A(2)(b).

Chronic disease. In #4A(2)(c), the patient has a chronic mental or physical disease, causing a severe loss of quality of life (where the burdens of life outweigh the benefits). Patients with advanced Alzheimer's disease, severe kidney disease or diabetes, or those in nursing homes fed by tubes may fall into this category.

These scenarios describe various degrees of incapacity. As a terminal condition, #4A(2)(a) is naturally the most serious. #4A(2)(b) and (c) may be terminal or nonterminal, and are slightly less serious. Nevertheless, many people would still prefer death over permanent unconsciousness or chronic disease as described in (b) and (c).

To give full meaning to choice #4A(2), which directs termination of life-sustaining treatment, you may choose as many subchoices as you wish. If you want to terminate life-sustaining treatment in terminal situations only, choose just #4A(2)(a). Add (b) and/or (c), as appropriate, if you want to terminate treatment in nonterminal cases as well.

Example: George has always been an active person who enjoys physical activities. His greatest fear is incapacity where he cannot be active. George makes a PAD and chooses 4A(2), plus subchoices (a), (b), and (c). With this selection, his life-sustaining treatment will be terminated at various levels of incapacity, from a terminal condition ((a)) to nonterminal cases ((b) and (c)).

If you choose #4A(2)(c), you can provide more detail for your choice in the spaces provided. This isn't absolutely necessary. But you may have some firm views on treatment you want respected.

Example: Like her father, Edith has diabetes. As her father struggled with the final stages of the disease, he developed circulatory problems and had a leg amputated. Edith doesn't want to go through an amputation. She makes a PAD choosing #4A(2) and subchoices (a), (b), and (c). She also adds an instruction in the space below subchoice (c) that she doesn't want amputation of limbs during treatment for diabetes.

Limits of Termination of Life-Sustaining Treatment

Whether you realize it or not, #4A(2)(a), (b), and (c) provide for types of passive euthanasia. Passive euthanasia is a way of hastening death by taking away treatment. Some people shy away from the concept of euthanasia.* But the fact is, these days passive euthanasia is well-accepted and noncontroversial.

The picture is far different for active euthanasia, where death is hastened by active means, such as fatal injection or drug dosage. Active euthanasia, which includes assisted suicide, is highly controversial, especially in Michigan. In response to Dr. Jack Kevorkian's assisted suicide campaign, Michigan adopted a temporary ban on assisting suicide in 1993. That law later expired, but a new permanent ban was re-enacted in 1998, making assisting suicide a felony. As a result, it's doubtful you can ask for active euthanasia or that your medical caregivers would provide it.

Do-Not-Resuscitate Orders

When a person goes into cardiac or pulmonary arrest, CPR can be given to restart the heart and lungs, restoring circulation of blood and preventing damage to the brain or other organs. CPR includes several therapies, including mouth-to-mouth resuscitation, administration of vasoactive drugs, tracheotomy with intubation, mechanical ventilation, and electric defibrillation. Some of these procedures are gentle and nonintrusive, such as mouth-to-mouth resuscitation; others, like defibrillation, can be violent, causing broken ribs or other trauma.

These days, CPR is given to almost every patient in cardiopulmonary

---

* Because it covers a wide range of end-of-life decisions—some controversial—euthanasia has a bad reputation. That's why many advance directive laws try to disguise the fact that they're authorizing passive euthanasia by calling it something else, such as death with dignity or natural death. Whatever the packaging, they all provide for some form of passive euthanasia.

arrest, whether a hospital in-patient or someone aided by emergency medical service (EMS) workers at home or in a public place. Some hopelessly ill patient would prefer to forego CPR, welcoming the chance to die and fearing the trauma of the procedure. To opt out of CPR, you must give a do-not-resuscitate (DNR) order to your medical caregivers.

CPR is really just one kind of life-sustaining treatment, and a DNR order is merely an advance directive about CPR. Ordinarily, these things could be dealt with in the main advance directive. The problem is, people are often stricken outside of health care facilities, and are treated by EMS workers who don't have immediate access to the advance directive, or the time to read it even it were available.

Michigan law allows you to issue a DNR order rejecting CPR. The order is legally binding on doctors, nurses, respiratory therapists, various EMS workers, and other "medical first responders" coming to your aid outside a hospital or other health care facility (nursing home or state mental health facility). During an emergency, these caregivers must determine if you have any

> ### MORE INFORMATION
>
> About passive and active voluntary euthanasia, contact:
>
> **Hemlock Society USA**
> P.O. Box 10180
> Denver, CO 80250
>
> Or call (800) 247-7421
>
> **Hemlock Society of Michigan**
> 902 Sunset Road
> Ann Arbor, MI 48103
>
> Or call (734) 663-1627
>
> For practical information about euthanasia, obtain:
>
> *Final Exit: The Practicalities of Self-Deliverance and Assisted Suicide for the Dying,* Derek Humphry, Secaucus, NJ: Hemlock Society, 1991.

vital signs (pulse or respiration). If all vital signs have stopped, and the caregiver finds that you have a written DNR order and/or a DNR bracelet, the caregiver must not administer CPR.

Why does a DNR order stop at the hospital door? As it happens, blanket DNR orders can create problems in a hospital setting, particularly during surgery. The anesthesia for surgery invariably depresses the cardiopulmonary system of the patient, making some degree of resuscitation necessary for recovery. A DNR order might be interpreted to prevent revival of the patient and make the surgery fatal.

If you want to give a hospital DNR order, for a nonsurgical situation, put it in your advance directive, perhaps in paragraph #4B of your PAD, as described below. For example, you might give a DNR order only after cardiopulmonary arrest during hospitalization, except while diagnostic or surgical procedures are being performed. Your doctor can advise you about the correct wording for a hospital DNR order.

Making Do-Not-Resuscitate Orders

Michigan's DNR law says that you or your patient advocate can give a DNR order rejecting CPR outside a health care facility (hospital, nursing home, or state mental health facility). The order can be written only, or both written and inscribed on a medical-alert bracelet.

Actually, there are two kinds of DNR orders: 1) general order 2) religious order. The general order is given for medical and/or personal reasons, after consultation with your attending doctor, who must also sign the order. The religious order is for members of churches or religious denominations practicing faith-healing. The religious order is executed by the patient or patient advocate alone, without participation of a doctor.

Both types of DNR orders are included in the forms section of this book, and there is a sample general order at the end of the previous chapter, on page 289. You must be 18 or older and of sound mind to make one. You sign the order as the "declarant," although signing by proxy (agent) is permissible if you are physically unable to sign (see "Executing a Living Will" on page 285 about how to sign by proxy and the correct form of a proxy signature).

The general order requires your doctor's signature. Each order must be witnessed by two adults, at least one of whom is not the declarant's spouse, parent, child, grandchild, sibling, or presumptive heir. The witnesses must also sign the order.

After execution of a written DNR order, the declarant-patient or a designee can attach a DNR bracelet to the declarant's wrist. The bracelet must be inscribed with, "DO-NOT-RESUSCITATE ORDER," the declarant's name and address, and the name, address, and telephone number of the declarant's attending doctor. Your medical caregivers can help you get a DNR bracelet, with this information.

Using Do-Not-Resuscitate Orders

The DNR law says that you must keep the original DNR order at home, where it will be available to EMS personnel. Some people tack the order on the door of their bedroom, for nighttime emergencies. If you got a DNR bracelet, you should wear it everywhere. For a general DNR order, the doctor who consulted with you must receive a copy of the executed order and put it in your permanent medical record.

If you want to revoke a DNR order, you or your patient advocate can revoke by any means showing an intent to revoke: 1) written revocation (by separate revocation document or by defacing the DNR order) 2) oral revocation (which must be recorded in writing by a witness and signed by the witness) 3) physical revocation, such as by destruction of the order and/or bracelet. After any kind of revocation, the original DNR order and all copies should be destroyed. Also, the bracelet must be removed immediately from the declarant's wrist.

Additional Written Instructions

In paragraph #4B, you may add any general instructions about health care you wish. For example, you may want treatment from a particular doctor, hospital or nursing home. This is the place for these practical instructions.

It's particularly important to give instructions about out-of-the-ordinary treatments. Otherwise, you will probably get customary treatment, which may be contrary to your personal views or religious beliefs.

> *Example:* Eugene joins the Jehovah's Witnesses church, which has a firm ban on blood transfusions. Eugene makes a PAD and forbids blood transfusions under any circumstances in paragraph #4(B).

Oral Instructions

Paragraph #4 permits oral health care instructions to your patient advocate. Needless to say, there are risks with this method. Your instructions may get garbled or misinterpreted. Or the patient advocate may choose to ignore them. That's why you should put all specific instructions in writing in the PAD.

Nevertheless, there is a role for oral instructions. Oral instructions are a good way to transmit the big picture to your patient advocate. Use them to describe your hopes, fears, personal or religious values, or philosophy of life. All this information provides a context for the specific written instructions you leave inside the PAD.

If your patient advocate knows you well, s/he may be familiar with this information. But it never hurts to go over it again. A good opportunity is when you ask your patient advocate if s/he is willing to serve.

How a Patient Advocate Designation Works

Whatever powers and instructions you give your patient advocate, s/he can't do anything while you're still healthy and capable. Like a living will, a PAD is dormant until you suffer an incapacity.* The PAD goes into effect when you are incapacitated by being "unable to participate in medical treatment decisions." Regrettably, the PAD law doesn't define this phrase. But it suggests a very serious incapacity since one must be gravely ill to be unable to participate in medical decision-making.

To avoid the trouble of going to court, the PAD law allows doctors to certify your incapacity informally. The law says that two doctors: 1) your attending physician 2) another physician or licensed psychologist, can examine you and determine incapacity. If it's convenient, they can make this determination in the doctors' statement in the PAD, or use another form. Either way, the doctors must state that they have examined you and, in their opinion, you're unable to participate in medical treatment decisions.

At that time, your patient advocate must sign the acceptance of designation, at the end of the PAD. Acceptance shows that the advocate is willing to shoulder all the responsibilities assigned in the instrument. After acceptance, the PAD is legally effective and ready to use.

---

* In addition, the PAD is durable to prevent any possible lapse during a period of mental incapacity.

Executing a Patient Advocate Designation

As with other advance directives, many people avoid making PADs because they deal with unpleasant topics like sickness, incapacity, and death. These people often wait until the last minute, when they are close to mental incapacity or actually suffering from a physical capacity, before they make PADs.

If you wait that long, you may need friends or relatives to help you with your PAD. That's fine, as long as you still have the mental capacity to make the instrument. Your friends or relatives can assist you while you make the PAD—by providing the form or information to fill it out—but the instrument must be your own choice. Otherwise, the PAD could be tainted by undue influence, duress or fraud.

Complete the PAD form by printing or typing. If you print, use a pen, instead of a pencil, to make a permanent document. This protects the document from alteration. It also helps convince others that the PAD is authentic.

A PAD doesn't have to be notarized. But otherwise, there are strict requirements for signing and witnessing. These rules may seem bothersome, but all must be followed or your PAD may not be enforceable.

Dating. When you sign the PAD, insert the date in the space provided in paragraph #7.

Signing. In paragraph #7, you must sign below the date, above the line marked "patient." If you are unable to sign easily because of a physical problem, you can scrawl your signature or even use a mark, such as an X.

At this point, your patient advocate doesn't sign the PAD. Later, after you are incapacitated, the advocate will sign the acceptance of designation before the instrument goes into effect.

Witnessing. Your signature must also be witnessed by several witnesses. The witnesses must watch you as you sign the PAD. Immediately afterward, they should read paragraph #8. The witnesses should sign their names in the spaces below the paragraph, and then print their names and addresses below their signatures.

As a check against undue influence, duress and fraud, the PAD law disqualifies anyone who might have an interest in you or your property. In all, the law prohibits the following people from witnessing your PAD:

- spouse
- parent
- child
- grandchild
- sibling (brother or sister)
- presumptive heir (person who would inherit from you if you died without a will)

- known devisee (person designated to take property in your will)
- physician
- patient advocate
- life or health insurance company's employees
- health facility's employees
- home for the aged's employees

As you can see, all your close relatives and most of your medical care-givers are disqualified as witnesses. This leaves your friends as probably the best choice as witnesses.* Friends make good witnesses because you're apt to stay in touch with them, so they can be located if they have to testify about the making of your PAD. Whomever you choose as witnesses, select individuals who are around your age or younger and in good health.

The PAD law actually requires just two witnesses. However, the PAD in this book asks for three witnesses as a precaution against having too few witnesses. As described above, many people are disqualified from serving as witnesses. If you have just two witnesses, and one turns out to be ineligible, your PAD might be unenforceable. By adding an extra witness, you reduce the chance of this happening.

After You Make a Patient Advocate Designation

At a time when more people than ever are making advance directives, there are disturbing reports that these instruments aren't always followed. A recent survey by the Department of Health and Human Services found that 40% of patients with advance directives didn't put them in their medical records, where doctors could find them.

This problem emphasizes how important it is to distribute your PAD. By distributing the instrument, you guarantee that it will be recognized and accepted by your medical caregivers.

The method of distribution depends on whether you plan to use the PAD now or later. If you plan to use the instrument soon, it must be put into effect and distributed without delay. But if you've made the PAD as a long-term planning device, store the instrument for later use.

If you expect to use the PAD soon, it must be put into effect by having: 1) two doctors certify your incapacity 2) the patient advocate accept designation as your patient advocate.

As mentioned earlier, two doctors: 1) your attending physician 2) another physician or licensed psychologist, must certify your incapacity. They can use the doctors' statement inside the PAD or another form. Either way, the doctors must examine you and state, in writing, that you are unable to participate in medical treatment decisions.

---

* But if you have given property to these friends in your will, they too will be disqualified from witnessing, as known devisees.

Then, your patient advocate signs the acceptance of designation at the end of the PAD. As required by law, the acceptance tells the patient advocate about some of his/her duties, and gets the advocate's consent. Your patient advocate should read the acceptance, date, and sign it. The signature doesn't need to be witnessed or notarized.

When your patient advocate refuses or is unable to serve, see whether the successor patient advocate is willing to take over. If so, the successor can read, date and sign the acceptance of designation instead.

After the doctors' statement (or a similar separate form) and the acceptance of designation sections of your PAD have been completed, make several photocopies of the document. According to the PAD law, copies must be distributed to:

- your patient advocate
- your attending physician
- any health care facility (such as a hospital, nursing home, or hospice) where you are located

As soon as your attending physician and health care facility receive copies of the PAD, they must put them in your medical record. That way, they will have evidence of the fact that your patient advocate can now make health care decisions for you. If you are being transferred between several health care facilities, you may have multiple attending physicians and medical records. Make extra copies of the PAD and distribute these to the other physicians and health care facilities where you are receiving in-patient treatment.

If you have made a PAD while you're still healthy, as a planning tool for future use, the method of distribution will be different. Because the instrument may be dormant for years, distribute it to just a few persons at first. Give copies to your patient advocate and personal doctor. Store the original document in a safe place, with your vital papers at home or in a safe deposit box at a financial institution.*

Later, when you become incapacitated, the PAD can be removed from storage and activated. The doctors complete the doctors' statement and your patient advocate signs the acceptance of designation, as described above. Afterward, the document can be photocopied and distributed to those listed above.

Acceptance of Patient Advocate Designation

PADs are a vast improvement over the previous ways incapacitated patients gave consent to medical treatment, so medical caregivers should be eager to accept them. All the same, the PAD tries to aid acceptance in

---

* If you use a safe deposit box, make sure that others have access to the box. For this reason, you may want to lease the box jointly with your spouse or others.

several ways. Paragraph #5 says that others can rely on the document, usually without liability. The formal requirements for making the PAD (dating, signing, witnessing) also make it more acceptable.

Nevertheless, some medical caregivers might hesitate to accept PADs, especially for important decisions like major surgery or terminating life-sustaining treatment. What caregivers fear is that the PAD has already terminated before the patient advocate uses it. Although the PAD law offers caregivers a degree of protection in this situation, they might still be nervous.

Luckily, the PAD law provides a way to ease their fear. It allows a patient advocate to make an affidavit stating that, as far as s/he knows, the PAD hasn't terminated. The affidavit should convince medical caregivers that the instrument is valid, and allow the patient advocate to exercise it.

The forms section has an affidavit in support of patient advocate designation, which your patient advocate can make for that purpose. As with any affidavit, the advocate must swear to and sign the form before a notary public.

Terminating a Patient Advocate Designation

The PAD law offers several easy ways to terminate designations. The law makes termination as easy as possible because it doesn't want you to get stuck with a PAD you no longer want.

The normal way to terminate a PAD is by revocation. The PAD law allows you to revoke anytime—even after you have become incapacitated. What's more, you can revoke by giving almost any sign that you want to revoke.

Despite this flexibility, by far the best way to revoke your PAD is in writing. You can use the revocation of advance directive contained in the forms section. You should date and sign the revocation, but it doesn't have to be witnessed or notarized.

When you are unable to make a written revocation, you can orally revoke the PAD. If you are incapable of speaking, you can give any kind of gesture signifying revocation. A nonwritten (oral or nonverbal) revocation must be witnessed by another person. Afterward, the witness must sign a written description of the revocation and, if possible, notify the patient advocate. The revocation of advance directive has a place for describing an unwritten revocation.

Example: George makes a PAD. Later, he suffers a stroke that leaves him speechless and almost totally paralyzed, but still alert. Through gestures, George indicates to Margo that he wants to revoke the PAD. With his brother also present, Margo asks George whether he wants to revoke his PAD, and George nods, "Yes." Margo records this nonverbal revocation, dates, and signs it.

Whether you revoke your PAD by written or nonwritten means, it's vital to give notice of revocation to your patient advocate, attending physician, and health care facility. Until this notice, your patient advocate may still be able to exercise the PAD with your medical caregivers. As a result, you'll want to give notice of revocation immediately.

To give your patient advocate notice, deliver a copy of the revocation document (such as a revocation of advance directive) to your patient advocate personally. If that's inconvenient, send a copy of the revocation document to the patient advocate by certified mail, return receipt requested. The receipt proves that the patient advocate got the revocation.

Notify your attending physician and health care facility of the revocation by delivering or sending copies of the revocation to them. Afterward, they must, by law, note the revocation in your medical record and bedside chart to prevent exercise of the revoked PAD.

After you revoke the PAD, destroy the original document and as many copies as you can find (but keep a copy marked "canceled" for your records). Destroying the designation leaves absolutely no doubt that you intend to revoke the instrument. Destruction also makes it impossible for someone to get the document and try to exercise it against your wishes.

Another way to revoke your PAD is to make a new one. The introductory paragraph says that, by making the instrument, you intend to revoke any prior PAD you might have made. Thanks to this provision, the last PAD you make is the one that's effective. Nevertheless, it's also a good idea to destroy any prior PAD (and all copies except yours) you have made, for the reasons described above.

Besides revocation, there are several other ways a PAD can terminate:

Death. The PAD ends at your death.

Recovery from incapacity. Your recovery from incapacity (by regaining the ability to participate in medical treatment decisions) makes the PAD ineffective. The PAD law doesn't say how recovery is determined, but presumably doctors decide this, just as they determined your initial incapacity.* Upon recovery, the PAD remains ineffective until doctors decide that you are incapacitated again.

Loss of patient advocates. The PAD terminates when your patient advocates dies or quits, and the successor patient advocate is also unable to serve.

Court order. If someone believes that your patient advocate is acting improperly, this person can ask the probate court to look into the situation. If abuse is found, the probate court can replace your patient advocate, or even dissolve the PAD entirely.

Expiration. The PAD can end by its own terms. For example, it's possible to have the PAD expire on a particular date or after a specific period of

---

* When the doctors certify your recovery from incapacity, they must do so in a separate document because there isn't space in the doctors' statement in the PAD.

time. However, the PAD in this book doesn't have an expiration provision because there's no telling when or how long you might need it.

Change of marital status. The PAD law conveniently suspends a designation when you have selected your spouse as patient advocate, and you are undergoing a divorce, annulment, or separate maintenance (Michigan's equivalent of a legal separation). If you obtain a final judgment of divorce, annulment, or separate maintenance later, the PAD automatically terminates, unless you have named a successor patient advocate. In that case, the PAD continues with the successor as your patient advocate in place of your ex-spouse.

Revising a Patient Advocate Designation

After you have made your PAD, review it periodically—perhaps every year or two—to see if any revision is necessary. A PAD can become easily outdated if you change your mind about your health care. Advances in medicine may also make it obsolete. Or you may simply want to change patient advocates.

When you want to revise your PAD, don't make revisions by crossing out old material and/or adding new material. After a designation is dated, signed and witnessed, it's complete and mustn't be altered. There are ways to amend the instrument, but amendment is a lot of trouble. Instead, the best way to revise is to make a new PAD.

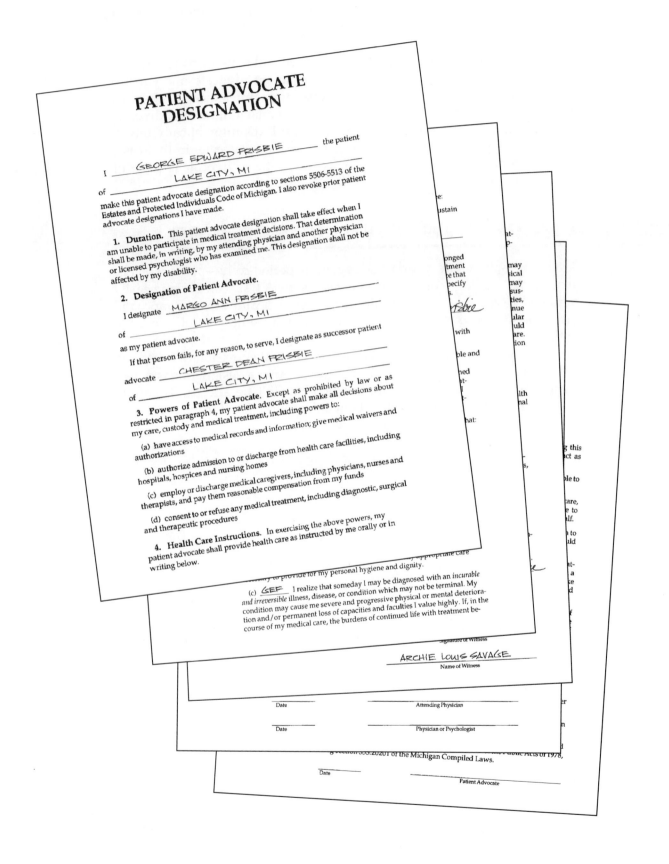

PATIENT ADVOCATE DESIGNATION

I _____GEORGE EDWARD FRISBIE_____ the patient

of _____LAKE CITY, MI_____

make this patient advocate designation according to sections 5506-5513 of the Estates and Protected Individuals Code of Michigan. I also revoke prior patient advocate designations I have made.

1. Duration. This patient advocate designation shall take effect when I am unable to participate in medical treatment decisions. That determination shall be made, in writing, by my attending physician and another physician or licensed psychologist who has examined me. This designation shall not be affected by my disability.

2. Designation of Patient Advocate.

I designate _____MARGO ANN FRISBIE_____

of _____LAKE CITY, MI_____

as my patient advocate.

If that person fails, for any reason, to serve, I designate as successor patient

advocate _____CHESTER DEAN FRISBIE_____

of _____LAKE CITY, MI_____

3. Powers of Patient Advocate. Except as prohibited by law or as restricted in paragraph 4, my patient advocate shall make all decisions about my care, custody and medical treatment, including powers to:

(a) have access to medical records and information; give medical waivers and authorizations

(b) authorize admission to or discharge from health care facilities, including hospitals, hospices and nursing homes

(c) employ or discharge medical caregivers, including physicians, nurses and therapists, and pay them reasonable compensation from my funds

(d) consent to or refuse any medical treatment, including diagnostic, surgical and therapeutic procedures

4. Health Care Instructions. In exercising the above powers, my patient advocate shall provide health care as instructed by me orally or in writing below.

(c) _GEF_ I realize that someday I may be diagnosed with an *incurable and irreversible* illness, disease, or condition which may not be terminal. My condition may cause me severe and progressive physical or mental deterioration and/or permanent loss of capacities and faculties I value highly. If, in the course of my medical care, the burdens of continued life with treatment be-

ARCHIE LOUIS SAVAGE
Name of Witness

_____ _____
Date   Attending Physician

_____ _____
Date   Physician or Psychologist

§ section 333.20201 of the Michigan Compiled Laws.

_____ _____
Date   Patient Advocate

AFFIDAVIT IN SUPPORT OF PATIENT ADVOCATE DESIGNATION

State of Michigan

County of _LAKE_

I, _MARGO ANN FRISBIE_ , being sworn, say:

1. I am the patient advocate of _GEORGE EDWARD FRISBIE_ under a patient advocate designation dated _JAN. 1, 2000_

2. I do not have actual knowledge that the patient advocate designation has been amended or revoked by the patient or by any other cause.

Margo Ann Frisbie

Subscribed and sworn to before me on _MAY 1, 2000_

Guy Frances Fisk
Notary Public

LAKE County, Michigan

My commission expires _7-7-02_

Glossary

ADVANCE DIRECTIVE—Instructions about future health care treatment. An advance directive may provide guidance about any health care decision, including termination of life-sustaining treatment.

Advance directives may be oral or written. Written advance directives include living wills, patient advocate designations (PADs), and do-not-resuscitate (DNR) orders.

ANATOMICAL GIFT—Donation of body parts (organ/tissue donation) or a whole body (gift of body) for transplantation, medical research, or education.

BASIS—Tax concept used to figure capital gain (or loss) when property is sold. There are several kinds of basis: 1) cost basis (purchase price) for property you buy 2) carry-over basis (the donor's basis) for property you receive by gift 3) stepped-up basis (usually the fair market value of the property at the date of the deceased's death) for property received from a deceased person by will, inheritance or nonprobate transfer. A basis may be adjusted for several factors, such as improvement or damage to property.

BOND—Fiduciary's promise to pay financial losses caused by his/her decisions. Frequently, the promise must be backed by a bonding company, or surety, which charges a premium for the guarantee.

CAPITAL GAIN—Profit from the sale of property. Ordinarily, capital gain is the difference between the basis of the property and the sale proceeds. Under current tax law, capital gain is taxed at lower rates than ordinary income, such as wages and salary.

CHILDREN—Michigan's estates code defines children, and this definition is used for distributions of property under the inheritance law and the Michigan statutory will. (The code definition of children is depicted in the chart on the next page.) In a handwritten will, you may accept the code definition of children or redefine them for special situations.

CODICIL—Amendment to a will changing or supplementing the will. A codicil must be in writing and executed in the same manner as wills (signed and usually witnessed).

COMMUNITY PROPERTY—A type of joint property between spouses. Community property (CP) gives spouses equal shares of the property, without rights of survivorship. When the marriage ends by death or divorce, each spouse gets half of the community property. Community property exists in nine states (not Michigan), mostly in the South and West.

CONSERVATOR—Manager of property of a helpless person, such as a minor child or incapacitated adult. Under prior law, a conservator was called guardian of the estate, and some old wills use this terminology.

Estates Code Definition of Children

	Man	Woman
(1) Children born during marriage*	Yes**	Yes
(2) Children born out of wedlock (illegitimate children)	Only if paternity is acknowledged***	Yes
(3) Children legally adopted	Yes	Yes
(4) Children over whom parents have lost parental rights in a termination of parental rights or adoption case	No	No
(5) Stepchildren	No****	No****
(6) Foster children	No	

*Children born during marriage are presumed to be husband's. But paternity can be disproved with strong evidence to the contrary. If so, child is illegitimate and falls under (2).

** Children born during marriage using assisted reproductive procedures, such as artificial insemination, are children of marriage if husband consents to the procedure.

***Paternity can be acknowledged by: 1) formal acknowledgment of paternity by both parents 2) order of filiation in a paternity case 3) father's joining with mother for correction of birth certificate 4) father's habitually treating the child as his own since the child's youth

****Stepchildren can be legally adopted by stepparent in a stepparent adoption. If so, adoptee falls under (3).

CUSTODIAN—Manager of a minor's property under the Uniform Transfers to Minors Act (UTMA).

DEATH CEREMONY—Ritual marking death, such as a funeral, memorial or committal.

DESCENDANT—Relative descended from you in a straight line, such as a child, grandchild, great-grandchild, etc. Unless your will says otherwise, the estates code definition of children is used to determine descendants. For example, a child adopted by your son or daughter is regarded as your grandchild and one of your descendants.

DEVELOPMENTALLY DISABLED ADULT—Adult with a permanent physical or mental impairment, such as mental retardation.

DISABILITY—See "Incapacity."

DOMESTIC ANIMAL—Animals are usually classified by species as either domestic or wild. Domestic species, such as dogs, cats, and horses, are peaceful and tame enough to live in human society. Wild animals, such as monkeys, bears, wolves, etc., are untamed and cannot live safely among humans. Within a species, individual animals can crossover to the opposite category. So, for example, a dog can become wild, or a wild monkey can become tame and be regarded as domestic.

Pets are a sub-category of domestic animals; see "Pet" for more about pet animals.

DOWER—Life-estate (property interest that lasts for the lifetime of the owner, and then expires) a widow (but not a widower) has in all the real property her husband owns during the marriage. Dower gives the widow a one-third life estate in this property. Dower is one of several marital rights widows have. Usually, they surrender it in favor of other rights.

ESTATE TAXES—Taxes imposed on the transfer of property at death. Michigan residents face two estate taxes: federal estate tax (FET) and Michigan estate tax (MET).

EUTHANASIA—Literally, a good or merciful death. Euthanasia is a general term covering a wide range of end-of-life decisions, from termination of life-sustaining treatment to various forms of suicide and even homicide.

Euthanasia is categorized as active (ending the patient's life directly) or passive (ending the patient's life indirectly), and voluntary (death with the patient's consent) or involuntary (death without the patient's consent).

EXECUTION—Method for making a document legally effective. Usually, execution requires dating, signing, and maybe witnessing or notarizing the document.

FAMILY RIGHTS—Include the marital rights (elective share and dower) depicted on page 98, plus several probate allowances: 1) $15,000 homestead allowance for a surviving spouse or minor/dependent children 2) family allowance in a reasonable amount up to a maximum of $18,000 for support of a surviving spouse or minor/dependent children during probate 3) $10,000 exempt property allowance in household property, personal effects, or other assets, for a surviving spouse or children. These allowance amounts will be adjusted for inflation annually in 2001 and thereafter.

FIDUCIARY—Someone holding a position of trust with respect to another person. Fiduciaries include personal representatives, guardians, conservators, UTMA custodians, trustees, and agents (including patient advocates).

FINAL DISPOSITION—Method for disposing of a body, such as burial, cremation, anatomical gift, etc.

GIFT—As used in this book, gift has a two-fold meaning:

Lifetime gift—Transfer of property during your lifetime, motivated by an intent to give the property, which is delivered from the giver (donor) and accepted by the recipient (donee).

Will gift—Transfer of property in a will. Under former law, will gifts of personal property were known as either bequests or legacies, and will gifts of real property were called devises. In the current probate code, all will gifts are technically devises. But because this term is unfamiliar to most people, this book uses will gift instead.

GUARDIAN—Custodian of a helpless person, such as an orphaned child or legally incapacitated or developmentally disabled adult, who takes care of the person's physical well-being. Under prior law, a guardian was called guardian of the person, and some old wills use this terminology.

HEIRS—Relatives who inherit your property if you die without a will. Wills sometimes use heirship to distribute property to remote takers, after all close relatives have died (art. 2.3 of the Michigan statutory will does this).

Michigan inheritance law defines heirs. Heirs are drawn from one relative-by-marriage (spouse) and the following close blood relatives.

- children and descendants (grandchildren, great-grandchildren, etc.)
- parents
- brothers/sisters and their descendants (nephews/nieces, grand-nephews/grandnieces, etc.)
- grandparents and their descendants (uncles/aunts, first cousins, first cousins once-removed, etc.)

Other more remote blood relatives, relatives by-marriage (in-laws), and all nonrelatives cannot qualify as heirs. The chart on the opposite page depicts who may become an heir and the shares they take.

It's a legal truism that a living person has no heirs. During your life, you have presumptive heirs (spouse and close relatives who might qualify as heirs if you died). But true heirs are established only at the time of death (as modified by the 120-hour survival rule). At that point, your heirs are fixed, and more remote relatives are excluded from heirship.

> *Example*: Dudley Mangrove dies in a plane crash, without a will. He is survived by his mother and two brothers. Dudley's mother takes his entire estate as his heir because she is his closest living relative according to the chart above. Dudley's brothers don't qualify as his heirs since they aren't as closely related to him as his mother.

INCAPACITY—A mental or physical problem preventing the victim from managing his/her affairs. Incapacity is the same as disability. Incapacity is the preferred term in this book, but disability is used in the power of attorney and PAD forms because that is what the law requires.

INHERITANCE—Distribution of probate property of those who die without a will. Michigan has an inheritance law specifying the pattern of distribution. Basically, the property goes to the deceased person's heirs.

JOINT TENANCY—A type of joint property. Joint tenancy (JT) gives each owner (joint tenant) an equal but undivided interest in the property. Joint tenancy also provides rights of survivorship, giving the surviving joint tenant full 100% ownership when the other joint tenant dies.

LEGALLY INCAPACITATED PERSON—Adult who can't take care of himself/herself because of a mental, physical, or personal problem.

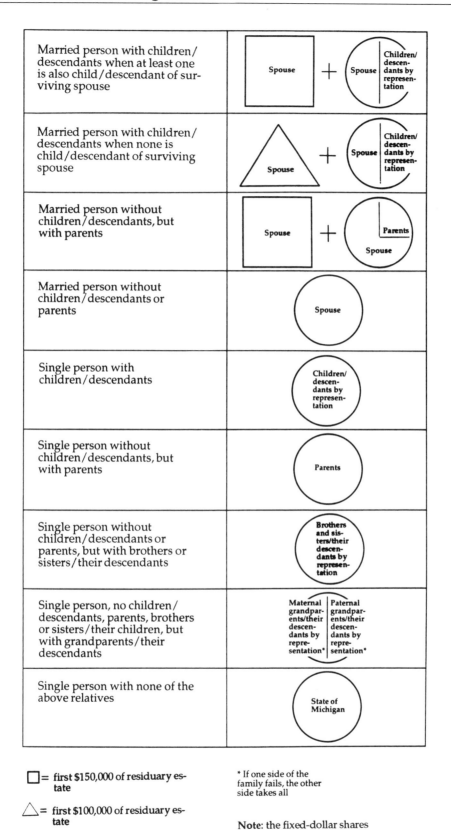

Married person with children/descendants when at least one is also child/descendant of surviving spouse	Spouse + Spouse | Children/descendants by representation
Married person with children/descendants when none is child/descendant of surviving spouse	Spouse + Spouse | Children/descendants by representation
Married person without children/descendants, but with parents	Spouse + Parents Spouse
Married person without children/descendants or parents	Spouse
Single person with children/descendants	Children/descendants by representation
Single person without children/descendants, but with parents	Parents
Single person without children/descendants or parents, but with brothers or sisters/their descendants	Brothers and sisters/their descendants by representation
Single person, no children/descendants, parents, brothers or sisters/their children, but with grandparents/their descendants	Maternal grandparents/their descendants by representation* | Paternal grandparents/their descendants by representation*
Single person with none of the above relatives	State of Michigan

▢ = first $150,000 of residuary estate

△ = first $100,000 of residuary estate

◯ = 1) any remainder of residuary estate after spouse's share has been deducted 2) otherwise, entire residuary estate

* If one side of the family fails, the other side takes all

Note: the fixed-dollar shares allotted to spouse will be adjusted for inflation annually

LIVING WILL—A type of advance directive giving health care instructions directly to medical caregivers. A living will may provide guidance on virtually any health care decision, but deals most often with termination of life-sustaining treatment.

NONPROBATE ESTATE—All the nonprobate property a deceased person had. A nonprobate estate passes outside of probate, according to its own rules, not by the inheritance law or the deceased's will. For example, joint tenancy property passes by right of survivorship, and life insurance proceeds and retirement plan death benefits go to designated beneficiaries.

NONPROBATE PROPERTY—Includes:

- joint tenancy and tenancy by the entirety property
- proceeds from insurance on your life received by someone other than your estate
- retirement plan death benefits received by someone other than your estate
- property held in a living (*inter vivos*) trust
- miscellaneous assets such as *Totten* trusts, pay-on-death (POD) bonds, and custodial accounts at banks or brokerages in POD form.

PATIENT ADVOCATE DESIGNATION—A type of advance directive in the form of a health care power of attorney. In a patient advocate designation (PAD), the principal (patient) assigns health care powers to an agent (patient advocate), which the patient advocate uses to make health care decisions for the patient. The patient may also add health care instructions to guide the patient advocate.

PERSONAL PROPERTY—Any property that isn't real property. Personal property includes ordinary things like clothing, jewelry, motor vehicles, etc., as well as financial assets such as bank accounts, stocks, bonds, etc.

PERSONAL REPRESENTATIVE—One handling the probate of a deceased person's estate. A personal representative also has some authority to carry out the deceased's written instructions about final disposition of his/her body and death ceremonies. Under prior law, a personal representative was known as either an executor or administrator.

PET—According to the customary view, a pet is a domestic animal kept by humans for pleasure. But this definition seems narrow, ignoring the deep bonds that many people form with pets. From a modern point of view, pets are domestic animals regularly receiving close personal attention and affection from their owners.

POWER of ATTORNEY—Legal instrument creating an agency between a principal and an agent. In a power of attorney, the principal gives the agent powers to act for the principal's benefit. There are many kinds of powers of attorney, including:

Durable power of attorney (DPA)—Assigns financial powers to an agent. If the instruments is made durable, it lasts during incapacity of the principal.

Patient advocate designation (PAD)—A health care power of attorney, giving health care powers to an agent, known as a patient advocate.

Custodial power of attorney (CPA)—Transfers custodial powers to an agent allowing the agent to take care of a dependent temporarily.

POWERS of PERSONAL REPRESENTATIVE—Powers a personal representative uses to carry out his/her duties. The powers may be assigned in a will or granted by law, in the estates code. In fact, the code gives personal representatives 32 separate powers, including:

- receive, retain, insure, or dispose of assets
- repair, develop, lease, or abandon property
- pay taxes and assessments
- handle legal matters
- perform, compromise, or reject contracts
- settle debts
- borrow money
- invest funds
- vote stocks
- employ agents, advisers, etc.
- operate a business for up to four months, or incorporate it
- distribute the estate

PROBATE—Has a double meaning. In one sense, probate refers to the filing and proof of a will as the willmaker's final and authentic will. In this regard, people often speak about probating a will.

The second, more accurate, meaning of probate is settlement of a deceased person's probate estate. During settlement, probate property is collected into a probate estate, charges against the estate are paid, and the remainder is distributed according to the inheritance law or will.

PROBATE ESTATE—All the probate property a deceased person owns, which passes through probate before distribution by the inheritance law or will. The Michigan statutory will calls the probate estate the willmaker's "assets."

PROBATE PROPERTY—Includes:

- property you own alone (solely-owned property)
- your percentage share of tenancy in common property
- proceeds from insurance on your life if your estate receives the proceeds
- retirement plan death benefits if your estate receives the benefits

REAL PROPERTY—Land and anything permanently attached, such as houses, buildings, demobilized mobile homes, etc. Real property is the same as real estate.

REPRESENTATION—A pattern of property distribution. Representation permits a deceased taker's children/descendants to stand in, or represent, him/her in the distribution (hence the name). In that case, the children/descendants split the deceased taker's share among themselves in some way, often equally.

Michigan representation is a modified *per capita* pattern of distribution, which is known as per-capita-at-each-generation. In this scheme, equal shares are allotted to takers equally related to the deceased, as in the following examples.

Example: Grover dies before Edith. At Edith's death, Grover is survived by wife Doreen and four children. According to representation, Grover's four children (Edith's grandchildren (= GC)) represent him in the distribution pattern and take his one-fourth share to divide equally among themselves.

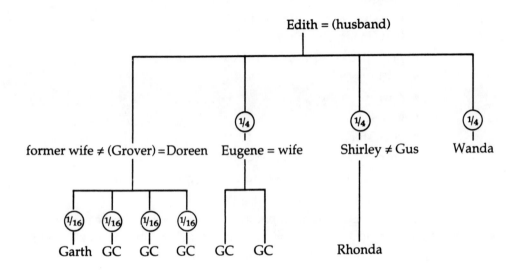

Example: In this case, Grover, Shirley and Wanda all die before Edith. Eugene gets one-third of the estate, and the five grandchildren, who are all equally related to Edith, split the remaining two-thirds share equally.

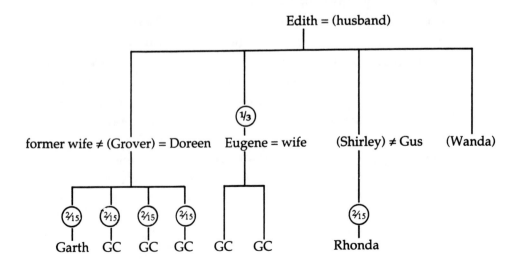

Example: In this scenario, all of Edith's children die before her. The seven grandchildren take *per capita*, and divide the estate equally.

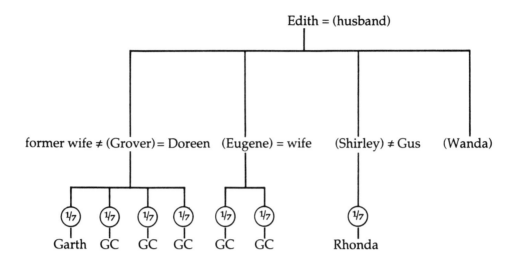

The inheritance law uses representation to pass the shares of deceased would-be heirs onto to their children/descendants. Wills often adopt representation to provide for complete distributions of property. For example, the Michigan statutory will uses representation to dispose of cash gifts and residuary estates in some situations. The handwritten wills in this book also use representation in similar ways.

There are other distribution patterns besides representation. *Per capita* and *per stirpes* distributions are the chief alternatives.

In a true *per capita* distribution, all takers get an equal share, without regard to how closely they are related to the deceased. In effect, the estate is divided by the number of takers, with each taker receiving an equal share. A *per capita* distribution in the first example above is:

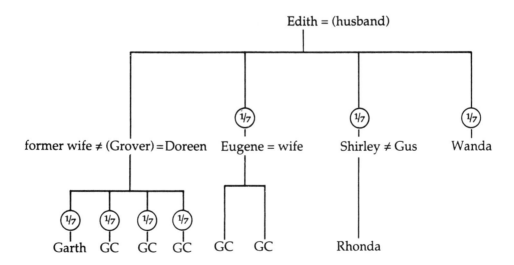

Few people want a pure *per capita* distribution, because the pattern ignores closeness of relation to the deceased. As explained above, Michigan representation is predominately *per capita*, but also considers the relationship of the takers to the deceased. Thus, if you want a *per capita* distribution, it may be better to stick with Michigan representation.

With *per stirpes* distribution, the estate is distributed along the branches of the family tree (these branches are known as *stirpes* in Latin). Descendants divide the share their deceased ancestor would have had, had the ancestor lived. For example, a true *per stirpes* distribution in the third example is:

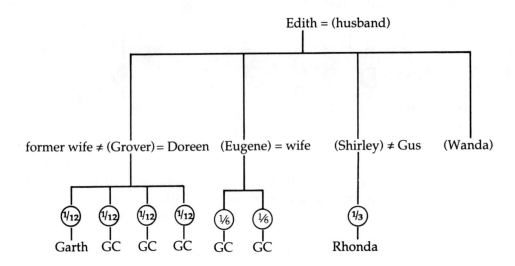

If you want a *per stirpes* distribution in your handwritten will, you must rephrase the gift of your residuary estate. For example, had George Frisbie wanted to give his residuary estate *per stirpes*, in instead of by representation, he would say:

> Two: I give my residuary estate to my wife Margo Ann Frisbie. If Margo Ann Frisbie fails to survive me, the residuary estate shall go to my children and descendants per stirpes.

Bear in mind that a *per stirpes* distribution can result in vastly unequal estate distributions, as in the *per stirpes* example above where grandchild Rhonda takes one-third of the estate while the other grandchildren get lesser shares. To many people, this kind of distribution is unfair.

RESIDENCE—Your permanent home.

RESIDUARY ESTATE—Remainder or residue of a probate estate after deduction, if any, of final expenses (costs of probate, final disposition, death ceremony, estate taxes, and costs of final illness), family rights, claims against the estate, and specific gifts. The Michigan statutory will calls this estate "all other assets."

SETTLOR—Creator of a trust.

SPECIAL JOINT TENANCY—A special kind of joint tenancy in real property only. A special joint tenancy (SJT) is actually a joint life estate between the co-owners, which gives the survivor full ownership of the property.

SPOUSE—Person to whom are legally married. Michigan authorizes two types of marriage: 1) ceremonial marriage (performed by most religious leaders and several types of government officials) 2) secret marriage (an obscure form of marriage performed by a probate judge for the benefit of: (a) people with a good reason to keep their marriage secret (b) children under the age of 16 in certain circumstances).

Common law marriage, in which couples informally agree to live together as husband and wife, was abolished in Michigan on January 1, 1957. Nevertheless, Michigan residents who began living together as husband and wife before that date might still have a valid Michigan common law marriage.

Michigan also recognizes out-of-state marriages. If a marriage is legal in the state where it began, it's legal in Michigan. Therefore, it's possible to have a valid common law marriage in Michigan if it began in one of the states still permitting this type of marriage. As of 2000, the District of Columbia and the following states permit common law marriages:

- Alabama
- Colorado
- Georgia
- Idaho
- Iowa
- Kansas
- Montana
- Oklahoma
- Pennsylvania
- Rhode Island
- South Carolina
- Texas
- Utah

TAXABLE ESTATE—Property of a deceased person subject to estate taxation. A taxable estate includes most probate property, much nonprobate property and some gifts and other lifetime transfers. Ordinarily, the taxable estate is the largest of all the estates (probate, nonprobate, taxable).

TENANCY in COMMON—A type of joint property. A tenancy in common (TC) gives each owner (tenant in common) a fractional share of the property, which is transferable by sale, gift, will or inheritance.

TENANCY by the ENTIRETY—Joint tenancy between spouses.

TRUST—Three-sided arrangement where a propertyowner (settlor) transfers property to another (trustee) to hold for the benefit of a third person (beneficiary).

Trusts are usually placed into two categories: testamentary trust (created in the settlor's will) and living trust (also called *inter vivos* trust) created by the settlor while alive.

TRUSTEE—The fiduciary who receives legal title to the trust property, and manages it for the trust beneficiaries.

WILL—Legal instrument transferring probate property after death. A will may also appoint fiduciaries, such as personal representatives, guardians, and conservators, and give final directions to survivors. There are several types of wills in Michigan: regular, statutory, handwritten, and international.

Update Offer

It's unlikely that the estate planning laws described in this book will change much before the next edition of this book is available, and this is why:

- Publication of this book coincides with new Michigan will and estate laws, which went into effect on April 1, 2000. Since these laws are new, they probably won't be revised for a number of years.
- Several of the dollar-amounts described in this book are self-adjusting. For example, most of the dollar-amounts in the Michigan inheritance law and the federal gift and estate tax law will be adjusted for inflation annually. These automatic adjustments reduce the need for amendment of those laws.

Nevertheless, estate planning laws are revised occasionally. If you want to know if any of the laws described in this book has changed since publication, send a self-addressed stamped envelope to us and request an estate planning book update. If there have been important changes, we will send you a notice describing these changes.

Forms

Statutory Will

Separate List

Self-Proving Declaration (for will execution)

Self-Proving Declaration (for previously-signed will)

Custodial Power of Attorney

(separate) Guardian Appointment

Living Trust Agreement (pet trust)

Quit Claim Deed

Transfer under the Michigan Uniform Transfers to Minors Act

Letter of Instruction

Anatomical Donor Document

Durable Power of Attorney

Attachment (to durable power of attorney)

Revocation of Power of Attorney

Living Will

Revocation of Advance Directive

Do-Not-Resuscitate Order (general)

Do-Not-Resuscitate Order (religious)

Patient Advocate Designation

Affidavit in Support of Patient Advocate Designation

Note: a double set of these forms is included for both spouses in a family.

MICHIGAN STATUTORY WILL

NOTICE

1. An individual age 18 or older and of sound mind may sign a will.
2. There are several kinds of wills. If you choose to complete this form, you will have a Michigan statutory will. If this will does not meet your wishes in any way, you should talk with a lawyer before choosing a Michigan statutory will.
3. Warning! It is strongly recommended that you do not add or cross out any words on this form except for filling in the blanks because all or part of this will may not be valid if you do so.
4. This will has no effect on jointly held assets, on retirement plan benefits, or on life insurance on your life if you have named a beneficiary who survives you.
5. This will is not designed to reduce estate taxes.
6. This will treats adopted children and children born outside of wedlock who would inherit if their parent died without a will the same way as children born or conceived during marriage.
7. You should keep this will in your safe deposit box or other safe place. By paying a small fee, you may file the will in your county's probate court for safekeeping. You should tell your family where the will is kept.
8. You may make and sign a new will at any time. If you marry or divorce after you sign this will, you should make and sign a new will.

INSTRUCTIONS:

1. To have a Michigan statutory will, you must complete the blanks on the will form. You may do this yourself, or direct someone to do it for you. You must either sign the will or direct someone else to sign it in your name and in your presence.
2. Read the entire Michigan statutory will carefully before you begin filling in the blanks. If there is anything you do not understand, you should ask a lawyer to explain it to you.

MICHIGAN STATUTORY WILL

of

_____
(Print or type your full name)

ARTICLE 1. DECLARATIONS

This is my will and I revoke any prior wills and codicils. I live in _____ County, Michigan.

My spouse is _____
(Insert spouse's name or write "none")

My children now living are:

_____   _____
(Insert names or write "none")

_____   _____

_____   _____

ARTICLE 2. DISPOSITION OF MY ASSETS

2.1 CASH GIFTS TO PERSONS OR CHARITIES. (Optional)

I can leave no more than two (2) cash gifts. I make the following cash gifts to the persons or charities in the amount stated here. Any transfer tax due upon my death shall be paid from the balance of my estate and not from these gifts.

Full name and address of person or charity to receive cash gift (name only 1 person or charity here):

_____
(Insert name of person or charity)

_____
(Insert address)

Amount of gift (In figures): $_____

Amount of gift (In words): _____ Dollars

_____
(Your signature)

Full name and address of person or charity to receive cash gift (name only 1 person or charity):

_____
(Insert name of person or charity)

_____
(Insert address)

Amount of gift (In figures): $_____

Amount of gift (In words): _____ Dollars

_____
(Your signature)

2.2 PERSONAL AND HOUSEHOLD ITEMS.

I may leave a separate list or statement, either in my handwriting or signed by me at the end, regarding gifts of specific books, jewelry, clothing, automobiles, furniture, and other personal and household items.

I give my spouse all my books, jewelry, clothing, automobiles, furniture, and other personal and household items not included on such a separate list or statement. If I am not married at the time I sign this will or if my spouse dies before me, my personal representative shall distribute those items, as equally as possible, among my children who survive me. If no children survive me, these items shall be distributed as set forth in paragraph 2.3.

2.3 ALL OTHER ASSETS.

I give everything else I own to my spouse. If I am not married at the time I sign this will or if my spouse dies before me, I give these assets to my children and the descendants of any deceased child. If no spouse, children, or descendants of children survive me, I choose 1 of the following distribution clauses by signing my name on the line after that clause. If I sign on both lines, if I fail to sign on either line, or if I am not now married, these assets will go under distribution clause (b).

Distribution clause, if no spouse, children, or descendants of children survive me. (Select only 1).

(a) One-half to be distributed to my heirs as if I did not have a will, and one-half to be distributed to my spouse's heirs as if my spouse had died just after me without a will.

_____
(Your signature)

(b) All to be distributed to my heirs as if I did not have a will.

_____
(Your signature)

ARTICLE 3. NOMINATIONS OF PERSONAL REPRESENTATIVE, GUARDIAN, AND CONSERVATOR

Personal representatives, guardians, and conservators have a great deal of responsibility. The role of a personal representative is to collect your assets, pay debts and taxes from those assets, and distribute the remaining assets as directed in the will. A guardian is a person who will look after the physical well-being of a child. A conservator is a person who will manage a child's assets and make payments from those assets for the child's benefit. Select them carefully. Also, before you select them, ask them whether they are willing and able to serve.

3.1 PERSONAL REPRESENTATIVE. (Name at least 1)

I nominate _____
(Insert name of person or eligible financial institution)

of _____
(Insert address)

to serve as personal representative.

If my first choice does not serve, I nominate

_____
(Insert name of person or eligible financial institution)

of _____
(Insert address)

to serve as personal representative.

3.2 GUARDIAN AND CONSERVATOR.

Your spouse may die before you. Therefore, if you have a child under age 18, name an individual as guardian of the child, and an individual or eligible financial institution as conservator of the child's assets. The guardian and the conservator may, but need not be, the same person.

If a guardian or conservator is needed for any child of mine, I nominate

_____
(Insert name of individual)

of _____ as guardian
(Insert address)

and _____
(Insert name of individual or eligible financial institution)

of _____
(Insert address)

to serve as conservator.

If my first choice cannot serve, I nominate

_____
(Insert name of individual)

of _____ as guardian
(Insert address)

and _____
(Insert name of individual or eligible financial institution)

of _____
(Insert address)

to serve as conservator.

3.3 BOND.

A bond is a form of insurance in case your personal representative or a conservator performs improperly and jeopardizes your assets. A bond is not required. You may choose whether you wish to require your personal representative and any conservator to serve with or without bond. Bond premiums would be paid out of your assets.

(Select only 1)

(a) My personal representative and any conservator I have named shall serve with bond.

_____
(Your signature)

(b) My personal representative and any conservator I have named shall serve without bond.

_____
(Your signature)

3.4 DEFINITIONS AND ADDITIONAL CLAUSES.

Definitions and additional clauses found at the end of this form are part of this will.

I sign my name to this Michigan statutory will on_____ , 19 _____.

_____
(Your signature)

NOTICE REGARDING WITNESSES

You must use 2 adults who will not receive assets under this will as witnesses. It is preferable to have 3 adult witnesses. All the witnesses must observe you sign the will, or have you tell them you signed the will, or have you tell them the will was signed at your direction in your presence.

STATEMENT OF WITNESSES

We sign below as witnesses, declaring that the individual who is making this will appears to be of sound mind and appears to be making this will freely, without duress, fraud, or undue influence, and that the individual making this will acknowledges that he or she has read, or has had it read to him or her, and understands the contents of this will.

_____   _____
(Print name)   (Signature of witness)

_____
(Address)

_____
(City)   (State)   (Zip)

_____   _____
(Print name)   (Signature of witness)

_____
(Address)

_____
(City)   (State)   (Zip)

_____   _____
(Print name)   (Signature of witness)

_____
(Address)

_____
(City)   (State)   (Zip)

Definitions

The following definitions and rules of construction apply to this Michigan statutory will:

(a) "Assets" means all types of property you can own, such as real estate, stocks and bonds, bank accounts, business interests, furniture, and automobiles.

(b) "Descendants" means your children, grandchildren, and their descendants.

(c) "Descendants" or "children" includes individuals born or conceived during marriage, individuals legally adopted, and individuals born out of wedlock who would inherit if their parent died without a will.

(d) "Jointly held assets" means those assets to which ownership is transferred automatically upon the death of 1 of the owners to the remaining owner or owners.

(e) "Spouse" means your husband or wife at the time you sign this will.

(f) Whenever a distribution under a Michigan statutory will is to be made to an individual's descendants, the assets are to be divided into as many equal shares as there are then living descendants of the nearest degree of living descendants and deceased descendants of that same degree who leave living descendants. Each living descendant of the nearest degree shall receive 1 share. The remaining shares, if any, are combined and then divided in the same manner among the surviving descendants of the deceased descendants as if the surviving descendants who are allocated a share and their surviving descendants had predeceased the descendant. In this manner, all descendants who are in the same generation will take an equal share.

(g) "Heirs" means those persons who would have received your assets if you had died without a will, domiciled in Michigan, under the laws that are then in effect.

(h) "Person" includes individuals and institutions.

(i) Plural and singular words include each other, where appropriate.

(j) If a Michigan statutory will states that a person shall perform an act, the person is required to perform that act. If a Michigan statutory will states that a person may do an act, the person's decision to do or not to do the act shall be made in good faith exercise of the person's powers.

Additional Clauses

Powers of personal representative

1. A personal representative has all powers of administration given by Michigan law to personal representatives and, to the extent funds are not needed to meet debts and expenses currently payable and are not immediately distributable, the power to invest and reinvest the estate from time to time in accordance with the Michigan prudent investor rule. In dividing and distributing the estate, the personal representative may distribute partially or totally in kind, may determine the value of distributions in kind without reference to income tax bases, and may make non-pro rata distributions.

2. The personal representative may distribute estate assets otherwise distributable to a minor beneficiary to the minor's conservator or, in amounts not exceeding $5,000.00 per year, either to the minor, if married; to a parent or another adult with whom the minor resides and who has the care, custody, or control of the minor; or to the guardian. The personal representative is free of liability and is discharged from any further accountability for distributing assets in compliance with the provisions of this paragraph.

Powers of Guardian and Conservator

A guardian named in this will shall have the same authority with respect to the child as a parent having legal custody would have. A conservator named in this will has all of the powers conferred by law.

MICHIGAN STATUTORY WILL

NOTICE

INSTRUCTIONS:

MICHIGAN STATUTORY WILL

of

_____
(Print or type your full name)

ARTICLE 1. DECLARATIONS

This is my will and I revoke any prior wills and codicils. I live in _____ County, Michigan.

My spouse is _____
(Insert spouse's name or write "none")

My children now living are:

_____   _____
(Insert names or write "none")

_____   _____

_____   _____

ARTICLE 2. DISPOSITION OF MY ASSETS

2.1 CASH GIFTS TO PERSONS OR CHARITIES. (Optional)

I can leave no more than two (2) cash gifts. I make the following cash gifts to the persons or charities in the amount stated here. Any transfer tax due upon my death shall be paid from the balance of my estate and not from these gifts.

Full name and address of person or charity to receive cash gift (name only 1 person or charity here):

_____
(Insert name of person or charity)

_____
(Insert address)

Amount of gift (In figures): $_____

Amount of gift (In words): _____ Dollars

_____
(Your signature)

Full name and address of person or charity to receive cash gift (name only 1 person or charity):

_____
(Insert name of person or charity)

_____
(Insert address)

Amount of gift (In figures): $_____

Amount of gift (In words): _____ Dollars

_____
(Your signature)

2.2 PERSONAL AND HOUSEHOLD ITEMS.

I may leave a separate list or statement, either in my handwriting or signed by me at the end, regarding gifts of specific books, jewelry, clothing, automobiles, furniture, and other personal and household items.

I give my spouse all my books, jewelry, clothing, automobiles, furniture, and other personal and household items not included on such a separate list or statement. If I am not married at the time I sign this will or if my spouse dies before me, my personal representative shall distribute those items, as equally as possible, among my children who survive me. If no children survive me, these items shall be distributed as set forth in paragraph 2.3.

2.3 ALL OTHER ASSETS.

I give everything else I own to my spouse. If I am not married at the time I sign this will or if my spouse dies before me, I give these assets to my children and the descendants of any deceased child. If no spouse, children, or descendants of children survive me, I choose 1 of the following distribution clauses by signing my name on the line after that clause. If I sign on both lines, if I fail to sign on either line, or if I am not now married, these assets will go under distribution clause (b).

Distribution clause, if no spouse, children, or descendants of children survive me. (Select only 1).

(a) One-half to be distributed to my heirs as if I did not have a will, and one-half to be distributed to my spouse's heirs as if my spouse had died just after me without a will.

_____
(Your signature)

(b) All to be distributed to my heirs as if I did not have a will.

_____
(Your signature)

ARTICLE 3. NOMINATIONS OF PERSONAL REPRESENTATIVE, GUARDIAN, AND CONSERVATOR

Personal representatives, guardians, and conservators have a great deal of responsibility. The role of a personal representative is to collect your assets, pay debts and taxes from those assets, and distribute the remaining assets as directed in the will. A guardian is a person who will look after the physical well-being of a child. A conservator is a person who will manage a child's assets and make payments from those assets for the child's benefit. Select them carefully. Also, before you select them, ask them whether they are willing and able to serve.

3.1 PERSONAL REPRESENTATIVE. (Name at least 1)

I nominate _____
(Insert name of person or eligible financial institution)

of _____
(Insert address)

to serve as personal representative.

    If my first choice does not serve, I nominate

_____
(Insert name of person or eligible financial institution)

of _____
(Insert address)

to serve as personal representative.

3.2 GUARDIAN AND CONSERVATOR.

    Your spouse may die before you. Therefore, if you have a child under age 18, name an individual as guardian of the child, and an individual or eligible financial institution as conservator of the child's assets. The guardian and the conservator may, but need not be, the same person.

    If a guardian or conservator is needed for any child of mine, I nominate

_____
(Insert name of individual)

of _____ as guardian
(Insert address)

and _____
(Insert name of individual or eligible financial institution)

of _____
(Insert address)

to serve as conservator.

    If my first choice cannot serve, I nominate

_____
(Insert name of individual)

of _____ as guardian
(Insert address)

and _____
(Insert name of individual or eligible financial institution)

of _____
(Insert address)

to serve as conservator.

3.3 BOND.

    A bond is a form of insurance in case your personal representative or a conservator performs improperly and jeopardizes your assets. A bond is not required. You may choose whether you wish to require your personal representative and any conservator to serve with or without bond. Bond premiums would be paid out of your assets.

    (Select only 1)

    (a) My personal representative and any conservator I have named shall serve with bond.

_____
(Your signature)

    (b) My personal representative and any conservator I have named shall serve without bond.

_____
(Your signature)

3.4 DEFINITIONS AND ADDITIONAL CLAUSES.

Definitions and additional clauses found at the end of this form are part of this will.

I sign my name to this Michigan statutory will on_____ , 19 _____.

_____
(Your signature)

NOTICE REGARDING WITNESSES
You must use 2 adults who will not receive assets under this will as witnesses. It is preferable to have 3 adult witnesses. All the witnesses must observe you sign the will, or have you tell them you signed the will, or have you tell them the will was signed at your direction in your presence.

STATEMENT OF WITNESSES
We sign below as witnesses, declaring that the individual who is making this will appears to be of sound mind and appears to be making this will freely, without duress, fraud, or undue influence, and that the individual making this will acknowledges that he or she has read, or has had it read to him or her, and understands the contents of this will.

_____   _____
(Print name)   (Signature of witness)

_____
(Address)

_____   _____   _____
(City)   (State)   (Zip)

_____   _____
(Print name)   (Signature of witness)

_____
(Address)

_____   _____   _____
(City)   (State)   (Zip)

_____   _____
(Print name)   (Signature of witness)

_____
(Address)

_____   _____   _____
(City)   (State)   (Zip)

Definitions
The following definitions and rules of construction apply to this Michigan statutory will:

(a) "Assets" means all types of property you can own, such as real estate, stocks and bonds, bank accounts, business interests, furniture, and automobiles.

(b) "Descendants" means your children, grandchildren, and their descendants.

(c) "Descendants" or "children" includes individuals born or conceived during marriage, individuals legally adopted, and individuals born out of wedlock who would inherit if their parent died without a will.

(d) "Jointly held assets" means those assets to which ownership is transferred automatically upon the death of 1 of the owners to the remaining owner or owners.

(e) "Spouse" means your husband or wife at the time you sign this will.

(f) Whenever a distribution under a Michigan statutory will is to be made to an individual's descendants, the assets are to be divided into as many equal shares as there are then living descendants of the nearest degree of living descendants and deceased descendants of that same degree who leave living descendants. Each living descendant of the nearest degree shall receive 1 share. The remaining shares, if any, are combined and then divided in the same manner among the surviving descendants of the deceased descendants as if the surviving descendants who are allocated a share and their surviving descendants had predeceased the descendant. In this manner, all descendants who are in the same generation will take an equal share.

(g) "Heirs" means those persons who would have received your assets if you had died without a will, domiciled in Michigan, under the laws that are then in effect.

(h) "Person" includes individuals and institutions.

(i) Plural and singular words include each other, where appropriate.

(j) If a Michigan statutory will states that a person shall perform an act, the person is required to perform that act. If a Michigan statutory will states that a person may do an act, the person's decision to do or not to do the act shall be made in good faith exercise of the person's powers.

Additional Clauses
Powers of personal representative

1. A personal representative has all powers of administration given by Michigan law to personal representatives and, to the extent funds are not needed to meet debts and expenses currently payable and are not immediately distributable, the power to invest and reinvest the estate from time to time in accordance with the Michigan prudent investor rule. In dividing and distributing the estate, the personal representative may distribute partially or totally in kind, may determine the value of distributions in kind without reference to income tax bases, and may make non-pro rata distributions.

2. The personal representative may distribute estate assets otherwise distributable to a minor beneficiary to the minor's conservator or, in amounts not exceeding $5,000.00 per year, either to the minor, if married; to a parent or another adult with whom the minor resides and who has the care, custody, or control of the minor; or to the guardian. The personal representative is free of liability and is discharged from any further accountability for distributing assets in compliance with the provisions of this paragraph.

Powers of Guardian and Conservator

A guardian named in this will shall have the same authority with respect to the child as a parent having legal custody would have. A conservator named in this will has all of the powers conferred by law.

SEPARATE LIST

for the Michigan statutory will of

_____

(Full name)   (Date of will)

According to sec. 2.2 of my Michigan statutory will and sec. 2513 of the Estates and Protected Individuals Code of of Michigan, I give the following personal and household items to the persons designated below:

I sign my name to this separate list on _____

_____

(Signature)

SEPARATE LIST

for the Michigan statutory will of

_____
(Full name)   (Date of will)

According to sec. 2.2 of my Michigan statutory will and sec. 2513 of the Estates and Protected Individuals Code of of Michigan, I give the following personal and household items to the persons designated below:

I sign my name to this separate list on _____

_____
(Signature)

SELF-PROVING DECLARATION
(for will execution)

I, _____ , the testator sign my name to this document on _____ . I declare under penalty for perjury under the law of the state of Michigan that this document is my will; that I sign it willingly or willingly direct another to sign it for me; that I execute it as my voluntary act for the purposes expressed in the will, and that I am 18 years of age or older, of sound mind, and under no constraint or undue influence.

_____
(Signature)   Testator

We, _____

_____

and _____

the witnesses, sign our names to this document under penalty for perjury under the law of the state of Michigan, and declare that all of the following statements are true: the individual signing this document as testator executes the document as his or her will, signs it willingly or willingly directs another to sign for him or her, and executes it as his or her voluntary act for the purposes expressed in this will; each of us, in the testator's presence, signs this will as witness to the testator's signing; and, to the best of our knowledge, the testator is 18 years of age or older, of sound mind, and under no constraint or undue influence.

_____
Date

_____
(Signature)   Witness

_____
Date

_____
(Signature)   Witness

_____
Date

_____
(Signature)   Witness

SELF-PROVING DECLARATION
(for will execution)

I, _____ , the testator
sign my name to this document on _____ . I declare under penalty for
perjury under the law of the state of Michigan that this document is my will;
that I sign it willingly or willingly direct another to sign it for me; that I execute it as my voluntary act for the purposes expressed in the will, and that I
am 18 years of age or older, of sound mind, and under no constraint or
undue influence.

_____
(Signature)   Testator

We, _____

_____

and _____

the witnesses, sign our names to this document under penalty for perjury
under the law of the state of Michigan, and declare that all of the following
statements are true: the individual signing this document as testator executes
the document as his or her will, signs it willingly or willingly directs another
to sign for him or her, and executes it as his or her voluntary act for the purposes expressed in this will; each of us, in the testator's presence, signs this
will as witness to the testator's signing; and, to the best of our knowledge, the
testator is 18 years of age or older, of sound mind, and under no constraint or
undue influence.

_____   _____
Date   (Signature)   Witness

_____   _____
Date   (Signature)   Witness

_____   _____
Date   (Signature)   Witness

SELF-PROVING DECLARATION
(for previously-signed will)

We, _____

_____

_____

and _____

the testator and the witnesses, respectively, whose names are signed to the attached will, sign this document and declare under penalty for perjury under the law of the state of Michigan that all of the following statements are true: the individual signing this document as the will's testator executed the will as his or her will, signed it willingly or willingly directed another to sign for him or her, and executed it as his or her voluntary act for the purposes expressed in the will; each witness, in the testator's presence, signed the will as witness to the testator's signing; and, to the best of the witnesses' knowledge, the testator, at the time of the will's execution, was 18 years of age or older, of sound mind, and under no constraint or undue influence.

_____   _____
Date   (Signature)   Testator

_____   _____
Date   (Signature)   Witness

_____   _____
Date   (Signature)   Witness

_____   _____
Date   (Signature)   Witness

SELF-PROVING DECLARATION
(for previously-signed will)

We, _____

_____

_____

and _____

the testator and the witnesses, respectively, whose names are signed to the attached will, sign this document and declare under penalty for perjury under the law of the state of Michigan that all of the following statements are true: the individual signing this document as the will's testator executed the will as his or her will, signed it willingly or willingly directed another to sign for him or her, and executed it as his or her voluntary act for the purposes expressed in the will; each witness, in the testator's presence, signed the will as witness to the testator's signing; and, to the best of the witnesses' knowledge, the testator, at the time of the will's execution, was 18 years of age or older, of sound mind, and under no constraint or undue influence.

_____   _____
Date   (Signature)   Testator

_____   _____
Date   (Signature)   Witness

_____   _____
Date   (Signature)   Witness

_____   _____
Date   (Signature)   Witness

CUSTODIAL POWER
OF ATTORNEY

I _____ the principal

of _____

make this power of attorney according to sec. 5103 of the Estates and Protected
Individuals Code of Michigan. I also revoke any prior power of attorney I may
have made dealing with the dependent's custody as described below.

I am either the parent of the minor child(ren) or guardian of the ward(s) (who
shall be referred to as the "dependent") named below:

Name	Date of Birth

1. Appointment of Agent.

I appoint _____

of _____

as my agent.

If that person fails, for any reason, to serve as my agent, I appoint as succes-

sor agent _____

of _____

2. Duration. This power of attorney shall take effect when I sign it, and
shall remain in effect for six months/until _____
This power of attorney shall not be affected by my disability.

3. Powers of Agent. Except as stated in paragraph 4, I transfer to the agent
all my powers regarding the care, custody and property of the dependent
named above, including powers to:

(a) provide for the dependent's medical treatment by consenting to or refusing any diagnostic, surgical or therapeutic procedures

(b) provide for the dependent's education

(c) manage the dependent's property

(d) other:

4. Restrictions on Agent's Powers. The agent shall not have the power to do anything prohibited by law, or as stated below:

5. Reliance by Third Parties. Third parties can rely on this power of attorney without liability to me or my estate, unless they have actual notice that the power of attorney has been amended or terminated.

6. Miscellaneous. This power of attorney shall be governed by Michigan law, although it may be used out of state. The singular nouns and pronouns in the power of attorney shall refer to plural principals or dependents as the case may be. Photocopies of this document shall have the same legal authority as the original.

_____   _____
Date   Principal

_____   _____
Date   Principal

Witnesses:

_____

_____

State of Michigan

County of _____

   This instrument was acknowledged before me on _____

by _____

                                   _____
                                                     Notary Public

                                   _____ County, Michigan

                                   My commission expires _____

CUSTODIAL POWER OF ATTORNEY

I _____ the principal

of _____

make this power of attorney according to sec. 5103 of the Estates and Protected Individuals Code of Michigan. I also revoke any prior power of attorney I may have made dealing with the dependent's custody as described below.

I am either the parent of the minor child(ren) or guardian of the ward(s) (who shall be referred to as the "dependent") named below:

_____
Name   Date of Birth

_____

_____

_____

1. Appointment of Agent.

I appoint _____

of _____

as my agent.

If that person fails, for any reason, to serve as my agent, I appoint as successor agent _____

of _____

2. Duration. This power of attorney shall take effect when I sign it, and shall remain in effect for six months/until _____
This power of attorney shall not be affected by my disability.

3. Powers of Agent. Except as stated in paragraph 4, I transfer to the agent all my powers regarding the care, custody and property of the dependent named above, including powers to:

(a) provide for the dependent's medical treatment by consenting to or refusing any diagnostic, surgical or therapeutic procedures

(b) provide for the dependent's education

(c) manage the dependent's property

(d) other:

4. Restrictions on Agent's Powers. The agent shall not have the power to do anything prohibited by law, or as stated below:

5. Reliance by Third Parties. Third parties can rely on this power of attorney without liability to me or my estate, unless they have actual notice that the power of attorney has been amended or terminated.

6. Miscellaneous. This power of attorney shall be governed by Michigan law, although it may be used out of state. The singular nouns and pronouns in the power of attorney shall refer to plural principals or dependents as the case may be. Photocopies of this document shall have the same legal authority as the original.

_____
Date

_____
Principal

_____
Date

_____
Principal

Witnesses:

_____

_____

State of Michigan

County of _____

   This instrument was acknowledged before me on _____

by _____

_____
Notary Public

_____ County, Michigan

My commission expires _____

GUARDIAN APPOINTMENT

I _____

of _____

make the following guardian appointments as authorized by the Estates and Protected Individuals Code of Michigan. I also revoke any prior guardian appointments I have made outside a will.

I. Guardian for Children

A. Guardian for Minor Children

If any of my minor children needs a guardian after my death, I appoint

_____

as guardian.

If that person fails, for any reason, to serve as guardian, I appoint as guardian

dian _____

B. Guardian for Legally Incapacitated Adult Children

I am currently serving as guardian for my legally incapacitated unmarried adult child(ren), and I appoint the following person to succeed me as guardian after my death _____

If that person fails, for any reason, to serve as guardian, I appoint as successor guardian _____

II. Guardian for Spouse

I am currently serving as guardian for my legally incapacitated spouse, and I appoint the following person to succeed me as guardian after my death

_____

If that person fails, for any reason, to serve as guardian, I appoint as successor guardian _____

_____   _____
Date   Parent or Spouse

Witnesses:

_____

_____

GUARDIAN APPOINTMENT

I _____

of _____

make the following guardian appointments as authorized by the Estates and Protected Individuals Code of Michigan. I also revoke any prior guardian appointments I have made outside a will.

I. Guardian for Children

A. Guardian for Minor Children

If any of my minor children needs a guardian after my death, I appoint

_____

as guardian.

If that person fails, for any reason, to serve as guardian, I appoint as guardian _____

B. Guardian for Legally Incapacitated Adult Children

I am currently serving as guardian for my legally incapacitated unmarried adult child(ren), and I appoint the following person to succeed me as guardian after my death _____

If that person fails, for any reason, to serve as guardian, I appoint as successor guardian _____

II. Guardian for Spouse

I am currently serving as guardian for my legally incapacitated spouse, and I appoint the following person to succeed me as guardian after my death

_____

If that person fails, for any reason, to serve as guardian, I appoint as successor guardian _____

_____   _____
Date   Parent or Spouse

Witnesses:

_____

_____

LIVING TRUST AGREEMENT

1. Creation of Trust. This is a trust agreement creating a living trust for the primary benefit of designated pet and domestic animals, as authorized by sec. 2722 of the Estates and Protected Individuals Code of Michigan (EPIC),

between _____

of_____ settlor, and

_____

of_____ trustee

   A. *Name of trust.* This living trust shall be named and be known as the

_____ Living Trust.

   B. *Trustee succession.* If the trustee named above cannot serve, that person

shall be replaced by _____

of_____

   C. *Trust enforcement.* If necessary, this trust shall be enforced by

_____

of_____

as provided by sec. 2722(3)(d) of EPIC.

   D. *Trust property.* The principal source of trust property shall be transfers from the settlor's will, receivable after the settlor's death. The trust may also receive nontestamentary transfers from the settlor after his/her death. This property, and any income from these assets, shall constitute the trust property.

   E. *Trust purpose.* The primary purpose of this trust is to provide funds for the care of the animal beneficiaries after the death of the settlor. Before then, the trust shall exist without trust property, and do nothing.

   F. *Beneficiaries of trust.* There shall be two classes of beneficiaries of this trust: 1) animals 2) individuals (people and organizations), who shall receive distributions from the trust as specified in section 2.

   (1) *Animal beneficiaries.* The following pet or domestic animals shall be the animal beneficiaries of this trust. (List additional animal beneficiaries in an attachment)

Name	Species and/or breed

(2) *Individual beneficiaries.* The following people or organizations shall be the individual beneficiaries of this trust. (List additional individual beneficiaries in an attachment)

Name

2. Distribution of Trust Property. To carry out the trust purpose, the trustee shall distribute trust property as follows:

A. *Regular distributions.* After the death of the settlor, the trustee shall pay reasonable amounts periodically to the owners or caretakers of the animal beneficiaries for their care as long as they live.

In making regular distributions, the trustee can spend unequal amounts for the care of the animal beneficiaries, and may exhaust all trust property in providing for their care.

B. *Final distributions.* After termination of the trust, any remaining trust property shall be divided into as many equal shares as there are then-existing individual beneficiaries of this trust, and the shares shall be distributed to these individual beneficiaries.

(1) *Termination at expiration of trust.* After the death of the last surviving animal beneficiary, the trust shall terminate and final distribution shall commence.

(2) *Advanced termination.* The trust shall terminate before expiration if the trust never receives any property from the settlor's will or nontestamentary sources after the settlor's death, or if trust property is exhausted by regular distributions.

3. Revocation or Amendment of Trust. The settlor may at anytime during his/her life, amend, revoke, in whole or in part, this trust agreement, by giving the trustee written notice of the amendment.

The settlor specifically reserves the right to change any of the beneficiaries of this trust, by attaching a signed and dated amendment form to this agreement, naming new beneficiaries and/or removing others.

4. Powers and Duties of Trustee. The trustee shall possess all the powers granted to trustees by sec. 7401 of EPIC.

The trustee shall have all the duties imposed on trustees by secs. 7301-07 of EPIC, except the trustee shall be excused from normal trust filing, reporting, registration, periodic accounting, separate maintenance of funds duties, as permitted by sec. 2722(3)(e) of the code.

Anyone serving as trustee of this trust shall do so without bond and without fees for services.

5. Miscellaneous. This trust agreement shall be governed by Michigan law, although it may be used out of state. The singular nouns and pronouns in this documents shall refer to plurals as the case may be. Photocopies of this document shall have the same legal authority as the original.

_____   _____
Date   Settlor

_____   _____
Date   Trustee

Witnesses:

_____

_____

State of Michigan

County of _____

This instrument was acknowledged before me on _____

by _____

_____
Notary Public

_____ County, Michigan

My commission expires _____

LIVING TRUST AGREEMENT

1. Creation of Trust. This is a trust agreement creating a living trust for the primary benefit of designated pet and domestic animals, as authorized by sec. 2722 of the Estates and Protected Individuals Code of Michigan (EPIC),

between _____

of _____ settlor, and

_____

of _____ trustee

    A. *Name of trust.* This living trust shall be named and be known as the

_____ Living Trust.

    B. *Trustee succession.* If the trustee named above cannot serve, that person

shall be replaced by _____

of _____

    C. *Trust enforcement.* If necessary, this trust shall be enforced by

_____

of _____

as provided by sec. 2722(3)(d) of EPIC.

    D. *Trust property.* The principal source of trust property shall be transfers from the settlor's will, receivable after the settlor's death. The trust may also receive nontestamentary transfers from the settlor after his/her death. This property, and any income from these assets, shall constitute the trust property.

    E. *Trust purpose.* The primary purpose of this trust is to provide funds for the care of the animal beneficiaries after the death of the settlor. Before then, the trust shall exist without trust property, and do nothing.

    F. *Beneficiaries of trust.* There shall be two classes of beneficiaries of this trust: 1) animals 2) individuals (people and organizations), who shall receive distributions from the trust as specified in section 2.

    (1) *Animal beneficiaries.* The following pet or domestic animals shall be the animal beneficiaries of this trust. (List additional animal beneficiaries in an attachment)

Name	Species and/or breed

(2) *Individual beneficiaries.* The following people or organizations shall be the individual beneficiaries of this trust. (List additional individual beneficiaries in an attachment)

Name

---

2. Distribution of Trust Property. To carry out the trust purpose, the trustee shall distribute trust property as follows:

A. *Regular distributions.* After the death of the settlor, the trustee shall pay reasonable amounts periodically to the owners or caretakers of the animal beneficiaries for their care as long as they live.

In making regular distributions, the trustee can spend unequal amounts for the care of the animal beneficiaries, and may exhaust all trust property in providing for their care.

B. *Final distributions.* After termination of the trust, any remaining trust property shall be divided into as many equal shares as there are then-existing individual beneficiaries of this trust, and the shares shall be distributed to these individual beneficiaries.

(1) *Termination at expiration of trust.* After the death of the last surviving animal beneficiary, the trust shall terminate and final distribution shall commence.

(2) *Advanced termination.* The trust shall terminate before expiration if the trust never receives any property from the settlor's will or nontestamentary sources after the settlor's death, or if trust property is exhausted by regular distributions.

3. Revocation or Amendment of Trust. The settlor may at anytime during his/her life, amend, revoke, in whole or in part, this trust agreement, by giving the trustee written notice of the amendment.

The settlor specifically reserves the right to change any of the beneficiaries of this trust, by attaching a signed and dated amendment form to this agreement, naming new beneficiaries and/or removing others.

4. Powers and Duties of Trustee. The trustee shall possess all the powers granted to trustees by sec. 7401 of EPIC.

The trustee shall have all the duties imposed on trustees by secs. 7301-07 of EPIC, except the trustee shall be excused from normal trust filing, reporting, registration, periodic accounting, separate maintenance of funds duties, as permitted by sec. 2722(3)(e) of the code.

Anyone serving as trustee of this trust shall do so without bond and without fees for services.

5. Miscellaneous. This trust agreement shall be governed by Michigan law, although it may be used out of state. The singular nouns and pronouns in this documents shall refer to plurals as the case may be. Photocopies of this document shall have the same legal authority as the original.

_____   _____
Date   Settlor

_____   _____
Date   Trustee

Witnesses:

_____

_____

State of Michigan

County of _____

     This instrument was acknowledged before me on _____

by _____

                            _____
                                  Notary Public

                      _____ County, Michigan

                      My commission expires _____

QUIT CLAIM DEED

, grantor(s),

of

quit claims to   , grantee(s),

of

the following real property located in the   of
County, Michigan:

for the sum of

This deed is exempt from transfer tax under:

Date _____

Witnesses:

_____

_____

☐ MCL 207.526(a) (gift)

☐ MCL 207.526(i) (transfer of tenancy by the entirety between spouses)

☐ MCL 207.526(q) (creation of joint tenancy when
grantor(s) is one of the joint tenants)

Grantor(s):

_____

_____

State of Michigan

County of _____

    This instrument was acknowledged before me on _____

by _____

_____

Notary Public

_____ County, Michigan

My commission expires _____

Prepared by: Return recorded deed to grantee, or other:

Send future tax bills to grantee, or other:

QUIT CLAIM DEED

, grantor(s),

of

quit claims to   , grantee(s),

of

the following real property located in the   of
                    County, Michigan:

for the sum of

This deed is exempt from transfer tax under:

Date _____

☐ MCL 207.526(a) (gift)

☐ MCL 207.526(i) (transfer of tenancy by the entirety between spouses)

☐ MCL 207.526(q) (creation of joint tenancy when
grantor(s) is one of the joint tenants)

Witnesses: Grantor(s):

_____   _____

_____   _____

State of Michigan

County of _____

   This instrument was acknowledged before me on _____

by _____

_____

Notary Public

_____ County, Michigan

My commission expires _____

Prepared by: Return recorded deed to grantee, or other:

                        Send future tax bills to grantee, or other:

TRANSFER UNDER THE MICHIGAN UNIFORM TRANSFERS TO MINORS ACT

I, _____

(name of transferor or name and representative capacity, if a fiduciary)

transfer to _____

(name of custodian)

as custodian for _____

(name of minor)

[until age _____]

under the Michigan uniform transfers to minors act, the following:

(insert a description of the custodial property sufficient to identify it).

_____   _____

Dated   (Signature)

_____

(name of custodian)

acknowledges receipt of the property described above as custodian for the minor named above under the Michigan uniform transfers to minor act.

_____   _____

Dated   (Signature of Custodian)

TRANSFER UNDER THE MICHIGAN
UNIFORM TRANSFERS TO MINORS ACT

I, _____

(name of transferor or name and representative capacity, if a fiduciary)

transfer to _____

(name of custodian)

as custodian for _____

(name of minor)

[until age _____]

under the Michigan uniform transfers to minors act, the following:

(insert a description of the custodial property sufficient to identify it).

_____

Dated

_____

(Signature)

_____

(name of custodian)

acknowledges receipt of the property described above as custodian for the minor named above under the Michigan uniform transfers to minor act.

_____

Dated

_____

(Signature of Custodian)

LETTER OF INSTRUCTION

I provide this information to my survivors to settle my estate. I also give the following instructions to my personal representative or others as permitted by sec. 3701 of the Estates and Protected Individuals Code of Michigan.

1. Important Personal Information

A. *Personal information*

Name:

  (Maiden name):

  Address:

  Date of birth: place of birth:

  Social security no:

  Citizenship:

Spouse:

  Date of marriage: place of marriage:

  Former spouse(s):

  Address:

Parents:

  Address:

Children:

  Address(es):

Brothers and sisters:

  Address(es):

Education: (List schools attended, degree and/or honors received, and date of graduation)

Occupation:

  Employer:

  Former employers:

Branch of military service:

  Dates of service:

  Commendations:

  Service no:

Rank at discharge:

Manner of separation:

Religious affiliation:

Local place of worship:

Clergyman:

Professional and fraternal memberships:

Civic and charitable activities:

Other activities, achievements, hobbies, etc:

My personal documents (birth certificate, marriage license, divorce papers, military service papers, etc.) are located at:

Safe deposit box at: box no:

At home in:

Other place:

Keys to my house, motor vehicles, safe deposit box, etc., are located at:

Pet animals I own or take care of:

I have made the following arrangements for care of these pets after my death:

The pets receive care from this veterinarian or animal hospital:

B. *Financial information*

I have these financial accounts:

Financial institution	address	type	account no.
Financial institution	address	type	account no.
Financial institution	address	type	account no.

I have these stock brokerage accounts:

Broker	address	type	account no.
Broker	address	type	account no.
Broker	address	type	account no.

My stockbroker is:

I have the following retirement plans or accounts:

Broker	address	type	account no.

Broker	address	type	account no.

Broker	address	type	account no.

My accountant is:

My financial adviser or planner is:

I have these credit and charge accounts:

Creditor	address	account no.

Creditor	address	account no.

Creditor	address	account no.

I have these outstanding loans:

Creditor	address	account no.

Creditor	address	account no.

Creditor	address	account no.

I have these insurance (life disability, long-term care, homeowners, automobile, etc.) policies:

Insurer	type of insurance	policy no.

Insurer	type of insurance	policy no.

Insurer	type of insurance	policy no.

My insurance agent is:

My financial documents (bank books, tax returns, stock and bond certificates, loan documents, retirement plan documents, insurance policies, deeds, mortgages, etc.) are located at:

Safe deposit box at: box no:

At home in:

Other place:

C. *Legal information*

My will and other estate planning documents are located at:

    Safe deposit box at: box no:

    Probate court at:

    At home in:

    Other place:

    My first-choice personal representative is:

    Address:

    My second-choice personal representative is:

    Address:

My lawyer is:

2. Final Disposition

For final disposition of my body, I request:

_____ Earth burial

Place of burial: (Attach deed to cemetery plot)

_____

Cemetery   plot no.   grave no.

Outer burial container:

   ____ I want the least expensive outer burial container

   ____ I want this outer burial container:

Grave-marker:

   ____ I want no grave-marker

   ____ I want this type of grave-marker:

     ____ Upright stone marker

     ____ Flush marker made of: ☐ stone ☐ metal

I want this inscription on my grave-marker:

_____ Entombment

Place of entombment: (Attach deed to tomb)

_____

Cemetery   tomb or niche no.

_____ Cremation, with the cremains or ashes:

Buried at:

Final container (urn or other container):

Placed in a columbarium at: niche no.

Final container (urn or other container):

Scattered (if permissible) at:

Other disposition of cremains or ashes:

_____ Anatomical gifts

_____ I have made an anatomical gift of body parts to:

The anatomical donor document is located at:

_____ I have made a gift of my whole body to:

The anatomical donor document/gift of body form is located at:

If my gift is rejected by the donee, I want final disposition by:

_____ I forbid any anatomical gifts from my body

_____ Other kind of final disposition by (burial at sea, etc.):

3. Death Ceremony

I want my death memorialized by: (Select as many as are applicable)

_____ Funeral

Before the funeral, I want my body preserved by:

_____ Embalming

_____ Refrigeration or other cooling (May prevent certain types of funerals)

I want this container for my body:

_____ Casket made of:

_____ wood

_____ metal: ☐ sealed ☐ nonsealing

_____ synthetic (plastic or fiberglass)

I want to: ☐ buy ☐ rent a casket

If a casket is bought, I want:

_____ expensive casket

_____ least expensive casket

_____ Other container:

The casket may be viewed:

Before the funeral:

☐ By all mourners ☐ by immediate family only ☐ open ☐ closed

During the funeral:

☐ By all mourners ☐ by immediate family only ☐ open ☐ closed

After the funeral:

    ☐ By all mourners ☐ by immediate family only ☐ open ☐ closed

The funeral service should take place at:

I want: or: to officiate
at the service.

I want the service to include: (Describe religious material, readings, music, etc.)

I want the following six persons as pallbearers:

I want flowers from:

___ Immediate family only

___ Anyone

___ No flowers, and gifts in lieu of flowers to:

Other funeral instructions:

_____ Memorial

The memorial should take place at:

I want: or: to officiate
at the memorial service.

I want the service to include: (Describe religious material, readings, music, etc.)

_____ Committal

I want: or: to officiate
at the service.

I want the service to include: (Describe religious material, readings, music, etc.)

4. Final Arrangements

I have made arrangements for final disposition and/or a death ceremony with:

_____ Funeral home:

Address:

_____ Cemetery:

Address:

_____ Memorial society:

Address:

_____ Direct disposition firm:

Address:

_____ I have prepaid the cost of these arrangements by the following plan: (Attach contract)

Additional information or instructions:

_____   _____
Date   Signature

LETTER OF INSTRUCTION

I provide this information to my survivors to settle my estate. I also give the following instructions to my personal representative or others as permitted by sec. 3701 of the Estates and Protected Individuals Code of Michigan.

1. Important Personal Information

A. *Personal information*

Name:

  (Maiden name):

  Address:

  Date of birth: place of birth:

  Social security no:

  Citizenship:

Spouse:

  Date of marriage: place of marriage:

  Former spouse(s):

  Address:

Parents:

  Address:

Children:

  Address(es):

Brothers and sisters:

  Address(es):

Education: (List schools attended, degree and/or honors received, and date of graduation)

Occupation:

  Employer:

  Former employers:

Branch of military service:

  Dates of service:

  Commendations:

  Service no:

Rank at discharge:

Manner of separation:

Religious affiliation:

Local place of worship:

Clergyman:

Professional and fraternal memberships:

Civic and charitable activities:

Other activities, achievements, hobbies, etc:

My personal documents (birth certificate, marriage license, divorce papers, military service papers, etc.) are located at:

Safe deposit box at: box no:

At home in:

Other place:

Keys to my house, motor vehicles, safe deposit box, etc., are located at:

Pet animals I own or take care of:

I have made the following arrangements for care of these pets after my death:

The pets receive care from this veterinarian or animal hospital:

B. *Financial information*

I have these financial accounts:

Financial institution	address	type	account no.
Financial institution	address	type	account no.
Financial institution	address	type	account no.

I have these stock brokerage accounts:

Broker	address	type	account no.
Broker	address	type	account no.
Broker	address	type	account no.

My stockbroker is:

I have the following retirement plans or accounts:

Broker	address	type	account no.
Broker	address	type	account no.
Broker	address	type	account no.

My accountant is:

My financial adviser or planner is:

I have these credit and charge accounts:

Creditor	address	account no.
Creditor	address	account no.
Creditor	address	account no.

I have these outstanding loans:

Creditor	address	account no.
Creditor	address	account no.
Creditor	address	account no.

I have these insurance (life disability, long-term care, homeowners, automobile, etc.) policies:

Insurer	type of insurance	policy no.
Insurer	type of insurance	policy no.
Insurer	type of insurance	policy no.

My insurance agent is:

My financial documents (bank books, tax returns, stock and bond certificates, loan documents, retirement plan documents, insurance policies, deeds, mortgages, etc.) are located at:

Safe deposit box at: box no:

At home in:

Other place:

C. *Legal information*

My will and other estate planning documents are located at:

Safe deposit box at: box no:

Probate court at:

At home in:

Other place:

My first-choice personal representative is:

Address:

My second-choice personal representative is:

Address:

My lawyer is:

2. Final Disposition

For final disposition of my body, I request:

_____ Earth burial

Place of burial: (Attach deed to cemetery plot)

Cemetery   plot no.   grave no.

Outer burial container:

___ I want the least expensive outer burial container

___ I want this outer burial container:

Grave-marker:

___ I want no grave-marker

___ I want this type of grave-marker:

___ Upright stone marker

___ Flush marker made of: ☐ stone   ☐ metal

I want this inscription on my grave-marker:

_____ Entombment

Place of entombment: (Attach deed to tomb)

Cemetery   tomb or niche no.

_____ Cremation, with the cremains or ashes:

Buried at:

Final container (urn or other container):

Placed in a columbarium at: niche no.

Final container (urn or other container):

Scattered (if permissible) at:

Other disposition of cremains or ashes:

_____ Anatomical gifts

_____ I have made an anatomical gift of body parts to:

The anatomical donor document is located at:

_____ I have made a gift of my whole body to:

The anatomical donor document/gift of body form is located at:

If my gift is rejected by the donee, I want final disposition by:

_____ I forbid any anatomical gifts from my body

_____ Other kind of final disposition by (burial at sea, etc.):

3. Death Ceremony

I want my death memorialized by: (Select as many as are applicable)

_____ Funeral

Before the funeral, I want my body preserved by:

_____ Embalming

_____ Refrigeration or other cooling (May prevent certain types of funerals)

I want this container for my body:

_____ Casket made of:

_____ wood

_____ metal: ☐ sealed   ☐ nonsealing

_____ synthetic (plastic or fiberglass)

I want to: ☐ buy   ☐ rent a casket

If a casket is bought, I want:

_____ expensive casket

_____ least expensive casket

_____ Other container:

The casket may be viewed:

Before the funeral:

☐ By all mourners   ☐ by immediate family only   ☐ open   ☐ closed

During the funeral:

☐ By all mourners   ☐ by immediate family only   ☐ open   ☐ closed

After the funeral:

☐ By all mourners ☐ by immediate family only ☐ open ☐ closed

The funeral service should take place at:

I want: or: to officiate
at the service.

I want the service to include: (Describe religious material, readings, music, etc.)

I want the following six persons as pallbearers:

I want flowers from:

___ Immediate family only

___ Anyone

___ No flowers, and gifts in lieu of flowers to:

Other funeral instructions:

_____ Memorial

The memorial should take place at:

I want: or: to officiate
at the memorial service.

I want the service to include: (Describe religious material, readings, music, etc.)

_____ Committal

I want: or: to officiate
at the service.

I want the service to include: (Describe religious material, readings, music, etc.)

4. Final Arrangements

I have made arrangements for final disposition and/or a death ceremony with:

_____ Funeral home:

  Address:

_____ Cemetery:

  Address:

_____ Memorial society:

  Address:

_____ Direct disposition firm:

  Address:

_____ I have prepaid the cost of these arrangements by the following plan: (Attach contract)

Additional information or instructions:

_____   _____
Date   Signature

ANATOMICAL DONOR DOCUMENT

_____

In the hope that I may help others, I hereby make this anatomical gift if medically acceptable, to take effect upon my death. The words and marks below indicate my desires.

I give:

(a) _____ any need organs or physical parts

(b) _____ only the following organs or physical parts

_____

Specify organ(s) or physical part(s)

For the purposes of transplantation, therapy, medical research or education:

(c) _____ my body for anatomical study if needed.

Limitations or special wishes, if any: _____

_____

Signed by the donor and the following 2 witnesses in the presence of each other:

_____

Signature of donor

_____

Date of birth of donor

_____

Date signed

_____

City and state

_____

Witness

_____

Witness

ANATOMICAL DONOR DOCUMENT

_____

In the hope that I may help others, I hereby make this anatomical gift if medically acceptable, to take effect upon my death. The words and marks below indicate my desires.

I give:

(a) _____ any need organs or physical parts

(b) _____ only the following organs or physical parts

_____
Specify organ(s) or physical part(s)

For the purposes of transplantation, therapy, medical research or education:

(c) _____ my body for anatomical study if needed.

Limitations or special wishes, if any: _____

_____

Signed by the donor and the following 2 witnesses in the presence of each other:

_____
Signature of donor

_____
Date of birth of donor

_____
Date signed

_____
City and state

_____
Witness

_____
Witness

DURABLE POWER
OF ATTORNEY

I _____ the principal

of _____

make this power of attorney according to sections 5501-5505 of the Estates and Protected Individuals Code of Michigan. I also revoke prior powers of attorney I have made dealing with my financial affairs as described below.

1. Appointment of Agent. I appoint as my agent

_____

of _____

If that person fails, for any reason, to serve as my agent, I appoint as successor agent _____

of _____

2. Duration. Choose one of the following sections (A or B), by writing your initials before your choice.

A. _____ *(Immediate powers)* This power of attorney shall take effect when I sign it. The power of attorney shall not be affected by my disability.

B. _____ *(Springing powers)* This power of attorney shall take effect upon my disability. For the purpose of this power of attorney, I shall be disabled when I am unable to manage my own affairs. This determination shall be made, in writing, by a physician.

If possible, the physician determining my disability, or recovery from disability, shall be _____

This power of attorney shall be suspended when I recover from disability. I shall be recovered from disability when a physician determines, in writing, that I am able to mange my own affairs again.

3. Powers of Agent. Except as stated in paragraph 4, the agent can do anything regarding my financial affairs that I could do, including powers to:

(a) *Property management.* Buy, sell, give (outright or in trust), hold, convey, exchange, lease, partition, improve, mortgage, option, insure, invest or otherwise deal with my real or personal property (my real property may be described in an attachment to this form, which may be revised from time to time). Make deeds, bills of sale, purchase agreements, land contracts, sales contracts, listing agreements, easements, mortgages, leases, options, security agreements or other documents with regard to my real or personal property.

(b) *Investment.* Invest or reinvest in stocks, bonds, loans, U.S. government obligations (including savings bonds and treasury bills) and other securities; receive dividends or interest from the securities; vote stock in person or by proxy; deal with the securities directly or through a brokerage firm; make any documents with regard to the securities.

(c) *Business management.* Operate, participate in, reorganize, recapitalize, incorporate, sell, merge, close, liquidate or dissolve a business that I might be engaged in; employ agents, officers or directors for the business; make contracts with regard to the business, including buy-sell or partnership agreements.

(d) *Borrowing.* Borrow money, unsecured or secured by my property; make promissory notes, mortgages, security agreements, guaranties or similar documents in connection with any borrowing.

(e) *Debts and expenses.* Pay bills, loans, notes or other debts owed by me or incurred by the agent for me; pay all expenses for the support and maintenance of me or my dependents; pay all expenses for the management of my property.

(f) *Financial institutions.* Open or close an account at a bank, savings and loan association, credit union or other financial institution; make deposits or withdrawals from the account, and make drafts, checks, receipts, notes or other instruments for that purpose; lease, discontinue, enter or withdraw contents from a safe deposit box at a financial institution; carry on any other transactions at financial institutions.

(g) *Taxes.* Pay federal, state or local taxes I owe, or any interest or penalty on them; make and file tax returns, reports, forms, declarations or other documents for these taxes; claim and cash any tax refund; handle any and all federal, state or local tax matters.

(h) *Employee benefits.* Exercise all rights, options, powers or privileges for any pension, thrift, stock option or ownership, profit-sharing or other employee benefit plan I am eligible for.

(i) *Government benefits.* Apply for and receive any government benefits, including social security, that I am eligible for; receive and cash or deposit any benefit check or draft.

(j) *Legal and administrative proceedings.* Begin, continue, defend, appeal, or settle any legal or administrative proceedings involving me or my property.

(k) *Insurance.* Obtain, redeem, borrow against, amend, cancel, convert, pledge, surrender or change any insurance I have; make any documents, forms or affidavits in connection with any insurance.

(l) *Motor vehicles.* Apply for or transfer the certificates of title to automobiles or other motor vehicles.

(m) *Agents and employees.* Employ and compensate real estate brokers, stock-brokers, advisers, accountants, lawyers, or other agents and employees.

(n) *Other powers.* I also give the agent powers to:

4. Restrictions on Powers of Agent. The agent shall not have the power to do any of the following things: a) make a will or codicil for me b) change the beneficiary of any life insurance c) have any power or incidents of ownership over life insurance I own on the agent's life d) exercise any powers that would make my property taxable to the agent for gifts, estate or income tax purposes e) other:

5. Compensation of Agent. The agent may receive reimbursement for actual and necessary expenses incurred in carrying out the above powers. Otherwise, the agent shall not receive any compensation.

6. Reliance by Third Parties. Third parties can rely on this power of attorney without liability to me or my estate, unless they have actual notice that the power of attorney has been amended or terminated.

7. Miscellaneous. This power of attorney shall be governed by Michigan law, although it may be used out of state. Photocopies of this document shall have the same legal authority as the original.

_____   _____
Date
                                                     Principal

Witnesses:

_____

_____

State of Michigan

County of _____

This instrument was acknowledged before me on _____

by _____

                                        _____
                                        Notary Public

                                        _____ County, Michigan
                                        My commission expires _____

Prepared by:

Physician's Statement

I _____

of _____

am a physician.

    I have examined the principal and it is my opinion that s/he is unable to manage his/her own affairs.

_____   _____
Date   Physician

DURABLE POWER OF ATTORNEY

I _____ the principal

of _____

make this power of attorney according to sections 5501-5505 of the Estates and Protected Individuals Code of Michigan. I also revoke prior powers of attorney I have made dealing with my financial affairs as described below.

1. Appointment of Agent. I appoint as my agent

_____

of _____

If that person fails, for any reason, to serve as my agent, I appoint as successor agent _____

of _____

2. Duration. Choose one of the following sections (A or B), by writing your initials before your choice.

A. _____ *(Immediate powers)* This power of attorney shall take effect when I sign it. The power of attorney shall not be affected by my disability.

B. _____ *(Springing powers)* This power of attorney shall take effect upon my disability. For the purpose of this power of attorney, I shall be disabled when I am unable to manage my own affairs. This determination shall be made, in writing, by a physician.

If possible, the physician determining my disability, or recovery from disability, shall be _____

This power of attorney shall be suspended when I recover from disability. I shall be recovered from disability when a physician determines, in writing, that I am able to mange my own affairs again.

3. Powers of Agent. Except as stated in paragraph 4, the agent can do anything regarding my financial affairs that I could do, including powers to:

(a) *Property management.* Buy, sell, give (outright or in trust), hold, convey, exchange, lease, partition, improve, mortgage, option, insure, invest or otherwise deal with my real or personal property (my real property may be described in an attachment to this form, which may be revised from time to time). Make deeds, bills of sale, purchase agreements, land contracts, sales contracts, listing agreements, easements, mortgages, leases, options, security agreements or other documents with regard to my real or personal property.

(b) *Investment.* Invest or reinvest in stocks, bonds, loans, U.S. government obligations (including savings bonds and treasury bills) and other securities; receive dividends or interest from the securities; vote stock in person or by proxy; deal with the securities directly or through a brokerage firm; make any documents with regard to the securities.

(c) *Business management.* Operate, participate in, reorganize, recapitalize, incorporate, sell, merge, close, liquidate or dissolve a business that I might be engaged in; employ agents, officers or directors for the business; make contracts with regard to the business, including buy-sell or partnership agreements.

(d) *Borrowing.* Borrow money, unsecured or secured by my property; make promissory notes, mortgages, security agreements, guaranties or similar documents in connection with any borrowing.

(e) *Debts and expenses.* Pay bills, loans, notes or other debts owed by me or incurred by the agent for me; pay all expenses for the support and maintenance of me or my dependents; pay all expenses for the management of my property.

(f) *Financial institutions.* Open or close an account at a bank, savings and loan association, credit union or other financial institution; make deposits or withdrawals from the account, and make drafts, checks, receipts, notes or other instruments for that purpose; lease, discontinue, enter or withdraw contents from a safe deposit box at a financial institution; carry on any other transactions at financial institutions.

(g) *Taxes.* Pay federal, state or local taxes I owe, or any interest or penalty on them; make and file tax returns, reports, forms, declarations or other documents for these taxes; claim and cash any tax refund; handle any and all federal, state or local tax matters.

(h) *Employee benefits.* Exercise all rights, options, powers or privileges for any pension, thrift, stock option or ownership, profit-sharing or other employee benefit plan I am eligible for.

(i) *Government benefits.* Apply for and receive any government benefits, including social security, that I am eligible for; receive and cash or deposit any benefit check or draft.

(j) *Legal and administrative proceedings.* Begin, continue, defend, appeal, or settle any legal or administrative proceedings involving me or my property.

(k) *Insurance.* Obtain, redeem, borrow against, amend, cancel, convert, pledge, surrender or change any insurance I have; make any documents, forms or affidavits in connection with any insurance.

(l) *Motor vehicles.* Apply for or transfer the certificates of title to automobiles or other motor vehicles.

(m) *Agents and employees.* Employ and compensate real estate brokers, stock-brokers, advisers, accountants, lawyers, or other agents and employees.

(n) *Other powers.* I also give the agent powers to:

4. Restrictions on Powers of Agent. The agent shall not have the power to do any of the following things: a) make a will or codicil for me b) change the beneficiary of any life insurance c) have any power or incidents of ownership over life insurance I own on the agent's life d) exercise any powers that would make my property taxable to the agent for gifts, estate or income tax purposes e) other:

5. Compensation of Agent. The agent may receive reimbursement for actual and necessary expenses incurred in carrying out the above powers. Otherwise, the agent shall not receive any compensation.

6. Reliance by Third Parties. Third parties can rely on this power of attorney without liability to me or my estate, unless they have actual notice that the power of attorney has been amended or terminated.

7. Miscellaneous. This power of attorney shall be governed by Michigan law, although it may be used out of state. Photocopies of this document shall have the same legal authority as the original.

_____   _____
Date

                                         Principal

Witnesses:

_____

_____

State of Michigan

County of _____

This instrument was acknowledged before me on_____

by _____

                                _____
                                                Notary Public
                                _____ County, Michigan
                                My commission expires _____

Prepared by:

Physician's Statement

I _____

of _____

am a physician.

   I have examined the principal and it is my opinion that s/he is unable to manage his/her own affairs.

| _____ | _____ |
| Date | Physician |

ATTACHMENT

Real property described as follows:

ATTACHMENT

Real property described as follows:

REVOCATION OF POWER
OF ATTORNEY

I_____ the principal

of _____

revoke my power of attorney dated _____[and recorded

on _____ at Liber _____ Page_____ in the office of the

Register of Deeds, _____ County, Michigan], and all the powers

given to my agent _____

in this power of attorney.

_____
Date   _____

                                                    Principal

Witnesses:

_____

_____

State of Michigan

County of _____

  This instrument was acknowledged before me on_____

by _____

                              _____

                                        Notary Public

                              _____ County, Michigan
                              My commission expires _____

Prepared by:

REVOCATION OF POWER OF ATTORNEY

I _____ the principal

of _____

revoke my power of attorney dated _____[and recorded

on _____ at Liber _____ Page_____ in the office of the

Register of Deeds, _____ County, Michigan], and all the powers

given to my agent _____

in this power of attorney.

_____
Date

_____

Principal

Witnesses:

_____

_____

State of Michigan

County of _____

   This instrument was acknowledged before me on _____

by _____

_____

Notary Public

_____ County, Michigan

My commission expires _____

Prepared by:

LIVING WILL

I _____

of _____

give the following instructions for my future health care. I also revoke prior living wills I have made.

1. Duration. This living will shall take effect when I am unable to make my own health care decisions. That determination shall be made, in writing, by my attending physician and another physician or licensed psychologist who has examined me.

2. Health Care Instructions. Those responsible for my health care shall provide such care as instructed by me orally or in writing below.

A. Life-Sustaining Treatment.

Sign *one* (1 or 2) of the following two statements with which you agree:

(1) I direct that all medically appropriate treatment be provided to sustain my life, regardless of my mental or physical mental condition.

_____
Signature

(2) There are circumstances in which I do not want my life to be prolonged by further medical treatment. In these circumstances, life-sustaining treatment shall not be initiated, and if it has been, it must discontinued. I recognize that these decisions could or would allow me to die. In the following section, I specify the circumstances in which I choose to terminate life-sustaining treatment.

_____
Signature

If you have signed statement (2), initial each of the statements (a,b,c) with which you agree:

(a) _____ I realize that someday I may be diagnosed with an incurable and irreversible illness, disease, or condition. If this occurs, and my attending physician and at least one additional physician who has personally examined me determine that my condition is *terminal,* I direct that life-sustaining treatment that would artificially prolong my death be withheld or withdrawn. I also direct that I receive all medically appropriate care to make me comfortable and relieve pain.

To me, terminal condition means that my physicians have determined that:
(Initial one choice)

____ I will die within a few days

____ I will die within a few weeks

_____ I have a life expectancy of six months or less

_____ I have a life expectancy of one year or less

(b) _____ If become *permanently unconscious*, and it is determined by my attending physician and at least one additional physician with appropriate expertise who has personally examined me, that I have totally and irreversibly lost consciousness and my capacity for interaction with other people and my surroundings, I direct that life-sustaining treatment be withheld or withdrawn. I understand that I will not experience pain or discomfort in this condition, and I direct that I receive all medically appropriate care for my personal hygiene and dignity.

(c) _____ I realize that someday I may be diagnosed with an *incurable and irreversible* illness, disease, or condition which may not be terminal. My condition may cause me severe and progressive physical or mental deterioration and/or permanent loss of capacities and faculties I value highly. If, in the course of my medical care, the burdens of continued life with treatment become greater than the benefits I experience, I direct that life-sustaining treatment be withheld or withdrawn. I also direct that I receive all medically appropriate care to make me comfortable and relieve pain.

(Paragraph (c) covers a wide range of possible situations in which you may have experienced partial or complete loss of certain mental or physical capacities you value highly. If you wish, in the space provided below, you may specify the conditions in which you would choose to terminate life-sustaining treatment. You might include a description of the faculties or capacities, which, if irretrievably lost, would lead you to accept death rather than continue living. You may want to express any special concerns you have about particular medical conditions or treatment, or any other considerations which would provide further guidance to those who may become responsible for your care. If necessary, you may attach a separate statement to this document or use section B to provide additional instructions.)

Examples of conditions that I find unacceptable are:

B. Additional Health Care Instructions: (You may give additional health care instructions here. If you need more space, you may attach an additional statement to this document.)

3. Revocation. I may revoke this living will anytime, regardless of my mental capacity, by any means I am able to show an intent to revoke.

4. Reliance by Third Parties. Third parties can rely on this living will as the authoritative expression of my health care instructions, without liability to me or my estate, unless they have actual notice that the living will has been amended or terminated.

5. Miscellaneous. This living will shall be governed by Michigan law, but it may be used out of state. Photocopies of this document shall have the same legal authority as the original.

6. Signature. I am of sound mind and sign this living will voluntarily and without undue influence, duress or fraud.

_____   _____
Date   Signature

7. Witnesses. We declare that the person who signed this document, or asked another to sign this document on his/her behalf, did so in our presence, that s/he is personally known to us, and that s/he appears to be of sound mind and free of undue influence, duress or fraud.

_____
Signature of Witness

_____
Name of Witness

_____
Address of Witness

_____
City   State   Zip

_____
Signature of Witness

_____
Name of Witness

_____
Address of Witness

_____
City   State   Zip

Doctors' Statement

I _____

of _____

am the patient's attending physician.

I _____

of _____

am either a physician or a licensed psychologist.

We have examined the patient and it is our opinion that s/he is unable to make his/her own health care decisions.

_____   _____
Date   Attending Physician

_____   _____
Date   Physician or Psychologist

LIVING WILL

I _____

of _____

give the following instructions for my future health care. I also revoke prior living wills I have made.

1. Duration. This living will shall take effect when I am unable to make my own health care decisions. That determination shall be made, in writing, by my attending physician and another physician or licensed psychologist who has examined me.

2. Health Care Instructions. Those responsible for my health care shall provide such care as instructed by me orally or in writing below.

A. Life-Sustaining Treatment.

Sign *one* (1 or 2) of the following two statements with which you agree:

(1) I direct that all medically appropriate treatment be provided to sustain my life, regardless of my mental or physical mental condition.

_____
Signature

(2) There are circumstances in which I do not want my life to be prolonged by further medical treatment. In these circumstances, life-sustaining treatment shall not be initiated, and if it has been, it must discontinued. I recognize that these decisions could or would allow me to die. In the following section, I specify the circumstances in which I choose to terminate life-sustaining treatment.

_____
Signature

If you have signed statement (2), initial each of the statements (a,b,c) with which you agree:

(a) _____ I realize that someday I may be diagnosed with an incurable and irreversible illness, disease, or condition. If this occurs, and my attending physician and at least one additional physician who has personally examined me determine that my condition is *terminal*, I direct that life-sustaining treatment that would artificially prolong my death be withheld or withdrawn. I also direct that I receive all medically appropriate care to make me comfortable and relieve pain.

To me, terminal condition means that my physicians have determined that:
(Initial one choice)

_____ I will die within a few days

_____ I will die within a few weeks

_____ I have a life expectancy of six months or less

_____ I have a life expectancy of one year or less

(b) _____ If become *permanently unconscious*, and it is determined by my attending physician and at least one additional physician with appropriate expertise who has personally examined me, that I have totally and irreversibly lost consciousness and my capacity for interaction with other people and my surroundings, I direct that life-sustaining treatment be withheld or withdrawn. I understand that I will not experience pain or discomfort in this condition, and I direct that I receive all medically appropriate care for my personal hygiene and dignity.

(c) _____ I realize that someday I may be diagnosed with an *incurable and irreversible* illness, disease, or condition which may not be terminal. My condition may cause me severe and progressive physical or mental deterioration and/or permanent loss of capacities and faculties I value highly. If, in the course of my medical care, the burdens of continued life with treatment become greater than the benefits I experience, I direct that life-sustaining treatment be withheld or withdrawn. I also direct that I receive all medically appropriate care to make me comfortable and relieve pain.

(Paragraph (c) covers a wide range of possible situations in which you may have experienced partial or complete loss of certain mental or physical capacities you value highly. If you wish, in the space provided below, you may specify the conditions in which you would choose to terminate life-sustaining treatment. You might include a description of the faculties or capacities, which, if irretrievably lost, would lead you to accept death rather than continue living. You may want to express any special concerns you have about particular medical conditions or treatment, or any other considerations which would provide further guidance to those who may become responsible for your care. If necessary, you may attach a separate statement to this document or use section B to provide additional instructions.)

Examples of conditions that I find unacceptable are:

B. Additional Health Care Instructions: (You may give additional health care instructions here. If you need more space, you may attach an additional statement to this document.)

3. Revocation. I may revoke this living will anytime, regardless of my mental capacity, by any means I am able to show an intent to revoke.

4. Reliance by Third Parties. Third parties can rely on this living will as the authoritative expression of my health care instructions, without liability to me or my estate, unless they have actual notice that the living will has been amended or terminated.

5. Miscellaneous. This living will shall be governed by Michigan law, but it may be used out of state. Photocopies of this document shall have the same legal authority as the original.

6. Signature. I am of sound mind and sign this living will voluntarily and without undue influence, duress or fraud.

_____   _____

Date   Signature

7. Witnesses. We declare that the person who signed this document, or asked another to sign this document on his/her behalf, did so in our presence, that s/he is personally known to us, and that s/he appears to be of sound mind and free of undue influence, duress or fraud.

_____

Signature of Witness

_____

Name of Witness

_____

Address of Witness

_____

City   State   Zip

_____

Signature of Witness

_____

Name of Witness

_____

Address of Witness

_____

City   State   Zip

Doctors' Statement

I _____

of _____

am the patient's attending physician.

I _____

of _____

am either a physician or a licensed psychologist.

   We have examined the patient and it is our opinion that s/he is unable to make his/her own health care decisions.

_____   _____
Date   Attending Physician

_____   _____
Date   Physician or Psychologist

REVOCATION OF
ADVANCE DIRECTIVE

I _____

of _____

have made the following advance directive: □ living will   □ designation of

patient advocate   □ do-not-resuscitate order;   dated _____

   I revoke this instrument, effective immediately.

_____   _____
Date

RECORD OF NONWRITTEN REVOCATION

I _____

of _____

witnessed _____

revoke the advance directive described above by doing: (Describe oral or nonverbal
revocation in space below)

_____   _____
Date   Witness

REVOCATION OF
ADVANCE DIRECTIVE

I _____

of _____

have made the following advance directive: ☐ living will   ☐ designation of

patient advocate   ☐ do-not-resuscitate order;   dated _____

I revoke this instrument, effective immediately.

_____   _____
Date

RECORD OF NONWRITTEN REVOCATION

I _____

of _____

witnessed _____

revoke the advance directive described above by doing: (Describe oral or nonverbal
revocation in space below)

_____   _____
Date   Witness

DO-NOT-RESUSCITATE ORDER
(General)

I have discussed my health status with my physician,

_____.

I request that in the event my heart and breathing should stop, no person shall attempt to resuscitate me. This order is effective until it is revoked by me.

Being of sound mind, I voluntarily execute this order, and I understand its full import.

_____   _____
(Declarant's signature)   (Date)

_____
(Type or print declarant's full name)

_____   _____
(Signature of person who signed for declarant, if applicable)   (Date)

_____
(Type or print full name)

_____   _____
(Physician's signature)   (Date)

_____
(Type or print physician's full name)

Attestation of Witnesses

The individual who has executed this order appears to be of sound mind, and under no duress, fraud, or undue influence. Upon executing this order, the individual has (has not) received an identification bracelet.

_____   _____
(Witness signature)   (Date)

_____
(Type or print witness' name)

_____   _____
(Witness signature)   (Date)

_____
(Type or print witness' name)

THIS FORM WAS PREPARED PURSUANT TO, AND IS IN COMPLIANCE WITH, THE MICHIGAN DO-NOT-RESUSCITATE PROCEDURE ACT

DO-NOT-RESUSCITATE ORDER
(General)

I have discussed my health status with my physician,

_____ .

I request that in the event my heart and breathing should stop, no person shall attempt to resuscitate me. This order is effective until it is revoked by me.

Being of sound mind, I voluntarily execute this order, and I understand its full import.

_____   _____
(Declarant's signature)   (Date)

_____
(Type or print declarant's full name)

_____   _____
(Signature of person who signed for declarant, if applicable)   (Date)

_____
(Type or print full name)

_____   _____
(Physician's signature)   (Date)

_____
(Type or print physician's full name)

Attestation of Witnesses

The individual who has executed this order appears to be of sound mind, and under no duress, fraud, or undue influence. Upon executing this order, the individual has (has not) received an identification bracelet.

_____   _____
(Witness signature)   (Date)

_____
(Type or print witness' name)

_____   _____
(Witness signature)   (Date)

_____
(Type or print witness' name)

THIS FORM WAS PREPARED PURSUANT TO, AND IS IN COMPLIANCE WITH, THE MICHIGAN DO-NOT-RESUSCITATE PROCEDURE ACT

DO-NOT-RESUSCITATE ORDER
(Religious)

I request that in the event my heart and breathing should stop, no person shall attempt to resuscitate me. This order is effective until it is revoked by me.

Being of sound mind, I voluntarily execute this order, and I understand its full import.

_____   _____
(Declarant's signature)   (Date)

_____
(Type or print declarant's full name)

_____   _____
(Signature of person who signed for declarant, if applicable)   (Date)

_____
(Type or print full name)

Attestation of Witnesses

The individual who has executed this order appears to be of sound mind, and under no duress, fraud, or undue influence. Upon executing this order, the individual has (has not) received an identification bracelet.

_____   _____
(Witness signature)   (Date)

_____
(Type or print witness' name)

_____   _____
(Witness signature)   (Date)

_____
(Type or print witness' name)

THIS FORM WAS PREPARED PURSUANT TO, AND IS IN COMPLIANCE WITH, THE MICHIGAN DO-NOT-RESUSCITATE PROCEDURE ACT

DO-NOT-RESUSCITATE ORDER
(Religious)

I request that in the event my heart and breathing should stop, no person shall attempt to resuscitate me. This order is effective until it is revoked by me.

Being of sound mind, I voluntarily execute this order, and I understand its full import.

_____   _____
(Declarant's signature)   (Date)

_____
(Type or print declarant's full name)

_____   _____
(Signature of person who signed for declarant, if applicable)   (Date)

_____
(Type or print full name)

Attestation of Witnesses

The individual who has executed this order appears to be of sound mind, and under no duress, fraud, or undue influence. Upon executing this order, the individual has (has not) received an identification bracelet.

_____   _____
(Witness signature)   (Date)

_____
(Type or print witness' name)

_____   _____
(Witness signature)   (Date)

_____
(Type or print witness' name)

THIS FORM WAS PREPARED PURSUANT TO, AND IS IN COMPLIANCE WITH, THE MICHIGAN DO-NOT-RESUSCITATE PROCEDURE ACT

PATIENT ADVOCATE DESIGNATION

I _____ the patient

of _____

make this patient advocate designation according to sections 5506-5513 of the Estates and Protected Individuals Code of Michigan. I also revoke prior patient advocate designations I have made.

1. Duration. This patient advocate designation shall take effect when I am unable to participate in medical treatment decisions. That determination shall be made, in writing, by my attending physician and another physician or licensed psychologist who has examined me. This designation shall not be affected by my disability.

2. Designation of Patient Advocate.

I designate _____

of _____

as my patient advocate.

If that person fails, for any reason, to serve, I designate as successor patient

advocate _____

of _____

3. Powers of Patient Advocate. Except as prohibited by law or as restricted in paragraph 4, my patient advocate shall make all decisions about my care, custody and medical treatment, including powers to:

(a) have access to medical records and information; give medical waivers and authorizations

(b) authorize admission to or discharge from health care facilities, including hospitals, hospices and nursing homes

(c) employ or discharge medical caregivers, including physicians, nurses and therapists, and pay them reasonable compensation from my funds

(d) consent to or refuse any medical treatment, including diagnostic, surgical and therapeutic procedures

4. Health Care Instructions. In exercising the above powers, my patient advocate shall provide health care as instructed by me orally or in writing below.

A. Life-Sustaining Treatment.

Sign *one* (1 or 2) of the following two statements with which you agree:

(1) I direct that all medically appropriate treatment be provided to sustain my life, regardless of my physical or mental condition.

Patient

(2) There are circumstances in which I do not want my life to be prolonged by further medical treatment. In these circumstances, life-sustaining treatment shall not be initiated, and if it has been, it must be discontinued. I recognize that these decisions could or would allow me to die. In the following section, I specify the circumstances in which I choose to terminate life-sustaining measures.

Patient

If you have signed statement (2), initial each of the statements (a,b,c) with which you agree:

(a) _____ I realize that someday I may be diagnosed with an incurable and irreversible illness, disease, or condition. If this occurs, and my attending physician and at least one additional physician who has personally examined me determine that my condition is *terminal*, I direct that life-sustaining treatment that would artificially prolong my death be withheld or withdrawn. I also direct that I receive all medically appropriate care to make me comfortable and to relieve pain.

To me, terminal condition means that my physicians have determined that:
(Initial one choice)

_____ I will die within a few days

_____ I will die within a few weeks

_____ I will have a life expectancy of six months or less

_____ I will have a life expectancy of one year or less

(b) _____ If I become *permanently unconscious*, and it is determined by my attending physician and at least one additional physician with appropriate expertise who has personally examined me, that I have totally and irreversibly lost consciousness and my capacity for interaction with other people and my surroundings, I direct that life-sustaining treatment be withheld or withdraw. I understand that I will not experience pain or discomfort in this condition, and I direct that I receive all medically appropriate care necessary to provide for my personal hygiene and dignity.

(c) _____ I realize that someday I may be diagnosed with an *incurable and irreversible* illness, disease, or condition which may not be terminal. My condition may cause me severe and progressive physical or mental deterioration and/or permanent loss of capacities and faculties I value highly. If, in the course of my medical care, the burdens of continued life with treatment become greater than the benefits I experience, I direct that life-sustaining treatment by withheld or withdrawn. I also direct that I receive all medically appropriate care to make me comfortable and relieve pain.

(Paragraph (c) covers a wide range of possible situations in which you may have experienced partial or complete loss of certain mental or physical capacities you value highly. If you wish, in the space provided below you may specify detail the conditions in which you would choose to terminate life-sustaining treatment. You might include a description of the faculties or capacities, which, if irretrievably lost, would lead you to accept death rather than continue living. You may want to express any special concerns you have about particular medical conditions or treatment, or any other considerations which would provide further guidance to those who may become responsible for your care. If necessary, you may attach a separate statement to this document or use section B to provide additional instructions.)

Examples of conditions that I find unacceptable are:

B. Additional Health Care Instructions: (You may give additional health care instructions here. If you need more space, you may attach an additional statement to this document.)

5. Reliance by Third Parties. Third parties can rely on this patient advocate designation, the doctors' statement or my patient advocate's decisions, without liability to me or my estate, unless they have actual notice that the patient advocate designation has been amended or terminated.

6. Miscellaneous. This patient advocate designation shall be governed by Michigan law, but it may be used out of state. Photocopies of this document shall have the same legal authority as the original.

7. Signature. I am 18 years of age or older and of sound mind. I am signing this designation of patient advocate voluntarily and without undue influence, duress or fraud.

_____	_____
Date	Patient

8. Witnesses. We are eligible to serve as witnesses. We have witnessed the patient's signature, and state that the patient appears to be of sound mind and free of undue influence, duress or fraud.

_____
Signature of Witness

_____
Name of Witness

_____
Address of Witness

_____
City   State   Zip

_____
Signature of Witness

_____
Name of Witness

_____
Address of Witness

_____
City   State   Zip

_____
Signature of Witness

_____
Name of Witness

_____
Address of Witness

_____
City   State   Zip

Doctors' Statement

I _____

of _____

am the patient's attending physician.

I _____

of _____

am either a physician or a licensed psychologist.

We have examined the patient and it is our opinion that s/he is unable to participate in medical treatment decisions.

_____   _____
Date   Attending Physician

_____   _____
Date   Physician or Psychologist

Acceptance of Designation

I have been designated as the patient advocate of the patient making this patient advocate designation. I accept that designation and agree to act as required by law and as stated below:

(a) This designation shall not become effective unless the patient is unable to participate in medical treatment decisions.

(b) A patient advocate shall not exercise powers concerning the patient's care, custody, and medical treatment that the patient, if the patient were able to participate in the decision, could not have exercised on his or her own behalf.

(c) This designation cannot be used to make a medical treatment decision to withhold or withdraw treatment from a patient who is pregnant that would result in the pregnant patient's death.

(d) A patient advocate may make a decision to withhold or withdraw treatment which would allow a patient to die only if the patient has expressed in a clear and convincing manner that the patient advocate is authorized to make such a decision, and that the patient acknowledges that such a decision could or would allow the patient's death.

(e) A patient advocate shall not receive compensation for the performance of his or her authority, rights, and responsibilities, but a patient advocate may be reimbursed for actual and necessary expenses incurred in the performance of his or her authority, rights, and responsibilities.

(f) A patient advocate shall act in accordance with the standards of care applicable to fiduciaries when acting for the patient and shall act consistent with the patient's best interests. The known desires of the patient expressed or evidenced while the patient is able to participate in medical treatment decisions are presumed to be in the patient's best interests.

(g) A patient may revoke his or her designation at any time and in any manner sufficient to communicate an intent to revoke.

(h) A patient advocate may revoke his or her acceptance to the designation at any time and in any manner sufficient to communicate an intent to revoke.

(i) A patient admitted to a health facility or agency has the rights enumerated in section 20201 of the public health code, Act. No. 368 of the Public Acts of 1978, being section 333.20201 of the Michigan Compiled Laws.

_____
Date

_____
Patient Advocate

PATIENT ADVOCATE DESIGNATION

I _____ the patient

of _____

make this patient advocate designation according to sections 5506-5513 of the Estates and Protected Individuals Code of Michigan. I also revoke prior patient advocate designations I have made.

1. Duration. This patient advocate designation shall take effect when I am unable to participate in medical treatment decisions. That determination shall be made, in writing, by my attending physician and another physician or licensed psychologist who has examined me. This designation shall not be affected by my disability.

2. Designation of Patient Advocate.

I designate _____

of _____

as my patient advocate.

If that person fails, for any reason, to serve, I designate as successor patient

advocate _____

of _____

3. Powers of Patient Advocate. Except as prohibited by law or as restricted in paragraph 4, my patient advocate shall make all decisions about my care, custody and medical treatment, including powers to:

(a) have access to medical records and information; give medical waivers and authorizations

(b) authorize admission to or discharge from health care facilities, including hospitals, hospices and nursing homes

(c) employ or discharge medical caregivers, including physicians, nurses and therapists, and pay them reasonable compensation from my funds

(d) consent to or refuse any medical treatment, including diagnostic, surgical and therapeutic procedures

4. Health Care Instructions. In exercising the above powers, my patient advocate shall provide health care as instructed by me orally or in writing below.

A. Life-Sustaining Treatment.

Sign *one* (1 or 2) of the following two statements with which you agree:

(1) I direct that all medically appropriate treatment be provided to sustain my life, regardless of my physical or mental condition.

Patient

(2) There are circumstances in which I do not want my life to be prolonged by further medical treatment. In these circumstances, life-sustaining treatment shall not be initiated, and if it has been, it must be discontinued. I recognize that these decisions could or would allow me to die. In the following section, I specify the circumstances in which I choose to terminate life-sustaining measures.

Patient

If you have signed statement (2), initial each of the statements (a,b,c) with which you agree:

(a) _____ I realize that someday I may be diagnosed with an incurable and irreversible illness, disease, or condition. If this occurs, and my attending physician and at least one additional physician who has personally examined me determine that my condition is *terminal,* I direct that life-sustaining treatment that would artificially prolong my death be withheld or withdrawn. I also direct that I receive all medically appropriate care to make me comfortable and to relieve pain.

To me, terminal condition means that my physicians have determined that:
(Initial one choice)

_____ I will die within a few days

_____ I will die within a few weeks

_____ I will have a life expectancy of six months or less

_____ I will have a life expectancy of one year or less

(b) _____ If I become *permanently unconscious*, and it is determined by my attending physician and at least one additional physician with appropriate expertise who has personally examined me, that I have totally and irreversibly lost consciousness and my capacity for interaction with other people and my surroundings, I direct that life-sustaining treatment be withheld or withdraw. I understand that I will not experience pain or discomfort in this condition, and I direct that I receive all medically appropriate care necessary to provide for my personal hygiene and dignity.

(c) _____ I realize that someday I may be diagnosed with an *incurable and irreversible* illness, disease, or condition which may not be terminal. My condition may cause me severe and progressive physical or mental deterioration and/or permanent loss of capacities and faculties I value highly. If, in the course of my medical care, the burdens of continued life with treatment become greater than the benefits I experience, I direct that life-sustaining treatment by withheld or withdrawn. I also direct that I receive all medically appropriate care to make me comfortable and relieve pain.

(Paragraph (c) covers a wide range of possible situations in which you may have experienced partial or complete loss of certain mental or physical capacities you value highly. If you wish, in the space provided below you may specify detail the conditions in which you would choose to terminate life-sustaining treatment. You might include a description of the faculties or capacities, which, if irretrievably lost, would lead you to accept death rather than continue living. You may want to express any special concerns you have about particular medical conditions or treatment, or any other considerations which would provide further guidance to those who may become responsible for your care. If necessary, you may attach a separate statement to this document or use section B to provide additional instructions.)

Examples of conditions that I find unacceptable are:

B. Additional Health Care Instructions: (You may give additional health care instructions here. If you need more space, you may attach an additional statement to this document.)

5. Reliance by Third Parties. Third parties can rely on this patient advocate designation, the doctors' statement or my patient advocate's decisions, without liability to me or my estate, unless they have actual notice that the patient advocate designation has been amended or terminated.

6. Miscellaneous. This patient advocate designation shall be governed by Michigan law, but it may be used out of state. Photocopies of this document shall have the same legal authority as the original.

7. Signature. I am 18 years of age or older and of sound mind. I am signing this designation of patient advocate voluntarily and without undue influence, duress or fraud.

---------------------------   --

Date   Patient

8. Witnesses. We are eligible to serve as witnesses. We have witnessed the patient's signature, and state that the patient appears to be of sound mind and free of undue influence, duress or fraud.

Signature of Witness

Name of Witness

_____
Address of Witness

_____
City   State   Zip

_____
Signature of Witness

_____
Name of Witness

_____
Address of Witness

_____
City   State   Zip

_____
Signature of Witness

_____
Name of Witness

_____
Address of Witness

_____
City   State   Zip

Doctors' Statement

I _____

of _____

am the patient's attending physician.

I _____

of _____

am either a physician or a licensed psychologist.

We have examined the patient and it is our opinion that s/he is unable to participate in medical treatment decisions.

_____   _____
Date   Attending Physician

_____   _____
Date   Physician or Psychologist

Acceptance of Designation

I have been designated as the patient advocate of the patient making this patient advocate designation. I accept that designation and agree to act as required by law and as stated below:

(a) This designation shall not become effective unless the patient is unable to participate in medical treatment decisions.

(b) A patient advocate shall not exercise powers concerning the patient's care, custody, and medical treatment that the patient, if the patient were able to participate in the decision, could not have exercised on his or her own behalf.

(c) This designation cannot be used to make a medical treatment decision to withhold or withdraw treatment from a patient who is pregnant that would result in the pregnant patient's death.

(d) A patient advocate may make a decision to withhold or withdraw treatment which would allow a patient to die only if the patient has expressed in a clear and convincing manner that the patient advocate is authorized to make such a decision, and that the patient acknowledges that such a decision could or would allow the patient's death.

(e) A patient advocate shall not receive compensation for the performance of his or her authority, rights, and responsibilities, but a patient advocate may be reimbursed for actual and necessary expenses incurred in the performance of his or her authority, rights, and responsibilities.

(f) A patient advocate shall act in accordance with the standards of care applicable to fiduciaries when acting for the patient and shall act consistent with the patient's best interests. The known desires of the patient expressed or evidenced while the patient is able to participate in medical treatment decisions are presumed to be in the patient's best interests.

(g) A patient may revoke his or her designation at any time and in any manner sufficient to communicate an intent to revoke.

(h) A patient advocate may revoke his or her acceptance to the designation at any time and in any manner sufficient to communicate an intent to revoke.

(i) A patient admitted to a health facility or agency has the rights enumerated in section 20201 of the public health code, Act. No. 368 of the Public Acts of 1978, being section 333.20201 of the Michigan Compiled Laws.

Date   Patient Advocate

AFFIDAVIT IN SUPPORT OF PATIENT ADVOCATE DESIGNATION

State of Michigan

County of _____

I, _____ , being sworn, say:

1. I am the patient advocate of _____

under a patient advocate designation dated _____

2. I do not have actual knowledge that the patient advocate designation has been amended or revoked by the patient or by any other cause.

_____

Subscribed and sworn to before me on _____

_____
Notary Public

_____ County, Michigan

My commission expires _____

AFFIDAVIT IN SUPPORT OF PATIENT ADVOCATE DESIGNATION

State of Michigan

County of _____

I, _____ , being sworn, say:

1. I am the patient advocate of _____

under a patient advocate designation dated _____

2. I do not have actual knowledge that the patient advocate designation has been amended or revoked by the patient or by any other cause.

_____

Subscribed and sworn to before me on _____

_____
Notary Public

_____ County, Michigan

My commission expires _____